Dedication

This book is dedicated to my wife, Glenora.

Without her many hours of selfless help this project never could have been made complete.

Acknowledgements

To my instructor in the advanced writing class at Mt. Hood Community College, Dee Lopez. I thank her for all the gentle admonishment and encouragement.

To my editor, Mr. David Kelly, who guided me so well through the peaks and valleys of writing this book. His patience and availability at all times is most appreciated.

To my mother who taught me to read when I was three, using phonics as a guide. She told me when reading a book I could place myself in the story and, by so doing, feel as though I experienced the adventure. Her advice has enriched my being and served me well for a lifetime.

Life, the Hard Way
or
Up From Poverty Flat

Eugene Curnow

Life, the Hard Way
Up from Poverty Flat

© 2007 Eugene Curnow
First Edition

Printed in USA

Library of Congress Cataloging-in-Publication Data

Life, the Hard Way: Up from Poverty Flat by Eugene Curnow
Includes photographs.
ISBN 978-09795189-3-5 (pbk) 447 pp.
1.   Memoir 2. World War II 3. Iwo Jima 4. Trains 5. Biography
6. The Great Depression
Eugene Curnow 2007
Bennett & Hastings Publishers www.bennetthastings.com
1(800)634-7392

Table of Contents

TABLE OF CONTENTS

PART II
WAR
(continued)

PART III
CIVILIAN LIFE

PART IV
LOVE

TABLE OF CONTENTS

PRELUDE

❖ A LITTLE SHAGGY DOG STORY ❖

The car skidded to a stop in front of our veterinary hospital and raised a cloud of dust that, caught by an east wind, whirled on by. Quickly, the driver was out of the car and around the front to the passenger side, where he flung open the door. From the front seat he scooped up a pink blanketed bundle and bolted across the sidewalk toward the hospital.

I had just sat down for the first time since my day of medicine and surgery had begun at 7:00 AM in our Portland, Oregon pet hospital. Jumping from the chair to open the front door, I glanced at my watch. It was nearly noon.

The man saw my nametag and his words gushed like a fountain as he nodded toward the blanket held firmly in his arms, "Dr. Curnow, our little dog Matilda, was just hit by a car. It happened a few minutes ago in front of our house over on Floral Place." I knew that address was not far from my veterinary clinic at 2965 N.E. Sandy Boulevard.

His words came with increasing speed, but his vocabulary impressed me as that of someone with an above-average education. Using the words "traumatic shock", "massive blood loss" and "her rate of respiration" Matilda's master obviously realized the seriousness of the accident and wanted to convey as much information as he could in a very short time.

I motioned for him to follow and within seconds Matilda lay on the examination table. I called for my kennel girl to assist "s.t.a.t." in the examining room.

The little white shaggy dog appeared to be a poodle mix. Her breathing was shallow and rapid, and she was not conscious. The left hind leg had an extra bend in it, indicating an underlying broken bone, and a rotating tire had torn away a large piece of skin from the muscle beneath. It remained attached on one side but had rolled into an odd shape. I lifted one of her lips and saw the gums and tongue were almost white instead of the normal pink. Though not bleeding now, a large amount of blood had soaked into the blanket. She was going into shock and shivered uncontrollably even though the temperature outside stood at ninety degrees. Through the stethoscope I heard a normal but frantic heartbeat.

"My name is Dolph. I live a few blocks away near Laurelhurst Park. Do you think you can save her? Please do everything possible," his forthright manner and voice carried the unusual quality of command.

"I can't promise anything Mr. Dolph but I'll sure do all I can." While speaking I reached for a vial of *Solu Delta Cortef*, a medication used to control shock in cases of severe trauma. (*SDC* was developed for the same use in humans, and the Upjohn Company had recently introduced it to the veterinary profession.) My assistant quickly shaved the hair from the frontal areas of the little dog's elbows. With perfect timing she closed an index finger over the vein to compress it. As I inserted the needle and administered the medication I asked Matilda's owner, who stood to one side and had watched every move, if he would like to sit down. Twelve years experience had taught me that a distressed pet owner could become lightheaded, or even faint and fall to the floor at the sight of a few drops of blood, or from seeing a needle enter a vein. Mr. Dolph refused.

"My wife will never forgive me if Matilda dies. I was trimming a bush beside our house. I thought she was right there with me. Then I heard tires screech and a yelp. I looked around and ran out front just in time to see a man carrying her to the grass of our parking strip. I thought she was dead, all limp and bleeding. The stranger offered to take Matilda to his veterinarian on the other side of town and pay for her care. He said she darted out in the street right in front of him and even though he locked his brakes there wasn't time to stop. I ran into the garage and got this blanket. I asked the man to give my wife his name and phone number, put Matilda in the car and came right over."

I let him speak without interruption. There was no doubt he

felt guilty and wanted to tell every detail in order to feel better. I finished injecting the medication, removed the syringe from the needle then taped it securely in place to remain in the vein for later use.

Mr. Dolph seemed near collapse. I asked my assistant to again offer him a chair. Thanking her he sat down and buried his head in his hands. In a few moments he sat upright, "What do you think her chances are?"

At this point I could not be optimistic. "Her condition isn't good. She might not survive. Whenever a three thousand pound car hits a ten pound dog, even if the car is only going five miles an hour, the kinetic energy of the one-and-a-half ton mass can do terrible internal as well as external damage."

He nodded understandingly. "Will you set the leg and sew up the skin now?"

"No, broken bones and flesh injuries are of no concern at this time. She needs to be brought out of shock and have the fluid volume from her blood loss replaced. To do this I'm going to give her what I call 'some liquid steak and eggs' through the same needle now in her foreleg. Whole blood or plasma was not readily available for pets, so in addition to the liquid steak and eggs I'll give her a massive injection of Vitamin B-12, which will quickly cause the bone marrow to replace a lot of red blood cells. An antibiotic injection will reduce the possibility of infection. Two attendants are on duty here all night so she'll be observed at all times. If her condition deteriorates at any time I'll be called and will return right away. Also in case of emergency, fire for example, all patients would be taken out of the hospital immediately by our two night people."

The man clung to every word. "Sounds like you've got everything covered, Doctor. I like people who plan ahead."

I nodded a silent "thank you" as I assured him, "We treat every pet as though it were our own."

After injecting the antibiotic and B-12, I carried Matilda to the kennel room (her owner following close behind) and put her in the "urgent care" kennel next to the open office door. I attached the I.V. line to the needle in her foreleg to begin the administration of saline and glucose (the "steak and eggs") and adjusted the flow. Though still unconscious her breathing had almost normalized, becoming slower and deeper.

When we re-entered the examination room to fill out the admission chart Mr. Dolph asked, "Will you phone my wife and give her your evaluation?"

"Certainly, how about at 4:30? By then I'll know if there's any change."

"That will be fine. I hope you will have good news."

From time-to-time, while working on his little dog, I observed the man. He appeared to be in his early seventies. About 5-feet 8-inches tall, he was stocky and muscular. He wore expensive gold-rimmed glasses and had an abundant head of gray hair. From the front window of the hospital I saw his car, a new top-of-the-line Cadillac. Because he lived near Laurelhurst Park, an upscale residential area of Portland, this seemed normal. Even while experiencing grief and concern he had the aura of a "take charge" person, used to having his wishes carried out. I had the feeling from the moment he said his name that somehow it had a significant association with something earlier in my life. "Dolph... Where have I heard that name before?"

With the paperwork finished he thanked my assistant and with a powerful grip shook my hand. As he went out the door he said, "It's going to be real quiet around our house. I hope you'll have an encouraging report at 4:30."

"So do I, Mr. Dolph."

I glanced at the clock. It was 1:30 PM, and I hadn't had lunch.

At the Dairy Queen on N.E. 28th and Broadway I could not shake the feeling about the man's name.

When I returned to the hospital just after 2:00 PM the change in Matilda was remarkable. Fully conscious, eyes open and alert, her ears wiggled normally as they picked up sounds from various parts of the kennel room: the meow of a kitten or the squeal of a happy puppy.

By 4:30 PM the bottle of I.V. solution ran out. Detaching it I left the needle in place in case it might be needed again.

Mr. Dolph and his wife each picked up a phone. Relief and happiness rang in their voices when I told them the good news. After further briefing I let them know Matilda would be the first patient I'd see the next morning.

Saying goodbye I asked them not to phone the next day before 11:00 AM.

The following morning I arrived at 6:45 anxious to see Matilda. To my surprise she stood on three legs, her tail briskly wagging. Offered some food, she ate eagerly. At that moment, for the first time since she came in, I felt sure she'd live.

As soon as my daytime assistant arrived I had her bring Matilda to the x-ray room to view the exact position and type of fracture: that would allow me to decide how best to immobilize it. The decision came easily.

The femur had a simple transverse fracture almost at the midpoint. It would require a routine open reduction and insertion of a stainless steel pin into the marrow shaft. This could be accomplished by cutting through the skin, moving aside the muscle overlying the fracture, exposing both ends of the broken bone (making it easy to see them) and aligning the pin.

Perfected by German physicians during World War II (WWII) this method of bone repair was used with great success on thousands of human casualties. In the 1940's it was adapted for use in veterinary medicine. Done under general anesthetic, a pointed, razor-sharp pin with a temporary handle attached is slowly twisted downward through the top half of the femur with a drill-like motion. The pin follows the inside of the marrow shaft and emerges at the surgically-exposed fracture point at the bottom half of the broken bone. That portion is then aligned by hand to receive the pin. Then, inserted its full length within the bottom half of the break, the pin is set solidly into hard, healthy bone at the very lower end. This forces the fractured ends to hold together tightly, in an exactly aligned position. One inch of the pin is left to protrude outside the skin above the hip, and the handle is removed. There is no pain, and the bone heals by primary union in twenty-one days or less. At that time, under light sedation, the pin is removed. No aftercare is required.

With the bone pin in place I aligned, flattened and freshened each side of the damaged skin, cutting a small amount of tissue from the edges and causing a little bleeding to enhance healing. Fifty-six simple interrupted, self-absorbing sutures completed the task. Matilda, though still groggy, appeared to be on her way to an uneventful recovery.

The Dolphs phoned promptly at 11:00 every morning. On day four the little dog appeared well enough to go home to continue recovering. When her master came to pick her up she heard him before he entered the kennel room. Barking and whining with joy, the newly pinned leg didn't diminish her enthusiasm. In a week she returned for a brief fluoroscopic examination. Both bone and skin were healing normally. On Day 18 after her brush with death, she returned to have the stainless steel pin removed. A case that began with a poor prognosis had been successfully resolved.

"She did remarkably well, Doctor. My wife and I are pleased with her recovery," Mr. Dolph said. "I guess it's time for me to bail her out," he joked.

He handed me a check, and it took only a moment for me to realize the significance of his name: imprinted in the upper left hand corner: ADM. S. Dolph USN, (ret).

Instantly I recalled the years during WWII when I had been a Navy Medical Corpsman. During that time, Admiral Dolph's name appeared on the liberty card of all Navy personnel in the 13th Naval District, which was located in the Western United

States and in the Pacific war zone. Every time I had gone on liberty, his signature on the card had allowed me to do it.

Momentarily astounded I asked the obvious question to which he answered, "Yes, I'm the Admiral whose signature allowed you to go on liberty. In addition, any legal order I gave had to be followed at once."

Having developed a good rapport over the weeks I jokingly replied, "For several years my life and 'liberty' were in your hands. Had we met on the street in uniform I'd have had to salute you with all that brass on your sleeves and the 'scrambled eggs' on your hat. What a switch this is Admiral. Now the life and liberty of your little dog, Matilda, has been in my hands and you had to take 'orders' from me."

The waiting room had no one in it at the time, and I asked him if he'd like to sit a few minutes and talk.

"I always enjoy an opportunity to have a conversation with anyone who served in the Pacific and returned home to become successful," he answered.

"Thanks Admiral. If I may I'd like to make an observation. What do you think the odds would be for the coincidence of us to meet under the circumstances; that you and I would live in Portland and you'd be less than half a mile away from this veterinary hospital when Matilda had desperate need for help?" He didn't speak as he shook his head sideways a few times indicating he felt the odds were very slim.

For half an hour or more we reminisced about the war in the Pacific. But now we conversed as equals.

I mentioned making the invasion of Iwo Jima as a medical corpsman on Blue Beach #2 with the 4th Marine Division that was wiped out as a fighting unit during that action and, as far as I knew, had never been and never will be, remanned. He didn't talk about any combat action he may have seen, and I suspect this was because he was still concerned but happy about Matilda's recovery.

Finally he stood with her in his arms, "I don't know what the chances would be that we would meet, especially under the conditions as they were that first day. I want you to know my wife and I are very pleased." He paused a moment as he walked to the door. Turning to face me he straightened up to full height, "Doctor, now it's my turn. I salute you."

Momentarily at a loss for words I bowed slightly, "Thank you Sir."

As was my policy, two weeks later I made the usual follow up phone call to check on Matilda. The recorded voice of a telephone operator came on the line, "The number you have reached has been disconnected and there is no new number." With great disappointment I replaced the receiver.

I had made the phone call at noon. All but one of my staff had gone out to lunch, and I sat alone in the peace and quiet of the office. In silence I glanced around at the surroundings. I looked at the gleaming desk made from oak, the nice carpet and the chair, upholstered with tufted soft leather. As the air conditioning system whispered comfort throughout the clinic on this hot, August day, I thought of my wonderful wife, two lovely daughters and rewarding profession. I had a lot to be pleased about. My quality of life at age 42 was excellent.

No one was being cut to pieces by flying shrapnel. No one was almost freezing in winter or being crushed to death under a load of telephone poles while riding on a railroad flatcar, and no one was almost starving.

I thought of the very small community called Olinda and of Whiskeytown, one mile west of Poverty Flat. I had lived in Poverty Flat as a child, with the constant gnaw of hunger in my belly. I thought of the tarpaper shack I had called home. The icy wind of winter was the only "air-conditioning" I had ever known early in life.

PART I
BOYHOOD

❖ A CYCLE OF LIFE ❖

In 1924 my dad, Harry, worked as an elevator operator in the Pittock Building in Portland, Oregon. Mother worked on the sixth floor as a secretary for Harrower Laboratories. They met through work, dated, then eloped and were married in Vancouver, Washington.

Early in 1928, when I was three, Dad, Mother and I lived in a cheap basement apartment in the southwest area of downtown Portland. From one window the hilly street outside our basement apartment could be seen. Being poor and having few toys , my wintertime entertainment became watching the cars (mostly Model T Ford's with skinny tires) try to climb the hill. I spent hours watching them attempt to go up the grade on snow and ice. Most made it about half way, lost traction and slid backward, twisting and turning while the driver fought the steering wheel trying to regain control. Many times I'd watch them crash into other cars that were stalled or parked at the curb. Traction chains were not commonly seen during the 1920's. The few cars that made it to the top had drivers who cut several short lengths of one-inch thick rope, looped them crossways over the rear tires and tied them tightly against the rim between the rear wheel's wooden spokes.

Our family life was not without its own entertaining slippery slopes. Mother, a devout Seventh Day Adventist and Dad, a non-practicing Catholic, had religions so diametrically opposed it's a wonder they ever got together. Adventists don't eat pork in any form, but my father breakfasted daily on bacon or ham and often wanted roast pork or chops for dinner. I remember listening, at the age of three, to their very loud arguments over this. To solve the problem Mother had two sets of cooking utensils, one for his pork and another for beef or lamb. I was given beef or lamb.

On payday Dad liked to gamble by playing the "counter punchboards." About 8-inches square the punchboards were made from 3/4 inch thick cardboard covered with colorful designs meant to attract attention. They had two hundred holes drilled in them, each having a tightly rolled slip of paper pushed downward inside it. Players used a round metal "key," cut flat and crosswise on one end, to continue pushing the tightly rolled paper out the opposite side of the board. Each "chance" cost a dime, and players might win from ten cents to one dollar, depending on what was written on the slip. Only one slip had the word "winner" written on it, and that person won the Grand Prize: a box of candy bars. Sometimes Dad wound up winning a box of twenty-four Milky Way, Butterfinger or Baby Ruth candy bars. Mother always reminded Dad the candy bars could have been bought at a store for a lot less money than he'd spent gambling to win them, but he wouldn't listen...and it seemed to me like Christmas every time he came home with the candy. I could hardly wait, and he made sure I'd get a bar or two right away even though Mother scolded him for ruining my supper.

In a dark out-of-the-way corner of the basement was a large locked "storage" room. In this room Dad operated an efficient moonshine still. It produced what he called "Nectar of the Gods." He distributed this to Portland nightclubs and speakeasies through his carefully established network of "trustworthy" taxi drivers. During the Prohibition years, it was illegal for individuals to make alcohol, but with time Dad's operation did so well that he quit his job running the Pittock Building's elevator. The job there had been mainly a cover-up and he used the extra time to produce more booze and a bigger profit.

In 1928 Dad made a business deal with a prominent and wealthy Portland physician who owned a brand new Franklin Air-Cooled car. The windows of the back seat's roomy interior came equipped with heavy black curtains that could be pulled down to completely hide the inside from view. The agreement was for Dad to make the moonshine, bottle it in one-gallon glass jugs and use the doctor's car to transport it to Oakland, California. The doctor would furnish all the necessary ingredients because during Prohibition a physician could buy hundreds of pounds of sugar and grain without arousing suspicion. Many doctors used these ingredients to produce legal medications for their patients, but "Revenooers" were always suspicious of anyone in the general public who bought large quantities.

Dad, a good carpenter, removed the cushioning and back seats from the big car and replaced them with a sturdy wooden frame able to hold 50, one-gallon glass jugs. He thickly padded the frame with rubber and un-sheared sheepskin. He then bolted it solidly to the floor to prevent it from bouncing loose if the car happened to hit one of the ever-present ruts or potholes in the roads of that era. In Oakland, due to the larger population and much greater demand, selling the liquor to owners of illegal after-hours clubs brought Dad and the doctor a much greater profit than it did in Portland. Soon we were able to move to the northeast, into a better part of town with nicer housing.

As time passed Mother would often become bothered with attacks of conscience. Although she enjoyed what the money bought, her strong religious belief made her very uncomfortable and every few months she'd report Dad's bootlegging to the police. The irony is that many officers who came to arrest him were either his customers or delivery people working for high placed politicians such as the Mayor, City Councilmen and Chief of Police. In addition, most of the Judges Dad appeared before were also his good after-hours buyers and most were on a first name basis with him.

In jail Dad spent only a few minutes each day in a cell, always unlocked, to satisfy the prisoner count and at night, unlike the others in jail, he always had a comfortable feather mattress, pillows and warm wool blankets. During the day he'd usually ride around in a Black and White patrol car, at times sharing a "nip or two" with a friendly officer. Some nights he'd be picked up at the police station in an official car, along with the police Captain, so they could mingle at parties given for influential people high in government. The booze drank at these get-togethers usually had been bought earlier from Dad by highly placed officials or "confiscated as evidence" by the Portland police when they arrested him.

Mother, a practical woman, knew from experience when Dad

was locked up there would be no income. As a result she always managed to "liberate" a few gallons of liquor from the stock before the police arrived, just enough to last until his release. She re-bottled it in pint flasks and hid them in the water tank of our toilet. In those days most water tanks were mounted on the wall six feet or more above and behind the bowl. A length of brass chain hung down and the wooden handle on the end had to be pulled to flush it. The expression, "Hey, you forgot to pull the chain" came about because of this arrangement of early day indoor plumbing. For a few days after Dad was arrested the toilet didn't flush very well due to the displacement of water by the pints of liquor concealed in the tank. When money for food ran low Mother would contact one of the cab drivers, sell a few pints and our life would continue.

I could tell when Dad would be coming home because with all of the flasks removed from the water and sold, the toilet again flushed perfectly. I remember how glad Mother would be to see him when he returned and flashed a large roll of greenbacks. She'd cuddle next to him and chide, "Where did you get all that money Harry?"

He'd tease, "It's a reward from the people downtown who were very happy because all the booze they confiscated as evidence arrived at the police station intact."

Dad's brother, Joe, a Captain with United Air Lines during this time, flew the route between Seattle, Washington and Oakland, California. When not on duty he stayed at a hotel in Alameda, a small town near Oakland. When Dad arrived in Alameda with the doctor's big car full of liquor, he would stay at the same hotel. Joe kept a Model A Ford at the hotel and used it to drive back and forth to the airport. One morning Joe's car wouldn't start, and he was due at the airport to fly back to Seattle. In those days the airlines were very strict about their flights being on schedule. This worried Joe. Giving up on starting his car he phoned Dad from the lobby. "Harry, can you give me a lift to the airport? My car won't start and I'm running out of time" Once inside the doctor's car Joe told Dad to drive fast.

Rushing toward the Oakland Airport through the Alameda tunnel a police officer on a motorcycle sped up behind them, red light flashing and siren wailing. Fifty, one-gallon glass jugs of moonshine were in the padded rack, behind drawn curtains in the rear of the big Franklin car. Joe became frantic. He thought he'd be implicated in the illegal bootlegging operation and would lose his job as an airline pilot.

"Good Lord, what are we going to do Harry? What if he wants to look inside behind the curtains? I should have taken a taxi—damn!!"

Dad, as usual thinking clearly under pressure, tried to soothe him, "Calm down now. You let me handle this." As soon as they were out of the tunnel, he pulled over to the curb. As the officer approached, Dad leaned out the window, "Boy officer, are we ever glad to see you. United Air Lines just called and ordered my brother Joe here to take a charter flight out to Seattle with some serum to save the life of a little boy."

The officer, at first suspicious, looked in and saw an authentic United Air Lines Captain in the passenger seat. Joe, extending his hand, introduced himself and the truth became obvious to the officer when he saw the silver wings on Joe's chest and the four stripes on the sleeves of his uniform.

Dad quickly continued, "We'd be forever in your debt if you'd give us an escort to the airport. If there's a fine for speeding I'll be glad to pay it to try and save the life of the little boy."

The mood of the officer instantly changed. Completely taken in by the story of the non-existent boy dying in Seattle the officer spoke.

"Captain, I'll be glad to escort you. Fellows just stay in close behind me."

With the police officer in the lead, they began driving much faster. Dad then worried that a jug might break. If the car hit a hard bump the pungent smell of alcohol would give everything away. He also became concerned that one of the rear window curtains, poorly secured in place by a small and inefficient clasp, would fly up and expose the fifty one-gallon glass jugs.

Red light flashing and siren screaming, chasing everyone off the road, the officer cleared the way for the big car right up to the main door of the airport. Joe said a quick goodbye, hurried into the building and on time, took his regularly scheduled flight out to Seattle.

The officer parked his motorcycle, turned off the engine and red light and strolled over to the car. Leaning on it he lit a cigarette. "It sure makes me feel good when I'm able to do something like this to help."

Obviously in no hurry to leave the big policeman continued to lean on the car with both arms and almost all his weight. On the running board his heavily booted foot jostled and bumped, shaking and rocking the car back and forth as he continued to chat with Dad.

Finally the officer left. Relieved, Dad sat a few moments watching the motorcycle weave back into traffic and disappear. Heading back to the hotel, Dad saw a diner and slowed the car to drive in for a cup of coffee. As he turned into the parking lot and gently applied the brakes the front tires hit the little bump at the first rise of the driveway. The tiny jolt caused the main curtain behind Dad's head to come loose from the poorly constructed latch. Instantly it rolled, flapping all the way up, fully exposing the rack and the fifty one-gallon jugs of moonshine. Dad drove to a vacant area at the far end of the parking lot, quickly got out and opened the back door. Reaching inside he pulled the black curtain down re-latching it as tightly as he could. The curtain could have flown up as the officer bumped the running board with his heavily booted foot, but it hadn't.

A few months later, after Dad just finished making a new batch of "Nectar of the Gods", Mother experienced another twinge of conscience, called the police, and the cycle began once more.

In 1929, unable to resolve the conflict within her she and Dad divorced. Mother and I moved to St. Paul, Minnesota to live with Aunt Clara, Uncle Pete Hansen, and their youngest son, Herbert.

❖ SKELETON IN THE CLOSET ❖

What family doesn't have a "Skeleton in the closet"? I first heard ours rattle, when I was a child living in Olinda California. Bits and pieces were whispered or spoken of in hushed tones. As I grew older I tried to discover the truth.

"Ma, what's this about Dad and Jack Davis?"

She'd reply nervously, "Oh, it's nothing, nothing," and quickly change the subject.

In the mid-1920's, Grandma Smith, Dad's mother, leased an apple orchard in Dee, Oregon. The ranch house and bunkhouse were located close together. From the northern flanks of Mt. Hood the large orchard-filled valley extended down to the Columbia River. In addition to apples, apricots and cherries this area, at that time, produced the greatest number of pears of any place in the United States. In the valley Dee is located on the east fork of the Hood River. Near the ranch an old wooden bridge crossed the east fork and a short distance downstream a big waterfall constantly thundered and frothed as the river poured into a deep black hole.

Grandma appointed my dad, Harry, as Superintendent of the orchard, so he and Mother moved from Portland to Dee. Dad needed a Ranch Foreman to help with the work. One evening, Grandma and Dad stopped at a local tavern for a few glasses of beer. In the tavern a six foot two inch, red headed Swede, Jack Davis, sat having a drink. In the congenial atmosphere the three met and talked. Jack said his last name really was Davidson, but he shortened it to Davis many years ago. Soon Grandma and Dad agreed that Jack, a loner with no family, had the qualities and experience needed to be a good Ranch Foreman.

Almost everywhere he lived, Dad put a still into operation. From experience he knew the art of politics. Using the outpourings of the still he made a point to "cultivate" the local police, from the man in charge to the most recently hired recruit. Because of Prohibition, when the local authorities became "thirsty" a free pint or two of Dad's booze, with its excellent quality and taste, quickly made them his friends.

On the outskirts of Dee the Hood River Valley Fruit Growers Association operated a packing plant. The town Sheriff was one of the major owners. A tall smokestack, badly needing a coat of paint, pierced the sky. Having worked as a high rigger on the construction of the Oakland Bay Bridge, Dad had the ability to move sure-footed and unafraid at great heights. Dad always attributed this ability to the habit of sampling his own booze: he might have needed the sample in order to bring on some "Dutch courage" but he always said that a pint or so "kept him steady on his feet." One day the Sheriff mentioned that the stack sure could use a coat of paint, and Dad thought of a way to "get in good" with the local law. Dad told him, "Maybe I could help. I was a professional high climber and rigger for many years."

Falling into the trap the Sheriff asked, "Harry, would you consider painting it?"

"Sure, if you'll help," Dad answered.

"I'll be more than glad to help. That stack's needed paint for a couple years, but we couldn't find anyone who'd work so high up. By golly Harry, I'm sure glad you decided to move here," the Sheriff grinned.

The opportune moment had arrived. "Do you take a little nip once in awhile…you know, the real hard stuff?"

Accompanied by a low chuckle came the cheerful answer, "Oh sure, I've been known to down a few now and then."

Early one Saturday, with the Sheriff helping and the boiler shut down for the weekend, Dad climbed the built-in steel ladder on the outside of the stack. At the top, he rigged the ropes, block and tackle, pulleys, bosun's chair and staging. The Sheriff drove to Hood River to get the paint while Dad carefully checked everything for safety. Returning, the Sheriff hoisted the paint to Dad at the top of the stack. Painting always begins at the top with the chair, staging and ropes set in such a way that the painter circles the stack, manipulating the ropes while progressing downward. By Saturday evening the job was nearly finished. By noon the next day, Dad and the Sheriff were removing the rigging and cleaning the area to make it ready for work. In his car, an old Star touring model, Dad had a gallon of his excellent booze for the Sheriff and a pint for himself.

"I brought you a little present," Dad said as he handed it over.

The Sheriff's eyes widened with delight. "Well, come on in the office awhile Harry, where we can sit and relax. We've put in some hard work and need a break," he smiled obviously anticipating the taste and feeling of warmth he'd get from the booze.

The next few hours in the packing plant office were spent quenching their thirst, smoking and talking. The Sheriff drank generously from the gallon jug. Neither had eaten lunch and the booze, warming their insides, produced an atmosphere of camaraderie.

About 4:30 in the afternoon Dad said, "I'd better be getting on home. Supper will be ready and I'll have to get washed up."

Totally drunk, the Sheriff, forgetting Dad had his own car parked nearby, rose unsteadily to his feet and slurred, "Can I give you a ride?" The question wavered from his lips.

Seeing the man could hardly stand, Dad answered, "No, thanks."

Parking his car behind the house, when Dad stepped inside, he heard piano music. He walked in and on the piano bench sat Mother and Jack Davis. By now Jack was treated like a family member. He could read music, and while sitting beside her he'd turn the page at the right moment and keep the paper flat so the music wouldn't be interrupted. As Dad entered he saw Jack leaning close to Mother while hesitating, getting ready to turn a page. In his intoxicated state Dad assumed Jack was making a play for her and his hot temper flared.

Dad always carried a loaded gun, an Army .45 caliber Colt

automatic. He pulled it from his pocket and leveled it at Jack, "Get the hell off that bench you backbiting son of a bitch. Go get your own woman and leave mine alone."

Both Jack and Mother tried to explain that Jack had only been turning pages of the new sheet music to hold it down because it wouldn't always stay flat. The explanation didn't register in Dad's alcohol-soaked brain. With the gun still leveled at Jack he told them both to go and get in the car. Going through the back door on the way outside to the car in the driveway, they had to pass through the kitchen. Here Jack saw his chance. When Dad wasn't looking he picked up a long bladed butcher knife, tucked it under the waistband beneath his belt and covered it with his baggy shirt.

In the front seat of the old Star, Mother sat between Jack and Dad, who carried the gun in his left hand jacket pocket. On the short drive to the east fork of the Hood River, the car weaved on the narrow road. Just before coming to a sharp right hand turn, only a short distance now from the old wooden bridge, a parking area had been bulldozed out by the original road-builders. Dad pulled in, parked and jumped out ordering Jack to get out too. He told Mother, "You stay in the car. This won't take long." With the gun in Jack's back Dad hustled him along the road. After a few yards they disappeared around the corner and onto the bridge.

A short distance downstream from the bridge is a waterfall that, pouring its torrents for centuries, has created below itself a huge dark pool called the Glory Hole. That name was given to it in covered wagon days, after a team of four horses, two men and a supply wagon tried to ford the river upstream and had been washed over the falls after the horses lost their footing in the rush of springtime runoff. Sucked under into the hole, horses, men and wagon disappeared forever without a trace.

The river, located in a geologic volcanic formation of Mt. Hood, has a huge subterranean lava tube running for many miles that slants gradually upward out of the bottom of the unusually deep hole. Downstream from the Glory Hole, water returns into the bottom of the river through many small openings in the top and sides of the large lava tube beneath, keeping the river flow constant. In winter, water rages over the falls into the depths of the huge hole. Tall fir trees with their roots and branches attached, after being torn from the earth by storms, crash into the pool and send spray high in the air before they are sucked under, never to be seen again.

Mother heard six shots fired in rapid succession. Alone now and obviously drunk, Dad weaved and stumbled back to the car.

"What did you do to Jack?" Mother questioned.

Dad replied, "He tried to kill me. He had a butcher knife and ran at me with it. I had to shoot him. It was self defense!!"

"Where is he now?" Mother asked.

"When I shot him he fell onto the road in the middle of the bridge so I grabbed his arms and pulled him over to the edge. Then I took my foot and pushed him off into the river. I saw him float away and go over the falls into the Glory Hole."

In disbelief Mother gasped, "Harry!! No, you didn't? You have to call the Sheriff right away and tell him what happened. If you don't and he finds out you'll be charged with murder."

Dad refused to make the call and as soon as they returned to the house he stretched out on the living room sofa and went to sleep. About one o'clock in the morning he awoke. Mother, still up, urged him to call the Sheriff. Finally persuaded, he picked up the phone.

"Bill," he said, calling the Sheriff by his first name, "This is Harry. I killed Jack Davis so you better come and arrest me."

The Sheriff, in no condition to talk because of a roaring hangover resulting from the "happy hour" with Dad, exclaimed,

"Aw, for Christ sake Harry, what the hell are you calling me at this hour for? It's after one o'clock in the morning!!"

"I just told you, I killed Jack Davis, so you better come and arrest me," Dad repeated.

"Good God Harry, go sleep it off" the Sheriff mumbled.

"If you don't come and arrest me now," Dad said, "I'll leave tomorrow and you'll never find me."

"O.K., O.K., Harry, call me in the morning and we'll talk."

"The hell I will," Dad growled slamming down the receiver.

Early the next morning Dad packed the car, locked the house, and he and Mother returned to their apartment at 1824 S.W. Market Street in Portland.

Grandma Smith made arrangements for someone else to operate the apple orchard, and as long as he lived, Dad never heard a word from the Sheriff of Hood River County.

The shooting incident between Dad and Jack happened in 1924, the year before I was born, so it was years before I was able to find out much about it. Dad and Mother divorced in 1928, when I was three, compounding my dilemma. Before leaving home at age 17 to join the Navy, I had heard only small fragments of the story from her standpoint.

After the war, when I was 21, I made my home with Dad in Seattle, Washington. Still curious about the incident, once in awhile I'd ask him a question about it; but he too gave incomplete and non-specific answers. Mother now lived in Tacoma, 30 miles away, and I'd visit her every month. I also continued to question her from time to time.

Finally, when she reached 70 years of age, I got my first specific answer while visiting one day. She admitted hearing six shots while waiting near the bridge in the old Star car. "I couldn't see the bridge, which was around a corner from the parking area. Because I didn't actually witness it I couldn't swear in court that Jack had been killed. Early the next morning when we were packing to go back to Portland I do remember that I couldn't find my favorite butcher knife. Later, Grandma Smith told me Jack never returned for any of his clothes or belongings that were left in the bunkhouse."

That day Mother reluctantly told me the rest of the story.

Years later I shared it with my wife and our two small daughters. In 1962 (before the State of Oregon built a new bridge of cement and steel over the east fork of the Hood River) I took them to Dee to look at the old, wooden bridge. I wanted to see whether the descriptions I had heard of it and the surrounding area were accurate.

I parked our car in the same open space provided by the original road builders and described so well by Mother. Brush, trees and the embankment that she had described prevented me from seeing the bridge, which was just beyond the sharp curve in the road. Making my way around the corner and onto the bridge I noticed, as Dad had said, that it had no sidewalks. The roadway, made from 4 x 8 inch heavy planking, was covered over with a 3-inch layer of Macadam paving. To prevent the roadway from twisting or warping, long thick steel rods, with threads and turnbuckles for adjustments, ran on each side raised 18 inches above the outer edges of the roadway planks. There were no obstructions or safety devices below the rods to prevent anything from falling into the river through this unprotected 1.5 foot space. I could see how easily someone, using his foot, could push a big man off of the bridge, underneath the steel rods and into the rushing water below.

Seeing this I had mixed emotions. Did Dad really do it? Am I the son of someone who got away with murder?

In 1956, at age 54, Dad had a stroke. As a result of its severity he remained confined to bed for the next 21 years, yet he never lost his sense of humor and his mind remained crystal clear. Well informed, he eagerly discussed politics and the latest local and world events. He always had at least one joke to tell whenever we'd visit him at the care center, a few miles south of Seattle in Federal Way. One example: "There were two dust-covered skeletons that hung side by side in a closet for more than 30 years. Finally one turned to the other and said, "You know, if only I had enough guts, I'd get the hell out of here."

In 1971, after our oldest daughter, Berniece married, I told the story about Jack Davis to her husband, 23 year old, Arvid Ivar "Bud" Anderson, a 6-foot 2-inch, red-bearded Swede. Dad had never met him, and together Bud and I formed a plan.

Taking Bud to the care center I had him walk into the ward unannounced. When he got beside Dad's bed he smiled and asked, "Are you Harry Curnow?"

Without hesitation Dad answered, "Yes."

Extending his hand, Bud said, "Pleased to meet you. I'm Bud Davis. Maybe you remember my Dad, Jack Davis."

My wife and I, with our daughters Yvonne and Berniece, were hiding behind the door in the hallway and heard Dad instantly shout.

"It was self defense, it was self defense!! He came at me with a knife!!"

It took almost fifty years for me to be absolutely sure of the truth.

❖ THE ROAD TO CALIFORNIA ❖

In 1931 Mother decided to move from St. Paul, Minnesota back to Portland, Oregon. Aunt Hattie and her husband Billy Moravec lived there in their big new house on Northeast 35th and Bryce Avenue. They had six young children and needed someone to help care for them.

Because of the Depression we couldn't afford to make the trip by bus or train, but Mother was not deterred. She checked the newspaper advertisements, where people who owned a car were sometimes offering to share a ride somewhere in exchange for payment of half the gasoline and oil expenses.

Mother made arrangements with a couple who had a new Model A Ford four-door sedan. They would be driving west as far as Spokane, Washington to visit their pregnant daughter. The luggage left very little room in the back seat for Mother and me, but I could tell by her smiles and cheer that she was happy to be returning to Portland. She would not have to endure any more harsh Minnesota winters.

We were able to stay on the road several days without interruption because both the husband and wife knew how to drive. In 1931, this was exceptional. One morning we were forced to stop in Wyoming, because the car was running low on fuel. It was only 6:00 AM, but "filling stations" were few and far between, especially in remote areas.

The station didn't open until 7:00 AM, and in those days there was no "self-service". Waiting beside the pump for almost an hour without the engine running the car's interior became uncomfortably cold. Ford's 1931 Model-A had no electric, fan-forced heating system. When the car moved ahead a metal shroud around the hot-exhaust manifold would channel warm air to a ducted opening under the dashboard and into the passenger compartment. No forward motion, no heat. Heavy rain spattering on the metal roof made the air seem even colder. As we waited my teeth chattered.

Finally, the station owner arrived. I watched fascinated as he went through the process of fueling our car: he hand-pumped a slightly red-colored fuel from an underground tank to a 10-gallon glass container atop the delivery tower. After the glass container was full he removed the fuel cap located on the car's hood, just in front of the windshield's centerline. Then he inserted the nozzle. I watched the silver metal ball of the dashboard gas gauge jiggle and roll slowly around from "E", the empty position, to 1/4th, 1/2, 3/4ths and then to the "F" mark indicating full.

While gasoline pumped slowly into the tank our driver had time to talk with the station owner. In 1931, many of the main highways were not good. In places, Montana and Wyoming for example, after a hard rain the highway often became little more than mud and ruts. Our driver asked, "What's the best and shortest route across the Rockies? We're on the way to Spokane."

The station owner gave his advice, "Well, from here there are two routes. I know only what the few travelers have told me in the last few days. Some said there are nearly impassable washouts on one route. Others said on the alternate route there are mudslides...some so deep in places, that if a car slid into one it would stay mired until spring. Everyone talked about rockslides on both routes. All these hazards are a hundred miles or more on down the road...if you can't get past them it will be too far for you to make the return trip back here and the next filling station is beyond all of that. I'm told the crews are doing the best they can to keep the roads open, but there's no guarantee you'll get through." Raising a large work worn hand he pointed a bent and crippled finger westward and continued. "You know, in the fall with all this rain and the possibility of snow, it's not a good time to be on any of the steep roads through those mountains. Hardly anyone is going over either route now. You folks and the youngster could be marooned for days."

As he wrapped up this lengthy description, the station owner removed the nozzle and replaced the fuel cap, then he offered another bit of information. "On either route you'll be starting up the steepest part in the dark."

I looked through the windshield to the road ahead. It led into a flat, boulder-strewn, treeless and desolate area. Though a main highway it was mostly mud- and water-filled ruts: to me it seemed impossible to drive through. In the distance loomed a bleak, gray mountainous horizon that did little to encourage hope. Rain continued to pour. Mother's voice sounded strained when she asked our driver, "Do you think we should try to go over such a steep road at night?"

"I think we'll be O.K. if we go slow. We want to be in Spokane in a couple of days for the birth of our first grandchild."

We said goodbye to the station owner, then started the car and drove out onto the muddy road, bumping and jostling our way toward the ominous, distant peaks.

After awhile, the rain stopped and the day went well. Toward evening, I tried to sleep, but it's not easy for a kid to doze off on an empty stomach. We couldn't find a place that served food, and I was hungry. Sleep finally overcame hunger and when I awoke it was dark.

I could tell by the sound that the car was in lower gears, climbing a mountain. The headlights reflected their beams off sheer, gray granite walls on the inside of the narrow road. I was watching them when we rounded a sharp curve and their beams shot into space, casting light across the canyon and onto an opposite wall. Its jagged profile extended down for hundreds of feet. The road had no guardrail for safety. I felt very small and isolated.

We approached a massive chunk of granite that hung out over the roadway. I remembered the warning about mudslides and rock falls, and I sensed Mother's apprehension. With the clarity of a 6 year old I could imagine the terrible consequences of a mudslide. Shifting soil could loosen the overhang and drop tons of stone slabs on top of the car...but, with good fortune, we passed safely through the dangerous area.

Two days later we arrived in Spokane. From there Mother and I took a Greyhound bus to Portland. With little money left she couldn't afford a ticket for me. She knew that children under age six rode free when accompanied by an adult. Taking advantage of my small, thin stature she told the ticket agent I was only five. She bought her ticket and before we got on in my ear she whispered, "If anyone asks, remember to tell them you were born February 8, 1926, which will make you only 5 years old." No one questioned us, and by not having to pay fare for me she had just enough money to buy us one glass of milk and one sandwich at a rest stop between Spokane and Portland. We shared them both.

During the trip an unpleasant odor seeped into the bus. It came from the leaky exhaust pipe of the big, inefficiently operating, gasoline engine under the long-nosed hood of the old Greyhound bus. I could hear the undulating whine of the engine and metallic clashing and grinding of gears whenever the driver shifted on hills. He'd obviously never learned to "double clutch" in order to shift smoothly. It's a wonder we got to Portland the way he'd either lug down or race the big old engine. Making matters worse, some passengers lit cigarettes. The combination of tobacco smoke, exhaust fumes, loud noise from the gnashing of gear teeth and swaying and lurching in this polluted atmosphere, caused some people to throw up, especially when rounding curves.

Hattie didn't need full time help with her six children, so Mother also went to work at Harrower Laboratories in Portland, where she had been a secretary before going to Minnesota. I was enrolled in Beaumont School on Northeast 42nd and Fremont Street. In St. Paul I had completed the first grade and half of the second. As a result I was now in class 2-B, the last half of the second grade.

That summer, in June of 1932, Mother decided I'd have a better life if I left the city to live with my uncle, Alfred Becker, on his small 11-acre ranch in Olinda, California. About 40 miles south of Mt. Shasta in northern California, Olinda is located 12 miles southwest of Redding. In a rural setting the very sparsely populated area consisted of various sized farms and only about

100 residents. Alfred hadn't quite finished building his house when I arrived, so for my first six months in California I boarded with a Seventh Day Adventist family, the Glassfords. Their home was in Cloverdale, another small community about ten miles from Alfred's ranch. That fall I was enrolled in third grade at the one-room Cloverdale school where Eddie Matchen, who later would become the famous heavyweight professional boxing contender, and his sisters also attended. As Postmaster in the tiny town of Oak, a short distance away, their father had a steady Government job.

There were several small communities in this area far out in the countryside. Many were only a wide spot in a dirt road with a house or two beside it. Most had no Post Office, store or filling station but many had a unique name. Igo, Ono, Oak, Churn Creek, Burnt Ranch, Whiskeytown and Poverty Flat to name a few.

Alfred finished his house in late December, and I left Glassford's to move in with him. He enrolled me in the Olinda school, where I would begin the second half of third grade as soon as Christmas vacation ended, in January 1933. Olinda Grade School also was a one-room country school. With eight rows of desks, each row seated the students of a single grade. Only one teacher, Mrs. Jordan, taught every subject in all the grades. In the middle of the room stood a wood-burning stove used for heat in winter. The schoolhouse was quite old and had a 12-foot ceiling. Above it was a generously sized attic space and a bell tower. In that dark environment lived hundreds of bats. One day my Cousin, Rex Moravec decided that it would be "fun" to climb into the attic and catch a baby bat. At the front of the room in the top drawer of her desk, Mrs. Jordan kept a few personal items: purse, some makeup and one medium size jar, made of opaque glass and having a screw on top. In it she kept rubber bands and thumbtacks. When Mrs. Jordan and all of the students were outside during lunch hour, Rex climbed into the attic and caught a tiny bat. With nobody in the room he put the squeaking baby inside the jar and loosely replaced the lid.

When classes resumed Mrs. Jordan became puzzled by a noise in the top desk drawer. Leaning back in her chair and opening it she recognized the sound as coming from the opaque jar. Curious now, as soon as she removed the lid the little bat "flapped" itself out of the bottle. On her lap it continued to flap and screech. Extremely afraid of bats, Mrs. Jordan leaped to her feet with a holler one could probably hear for at least half a mile. The bat dropped to the floor and quickly disappeared. But for a long time Mrs. Jordan kept right on "sweeping it off" herself with both hands, as she continued to wail.

Extremely intelligent, Uncle Alfred graduated from Carleton College in Northfield, Minnesota, Class of 1913, with a major in mathematics and a minor in philosophy. Northfield is known historically for being a primarily Swedish community where the famous Northfield Raid occurred. In that incident, the infamous James/Younger gang was cut to pieces by a bunch of storekeepers with Winchesters, proving that if you are smart you don't mess with Swedes! Carleton was, and still remains, a most distinguished college in the Midwest.

Soon after graduation Alfred went to work for a young government agency, the Internal Revenue Service. When the United States became involved in World War I (WWI), he joined the Army. As a member of the Quartermaster Corps, he was sent to France where he was devastated by the influenza epidemic and almost died. Returning home to St. Paul he took a job as a bookkeeper in a barrel factory.

Alfred wanted to become a schoolteacher in Minnesota but after returning from overseas the "true love" of his life, rejected him. Brokenhearted, in 1931 he moved to California and bought 11 acres of raw land for 11 cents an acre, a total of $1.21. (The family still has the original Bill of Sale.) In 2002, the land was selling for $25,000 an acre, situated in a prime living area. Alfred never married, and I became his only student. Because of Alfred's teaching and encouragement, which began with me at age six, Mrs. Jordan had me skip both the fifth and seventh grades.

Graduating in 1939 from the eighth grade at Olinda School in a class of three, I became the "valedictorian."

As it turned out, having been sent to live with Uncle Alfred at an early age became a terrific stroke of luck. With his superb education he exposed me to "big words". He made learning new things easy and enjoyable, and he loved the experience of teaching. His efforts were rewarded and especially fruitful later in life, when I attended Seattle University, University of New Mexico and Washington State University, having earned three advanced degrees.

When I moved in, nearly all of Alfred's land was overrun with the low growing shrub called chaparral. Scrub oak and manzanita, as well as large white oak, black oak and Digger pine, made up the rest of the vegetation. Arising in the southwest corner of his land a small stream that ran all year, fed by a natural spring, coursed through an ever-deepening gully that bisected the ranch. Lush wild blackberry vines producing large fruit, juicy and sweet, thickly lined both banks.

Before the land could grow crops it had to be cleared. Though hard work I remember it as being fun. It became much easier to rid the land of trash vegetation after a day or two of pouring rain. The water-soaked soil made the surface roots of the chaparral less difficult to pull out by hand. We stacked the brush in a huge pile in the center of a clearing. When it towered 15 feet or more, Alfred would set it on fire. Another name for chaparral is "greasewood," and it lives up to its name. Even when fresh and green, when set on fire, it almost explodes into flame. He always set it ablaze at dusk so that distant neighbors would see the glow in the evening sky and know he was making progress clearing his acreage. During the process he cut down and saved the larger trees and manzanita to burn for firewood in the stove used for both cooking and heat.

Alfred instilled in me at the age of six, while we struggled to clear his 11 acres, that the feeling of satisfaction and accomplishment from work well done is its own reward. He expressed the work ethic this way, "Something accomplished, something done, to earn the night's repose." He also expressed another idea about work, "Any job worth doing is worth doing well." Wise words, worth remembering: they helped me shape a successful life.

It took from the end of December until the following March to finish digging out the stumps and removing rocks to prepare the soil for plowing. Alfred borrowed a gentle old mare named Dixie and a plow and a harrow from our neighbor, Ed Everson. We took turns walking behind the mare and using the tools to break new earth, and in a few days the soil was ready for a crop. The first thing planted were five acres of Marshall strawberries. The iron rich, semi-volcanic red soil of Olinda is unsurpassed for raising them. Never have I tasted strawberries, many double or triple in size, with the sweetness, juiciness and unique flavor of a "dead ripe" Marshall. Crushed in a bowl they needed no extra sugar. Covered with thick rich cream, given us by a kindly neighbor, they were exquisite. Whenever I ate this harvest time treat, I felt rewarded for work well done. The flavor carried with it a feeling of success and accomplishment.

Where did the Marshall's go? I've never seen them in stores anywhere since leaving California in 1942. Today's strawberries aren't sweet, have little juice, taste or aroma. White and pithy, inside they are almost as hard as apples. Good for shipping long distances, they are absolutely no good to eat—especially for someone spoiled at an early age by the delicious Marshall's, topped with fresh, thick cream.

❖ OLINDA ❖

In 1933, after living with Alfred for more than a year, the five acres of strawberries we had planted brought in some much needed cash. Strawberries are a very work-intensive crop, so Alfred wrote to Mother in Portland saying he needed the help of a full-time cook and housekeeper. She agreed to move to Olinda.

Alfred's bachelor diet, mostly starch with a little pork or beef, didn't suit Mother at all. "To cook properly, I need milk."

To have milk and cream we needed a cow. During WWI, in France, Alfred had suffered a severely debilitating case of influenza. He had a small but steady pension of $23.00 a month. For $7.50 he bought a five-year old Holstein. He named her Violet. Holsteins give a lot of milk but the cream content is much less than that of a Jersey or Guernsey. To provide feed for the cow, 2.5 acres of millet and 2.5 acres of alfalfa were planted. Harvested and stored in a small, newly built barn, it saved a lot of money and became Violet's main daily feed, along with her supplement of costly rolled oats. This came in a 100-pound burlap bag. We emptied it and stored the oats in a clean 50-gallon steel drum inside the shed next to the house. The shed door always— and without fail—had to be secured from the outside using an old-fashioned but very efficient wooden-bar latch that Alfred made of scraps from 2 x 4's. If Violet broke out of her pasture, got in the drum full of oats and overate, she would bloat and die within a few days. Alfred warned me, while making a humorous play on words, "Always remember to securely replace the lid and lock the snap ring on the drum in the shed. In addition to the latch on the shed door, this will be her second line of 'de fence' if Violet gets loose."

Milking the cow morning and evening became my job. Before going to the barn, I'd fill an empty three-pound coffee can with oats. With this in one hand, in the other I would carry the stainless steel milk pail containing a gallon of warm water (the bail always wrapped in a clean, dry flour sack.) About a hundred yards from the house I'd enter the small barn. Violet always hurried to greet me and from her feed box, eagerly ate her "treat" of rolled oats as I sat on a one-legged stool, washed her teats and udder with the warm water, dried everything and milked her. Alfred said the treat of oats made her "let down her milk." I didn't care about that. Grumbling to myself I only knew that at 6:30 AM, when other kids were still asleep...or at that time in the evening when they were out playing...I had to be in the barn milking the cow.

Milking the cow and cutting wood was called "doing my everyday chores". Now that mother cooked full-time for three, more fuel had to be supplied for the old-fashioned, wood burning stove. Fortunately, lots of large dead manzanita, free for the taking, lay in no man's land just outside Alfred's back fence. I had a red wagon, a "Radio Flyer", Alfred bought me for Christmas my first year on the ranch. He'd told me, "It's your reward for doing good work helping me clear the land." I used my wagon to gather firewood. Everyday I put the sharp, double bladed ax and a few lengths of strong rope in the wagon, then pulled it out the back gate to forage for the daily load. I'd cut lots of fast-burning, high-heat-producing manzanita and some slower-burning black oak. Alfred's oft-repeated quotation about the work ethic, "Something accomplished, something done, to earn the night's repose," inspired me...but repose was still the most attractive. On each trip I wanted to carry as much as I could. At first, I would pile the 4-foot to 6-foot long branches on the wagon as high as possible then tightly tie them with the rope, circling it around both the wood and wagon. Thus the neatly-arranged branches became top-heavy loads, and they often tipped over as I took a quick turn as I hurried along. I then spent a lot of time restacking and re-tying the wood. It didn't take long to learn "The faster I went, the behinder I got." Going slower always resulted in less work, frustration and waste of time.

Once home each branch of the dry and brittle manzanita had to be cut to stove length. When incorrectly hit with the ax a newly cut stick would break off and fly at my head, as if propelled by a giant steel spring. With a "crack" it slammed against my skull. This was truly the school of hard knocks. It took only a few times to learn that a massive bump on the head, a pair of black eyes or a bloody nose would be my reward if I did not place the branch properly across the big oak log used as a chopping block.

On a very hot day during the second week in May of 1934, Cody William Stamps walked into our lives. Alfred, Mother and I were out in the five-acre field picking strawberries, which were to be sold wholesale to the stores in Redding the next day. With a bedroll and pack on his back, sweating and thirsty, Cody stopped to ask for a drink of water. When finished, he thanked Alfred then asked, "Could you use someone to work on your place? In return I'd only want a place to sleep and meals."

Because of his bout with influenza during WWI, and in spite of working in the clean country air of Olinda, Alfred was not in good physical condition. Thin in both face and body, his muscles were poorly developed. He was so thin that he looked taller than 5-feet 7-inches. The hectic work season of strawberry harvest had just started, and he welcomed this tall, well-mannered, broad-shouldered young man.

"Can you go to work right away?" Alfred motioned toward the field, "The berries need to be picked as soon as possible to keep from getting hot, overripe and spoiling before we can get them to the stores in Redding every morning."

Cody slipped off his pack and bedroll saying, "Just show me how you want them to be picked and where to start."

When Mother, a petite and attractive blue-eyed blonde came in from the field and saw the handsome stranger she became "all a' twitter" and immediately engaged Cody in conversation.

"Where are you from? What kind of work do you like?" she asked. I noticed she smiled and laughed more than usual while talking with him. Mother's interest was obvious.

When he had a chance to speak he said he came from Oklahoma, was 35 years old and had ridden the freight trains out west to find work.

Cody stood 6-feet 2-inches tall. He had thick, black wavy hair and brown eyes that always seemed to be smiling when looking at anyone. Half Cherokee Indian, he was very muscular and had a deep but soft voice. Talented and practical, he said he could do almost any kind of work or fix just about anything that needed repair. I, too, liked him right away.

Later in the week I became aware that our meals had improved after Cody came to eat with us.

Cooking full-time now for four, Mother said we needed two cows because when Violet "went dry" there would be no milk with which to make good meals. A farmer in Churn Creek, a tiny town about 15 miles away, had one for sale; she cost $10.00, and he agreed to deliver her at no extra charge. A Guernsey, she gave less milk than Violet but it contained almost twice as much thick, rich cream.

Our new cow had to be given a name: the name she brought with her, Tilley, just didn't seem right. One evening after supper as we sat relaxing, Alfred said, "Shall we name her Rosy? What do you think, Gene?"

Turning toward Cody I asked," How would Tootsie sound?"

He thought quietly for a moment then said, "Don't you all think a cow that looks like her would like to be named Bessie?" Looking at Mother, "What do you think, Frances?"

Without hesitation she replied, "Oh yes, she really does look like her name should be Bessie." Mother did a lot of instant agreeing these days when Cody presented an idea.

At her home in Churn Creek, Bessie had grazed for years in a pasture of soft clover and alfalfa. From lack of normal wear her hoofs were long and misshapen, making her lame. She limped badly. Cody used an ordinary hacksaw to cut off their excess length. With a coarse steel file he rounded off and smoothed the ends, returning them to their natural shape. In a few days she walked normally. "It's easy to do and painless, just like cutting our toenails." As usual, it impressed Mother and Alfred was delighted at having saved the cost of a veterinary bill.

I now had two cows to milk, when both were producing. At times we'd have too much milk and some spoiled because in Olinda we had no electricity, nor did we have any kind of refrigerator. Fresh from the cow we placed the milk in "milk pans". They were made of tin 10-inches in diameter and 4-inches deep. Covering them with a piece of clean white cloth kept out flies and other insects. But with air temperature as high as 121 degrees, even placed in the shade outside on the back porch, milk soured fast.

After Cody saw my mother throw away spoiled milk. he told Alfred that he knew how to build an inexpensive "cooler" that would keep out flies and insects *and* lower the temperature so the milk would stay sweet and usable for a longer time. As Alfred listened to Cody explain how it would work, he realized having a cooler would be a great idea. Alfred agreed to buy the material. He also thought that accepting Cody's offer to work on the farm in exchange for room and board had to be one of the best decisions he'd made in a long time.

Though very intelligent, Alfred could not learn to drive. The year he planted the 5-acres of strawberries he bought a 1923 Model T Ford Coup. He intended to use it to deliver crates of strawberries to the stores in Redding. But no matter how many times someone showed him, Alfred couldn't learn to control the three foot pedals and the steering column devices, combination emergency brake and neutral lever, spark and gas feed handles in the right sequence. So for two years the car sat unused under a tree behind the house.

Cody knew how to drive well. Checking the car, he filled the battery and radiator with water, cleaned and set the spark plugs, inspected the oil level and the gasoline tank, located underneath the seat, set the vibrator points on each of the four ignition coils and, with an old hand-operated pump, filled the tires with air. The battery, unused for so long, was dead. Attempting to start the old car using the hand crank proved unsuccessful so we pushed it out the front gate to the road on the brow of a nearby hill. Cody got in the drivers seat. "O.K., push her on over and we'll see if she'll still run after sitting so long."

Sputtering and coughing, the car began rolling faster and faster downhill. Even though everything was being done right, the engine was not catching. Reluctantly, with the bottom of the hill fast approaching...at the very last moment...it started. When the engine warmed up it ran smoothly. Smiling with pleasure, Cody drove it back to the house where he allowed it to continue running at a moderate speed for half an hour, charging the dead battery. Alfred laughed with delight and clapped his hands knowing he now had his own transportation. He would no longer have to depend on our good neighbor, Ed Everson, to take the strawberries to Redding.

Alfred stayed home while Cody and I drove to the Diamond Match Company in Anderson, 6 miles away, to get the material to make the cooler. When we got back to the ranch, Cody first made a box 8-feet long, 3-feet wide and 1-foot deep. It needed no top. He caulked all the seams to make it water tight. Small holes were drilled 2 inches apart on all four sides, 1 inch up from the bottom: each hole perfectly fitted to an old-fashioned wooden kitchen match, which was inserted with the head sticking outward. The open-topped, 1-foot deep box became a leakproof container with a variable system to let water drip out in controlled amounts. Pulling a matchstick outward a small distance increased the flow and pushing it in decreased it. Using 4 x 4's, Cody next built a strong frame, 8- by 4- by 3-feet, and set it on sturdy legs. Within the frame two shelves were added. On one side two doors, each a foot in width and covered with galvanized chicken wire and burlap, were hung to swing outward. Galvanized chicken wire and a double layer of burlap (used oat sacks) were then stretched around the rest of the frame. With the leakproof box placed on top, filled with water and adjusted by tweaking the matchsticks, the burlap sides became soaking wet. The cooler was placed in the shade of an oak tree close to the house. With the water on the wet burlap rapidly evaporating in the nearly constant north wind, the temperature of the milk inside became much lower.

Raw milk, however, always contains some bacteria. Even in the cooler it soured in five or six days, but this was much longer than when it spoiled in three days. Mother now could usually use it all for cooking or drinking. Once in awhile a pan full did sour, but because there were no flies in the cooler to introduce harmful bacteria Cody showed us how the thick Jell-O-like milk could be safely eaten. He called it "clabber milk", and it tasted a lot like today's natural yogurt. With a little salt and pepper sprinkled on, it tasted so good, I'd often eat half a milk-pan full. A wonderful treat for an always hungry young boy!

❖ THE OCARINAS ❖

Aunt Hattie's family moved onto a farm adjoining Alfred's. They too were poor, but her home always rang richly with good music. Mother played the old foot-pumped organ. Hattie and one of her sons, Jesse, each played violin. Her oldest son, Bud, played clarinet and a daughter, Muriel, played the ocarina. Rex and I, the younger children, called it a "sweet potato" because it resembled one in shape and size. Ocarina's are typically terra cotta—made of pottery that is glazed, fired and fragile.

When not in use all the musical instruments rested on a lace runner on top of the organ. One Saturday morning as my cousin Rex and I ran through the house to go outdoors, one of us caught a finger on an edge of the lace. Before we could stop it Muriel's ocarina, the only casualty, fell to the floor and shattered. Though a dollar or two could replace it, in 1936 our family had no spare money. Rex's mother, Hattie, was standing at the stove cooking and heard the noise. "Oh, what did you do?" Muriel saw the pieces on the floor and disappointed at her loss scolded, "Look what you've done. You two should be more careful. You're always causing trouble!!"

"We're sorry, it was just an accident," we told Muriel.

Always the peacemaker, Hattie said, "You boys go on outside. Muriel and I will take care of this."

Before we left the house Rex and I picked up the pieces and put them in a paper sack. We included a small glass bottle of Le-Pages glue, which was popular and the most inexpensive brand available at the time. Only 11 years old, Rex had exceptional hand/eye coordination, showing great talent in both fine art and mechanics.

"Maybe we can glue it together temporarily and use it as a pattern to make a new one. This bottle of stuff isn't strong enough to hold it together so it can be used again," he said. We sat on the porch thinking about what to do and not giving up hope. Rex thought a solution could be found.

"How about trying to make a new one out of that sticky clay the dredge picks up and dumps beside the pond down in Spring Gulch?" he asked. "It's a lot like the modeling clay we have at school. Do you think it might work?"

I answered, "It's worth a try."

Our homes, on small farms far out in the country, 12 miles southwest of Redding, California, were in an area which still remained popular for commercial gold dredging in the surrounding canyon streams. Rex's oldest brother, Bud, had a job on a dredge operating only a few miles from our home. He ran the big scoop bucket called a "dragline." This machine would dig up several yards at a time of gold-bearing, creek bed gravel and place it in a hopper to be processed for extraction of gold. Below the creek bed gravel was a thick layer of sticky clay. It was avoided as much as possible because it contained no gold, but a scoop or two sometimes got into the dragline bucket and passed through the hopper. Rex seemed convinced that this easily shaped clay could be used to make a new ocarina. When Bud came home from work that evening Rex asked if he knew any place close where the dragline had dug up clay.

Bud said, "Yes, there's a whole bunch in Spring Gulch, about two miles up the canyon. It's on all sides of the pond where we've recently finished working."

The next morning, we took the paper sack containing the pieces of broken ocarina and glue and walked to the pond. Beneath the shade of an oak tree Rex worked carefully to reassemble the shattered ocarina. He first glued together the largest pieces then the smaller ones of the broken "sweet potato". LePages glue, made for use on paper only, did not have enough strength to hold the ceramic material together very well, and we both handled it with great care after Rex skillfully made repairs.

Placing the fragile reconstructed ocarina on the paper sack in the hot sun, we decided to let the glue dry for about an hour. While waiting we went to the edge of the pond, waded in a short distance and scooped up large chunks of wet clay. Then we returned to the welcome shade of the oak tree, where our real work began. A gentle breeze, carrying a slightly "lemon-like" aroma from the chaparral bushes drifted around us. As we worked, the sticky clay dried and hardened on our cheap, "U.S. Keds" brand canvas shoes, the only things we wore when wading naked into the pond. We wiped our hands on our bib overalls, the only other clothing we had.

Using the fresh clay Rex carefully began duplicating the original ocarina, which rested between us. The shape had to be exactly the same. Each hole, where a finger of the player fit, had to be as close to the exact position of the original as possible. This would make sure the tone of each note would be correct. We had no tools to measure with, so we worked on this by "eyeballing" and adjusting every hole over and over until all of them looked perfectly aligned. Rex chose to duplicate the size of the original instrument. Because it would be less of a challenge, I chose to make one about half again larger.

Patting the pliable clay into about a 1-foot square and 1/2-inch thick sheet, Rex shaped it into a hollow form. It took several tries before the very moist clay would remain in shape without sagging. After letting it dry awhile in the sun, it remained rigid, and I successfully followed Rex's example. With the hollow body finished, the mouthpiece became the most difficult part to form. About 1.5 inches long, when connected to the hollow bulging body, the mouthpiece had to be positioned so that air blown through it would pass across the "sound port." This was a moderately large hole, about the size of a nickel, with a sharp edge at the back portion. Air passing over it caused the characteristic whistling sound. The air channel inside the mouthpiece had to be absolutely flat to spread the air evenly against this sharp back edge: this was critical to producing the correct key on the musical scale. The materials for making the mouthpiece were our hands, a small penknife and a thin piece of wood. From a dry scrap stick he found on the ground, Rex carved the correct shape. He pushed this through the mouthpiece to produce the thin, flat internal opening. Using the penknife's smallest blade, he cut finger holes into the body. Finally, an opening was made in the hollow chamber and the mouthpiece attached.

After hours of exacting but happy work, we finished the ocarinas. They were now ready to dry. Scouting around for a space, we hiked high up one side of the canyon, far from any road. We chose the south side of a large boulder, where we knew our prized work would get full sun and lots of heat. We carefully placed them there, atop the flattened paper sack, and then we went home. Early June in Olinda often brought temperatures far above 100 degrees so we knew the clay soon would set like cement.

School was still in session, so we had to delay our return to the site for a week, but when we got there we found the ocarinas had dried as hard as stone. Placing his fingers over all but one of the holes used to produce the notes of the musical scale, Rex gently blew into the mouthpiece of his replica. How excited we became hearing the clear mellow sounds! Trying my larger ocarina I found it made rich, but lower tones. Using both instruments simultaneously we tried several notes together. To our delight they blended and were musically correct.

Grinning with the pleasure of success and our good luck, we returned late in the afternoon to Rex's home where my Mother was visiting. Hattie recognized something amiss. "Well, you two look like the cats that ate the canary."

Excitedly speaking at the same time we chorused, "We've got a surprise here in the sack."

Muriel looked at us questioningly. Rex took the ocarinas from the sack, gently placing them on the kitchen table. Proudly, he announced to her, "Gene and I each made one."

Obviously impressed, Muriel picked them up and made an inspection. "Do they work?" she asked.

Eagerly we urged, "Go ahead, try them, try them." Anticipating that she'd be asked to provide accompaniment, Mother sat at the organ and started to play "Over the Waves", a family favorite. When Muriel began to play, the tone matched perfectly in the key of C, exactly the same key as her broken original. Muriel switched to the larger ocarina as Mother played "La Paloma". That ocarina had a lower tone, an exact match with the organ in the key of G. The keys of C and G are complimentary on the musical scale: that is why they sounded so good when Rex and I tried them at the same time in the shade of the oak tree. How pleased Rex and I were with the results of our labor when Muriel commented, "They sound pretty good, and I forgive you."

I don't know what became of the handmade ocarinas, but I'll never forget the pleasure of two 11-year old boys as we listened to their mellow tones while Muriel played them during many more family music sessions.

❖ THE FIRES ❖

In 1938, Olinda's spring and early summer were the driest in years. Evening storms without rain but with thunder and lightning strikes, started fires in the dense brush and tinder dry range grass. Nature produced fires were not uncommon in the area where Mother, Cody and I lived with Alfred. Some fires, however, were not caused by nature.

Rex and I, cousins and neighbors, were both 13 years old. We were almost always together. The largely spread out farming community of about 100 people provided nothing for us to do for fun. A movie theatre in Redding, 12 miles away, presented a matinee every Saturday and Sunday, but for Rex and me it might as well have been on the moon. Neither of us had 15 cents for admission nor any transportation...so we often created our own fun and excitement near where we lived.

In the southwest corner of Alfred's land stood half an acre of 3-foot tall native 'bunch grass'. Carrying our .22 caliber rifles or High Standard pistols, we'd often go hunting in it for rattlesnakes or rabbits. In late spring the tall bunch grass stood dead and dry, surrounded by shorter range grass that remained lush and green because the underground spring, seeping all year, always kept that small part of the farm moist. For fun and excitement Rex and I planned to set the tinder dry grass on fire some evening when the weather became clear and without wind. Because of the damp area around it, we knew the fire would remain safely within the isolated island of dry bunch grass, doing no damage but creating a lot of worry and anxiety among the adults.

Earlier in the spring Alfred had paid Rex and me five cents an hour, each, to create a 6-foot fire break that would protect his fence's cedar posts. We cut away all vegetation for 3-feet on each side of the fence. The firebreak was also supposed to protect the farm by preventing any range fire from jumping in and onto the property.

The dry bunch grass presented a great temptation. It seemed almost to beg to get set on fire. We knew that many people in the area would see the flames and wonder what could be burning. We formed a plan to make sure no one would suspect us, because Rex and I usually were blamed for almost everything. The challenge: how could we set ablaze about a half-acre of tinder dry bunch grass some evening without being blamed?

Six months earlier, in an abandoned barn, Rex and I had found half a box of old dynamite, a 100-foot roll of fuse used to ignite it and a can of blasting caps. In addition we found a full can of gunpowder in granular form, used by hunters to reload shells. A few months earlier Cody had told us that one of the many jobs he held in the past was "powder monkey" in a hard-rock mine. The powder monkey is the person who sets the sticks of dynamite into place on the rock face that is to be blasted away. Each "charge" must have in it a cap and fuse crimped solidly together and gently pushed into one end of a dynamite stick. "Kids, don't ever play with old dynamite or caps," he warned. "An old cap can be so unstable, just picking one up and turning it end-for-end might cause it to explode and blow your hand off." Continuing he told us "Dynamite is made from sawdust soaked in nitroglycerine. When it gets old it can form pools at the lowest points of the stick and no matter what position it's in, even the gentlest touch or slight bump can set it off."

Rex and I remembered this warning and were very careful not to bump them when we took the gunpowder, caps, dynamite and fuse from the barn. Because we were scared, it seemed like it took forever as we walked slowly and carefully home with our "liberated" treasure. Not knowing when it would come in handy, we hid it in the hayloft of Rex's family barn.

The evening finally came when all conditions were perfect for setting the dry bunch grass on fire. The roll of fuse we found in the abandoned barn played its part in our plan. After dark, from the storage shed behind Alfred's house, we took an empty, white cloth flour sack and a one-pint glass jar having a 'screw on' lid. After filling the jar with gasoline from the five gallon can in the shed and tightly capping it, we went to Rex's barn, climbed to the loft and cut 50 feet of fuse from the roll. Instructions on the spool informed us that it would burn at the rate of a foot a minute. With the fuse and jar of gasoline in the flour sack and some wooden kitchen matches in my pocket, on a clear, moonless night we made our way to the half-acre of bunch grass. Quietly we broke off handfuls of the tinder-dry grass and stuffed it into the sack. We poured half the gasoline over it, then pushed one end of the fuse inside to the bottom. We placed the sack about 5 feet within the area of dry bunch grass then poured the rest of the fuel over it. From that point we rolled out the remaining fuse, pulling it away from the dry bunch grass into the lush green damp area. According to our plan this would make sure that the blaze would not set fire to any dry range grass. We had thought of everything. No one would ever suspect Gene and Rex!!

Lighting the fuse we hurried to the road, where less than a quarter of a mile away was the home of Rex's grandmother. A diminutive lady of 85, born in Bohemia, Grandma Moravec stood only 4-feet, 9-inches tall. She had salt-and-pepper hair that she rolled into a big bun at the back of her head: when she let it down to be washed it almost touched the floor. She was always happy to see Rex and me. Whenever we'd visit she'd give each of us one of her delicious ethnic treats: a Buchtah, which is something like a cinnamon roll with thick frosting...although Buctahs are much tastier. She baked them fresh every evening.

When we walked into her home that evening she greeted us with hugs, a smile and warm, fresh-from-the-oven Buchtah. Grandpa Moravec greeted us in his thick German accent, "Hello boys." Their adult children, Frank, Rob and Helen, nodded to us in recognition.

Sticking to our plan Rex asked, "Grandma, what time is it?"

She answered, "It's 7:30, Rexie."

"I've got to be home by 9:00," Rex told her.

Our plan seemed to be working perfectly. With our timeline now clearly established with five adults, surely no one would suspect us later...when the fire broke out. It was still awhile before the hissing and sputtering fuse would ignite the flour sack full of gasoline-soaked, dead grass.

More than half an hour went by when Grandpa Moravec looked out the kitchen window. Seeing massive flames shoot skyward, he pointed to the conflagration and exclaimed, partly in German, "Mine Gott something outside ist on fire over dere." Rex and I glanced at each other and knew the incendiary device we lit 50 minutes ago had worked perfectly.

From Alfred's open-air porch, he, Cody and Mother saw the fire and hurried out to it. It didn't threaten anything so they watched it burn awhile then went back to the house.

We were delighted because just as we'd planned, the spectacular, fast burning fire did no harm. But seeing the bright glow in the sky and thinking maybe someone's house was on fire, neighbors drove from miles around to come and look...just as we thought they would.

On the way back to the house Alfred mumbled to my mother, "Frances, you know, I'll bet Gene and Rex had something to do with this!!"

We were fortunate to have never been caught.

One day, Cody said it would be a good idea to have some chickens and a rooster. "By having a rooster," he said, "The eggs will be fertile and once in awhile we can let a hen keep a clutch. Soon we'll have more chickens and extra eggs to eat."

Mother said she wanted brown eggs, because they tasted better.

So Cody suggested that Alfred buy Rhode Island Reds. From a man on another farm we got a rooster and twelve laying hens. The rooster, a large bird, didn't like me and sensed my fear. Though I fed him along with the hens, he rushed at me every day trying to jab me with his long sharp spurs. Frightened, I always ran to get out of his way.

Cody told me, "That rooster knows you're afraid. He'll keep running at you unless you stand your ground and show him you're the boss. Next time you go to collect the eggs take something to scare him with and he'll back down."

The next morning before going to feed the chickens I took the antique, long leather buggy whip out of the shed and carried it with me. As usual, this monstrosity of a bird rushed at me with both wings outstretched and flapping. This time I stood still. When he got in range, about five feet away, I let him have it. My first swing missed, but not the second. The thin tapered end of the leather tip wrapped itself around one of his outspread wings. I jerked on the whip but it didn't come loose. It spun the rooster around flipping him on his back in the dust. Surprised, his big yellowish-brown beak flew open and he let out a gurgling scream while rolling onto one side flapping his wings trying to get up. He struggled so violently I worried that he'd break the entrapped wing and end up dead. As I thought about letting go of the whip it came loose. The rooster jumped up, looked at me with his big yellow eyes, let out another raucous squawk and shaking his feathers, raced away in a cloud of dust to disappear behind the hen house. After that, when I fed the chickens or gathered eggs all I ever saw of him was his head, with its big floppy red comb and wattles and two yellow eyes peering with suspicion at me from behind a corner of the chicken coop.

In late summer of the same blistering hot and dry year, Rex and I went out one morning to gather fresh eggs from Alfred's chicken coop. We found three brown eggs from the Rhode Island Reds, and I carefully put them in my bib overalls' side pocket. In another pocket, as usual, were several old-style wooden kitchen matches. Alongside the path to the chicken coop, thick mats of dead, dry "clump grass" lay tightly flattened against the dusty, red-colored earth. An area of bare dirt surrounded each tuft of the thick, flattened clump grass. Because it pulled so much nutrition and moisture from the soil nothing, including the plain, dry native range grass, grew for nearly a foot around it. For a moment Rex and I paused, looking at one of the thick, flat clumps. With no conversation needed (he and I almost always knew each other's thoughts) I took one of the old style wooden kitchen matches from my pocket. Seeing it Rex spoke the thought that had already formed in my mind, "Why don't we light it and drop it on one of those dry clumps, let it burn a little, then stomp it out?"

Without hesitation I struck the match by whipping it across the back of one leg of my overalls. Fascinated, we watched for a moment as it hissed to life as a small, bright flare. When dropped on one of the smaller dry clumps, tiny tongues of golden fire soon shimmered, danced and spread. The danger we were playing with thrilled us, yet we seemed to be in perfect control. In a few moments I'd stomped out the small flames. This seemed so easy we decided to try it on a bigger clump. With ease, Rex stomped out the second fire. I set ablaze another clump, the biggest so far, and again we were enthralled by the danger.

But this time we waited too long. Suddenly, the larger mass of dry clump grass exploded with flame. Fire jumped across the bare area next to it, rapidly igniting the surrounding dry range grass. No matter how fast we stomped on both the burning clump and range grasses we couldn't put the fire out. The rapid stomping created a draft under foot and with each action more flame shot in every direction from beneath our shoes.

In seconds, despite our efforts, the fire flashed out of control. We ran to the house to alert Alfred and Cody. My Mother looked out the back door, saw the rapidly spreading flames, gasped and put a hand to her mouth but said nothing.

In Olinda everyone knew how to fight grass fires, and we were always prepared. We each grabbed an empty gunnysack from the shed behind the house. Several five gallon buckets were filled with water, quickly hand pumped from the well. Carrying the water and gunnysack we hurried to the fire and spread out along its course. Submerging the sack in the water bucket until it became fully soaked and sopping wet, we'd tightly grab one end then slam the other water logged end to the ground directly on top of the flames. A gunnysack, heavily soaked full of water, is an effective way to put out a grass fire. But no matter how fast we dipped and slammed down the water laden sacks, we couldn't get this fire under control. It moved rapidly through the tinder dry grass. In all directions it sped over the ground and the lines of bright yellow flame darted everywhere like angry shimmering snakes out of control.

Seeing our efforts were ineffective, Alfred called to Cody. "We're not going to be able to put this out. It's moving too fast. Let's call the fire department in Anderson."

Cody moved away from the fire and spoke over his shoulder, "I'll go call them and see if they'll come and help."

The Model-T Ford started with only one turn of the crank, and Cody quickly drove the 2 miles to Ulbergs, the general store. Inside, anchored to the wall, hung a big, old-fashioned, wood encased, crank- and dry cell-battery operated phone. Olinda was on a party line, which meant that one circuit served all the households: rather than dial tone, when you picked up the receiver you would be instantly linked into any existing conversation. When Cody picked up the receiver the phone, as usual, was busy. He cut in, asking the people to clear the line for a fire emergency. Without hesitation it cleared: everyone knew the danger fire held if it raced unchecked through the greasewood, manzanita, scrub oak and tinder-dry range grass.

All homes could be threatened. Although that spring Rex, Alfred and I had cut away all grass and brush within 100 feet of the house, barn and chicken coop, other people had not done the same. Dry grass, scrub oak and greasewood stood dangerously close to their homes and farm buildings.

Greasewood posed the greatest threat. Fire needs three things to exist: fuel, oxygen and ignition. When greasewood ignites, even the green leaves of spring and early summer appear to explode. An intense fireball erupts and rapidly creates a powerful updraft. This sucks more and more oxygen from the air under every bush. With a roar the almost white-hot flame springs skyward, as high as 100 feet, while thick black smoke rises above.

Cody made the call at Ulbergs and within 30 minutes the first tanker trucks from Anderson (six miles away) arrived at Alfred's farm. By then the fast moving flames had reached our 6-foot wide firebreak at the back fence line and jumped across it. Uncontrolled fire roared away, consuming thick stands of brush across the open rangeland. Clouds of black and gray smoke, visible for miles, billowed skyward.

Within two hours of Cody's phone call, nine more tanker trucks arrived from Redding, which was twelve miles away. Firemen cut a large opening in the back fence and then drove several tankers through and over the carpet of smoldering embers that led to the fire, burning uncontrolled about a mile away. Other tankers raced off in another direction. They would attempt to intercept and outflank the fire before it approached a road five miles west.

Meanwhile, more tanker trucks from Anderson arrived and spread out on Alfred's farm, where fire still burned. In less than an hour they had it under control. I watched as firemen equipped themselves with 5-gallon metal tanks made by the Indian Fire Suppression Company. Each tank sported a hose and hand pump nozzle. Firemen strapped the heavy tanks onto their backs and walked around spraying water on any remaining, smoking hotspots or flame.

Alfred was so impressed by the water delivery system, the next time he and Cody went to Redding in the Model T Ford, he bought one at the Western Auto hardware store. Fortunately, there never would be another fire on his land, so his fire-suppression tank would sit unused the remainder of Alfred's life.

The firemen from Redding were unrewarded in their heroic work at the road 5-miles distant. There they started a "backfire," a controlled fire that spreads upwind from the opposite direction toward a fire that is uncontrolled. The backfire consumes everything in the path that the uncontrolled fire needs to continue burning. The uncontrolled fire, as a result, dies from lack of fuel. It's a great idea, but this time it didn't work: flaming embers shot into the air and were tossed across the road by the power of the updraft.

After jumping the backfire and road, the flames raced on, burning fiercely for three more days. At night the glow in the sky to the west reminded me of my stupidity. Only because of good luck, no one was hurt and not one building burned. However, a lot of cedar fence posts were deeply charred to ground level and had to be replaced by angry and disgusted farmers.

Soon after the first tanker trucks from Anderson arrived I had gone back to the house, exhausted from trying for so long to put the fire out by swinging the heavy, water soaked gunnysack. Rex, muscular and much stronger, remained on the line. I felt deeply ashamed because I knew my foolishness caused the fire. I lowered my head with fatigue and remorse.

When I walked into the house, Cody and Alfred were already inside, seated at the kitchen table. Nodding toward me Cody questioned, "What do you think we should do with him?" As he spoke, he unbuckled his two and a half-inch wide leather belt. Corporeal punishment was not out of the question. Inwardly I winced, anticipating the severe whipping I deserved.

I was too tired to look up. Alfred sensed my deep remorse, "Let's just leave him alone. He's punished himself enough already." Replacing his belt, Cody agreed.

Several days after the fire, pointing a finger at me Mother admonished, "Your conscience should prick you for your foolishness." It did.

After all the firemen left Alfred's place, I stepped out onto the back porch. I noticed that the three eggs I'd gathered before starting the fire had broken in my pocket. Their contents had run down my leg and into one of my cheap, U.S. Keds canvas shoes. As I slowly sat down on the steps, their shattered shells made a crackling, crunching sound in my pocket.

❖ HUNGRY BOYS ❖

Young boys are always hungry. My cousin Rex and I, both 13 years old, were hungrier than most. The Great Depression, which started in 1929 and continued through the 1930's was severe. In 1938, we had barely enough food to survive. We had strawberries in May and June. In early summer, a kitchen garden provided some potatoes, onions, tomatoes, radishes and okra. In the fall, nectarine and peach trees Alfred planted a few years earlier provided ripe fruit. During the rest of the year, we nearly starved on a bare subsistence diet.

To make the most of his small pension Alfred would buy a 100 pound gunnysack of Turkey Red, a hard wheat sold primarily as inexpensive feed for chickens. At our house it fed people. Since it was not packaged for human consumption, mixed in with it were many inedible stems and tassels. Before being used as food for the family it had to be carefully cleaned. Cleaning the wheat became one of my chores, in addition to milking the cows and chopping the wood.

Thinly spreading the wheat onto a clean, white cloth made it easy to see and pick out the debris. I would spread a clean, white flour sack across the kitchen table then seat myself there with the bag of wheat. Every single kernel had to be handled individually and pushed aside into a pile. The stems and tassels, pulled to the table edge, were dropped to the floor and swept up later. On a weekend, working six hours a day, it took nearly two days for me to clean one hundred pounds.

Mother made several things from the wheat. After soaking in water over night to soften, we used it as a whole grain breakfast food. Boiling it for fifteen minutes the next morning made it even softer and ready to eat. We called it "wheat buds". Served with a sprinkle of brown sugar, some canned-condensed or fresh milk, it provided a moderately substantial meal.

Alfred and Cody would remark, "It sticks to the ribs," meaning they didn't get hungry as soon and could work outside longer before coming in to eat. Once in awhile we would have fried "bacon ends" with it. This cheap, hog jowl meat is given a bacon cure at the packinghouse then sold in chunks and uneven slices at the grocery store. A lot more fat than lean, but always a treat in our sparse diet, it crackled pleasantly when chewed and tasted like real bacon.

Alfred owned a small, cast iron, hand-operated grain grinder with three different size grinding burrs: coarse, medium and fine. When we ran out of coffee and had no money to buy more, Mother had me put on the coarse burr and grind some of the wheat, making it the size of coffee grounds. She'd spread it thinly on a metal baking sheet and place it in the oven of the wood-burning stove. She'd then scorch it by putting a few extra sticks of hot burning manzanita wood in the fire. In the percolator and used just like coffee grounds, it made a hot drink having a pleasant nutlike flavor. With some brown sugar, canned-condensed milk or real cream added, all coffee drinkers were satisfied. On cold days I'd drink it too.

We had two cows but sometimes—when one cow was dry—there wasn't enough milk or cream for the four of us. As a supplement Mother always kept on hand a few cans of Alpine condensed milk. The cans were sold in two sizes and each had a coupon printed on the label. A one-point coupon was on the full size can and a half-point on the smaller size. The Alpine Company sent Mother catalogs from which to select premiums in exchange for the coupons. She ordered various green, yellow and pink dishes made from what is now called "Depression glass". She had several complete sets including the large, loop-handled, glass-covered cake dishes that rested on a pedestal.

With the smallest burr Mother had me grind the wheat into fine flour. She used this to make a staple we called "wheat bread". To the wheat flour she would add Crisco shortening or lard, a bit of salt, some brown sugar and water. We were too poor to buy yeast to make it rise. Mother would spread the dough on a lightly greased, shallow pan then bake it in the oven until golden brown. Similar to corn bread, it was cut into small squares. For days at a time we had no food except the homemade wheat bread and a glass of milk or "fake" coffee. When we'd run out of the scorched wheat with which to make the hot coffee-like drink, Mother would make "cambric tea" as a substitute. This is a cup of hot water into which a little sugar and a few tablespoons of canned, condensed milk are added. It satisfied the desire for something hot to drink at breakfast and got everyone going on chilly mornings.

We never had enough money to buy anything to spread on the thin squares of wheat bread. I always felt poor when grade school started in the fall, because all I had to bring for lunch were four small squares of dry wheat bread...and a peach or nectarine when in season. I carried my meager lunch in a clean two-quart pail that came with a wire handle attached.

Peanut butter, white flour, lard and some other staples were sometimes given free to people who were so poor they were close to starvation. My lunch pail had been full of lard when we received it from the welfare department in Redding. Even though we were in the wake of the Great Depression, welfare had a stigma. People who accepted items from the Government were often looked down on as "poor white trash". To survive we swallowed our pride and lived on welfare. We had to "go on the dole" as our folks called it, to survive, although we detested having to do so.

Everyone else in school had a store bought lunch pail or at least a brown paper sack. In my lard pail I carried a little tin cup that I would fill with water from the hand-pumped schoolyard well. Embarrassed by having such inadequate food and knowing the other kids would recognize the lard pail as government issue, I felt miserable. I dreaded the scene as noon approached.

Olinda had a one-room school. Eight rows of desks in the single room were arranged side by side, each one representing a grade. Mrs. Jordan taught all eight grades. In our school was a classmate whose parents had a good income. We nicknamed him "Fats" because, at age 13, he weighed almost 200 pounds. For lunch he always brought four thick, juicy sandwiches made with store bought, sliced, white Wonder Bread. Piled in each sandwich were fresh crisp lettuce leaves, tomatoes, processed meat slices (like salami, bologna, and olive loaf) and cheese, all thickly slathered with mayonnaise. For desert Fats had two bananas, a bunch of grapes, half a dozen cookies and a big slice of thickly frosted cake. Of all the things in his lunch box, to me the sandwiches looked the most delicious. How I wished I could have such a sandwich. Fats sometimes took a long look at the squares of dry wheat bread I had to eat, and I noticed it. I thought he was getting ready to make fun of my poor lunch…but one day while we were eating together he said, "Hey, would you trade me a piece of that wheat bread for one of my sandwiches?"

I couldn't believe he'd want any of my dry bread but I quickly answered, "Sure." And we made the exchange. It turned out that Fats loved the taste of my simple food and couldn't seem to get enough, while I eagerly ate his thick meat- and cheese-sandwiches full of juicy, vine ripened tomatoes and crisp lettuce dripping with mayonnaise. Fats told the other kids how good he thought my wheat bread tasted and sometimes they too traded me slices of frosted chocolate layer cake, bananas, or a peanut butter and honey sandwich. For the last two years of grade school—while Fats and I were there together—I had wonderful lunches. He never tired of trading me a sandwich for a square of dry wheat bread. Sometimes I wonder whether Fats had told his parents about my poor, inadequate, dry lunches washed down with water and if—out of pity or kindness—they had instructed him to ask me to trade food. And I wonder if he told the other kids to do the same.

Fats enjoyed playing tricks. He often rode to school on a big white mare, a slow moving draft animal used for plowing. He rode bareback using only a bridle, bit and reins to guide her. As a draft horse she didn't know how to "neck rein" and had to have the bit in her mouth pulled one way or the other to make her go right or left. During noon hour one day he asked me if I'd like to ride the mare. I always wanted to ride her and having no fear at that time, accepted his offer immediately.

He boosted me up and as I sat astride the wide back of the mare her pungent sweet odor, coupled with the semi moist feel of her hair on this very hot day, seemed grand.

"Just kick her sides lightly with your heels and say 'giddiyap', then steer her by pulling one way or the other on these," he smiled handing me the reins.

Good instructions that didn't work because he had placed the bit upside down in the mare's mouth and she hated this. As soon as I kicked her and put a little tension on the reins she began to "crow hop". Up she went, front feet high in the air, then she came crashing down. Next, her hindquarters did the same, something like being on a giant living rocking horse. Riding bareback and with her mane so far forward, I had nothing to hold on to and several times almost fell off. Pulling on the reins had no effect on her direction, except "up". Each tug made matters worse: she'd jump even higher.

A large oak tree stood close to one end of the full-length front porch that graced the Olinda schoolhouse. Many of us often climbed that tree to eat lunch while sitting on one of the lower, sturdy branches. The mare continued to jump up and down wildly, and we were getting closer and closer to the tree. If I were lucky I might jump off onto it, but I didn't see the low branch until too late. As the mare ran under it the branch hit me squarely across the chest flipping me over backward. I fell to the ground in an uncoordinated heap. I looked up and saw the two massive rear hoofs, within less than an inch and kicking in my direction. By grace or good luck, I was not harmed.

Fats and the rest of the boys laughed. Someone taunted, "What happened Gene, can't you even ride a tame, old plow plug?" A lot of girls on the porch snickered thinking it a great joke. I suffered great embarrassment, but even worse, I developed an overwhelming fear of horses. My misadventure, at age 13, left its mark on me for life. Many years later, though I greatly enjoy looking at and admire a beautiful mare or stallion, I am still extremely afraid to be near one.

In early spring of 1938, the rolling hills around Olinda were carpeted with beautiful, lush green range grass. Brilliant white clouds floated in the blue sky like puffed up cotton balls. And the temperature usually stood near 78 degrees. It seemed far too beautiful to be in school.

Rex and I had never missed a day of school before, but one day we decided to play hooky. We planned to go hunting and eat for lunch, anything we got. From the cupboard in Rex's house we snuck some salt, pepper and Crisco shortening, which we wrapped in waxed paper. In my pocket I carried, as I almost always had from age 6, a few wooden kitchen matches. We also took a small piece of cloth salvaged from a washed, cotton flour sack. When soaked in Crisco, we planned to use it, tied to the end of a small stick, to baste any game we might get. We took along our homemade slingshots. We had made them from the 'Y' crotch of a scrub oak tree. Two, one-foot long, thick black rubber bands (that we cut from a discarded Model T Ford inner tube) and a piece of leather from the soft and pliable tongue of one of Cody's worn out work boots provided the power.

We first wandered into Spring Gulch where a small creek flowed: we were hoping to find a rabbit or squirrel getting a drink. Having no success we climbed to the top of a steep rise on one side of the canyon. We were on a large, flat plain covered with oak and pine trees as well as manzanita. In a grove of brush we heard a flock of robins chirping noisily. Most of the people in our area hunted and ate quail, which were abundant and delicious. We were hungry, and in our imaginations the robins looked like small chickens. We thought that robins might taste as good as quail.

Stones from our homemade slingshots hit their mark. Soon, we had two Robins cleaned, dressed and slowly turning over a small fire on a roughly fashioned spit. Not knowing how long to roast the birds I cut into them every few minutes with my jack knife to see if the meat looked done. While roasting for about ten minutes, we basted them with the Crisco soaked rag at the end of a stick. Sprinkling on some salt and pepper we assumed they were ready to eat. They looked so good, glistening golden brown. They smelled absolutely delicious—and tasted worse than horrible!!

As I bit into my robin I made such a scowl Rex asked, "What's wrong?"

"Boy," I answered, "Try yours and see if it tastes as bad as this one."

Cautiously he took a bite and instantly spit it out. "How can anything that smells so good taste this bad?" he questioned as we threw them into the fire.

Even with the flavoring of wood smoke, pepper and salt they were inedible. After taking only one small bite our appetites left. Carefully putting out the fire, we walked back to the edge of the canyon.

Like most kids who grow up in the country without a watch, we could tell time quite closely by looking at the sun, noting how far it stood above the horizon and observing the length of a shadow made by a tree. It wasn't time to go home, and we knew if we arrived early our parents would suspect we skipped school and give us a spanking. To pass the time, we lay down on a patch of green grass in the shade of an oak tree.

Looking up we tracked the progress of some brilliant, white cotton clouds as they marched slowly across the great, blue sky. Gazing between the oak's branches made the tree appear to be falling, an optical illusion caused by watching the moving clouds through stationary limbs. In the warm, crystal clear air and bright afternoon sunshine, all was peaceful and hushed except for some sparrows chirping in the distance. For awhile we lay relaxed watching the movement of clouds and trying to find in them various forms of shapes or faces.

Rex offered a pearl of wisdom and truth, surprisingly prescient for a 13-year old, "You know, as long as we live we'll remember this day and this time as some of the most happy and carefree moments we've ever had." He was right.

For a cow to give milk she must be bred and have a calf. In

the Olinda area only one farmer, Mr. Pratt, had a mature breeding bull, a "proven sire". A mean, wild and dangerous Holstein, he had the reputation of "doing good work", which meant he had been able to produce a calf every time. For this reason Mr. Pratt commanded the highest price of anyone for many miles around, $2.00 cash, for his bull to "service" a cow.

In 1938, Violet went dry, had to be bred and have a calf so she'd again produce her great quantity of milk. That year I was a freshman in high school, and I had suddenly discovered girls. How embarrassing it became for me to lead Violet along 4 miles of dusty, dirt road to visit the bull. My embarrassment was primarily due to the fact that the country road passed right in front of Ulbergs (the general store) and *that* was adjacent to the Ulbergs' big house. The Ulbergs, a Norwegian family, had a beautiful daughter, graced with sparkling blue eyes set off by lush, brunette hair. Marian and I were both 13-years old.

Violet led easily but didn't walk as fast as I wanted. With the impatience of youth I tugged and jerked on her lead rope, urging her to go faster, especially past the Ulbergs' home. The uncooperative cow had only one speed—extra slow!! Adding to my misery, about every 10 feet Violet let out a roaring bellow, as cows ready to breed always do. Mile after seemingly endless mile I trudged along barefoot in the heat. The blazing California sun had hiked the temperature to 115 degrees, but I could still feel the flush of embarrassment as we approached the Ulbergs' home. Violet's clanging cow bell and forlorn bellow created a cacophony. The raucous noise coming from this miserable monstrosity of a cow made the trip past the Ulbergs' house a nightmare. I felt sure the beautiful young girl I recently discovered would think me a fool, or at least very undesirable, if she saw me walking by with that cow.

I never did find out whether Marian saw the "parade", but if she did it must not have mattered. We enjoyed each other's company more and more all through high school. As modern kids say, we kind of became "an item". As a couple we were somewhat unusual. Remarkably, we both had been born on February 8, 1925–at exactly the same time.

Violet bred successfully. Mr. Pratt got his two dollars cash, and I walked the 4 miles home, hot, thirsty, barefoot, sunburned and embarrassed. But the cool reward of great quantities of milk and cream made the ordeal well worth the effort.

❖ BOOTS, SMOKEY AND ADOLPH ❖

Rex named his 2-year old dog Boots. I named my 7-year old dog Smokey. Boots, a large, light brown, curly haired Airedale mix, had an inherent stupid streak. Smokey, medium sized, was a brown and black, straight haired Australian Shepherd cross. He had only one good eye having lost sight in the other to a cataract early in life. But what he lost in vision he more than made up in brains. Both dogs were self sufficient, catching and sharing their food from the abundant supply of small animals such as kangaroo rats, squirrels and rabbits in our area. Getting rid of these critters meant our garden wouldn't be destroyed. So in addition to being good pets, the dogs provided a service.

On the open rangeland behind Uncle Alfred's farm there were many wild rabbits and plenty of brush, providing lots of places for them to hide. They made trails between their places of safety, such as a burrow or a thick clump of tall Johnson grass. When either dog spotted a rabbit the chase began. Most trails were generally circular and several hundred feet long. On the trails, chasing their elusive prey, the dogs ran round and round. Smokey, older and smaller, tired quickly so Boots almost always caught and ate a lot of the rabbit. After a few months we noticed something unusual happen between the two eager hunters. Rex and I wondered what had changed because now Smokey most often returned to the house with the rabbit. One afternoon when we were hunting rattlesnakes in the brushy area we found the answer.

The chase began when Boots flushed a rabbit. Making the loop around its safety trail three times Boots continued running as fast as he could, mouth open and tongue lolling out the side of his mouth. We watched amazed as Smokey, following Boots, suddenly stopped. He crouched close to the trail flat against the ground behind a tall clump of Johnson grass. Unable to be seen behind the grass he correctly anticipated that his unsuspecting prey would soon come racing by. Streaking toward Smokey's hiding place, the rabbit didn't have a chance. It saw nothing as it ran full speed into Smokey's open mouth and the jaws of the waiting dog snapped tightly around it. Rex and I never knew how Smokey thought out this strategy, but he had an intelligence that served him well.

Someplace I heard this story that was an example of the difference in intelligence of youth compared with that of the old and experienced.

There were two bulls, one young and eager, the other old and wise, grazing together high on a hill. Several miles away, in the valley below, the young bull noticed twenty beautiful heifers each ready to be bred.

"Wow!" exclaimed the young bull. "Do you see what I see?" He panted and motioned wildly toward the valley floor.

"Yes I do," answered the old bull.

"Gee whiz, man oh man," the young bull cried, "Let's run down real fast and breed one, O.K.?"

The old bull slowly looked up from his grazing and replied, "Young fella, why don't we just walk down and breed them all?"

Perhaps Smokey had lots of good sense, like the old bull. Boots never caught on, but he shared in the spoils and never went hungry.

Spring is mating time for birds. Rex and I discovered a crow's nest in the top of one of the tallest pine trees near Alfred's farm. A few days after the eggs hatched we could see the adults feeding their young. Someone told us that a baby crow taken from the nest very early in life and fed by people will imprint and accept the human as its parent. We absolutely had to have a baby crow and make it our pet.

We drew straws to see who would have to shinny up the branchless first 20 feet of the 60-foot tree, then climb 40 feet more among the gnarled limbs and up to the nest. Rex lost.

A strong north wind blew that day, and it was a dangerous climb because the top of the tree swayed back and forth. We also had to find a way to get the baby crow safely down. Rex couldn't use one of his hands to carry the baby bird because he'd need both as he climbed down the wind-whipped tree. Even more challenging would be the descent: the bird couldn't be put in a shirt or pants pocket without being crushed as Rex shinnied to the ground. We got an idea: in Alfred's shed we found a small cloth sack that had a "pucker string" to close the top opening. We tied one end of a piece of clothesline rope to the sack and on the other end of the rope formed a loop big enough to go over Rex's head and hang loosely around his neck. The baby crow could ride safely down in the sack, slung across Rex's back.

Coming down the swaying tree was slow but successful, and we had our baby crow. Opening the top of the sack we eagerly looked at the tiny spindly-feathered creature and I asked, "What shall we name him?"

Without hesitation Rex said, "How about Adolph?"

"Sounds good to me," and our new little pet had his name.

He grew rapidly and tamed easily. Being only a day or two old when we took him from the nest, he never learned fear. He was the biggest in the nest so we assumed Adolph was a male. From the time we got him to Rex's house, we found his appetite almost overwhelming. We fed him piles of earthworms gathered by digging them out of the five-acre clover field. We swatted hundreds of flies inside the house as they crawled up the glass of the windows. We chased grasshoppers, lunging at them with cupped hands only to have many spring to freedom at the last second. In the pasture we turned over dry cow splatters to catch beetles and the ever present, segmented, gray colored "sow bugs". Sometimes we fed him bread and milk.

Rex's house sat on a steep hillside and had been built on stilts over a spring that ran all year. The water kept the area under the house cool, and we thought as soon as he grew old enough we could move him beneath the home, which would provide a safe place for Adolph to roost at night. The area under Rex's house had a tightly closed door for protection, so it gave us a sense of security for our pet. We each handled, fed and talked to Adolph every day, and wondered if he could be taught to speak. We heard if you split the tongue of a crow it will learn to say words. We opened his beak and looked at his little dry black tongue. He wiggled it a few times as he looked pointedly at us with bead-like, shiny black eyes. Seeing this, we quickly dropped the idea.

Growing rapidly he remained tame and like a dog, came to either of us when we'd call, "Here Adolph, here Adolph." He enjoyed riding on a shoulder, and it soon became obvious he'd rather be carried than fly. In summertime, when we went shirtless, many times Adolph rewarded us with a smelly, gooey deposit on our flesh...but the fun and laughs he provided outweighed this indiscretion, and we always forgave him as we took a quick bath in the cool water of the irrigation ditch nearby.

That summer I worked cutting firebreaks around the fence line of Alfred's property. Working 12 hours a day in sweltering heat (usually between 105 and 118 degrees) I earned five cents an hour. With $5.00 I bought an old 1927 Chevrolet pickup. I had learned to drive at age nine in order to help out on the farm. This was not unusual: most kids in our very rural area learned at an early age but could not be licensed until they were 17 years old.

Rex and I taught Adolph to ride on the front of the pickup's roof while holding on with his sharp claws to the black cloth top. We enjoyed watching him struggle valiantly, resisting the rush of air as we drove along. Although he always could have flown faster than either Rex or I drove, he preferred to ride. We suspected he might have been a little lazy reinforcing our idea that he was probably a male.

One day we decided to see how fast we could drive before he'd lose his footing and be forced, by the fast moving air, to fly off the top of the pickup. Rex, on the passenger side, leaned out and watched Adolph from the open window. The red dust of the road billowed behind us while I drove ever faster. Through ten, then fifteen and finally twenty miles an hour, Adolph held on, digging his claws into the cloth of the padded roof. Once in awhile he'd loose the grip of one foot and pop open a wing while bringing the foot back down to the rooftop. Finally at 22 miles an hour he could no longer hang on. He spread both wings to glide about five feet above the pickup. As soon as we slowed he'd land back on the front edge of the roof, just above the windshield, as we continued on our way.

Adolph never offered to fly away to join the many flocks of crows that called with their scratchy, raucous voices as they flew around our area, and he never learned to answer. Sometimes he'd perch in a nearby tree cocking his head from side to side watching, as Rex and I dug fire trails around the fence lines of the family farms. His lazy streak remained obvious because at quitting time he always flew to one of our shoulders to ride back to the house.

Two years old and fully-grown, Adolph acted like a member of the family. He would perch on the branch of an oak tree near the house and preen his glistening black feathers. He would stay there for hours, waiting for us to come outside. By turning his head in any direction his shiny little black eyes followed us whenever we were near. We always had to feed him, because he never learned how to get worms, grubs or anything as food.

During the stifling hot months of June through September, Rex and his family slept outdoors, under a group of big oak trees next to their house. Adolph slept under the house, on his roost located over the cool water of the natural spring. About two o'clock one morning Rex heard him make a loud cry. He assumed a rat or mouse had disturbed Adolph. Moments later he heard another squawk coming from a distance down the canyon behind the house. Then the cries grew faint, far away and stopped.

Early that morning Rex came to my house, "Something got Adolph last night and carried him down the canyon. I heard him squawk, but I couldn't follow because it was too dark. I think we should go and try to find out what happened."

Overwhelmed by sadness, we couldn't figure out how the predator got into the roost area: the door remained tightly closed, and we found no other possible entry. Following the trail of shiny black feathers, a long way down the canyon we found a wing, a leg and many feathers beside a pool. We assumed a raccoon got him, since they do dip their food in water before eating. (It is a common belief that they are washing their food. This is not true. The real reason is because they do not have salivary glands and must first get adequate moisture into their mouth before they can swallow. Without the moisture they could choke and die.)

We were saddened by the loss of our friend, this funny crow we had taken from his element and introduced to the uncertain world of man. But I am happy knowing that he had more adventures than any of his nest mates, and I believe in his short life he enjoyed us as much as we enjoyed him.

❖ REVENGE OF THE SNAKE ❖

While still in the grip of the Depression, in 1939 we were so poor my family couldn't spare 15 cents for me to go to an afternoon movie in Redding, 12 miles away.

I was a freshman at Anderson High School when our English teacher, Miss Letson, required her students to attend the classic, very long movie, *Gone With The Wind*. The school paid the admission and a school bus took our entire class on the trip so all would see the movie at the same time. For most of us, it was the first film we saw in color.

In any high school class there usually is at least one, so called, character. Because the show was four-hours long, many in our group, including the clown, became bored. Near the film's end the heroine, midway down a winding staircase, paused for a moment then tripped and fell. She rolled to the bottom where she lay, apparently unconscious.

Jumping up from his balcony seat the class character yelled, "Hey, grab her while she's still warm."

The implication was clear. Bored no more almost everyone in our class (as well as many of the other people in the crowded theater) went wild with laughter.

Many people in Olinda were of the opinion that my cousin Rex and I also were "characters"…because we were known to create our own fun and jokes.

All roads in our area were nothing but red dirt, and in hot weather dust at least two inches deep and as fine as face powder covered them. During the summer Rex and I would each find a discarded worn out tire, tilt it upright and scoop large quantities of the extremely fine dust into its open bottom. We'd then roll them as fast as we could down the road, while clouds of dust poured out, settling on us and everything else along the way. We thought it looked like red smoke, and the faster we ran the more dust billowed from inside the tire and the more fun we had watching it being carried away on the wind.

On the small farm immediately south of us, in a house very close to the road, lived two unmarried sisters, Evelyn and Alberta Logan. They were between 20 and 25 years old. Many times the Logan sisters scolded us when we ran by rolling the tires. They didn't appreciate the huge amounts of red dust that, carried by the wind, blew into their house through open door and window screens. It settled thickly everywhere, and they asked us many times not to roll the offending dust-belching tires past their house...but we ignored them and did it anyway.

In the garage adjacent to their house, the sisters stored their home canning: peaches, pears, olives and lots of strawberry jam. One day, not long after they had once again loudly and thoroughly scolded us for causing so much dust to drift into their house, they discovered several jars of newly made jam were missing. They told the neighbors they were absolutely sure, "Gene and Rex stole it because we've seen them look in the open door of our garage as they run by on the road rolling those dust-belching tires."

The truth is we didn't steal the jam. As soon as we found out we were suspects, we went to the Logan's and told them we didn't take it. But they continued to tell their friends that they "just knew we were guilty."

We were humiliated at their falsely accusing us: we attended the same church, and I sang solo in front of the congregation almost every week. We couldn't believe they would consider us to be thieves. Rex's mother and mine were excellent parents, and we were raised to never lie or steal. My stepfather, Cody, a half Cherokee Indian, also taught me that my word should be a sacred trust and an unbreakable bond. We found the Logan sisters' accusations even more insulting because they knew how we were brought up.

In our young minds Rex and I thought we had to find a way to "get back" at them for this injustice. It wasn't long before the fauna of our area provided us the perfect opportunity.

A variety of large snakes, poisonous and non-poisonous, made their homes in the habitat around Olinda: there were black-and-white ringed King snakes, brown lowland Diamond Back rattle-snakes, some very thick and short, greenish colored High Mountain rattlesnakes and the common Bull snake. Brown in color, the Bull snake looks much like the lowland Diamond Back but it has no rattles and, although often quite large, is harmless.

A few days after being accused of stealing the jam, we were walking along the dirt road close to home one evening, and the biggest Bull snake we ever saw started to slither across in front of us. The nearly unthinkable idea of what we should do with this monster came to us both at the same moment. Gleefully we recalled how one time we heard the Logan sisters mention that they were deathly afraid of all snakes. We needed no more incentive than this.

Quickly killing it with rocks, we hid it in Uncle Alfred's shed and that night I slept at Rex's house. Sometime near midnight when we felt sure the Logan's were asleep, we sneaked out of bed, took the snake and some strong cotton cord from the shed and walked quietly up the road to the their house. We saw no light inside indicating the sisters were in bed. We tied one end of the cord to the tail of the dead snake. Creeping quietly onto their small front porch I suspended the fat monster its full six-foot length while Rex "boosted me up" so I could tie the free end of the cord under the overhang in front of their screen door. I hung it just far enough away so when the door opened it would not hit the snake. With the task complete we crept away.,

Back home in bed, with the thrill of anticipation, Rex and I lay awake most of the remainder of the night. We knew the Logan's usually got up just after sunrise so about an hour before it started to get light we returned to the scene. At their house the question became, how do we get the sisters to come rushing out? We decided both of us would step up on the front porch, pound our fists on the screen door, yell, stomp our feet and in general make a terrible commotion for a few moments. After doing this we'd jump off the porch and hide behind some thickly matted, low growing shrubs and wait.

The plan worked. Evelyn, wearing only her very thin pink rayon full-length summer nightgown, rushed out. As she threw open the screen door, in the very dim light she failed to see the huge dead snake dangling full length in her path. Rushing forward, her upper torso and face collided with its fat body. Hitting it so quickly caused the snake to violently flip-flop on the end of the cord and it ended up draped around her neck. Her screaming and hollering could, I'm sure, be heard a mile away. Evelyn's arms and legs uselessly flailed the air in four different directions as she lost her balance and fell off the porch into a big, thorny and mature rosebush. They say good Christians don't swear, but Rex and I heard words early that morning we'd never heard before.

Her sister, Alberta, appeared at the door carrying a double-barreled shotgun. When she saw the monstrous snake hanging by the tail in front of her, its dangling body still swinging from Evelyn's collision with it, she gave a single, deep throaty yell that sounded like a cow bellering. She jumped backward into the house and never came out. Evelyn, bleeding, cussing and moaning all at the same time, painfully extracted herself from the long, wood-like thorns of the rosebush. In tears, she managed to crouch low on the porch, creep past the big snake and get back in the house.

Neither Rex nor I had anticipated such a scene: clamor, screams, torn clothing and bleeding flesh. Our vengeful little joke had gotten out of hand, and we found ourselves feeling both sorry and scared. We continued crouching behind the thick low shrubs until we felt sure both ladies were attending to other matters and not looking out a window. Then we stood up and ran as fast as we could back to Rex's house where, unseen, we quickly got back into bed.

A few days later Rex's 60-year old uncle, Rob, admitted to the Logan sisters that he had stolen the jam. He denied, however, hanging the dead snake in front of their door and then luring them out of the house with noise. For many years he tried to convince them of his innocence but they never believed him. All of them have passed away, but maybe their children will come across this story some day and finally learn the truth.

❖ THE RIFLE ❖

In 1936, most boys in Olinda owned a .22 caliber rifle by age 8. In early 1936, at age 11 I still didn't.

One day a friend of my step dad, Cody, gave him an old .22 caliber pump action Remington that was missing a rear sight. Where the rear, "open sight" originally had been, there remained only a hole drilled by the manufacturer into the area close to and above the cartridge chamber. Threaded on the inside, the hole had once accommodated a screw that tightly held the missing rear sight. The front sight remained in place and had a metal bead painted bright red at the tip.

Cody often jokingly called himself, "A Jack of all trades, but master of none." The truth is he excelled in many fields requiring the talent to work well with his hands. The Pacific Gas and Electric Company had put in poles and wires, bringing electricity to Olinda that year. After linemen finished their job and moved on, many short pieces of scrap copper wire remained scattered about on the ground. One evening Cody brought home a short length of the thick, single strand wire. He took the rifle from its place on the wall and placed the square-cut end of the wire at the opening of the threaded hole to see if it would fit. It was only a little bigger in diameter than the hole, but slightly less in size than the deepest part of the threads inside; it fit perfectly. He then cut a one-inch piece off the soft copper wire scrap. To see if it would "thread itself" he rotated it while pushing it downward into the hole. The gun barrel had been heat-treated making the metal exceptionally hard. As Cody rotated and pushed the short piece of wire into the hole it "self-threaded" all the way to the bottom where it became permanently secure. Using a file, he shaped the wire that protruded out of the threaded hole. His work produced a sharp wedge shape on top with the long axis crossways to the barrel. Using a thin "knife file" he cut a centered narrow notch in the top of the sharpened wedge, making it look much like the Remington original. He let the wire stick out far enough so he'd be able to make changes after test firing.

To "sight in" the rifle, Cody and I went to the shed and carried out a sturdy workbench with a medium size vise solidly attached. Protecting the gun with some gunnysack material he placed the rifle in the vise and locked the jaws. On a two-foot square of cardboard he painted a target, which he tacked onto a fencepost about 30 yards away. Cody mounted the rifle in the vise, to hold the rifle rock steady when fired. He squinted through the notch in the homemade rear sight and perfectly aligned the notch bottom with the front sight's red bead. He fired, then checked the target. To compensate for inaccuracy, Cody then cut the wedge lower, and repeated the test. He moved the notch to the right or left or made it deeper as necessary. After firing ten rounds and with only a few changes, the rifle, fully adjusted, was totally accurate.

Cody didn't let me have the rifle without first giving instructions about using it efficiently and safely.

"Sonny boy," he said, "before shooting I want you always to remember. Never keep a live round in the chamber if you're going to carry the rifle, even for a short distance. Either leave a spent shell in or unload it. Even if you know for sure the rifle is empty, make it a habit to always set the safety lock to the 'on' position."

Handing it to me he said, "It's all yours. I know you'll have fun with it, but I want you to remember it isn't a toy. It can do a lot of damage."

After going over the instructions several times he asked, "Would you like to fire it now?"

The truth is, I could hardly wait!

Only a few of my first shots hit the target and others were a long way from center. Cody never chided, hurried me or became impatient. If I reacted slowly while learning he still gave praise, and I tried harder. Noticing that I always took a deep breath and held all of it in before pulling the trigger he advised.

"Sonny Boy, as you aim just breathe normally. Then, for greatest stability, a moment before you pull the trigger take in only half a breath and hold it. This won't distort your body like a full one can. As a result your accuracy will be better. Another secret of good marksmanship is to make sure to move nothing but your trigger finger when you fire. Squeeze gently and think of it as not even being attached to your hand." He emphasized, "Never jerk the trigger, remember, squeeze the one finger only. Finally, if you have time, take a lean on a stable object, like a tree or post. Combine this with half a breath then squeeze the trigger gently and you'll probably hit whatever you aim at."

The chicken yard and our small barn were located close together about one hundred yards from our house. Sitting inside alone one day with everyone away at the store, I heard the chickens begin to screech. Looking out the back door I saw a large hawk perched on a lower branch of the tall pine tree close to the chicken coop. I knew it might swoop down and catch one. I also knew that Cody would want me to shoot it.

Taking the rifle from the wall I loaded it with three cartridges. With it cradled under my arm I made my way quietly toward the frightened, noisy chickens. Within less than thirty yards of the unsuspecting predator I stopped. The overwhelming thrill of the moment, caused by my very first encounter with live game, swept through me. (Cody later described the sensation as "buck fever".) As Cody had instructed, I took a lean on a solid fence post, drew in half a breath, lined the sights on the center of the hawk's chest and gently squeezed the trigger. The bullet went through its heart killing the hawk instantly. Without a flutter it fell to the ground, where I left it.

The rear sight Cody made from a scrap of discarded copper wire worked perfectly. Elated, I returned to the house, unloaded the rifle and hung it back on the wall.

When everyone came back from the store I excitedly explained what had happened. Cody said, "You did good Sonny Boy. Let's go out and see what kind of a hawk it is." His encouragement made me feel proud.

Under the pine tree Cody told me that this species of Red

Tailed hawk killed chickens and most likely would have gotten one of ours. Then he added, "You keep shooting like that and some day you'll be a marksman." Prophetic words.

During the following six years all us boys competed to see who could hit the can, rock or bottle, firing our rifles from various distances. We also shot jack rabbits, squirrels, lizards and rattlesnakes. As a result we become exceptionally good shots. The rear sight remained stable, and I used the rifle constantly for six years, until I left Olinda at age 17.

I left the rifle behind, but I carried Cody's advice with me. During WWII, I would find his advice to be absolutely correct.

On Monday morning, December 8, 1941, President Roosevelt declared war with Japan.

On June 5, 1942, at age 17, I graduated from Shasta Union High School in Redding, California. The draft, the induction of all able-bodied men from the age of 18 to 26 into the Armed Forces, was in effect. The only way to make sure I could choose the branch of service I wanted, the Navy, I had to volunteer before my next birthday. Mother had to sign authorization papers so I could enlist

I entered "boot camp" with 199 other recruits. We were sent to the Naval Training Station on Point Loma in San Diego, California, to receive intense physical training and learn seamanship skills. For two months we would not be allowed to leave the base. Day after day we practiced the naval communication skills of Morse, semaphore flag, and blinker light codes. We learned how to identify planes and ships, both in daylight and in darkness. To qualify for the award Swimmer, Second Class (a prerequisite to being assigned sea duty), we had to be able to swim under water through a 50-foot obstacle course, jump off a 100-foot tower into deep water (that simulated leaping into the ocean from the main deck of a battleship or the flight deck of an aircraft carrier) and learn many other skills needed for survival in the ocean. Learning how to shoot a rifle would be our final training.

Many recruits had never held a rifle in their hands, but all of us eagerly looked forward to it because it meant a welcome all-day outing away from boot camp. For rifle instruction we would be taken by bus to the Marine Corps base at Camp Pendleton, a few miles north of San Diego.

Several weeks before getting this training, a lot of recruits made bets about who would be the best shot among our group of 200. We all knew each other's hometown, and a lot of speculation was done based on that piece of information. I had enlisted from Seattle, my Dad's hometown, where I had moved to attend college right after graduating high school. The betting men assumed that I was a "city kid".

All through training one of the recruits, Homer Bylan, an 18 year old from Arkansas, bragged constantly.

"I'm a country boy and I'll beat the ass off any of you in 'shootin'." Over and over he told tales of his lengthy experience as a hunter: how he'd 'chased along' behind Coon Hounds and shot game ever since he'd been a little kid. Finally fed up with his stories, one evening in the barracks (in front of most of the group) I told him I'd beat him hands down in shooting. No one believed a "city slicker" like me could shoot, and I never told anyone why I could.

It was an excellent day for competing. At Camp Pendleton the sun shone brightly while a warm, gentle sea breeze stirred the clear air. A big Marine Sergeant lined us up in twenty groups of ten. We were each issued a Springfield 30-06 caliber rifle perfectly "sighted in" and having a stabilizing leather sling attached. Our targets were 100 yards away. The Sergeant explained if we'd center the front sight in the middle of the hole in the rear "peep sight" then place the ball of the front sight at exactly the "six o'clock" position at the bottom of the black bulls eye on the target, the bullet would hit it dead center. We'd shoot 14 clips, each containing five rounds. The first 11 clips (55 rounds) were to be fired within an allotted time. We'd first shoot in rapid fire then in slow fire mode. He added that we would also be required to shoot in standing, sitting and prone positions. The last rounds, however, could be fired in the position of our choice with no time limit. A perfect score would be 140 points for the 70 rounds fired. A bulls-eye would earn two points and an American flag would be waved across the target. Just outside the bulls-eye, in a one inch wide white circle, a hit earned one point and a green flag would wave. A hit anyplace else on the target earned no points and a pair of "Maggie's drawers" (old ladies bloomers) would wave across it. A shot that entirely missed the target would be acknowledged by the repeated, rapid waving of a big, red "Jap meatball" across it, accompanied by loud jeering and booing.

Homer and I were in the last group of ten to shoot. Positioned on my right eight recruits away, I could easily glance over and see him. His shooting proved to be as good as he bragged. We both had finished firing the first 65 rounds, every one a bulls-eye. We had only five more left. Both of us had perfect scores, and the Marine Sergeant took notice. When the break came to load our last five cartridges he came over to me and in a slow southern drawl asked, "Where ah' yuh' all from Son?"

"Seattle, Washington Sir."

"Yuh' don't act like a city kid or a new recruit and yuh' sure as hell don't shoot like one—congratulations!!" He then spoke with Homer. I couldn't hear the conversation, but by the way Homer looked he too must have been given a compliment.

The rest of our group had finished shooting. Only the last ten, Homer and I along with eight others, remained on the line. As red-blooded sailors often do if they think they can win some money, many were excitedly making bets. I noticed the Sergeant and his helpers were also joining in, and while he held up the final firing of our last five rounds (until all bets were made) a Jeep drove up. A Marine Major got out and rapidly approached.

"What's going on here Sergeant?" he asked crisply, noticing an unusual stirring and chatter among the betting personnel.

"We got quite a show goin' on here Sir." Pointing to Homer and me he added, "Those two have perfect scores. They're gonna' be shootin' their last five rounds now in the position of their choice with no time limit."

The Major, immediately interested, ordered, "Carry on Sergeant." As he stepped into a position by the Jeep to watch he motioned his driver to shut off the engine.

To shoot our final rounds Homer and I both chose the sitting position. Through the megaphone the Sergeant told us to load our last rounds then ordered, "Ready." After a short pause he called, "Begin firin'." Eight other recruits on the line were shooting, but I paid attention only to the shots from Homer's rifle and my own.

Crack! An American flag waved. Homer's first shot slammed into the target dead center.

Crack! My first shot, a bulls-eye, also drew an American flag. Our next two shots each were acknowledged with American flags. Three of our final five rounds were expended.

Crack! Shot number four rang out. A green flag waved across Homer's target. It hit a fraction outside the bulls-eye in the one inch wide white ring. In war a good "killing shot" but a miss in competition.

Crack! The kick of the rifle jolted against my shoulder and a green flag appeared in front of my target.

One more round waited in our rifles. The Sergeant and most of the recruits fell almost silent as we prepared for shot number five. I saw Homer look toward me just before he fired his fifth and last round.

Crack! His rifle belched a little smoke and flame. For a few moments the Marine in the safety area below the targets ("the butts") hesitated as he checked. It seemed like we waited forever, then an American flag waved. Homer finished with a bulls-eye. Almost everyone cheered and clapped their hands

With only one shot left I couldn't beat Homer for a win. We could only finish in a tie, or I could lose.

Pulling on it as hard as I could I tugged the leather sling of the rifle around and under my left upper arm for greatest stability, as the Marine instructor had showed us. I remembered the day many years before when Cody had taught me to take only half a breath so it wouldn't distort my body. I looked through the rear peep sight of the 30-06, centered the front sight at the top of the black bulls eye then slowly lowered it to exactly the six o'clock position. In memory I was again 11 years old. In my mind I held the old .22 caliber Remington pump-action rifle steady on the lean of a solid fence post. I could hear our chickens cackle wildly as they fluttered and ran for shelter to avoid the hawk. I saw the red bead of the Remington's front sight resting in the bottom of the notch that Cody cut in the copper wire of the home made rear sight. All were perfectly in line with the center of the hawk's chest.

Crack! Only my index finger moved as I gently squeezed the trigger. A wild yell came from more than two hundred throats when without hesitation an American flag waved back and forth across the face of the target. My shot had hit dead center. I glanced to my right and saw Homer grin. In the noise, before returning to his Jeep, the Major spoke to the Sergeant, who walked over to Homer and me motioning for us to follow.

In the hut that served as his office we were offered a chair. Sitting behind the desk the Sergeant opened a drawer. Taking out a multi-form pad he wrote on it our name, rate and serial number. To this he added the name of our camp, John Paul Jones, and the name of our commanding officer, Captain H. C. Gearing. The form authorized Homer and me to be issued and wear, a short distance up from the wrist on the left sleeve of our dress blue uniform, the Navy insignia for expert rifleman.

Hands clasped behind his head and leaning far back in his swivel chair the Sergeant said, "Yuh' gave us quite a show out there. If either of yuh' boys had hit all bulls eyes yuh' all would have beaten the camp record for our new Marine recruits on their first time out rifle shootin'. What's so unusual is that yuh' all are the first Navy recruits during the whole time I've been here tu' equal our record. For two of yuh' tu' do it the same day is amazin'." He laughed, "Yuh' all should make a transfer tu' the Marine Corps."

Results were posted in our barracks the next day. In alphabetical order: *Bylan, Homer*, appeared at the top with *Curnow, Eugene*, just below it. Beside our names were identical scores, 139. Tied for first place, we each scored 69 bulls eyes out of a possible 70, and had one very near miss. Reading the roster we found several shooters missed with every shot and earned a score of zero.

Not long after this, boot camp days were over and all of us went separate ways. Though Homer and I won our expert rifleman award together and were complimented by the Marine Sergeant, we never became friends. We avoided each other as much as possible, and this may have been more my fault than his. However, as we left Camp John Paul Jones for the last time, each on a different bus, he and I glanced at each other and nodded in admiring recognition.

Ironically, I went on to become a medical corpsman. I would be associated with the Marines in the Pacific making the invasions of Iwo Jima and Okinawa. Medical corpsmen are noncombatants and do not carry a gun. Though I proudly wore the insignia for the Navy version of expert rifleman on my left forearm just above the wrist of my dress blue uniform, I've never fired a rifle again.

❖ THE TRAIN TRIP ❖

PART I

From the time Rex and I were 7 years old in 1932, whenever we went to Redding with our parents, while they were shopping he and I walked the few blocks to the railroad yard. There we first saw the massive iron monsters shooting fire, belching smoke, and hissing steam. Malleys, the biggest and most powerful engines ever built for the Southern Pacific railroad, with their tenders were 125 feet long. Each combination weighed more than one million pounds. On flat land it required only one to pull a passenger train 75 miles an hour. In the Siskiyou Mountains north of Redding it became an entirely different kind of railroading, slow going through long tunnels having with steep grades. It took great power to get heavily loaded freight trains up the Sacramento River canyon and across the Siskiyou Mountains beyond. In Redding two Malleys were coupled on the front. One more engine, usually a Mountain type or a Northern, was cut in about three quarters of the way back to help push. At the end, as a final helper, was another Malley pushing and the caboose.

In the slang of the day the huge engines were called "Mountain Malleys". That name derived from that of their French inventor, M. Anatole Mallet. The exceptional power of the enormous engines came from steam pressure of 200 pounds per square inch in the earlier model and 250 pounds in the later design that operated four sets of very large pistons. Also called Cab First's and Cab Forward's, all controls for the engineer and fireman were housed inside a cab in front of the boiler and smokestack instead of in back as is the case with all other steam driven railroad engines. The unique cab in the front made Malleys look like they were always running backward. The unusual design protected the crew from the possibility of death by suffocation from billowing clouds of choking black smoke and carbon monoxide as the powerful engines moved slowly, under full throttle climbing steep mountain grades pulling heavy loads.

It also assured that in every tunnel the tracks ahead could be clearly seen smoke free, by the engineer and fireman.

Every time Rex and I went to the rail yard we stood in awe watching the monsters. When coupled to the front of a train ready to go, the oil fueled fire, visible through holes incorporated in the design of the firebox, roared as tongues of flame flicked out in all directions. Sometimes an engineer watching us had a sense of humor. As we'd pass near one of the sets of pistons, he'd open a valve inside the cab for a moment causing a massive release of white steam. With a raging hiss it shot out near us. Frightened, we'd jump away. But fascinated by the many rods, pipes, levers, thumping steam-driven pumps and other machinery, we'd soon go back to get another close look at the fire-breathing giants. In time, by listening and observing, we learned that two short blasts from the unique six chime whistle of the lead engine and the urgent clanging of the big bronze bell, meant the engineer had his orders, the conductor in the caboose had given the "highball wave", and the train soon would leave.

With many heavily loaded freight cars to pull, at times it became difficult to get a train moving. The two leading Malleys moved slowly ahead taking up the slack in the couplers between the cars. Although each engine with its tender weighed more than one million pounds, sometimes one of the leading engines trying to move the heavy train would suddenly lose traction. All 16 driving wheels then began to spin wildly. The engineer quickly closed the throttle to stop the uncontrolled spinning. To add traction, he would then open a valve in the cab and shoot dry sand beneath the 63-inch high drivers, and then he'd try again. With exceptionally heavy trains, it could take several minutes for engineers in the two leading Malleys to synchronize their efforts to start the train moving. As youngsters, we knew we were watching a wonderful show of skill and precise cooperation between the engineers, and were thrilled seeing the lead engines labor strenuously as the train slowly pulled away. Being fascinated by locomotives of all kinds from childhood this interest has, during my lifetime, prompted me to learn as much as possible about them.

In June of 1940, when Rex and I were both 15 years old we decided it would be fun to hop a freight train in Redding and go to Portland, Oregon to visit our Grandma Smith and our childhood friends, the Closes. As we did every year, we worked 12 hours a day for five cents an hour, cutting fire breaks six feet wide in the tall dry grass and vegetation on both sides of the wooden post fence line surrounding Alfred's farm. We used this money to finance the adventure. Some days the temperature stood at 121 degrees. In spite of the blazing heat we worked every day. Alfred knew that having two healthy boys each willing to do back breaking labor for five cents an hour was a bargain and eagerly "hired" us. By August we both had saved $5.00 and were ready to leave. On Friday, in the shed behind Alfred's house we found two clean gunnysacks. In them we put a few pair of socks, some underwear, two shirts, a pair of rivet jeans, warm stocking caps and our Melton jackets. That night we hid the sacks of clothing under the hay in Alfred's barn. On Friday evening we walked 2 miles to Ulbergs general store and asked their 18 year old son, Carrol, if he'd give us a ride to Redding in a couple of days. After hearing our plan Carrol agreed to meet us by the bridge in Telephone Gulch a mile from our homes at ten o'clock the following Monday morning.

With our gunnysacks slung over our shoulders on Monday we climbed over the back fence and left Alfred's ranch. To protect our five-dollar bill we folded it between two thin pieces of cardboard that we placed beneath a sock in the heel of our shoe. By the bridge in Telephone Gulch, Carrol waited.

On the way to Redding, in his old open topped Maxwell car he asked, "Do your parents know?"

I told him, "No, but just to make sure they won't worry, will you stop on your way home and tell them? Let them know we'll be gone about two weeks."

"O.K., I'll tell them. How come you're doing this anyway?"

"We've wanted to do it for a long time and now it just seems right."

In Redding, Carrol parked in front of the main Post Office, about half a block from the railroad tracks. We waved a brief goodbye as the old Maxwell clattered slowly away.

Standing beside the tracks we watched the two Malley's being coupled to the front of a long freight train. Fireboxes roared, visibly belching flame, to produce the full head of steam needed to pull the heavy load around the many curves and up steep grades in the Sacramento River canyon.

We became apprehensive and for a moment a shiver shook me. The train looked so long and somehow the big Malleys now seemed much less friendly than in the past. They sounded like a pair of hissing, fire breathing dragons. From where we stood we counted 116 cars.

Shimmering heat waves engulfed everything as the temperature hit 118 degrees at noon that Monday in August of 1940. Fascinated, my cousin Rex and I watched the two giant hissing steam engines being made ready for the northbound trip. They were Mountain Malleys, and they were now at the front of a fully loaded freight train.

We wondered if our idea to hop a train that day might be foolish. Feeling both excitement and apprehension we looked down the track at the serpentine array of cars trying to decide where and which kind to get on for our secretly planned 450-mile ride to Oregon.

"How about riding halfway back?"

Rex squinted into the sun, "No, too close in front of that high wheeler helper that's about twenty cars from the end. The engineer might see us. Some place behind that engine would be better."

"True," I said. "But there's that Malley helper just ahead of the caboose. That engineer, or the conductor in the caboose, might see us."

Rex paused studying the many kinds of freight cars. Finally

he said, "You know, if we get on a tank car in front of a boxcar and we're between that high wheeler and the final Malley and the caboose, no one will be able to see us."

"Yup, I think you're right."

We tossed our gunny sacks containing the extra clothing over one shoulder. Carefully picking our way along the crushed rock ballast of the rail bed, we walked slowly past the high-wheeled engine and saw no one in the cab. Continuing along the rough roadbed, near the end of the train we reached our objective, a black tank car in front of a well-weathered, dull red boxcar.

"This should be good," Rex said. "From this far back we'll be able to watch the two leading Malley's working hard going around curves and climbing grades."

Here we faced the final decision. "You think we really should do this?"

Rex didn't voice his answer. Often while growing up we needed no words to communicate. Glancing at each other for only a moment we silently agreed. "Let's go."

Putting his gunnysack on the ground Rex grasped the rail beside the short steep steps near the back of the tank car and climbed up. Moving across the wooden platform he stomped on it, checking it for strength.

"Toss the bags and come on up. Everything looks O.K.," he extended his arms ready to make the catch.

Standing on the rear platform we examined the big iron wheel of the hand-operated emergency brake. Between the cars we looked down at the sturdy air hoses with their quick release, "glad hand" connectors hanging next to the drawbars and couplers that held the freight cars together. Last, we explored the outer sides of the tank car. Walking all the way around on the 18 inch wide wooden catwalk we held on to and tugged at the chest high galvanized pipe safety railing to be sure it wasn't loose. Satisfied with what we saw we returned to the rear platform.

Sweating profusely from heat and apprehension we heard two

short blasts from the whistle of the lead Malley and the start of urgent ringing from its big bronze bell. Excited, we knew we soon would be on our way!

Suddenly, a loud metallic slamming sound rushed toward us from the front of the train.

Startled, Rex turned quickly toward me, "What's that?"

I had no time to answer before a resounding jolt hit the tank car.

During the eight years we had watched the trains every time we'd go to Redding, we never saw one railroad policeman, also known as a yard bull. So we decided, on that blazing hot day in August that after the train started we were going to ride on the 18-inch wide wooden catwalk that circled a tank car located in front of the dull red boxcar. The loud, rapidly approaching slamming sound we heard had been caused by the slack between each set of couplers being taken up with a metallic bang as each car in-turn suddenly jerked to a start. The noise started at the front of the train and rolled toward the back as both leading engines began to slowly move. It took a few moments to reach us. Then, suddenly, the tank car jolted violently forward. We were still standing on the rear platform and Rex, facing the back of the train, lost his balance. Pitching headfirst he fell toward the front face of the boxcar in back of us. With his body arched almost full length between the two cars, both of his hands were pressed firmly against the front end of the boxcar behind while his feet were tightly wedged against the wooden platform of the tank car. If any other kind of freight car, except the kind that have a flat wall, had been behind us he'd have had nothing to catch himself against and would have fallen to the rail below directly in the path of the wheels.

Now, because of the length his body was arched, Rex found it impossible to pull himself upright. Hopelessly stuck in this position, while the train lurched and jerked gathered speed, with fright in his voice Rex yelled, "Hey, give me a pull up out of here!!"

Looking down at the mirror smooth ribbon of rail glistening in the sun, I was terror-stricken. I couldn't speak or move.

In high school everyone called me, "Birdie Muscles" because at age 15, I weighed 103 pounds. My arms were small and very weak. Rex, one of the strongest boys in school, had muscular, well-developed arms and weighed 150 pounds. Only because of the strength in his arms could he keep his body arched and prevent himself from falling to the rail below in front of the ever faster rolling wheels.

Only seconds passed but it seemed like a long time before I could act. As is sometimes the case, when extreme fright is involved, for a few moments a very weak person becomes exceptionally strong. With my left hand I grabbed and held on to the iron emergency brake wheel, and leaned forward over Rex as far as possible. Then with one smooth motion I reached out with my right hand, grasped the back of his clothing just below the neckline and pulled him upright. Because of the weakness of my arms, even if I'd have been able to use both of them at once, under ordinary circumstances I could never have pulled his 150-pound weight upward from his arched position.

"Boy, how'd you do that?" Rex appeared a little shaken.

"I don't know. I just did it," was all I could say.

We had witnessed a miracle and for awhile remained quiet, thinking how tragically our journey could have ended.

Seated on the 18-inch wide catwalk on the side of the tank car, we left Redding about two o'clock in the afternoon. Deep within the canyon beside the Sacramento River, the rail line ran north around challenging curves and over many bridges. Shasta Dam had not been completed and the new mile long trestle at Redding, that eventually would re-route the railroad, had not been put in service. Because of this the train we rode ran on the original tracks, following the course of the river in the bottom of the canyon.

From our vantage point we watched the sun play hide and seek among newly forming, fluffy white thunderheads over the Coast Range . A clean, fresh fragrance from tall ponderosa pine, fir and cedar trees drifted in the air. Manzanita, chaparral and scrub oak added paintbrush shades of green, pleasantly contrasting with the blush of the iron rich soil. In the shade at the bottom of the deep and narrow canyon the crystal clear, ice cold water of the river, fed by the ever-present snow on nearby Mount Shasta, tumbled along, cascading in white foam over submerged boulders. The slow rhythmic, click-clack, click-clack became pleasantly hypnotic as first the front then the back wheels passed over the joints in the rails. Rex and I felt a sense of accomplishment knowing for the first time in our lives we were unbound spirits, free to make our own decisions.

Nearly 50 miles from Redding in Dunsmuir, a small town in the bottom of the ever-narrowing canyon. We were well into the Siskiyou Mountains near the headwaters of the Sacramento River, when the train stopped. A division point, here crews were changed and the engines serviced.

We threw our gunnysacks to the ground and jumped off the tank car. Not thinking to bring a container of water with us and because of the intense August heat, our throats were parched. We walked a short distance to the small passenger station. Inside stood a drinking fountain made of white marble. From it, sparkling ice-cold water continually ran. The clock on the wall read 5:30 as we eagerly drank and splashed water on our face.

"It tastes like Dunsmuir water" became the highest compliment any water in California could be given, and in those days all water in the State was compared with it. Passenger trains don't stop at Dunsmuir anymore, and the station has been torn down. But the city officials had the foresight to remove and preserve the marble fountain. It can be found in a gazebo on the edge of a park next to the main street. There, in the heat of summer, it continues to bubble and refresh with its generous supply of cold, sparkling Dunsmuir water.

At a small grocery store nearby, we wanted to get the best possible buy on food. We looked over several possibilities, and we decided on a 19 cent, two pound package of thickly frosted cinnamon rolls. I washed mine down with a five-cent bottle of grape soda pop. Rex drank orange.

Attempting to return to our train, still waiting on the northbound tracks, we discovered that another freight had pulled alongside it and now waited on the southbound tracks. We wanted to return to the tank car we rode on coming north, but to get to it we would have to crawl across the tracks underneath the southbound train. Furthermore, our tank car was now too close to the vision line of the southbound engineers and conductors. To make sure they could not see us, we would have to crawl across the tracks near the southbound train's center and then walk between the two trains to get on board our tank car.

Talking it over we made our decision.

"You know, crawling across tracks under a freight train that might start to move is kind of dangerous," I observed.

Rex agreed, "Yea, but if we do it real fast and go exactly under its center, you know between the front and back sets of wheels, no matter which way the train might go we'll have time to get out from under it and away from the rail on the other side without being run over."

"O.K. But let's look up underneath the car real good to make sure nothing is hanging from it that could catch on our clothes and trap us. Boy, it still seems dangerous to me but I guess we'll have to do it to get back to the same tank car we rode in on."

We heard the two short blasts of a whistle telling us one of the trains had orders to move. But the echo from the steep canyon walls prevented us from knowing from which train the sound came. Because the southbound train had arrived after our northbound freight came in, we assumed it was our northbound train signaling it would soon leave.

Not wanting to miss it we crawled rapidly across the rails under a boxcar on the southbound line. Moments after our legs came from under the boxcar and cleared the second rail, with a metallic bang and a sudden jerk the southbound freight began to move. while We were still on hands and knees between the two trains. There is little room between trains on adjacent tracks and the movement caused unexpected dizziness. We sensed the danger of trying to stand up and walk between the two as the southbound train bumped and jarred along beside us shaking the earth. Though we were trapped between them, somehow common sense prevailed.

Rex motioned toward the moving train. "Let's sit right here until this one gets by."

As we squatted on our gunnysacks I muttered, "Look at those wheels, they're so close. If one of them jumps the track we'll be crushed."

"Yea, they sure are close," Rex agreed.

Gathering speed, the train rolled by. The intensity of noise increased and the steel flanges on the wheels shrieked while contacting the inner surface of the rail as metal scraped bare metal. On our gunnysacks, we were almost immobile with fear. Finally the southbound freight passed, and we knew that crawling under a train waiting to go on a main line is not something we'd ever do again. Climbing back to the relative safety on our same tank car, two short blasts from the whistle of the leading Malley alerted us that we too would soon be on our way.

Six miles north of Dunsmuir we were treated to something few people ever experience: the Cantera Loop. Here our 116-car freight traveled in three directions, north, east and south, at the same time. Making the 180-degree turn it crossed the last railroad bridge over the Sacramento River, struggled up the steep grade and climbed out of the canyon. This configuration, around a half circle of track on a steep grade, is not common. The sight overjoyed us as we watched from our open-air vantage point on the tank car. We could see, up on the grade and across the river, the two leading Malleys far ahead, under full throttle, gushing clouds of black smoke. The rest of the train followed, snaking around the half circle. A short distance ahead of our tank car the high wheeler helper engine noisily labored as it too helped push.

Looking back to the end of the train we saw the final Malley, with the caboose behind: it pushed as the engineer applied just the right amount of power needed to successfully make the turn. Two helper engines pushing were a necessity at the Cantera Loop: without them the Malleys' massive power at the front end could cause one or more freight cars on the bridge located at the center of the half circle, to be pulled sideways off the track and into the river.

Fifty-one years later in July of 1991, this did happen. A tank car full of weed killer derailed on the bridge and fell into the river, spilling 19,000 gallons of Metam Sodium. The chemical killed all aquatic life, both fish and vegetation, and caused the evacuation of Dunsmuir as well as all residents 42 miles downstream, to where the river empties into Shasta Lake. Ironically, this accident happened after the Southern Pacific had retired all its huge steam driven Mountain Malleys known in railroad terms as the "Cab Forward, 4-8-8-2's". The engines that powered the hapless freight train involved in the 1991 accident were the new Diesel-Electric, "Black Widow" units whose crew apparently found themselves short, simultaneously, of both experience and finesse at the controls.

About nine o'clock that night, we stopped in Grass Lake. Jumping from the tank car in the reduced light, we watched, from a distance, the tenders being filled with water. Men with large, long necked oil cans worked outside the engines to fill reservoirs and lubricate rods and slides: a lot of lubrication for the engines comes from a pressure device activated by a crewman in the cab but at almost every stop a lot still had to be done by hand.

Judging by the previous stop in Dunsmuir we expected to be here more than an hour. Rex pointed to a small café close to the tracks. "Let's go and have something to eat while they work on the train." As we walked toward the café he chided, "Boy, your face sure is dirty."

"Yea, well yours ain't so clean either," I shot back.

When we entered, clutching our dirty gunny sacks, the

Chinese people who ran the café stared. Rex and I were the only customers. We sat down at a deeply marred wood-topped table spotted with many char marks where cigarettes had been carelessly placed. We weren't greeted. After a few minutes I leaned toward Rex, and said in a low voice, "Maybe it would be a good idea, because of how dirty we are, to put some money on the table so the man staring at us will see it. You noticed the unfriendly way he looked when we came in...like he didn't want us here?"

Rex took two one-dollar bills and some coins from his pocket and put it on the table. Seeing this, the Chinese man, wearing a grease-spotted gray apron that once had been white, hurried over. In a thick accent he asked, "What I can get for you?"

"Could we have breakfast now even though it's time for supper?" Rex asked.

Looking at the money, he answered immediately. "Oh yes, sure. Breakfast here you get any time of day." He smiled, showing a dental disaster: one solid gold tooth in front among many snags black with decay.

Rex and I looked at each other, and silently agreed about two things: money talks, and this guy really needs to see a dentist.

We ordered bacon and eggs, pan-fried potatoes, toast and jelly and a large glass of milk. Meals big enough to feed a starving logger soon arrived. We were each given a pile of bacon on a separate plate. On another there were three eggs and a heap of potatoes. By their wonderful taste, they were obviously cooked in the bacon grease. In addition we each had six slices of toast, a jar of jelly, a quarter of a pound of real butter and a tall glass of cold milk. During the meal our glasses of milk were refilled twice at no extra charge. The cost for all this was sixty-nine cents each.

What a joy to eat delicious food until we were not only full but so stuffed that our stomach's hurt. At home for breakfast, our fare might be fried corn meal mush or boiled and softened whole grain wheat covered with thin syrup, homemade from brown sugar and hot water. Many times we had only a bowl of soupy watered down oatmeal.

This first meal that Rex and I bought with money we had earned ourselves, stood in extreme contrast to our poor diet at home. In our minds the same thought formed. "If we have only 69 cents we can eat well." Earning enough money was essential, and that meant we must develop a saleable skill. The conclusion we came to that night in a small out-of-the-way Chinese café, perhaps "on the wrong side of the tracks", helped shape for life our positive attitude toward work.

We left the café about 10:30 PM. The railroad men were nearly finished taking off one Malley from the front and both engines that helped push, and were re-attaching the caboose. The steep grades and sharp curves were behind us, so the train needed only one of the powerful engines to bring it north into Oregon.

Now in darkness, we used the lights of the rail yard and the light of the moon to choose a boxcar in which to ride. Inside, strewn on the floor, we could see lots of clean, heavy, shipping paper. We wrinkled it and made a pile about three feet deep, which provided for us a makeshift bed. In the high elevation of the Siskiyou Mountains it was cold. We put on the thick stocking hats and Melton jackets that we carried in our gunnysacks. Then, with a leap, we flopped down in the middle of the thick pile of paper. With full stomachs we burrowed into our rats' nest of crumpled shipping paper and drifted off to sleep listening to the steady rhythmic click clack, click clack of the rails.

When we woke the train wasn't moving, and it was so cold we could see our breath. The engine, nowhere in sight, had left our boxcar and a few others on a siding. From the open door, close by we saw the lights of a town. With our gunnysacks we jumped to the ground then walked across the many tracks of a railroad yard. Once in town, we read a storefront sign and found we were in Klamath Falls, Oregon. The hands of a lighted clock on a bank stood at 3:00. In the early morning, even in August, hoar frost covered everything. Our stocking caps and Melton jackets were inadequate against the chill. Finding, in town, a Standard gasoline station that stayed open 24 hours a day, we sneaked into its heated rest room. After half an hour we were warm enough to return to the rail yard and look for another northbound train. Outside once more, our teeth soon chattered.

On the far side of the rail yard we saw a small shack that appeared to be deserted. I suggested, "Let's go over and see if we can get inside. We can wait there until daylight before we try to find another train."

"Sure would be a lot better than being out here in this cold," Rex agreed.

We found the door unlocked, slowly opened it and looked around. Seeing no one in the dimly lit interior we cautiously entered. In the glow from some outdoor floodlights, we saw inside the shack a 6-foot long bench built in against one wall. There were also three chairs, a small table and best of all, an "airtight heater" stuffed with paper, kindling and chunks of wood. Piles of folded newspaper, more kindling and lots of wood lay in a sturdy wooden box a short distance away. On the table stood a kerosene lantern and beside it lay a box of wooden Diamond Brand, kitchen matches. I lit the lantern and saw on the table two half filled ashtrays, current newspapers and magazines indicating the shack had daily use.

Rex stood nearby with a match already in his hand, shivering. "Shall I light the stove?" Needing no answer, he lit it. A fire soon crackled cheerfully. The interior of the small building rapidly became pleasantly warm and we realized we were exhausted.

"Let's lie down and sleep awhile."

I agreed, "That's a real good idea. We can rest and then get out of here before anyone comes around and catches us."

Rex curled up on the floor, facing the wall, using his gunnysack as a pillow. I blew out the flame in the lantern then stretched out, face up, on the built in bench. Soon we drifted into warm, deep sleep.

The sounds of men talking outside then the squeaking hinges

of the door woke us as three railroad men entered. One struck a match and lit the lantern. Then they saw us.

"Hey, what's this!" one exclaimed.

"Shall I call the yard people?" the other asked.

The third man, obviously the boss, leaned over to look closely at our faces. I'll never forget his comment.

Seeing we were very young and didn't even need to shave he said, "No, let them sleep. They're just a couple of chickens trying to grow some feathers."

The purpose of the shack soon became evident. Here trains were coupled together and made up for their run. A small yard engine brought a few freight cars at a time to the rails outside the shack to be weighed on a huge scale. In the shack the figures from the scale outside were read and tallied. The total weight of the train, and whether it would travel over mountains or flat land would determine the kind of engine needed to pull it. This noisy activity continued for nearly two hours while Rex and I pretended to sleep.

It became extremely difficult for me to remain face up for this length of time. After half an hour I wanted so badly to turn on my side that it became absolute torture to stay still. Rex, on his side facing the wall, remained comfortable.

Finally, after bringing the last few cars to be weighed, the yard engine chugged away. With one eye I cautiously peeked at the boss as he put a couple of extra chunks of wood in the stove. Placing a finger to his lips he motioned for the others to leave.

Looking at Rex and me one more time, for a moment I saw a smile cross his face. Lowering the wick of the lantern, he pushed down the lever lifting the glass chimney. With a strong puff of air he blew out the flame, walked slowly out of the shack and quietly closed the door.

❖ THE TRAIN TRIP ❖
PART II

Warm and rested, early that morning we left the shack. Sunshine banished the chill from the air and the frost. By ten o'clock we had boarded a northbound train pulled by only one smaller engine. Our equipage was a brand new, slat-sided boxcar. Eventually it would be a cattle car, but that morning the aroma was as fresh as its brand new, bright red paint.

The clear blue water of Klamath Lake sparkled as our train journeyed mile after mile along the eastern shore, past extensive wetlands that was shelter for hundreds of waterfowl.

After a few hours the ride became monotonous. Resting our heads on our clothes-filled gunnysacks, we lay on the hard-planked floor and dozed. The constant jiggling and bumping of the cattle car floor took its toll.

"Sure wish we had a bunch of that clean shipping paper in here like we had in that other box car," Rex said.

"Yeah," I agreed. "Are your hip bones as sore as mine?"

The day grew hot, and we became thirsty. Once more we had forgotten to bring drinking water. Looking at the sparkling lake made our thirst intense. We decided at the next stop we would try to find a container, fill it and carry it along.

The train stopped in Chemult. The engineer positioned the tender below the water tower. From a huge spout thousands of gallons, to be used by the engine on the journey over the Cascade Mountains, quickly poured. We knew from previous stops that it took about fifteen minutes to fill the tender. Carrying our gunnysacks we moved quickly from the cattle car to search beside the tracks for a suitable container. We were almost ready to give up when Rex found a green glass bottle that had originally contained cheap, "rot gut" wine. Running to a tap under the tower we drank our fill, rinsed out the bottle, topped it off with cool water and

THE TRAIN TRIP, PART II

screwed on the cap. Two short blasts from the engine's whistle alerted us the train had been cleared to go. As it began to move we realized we were too far from the new cattle car. We tossed our gunnysacks on the nearest freight car and quickly climbed aboard. Strewn on the floor were big piles of clean brown shipping paper. Smiling, but without having to speak, we each knew the other felt lucky. We'd sleep well that night.

Much of the trip from Chemult to Eugene is downhill, through tunnels and around sharp curves. As the grade became steeper it seemed to both Rex and me that the train traveled much too fast to be under control. Racing around even the lesser curves, we thought it might jump off the rails. The air brakes came on and released but didn't reduce our speed. We sensed we were going much too fast for safety.

Worried, I asked Rex, "Don't you think we're picking up a lot of speed going down this hill?"

"Uh huh, I feel the brakes trying to work, and it seems like they don't slow us down at all," he agreed as the train rushed along.

Stepping to the open boxcar door to look forward at the engine we leaned out a short distance across a waist-high, hardwood 2 x 6 safety bar. The train bumped and jerked wildly as it sped down the grade. My strange sense of humor took over, and I saw a chance to play an exceptionally good practical joke on Rex.

The idea formed as the train plunged into an inky black tunnel. I planned that in the next tunnel I would step back from the wooden safety bar, creep on hands and knees to the opposite side of the boxcar, crawl under the big pile of shipping paper and disappear.

To set Rex up, as we leaned out across the wooden bar to watch the engine I said,

"You know, this thing is swaying sideways so bad a person could get dizzy in one of these real dark tunnels and fall out. So don't lean too hard on this wood bar."

Continuing to look ahead he nodded in agreement.

A few moments before we sped into the next tunnel I stepped around in front of Rex so he'd have to look past me to watch the engine enter. Taking advantage of the last light of afternoon I glanced backward to the other side of the boxcar and judged the distance to the heap of paper. In the blackness of the tunnel I crouched and crept backward a short distance then turned around. On hands and knees I continued to make my way to the paper, then buried myself under it.

From a small opening beneath the paper I watched Rex as the train sped out of the tunnel into daylight. He noticed right away that I wasn't in front of him. I saw the puzzled expression on his face while his gaze swept the boxcar's interior. Not seeing me, he panicked. His eyes bulged and opened wide as he ran a few steps forward then a few steps back. This useless motion obviously not the result of a plan or logic.

"Gene—, Gene—?" he called.

Because of the speed I knew he wouldn't jump off to go back and look for me. He leaned far out over the wooden safety bar, looking back to see if he could spot my body anywhere along the tracks. Frightened at seeing nothing, he again paced in all directions. Several times his ankles came so close I could have reached out and grabbed one. From my hiding place I continued to watch and wanted the joke to go on forever. But my sense of mirth was overpowering, and I soon exploded in fits of laughter. Standing up I jeered, "Boy, I sure fooled you this time!!"

Rex seldom swore, even under trying circumstances. However, the moment he saw me jump from under the shipping paper laughing and pointing a finger at him, he blurted out, with great relief, "You bastard!!"

That night we slept comfortably, again in a "rats nest" of clean shipping paper.

In the morning we awoke in Eugene. The boxcar had been shunted to a siding nearly a mile from the main yard where other trains were being made up. It took until noon to find one heading north. Since it was a beautiful day we decided to ride again on the wooden catwalk of a tank car that provided an unrestricted view.

Our train was rolling down the Willamette Valley toward Portland, and we were enjoying the scenery when a cinder flew into my right eye.

"Ouch," I yelped as I threw my hand over it.

"What happened?" Rex asked.

"Something blew in my eye, and it hurts!"

"Keep your hand over it awhile and the tears will wash it out."

The rush of wind on my face added to the discomfort. However, some relief came when the train slowed to about 10 miles an hour as it passed through Salem. In town, the long freight crept along for many blocks on tracks embedded in the center of a main city street just as a trolley might do. Friendly people of all ages waved and smiled. As we left Salem, tears washed the cinder from my eye.

We knew we'd soon be seeing Grandma Smith and the Closes, and we were happy and excited at the prospect of our journey's success.

We had left our green, glass water bottle in the boxcar in Eugene. As the train arrived in Portland, heading for the Brooklyn rail yard, we were taunted by the sprinklers at the Eastmoreland Golf Course. Rotating irrigation heads sent jets of cool water high in the air. The view of that made our thirst more intense than we could endure. As the train slowed we threw our gunnysacks to the ground and jumped. I ran through the nearest overhead shower, stopped the sprinkler action, and we drank. How good the water tasted and how happy we were to be in Portland!

Before jumping off the tank car we noticed a small grocery store close by. We made our way to it. For some reason, a craving for lettuce and mayonnaise overwhelmed us. We bought that, plus a two-pound package of delicious, thickly frosted cinnamon rolls. Groceries in hand, we headed for the small park across the street from the store. At one end stood a tall, outdoor advertising sign that cast an inviting shadow: we headed for its shade, which promised some relief from the heat of an August afternoon.

Our thirst was quenched, but we wanted more water to have with our cinnamon rolls. En route to the shade, we found two empty beer cans. They looked new so we picked them up, took them to a nearby spigot and filled them.

Seated in the shade, we used my jack knife to cut the lettuce into chunks. We slathered them with mayonnaise and devoured all of them. Having no spoon, we found a flat stick and used it to get every bit of mayonnaise from the jar. We may have looked like vagabonds, but something about our intense craving made that lettuce and dressing feel like the main course at a king's banquet.

More relaxed, we began eating the dessert course: cinnamon rolls and an occasional drink of water from the beer cans. For awhile all went well...and then in came the clowns.

We hadn't thoroughly rinsed out what we thought to be clean beer cans. Pressing them tightly to our lips we threw our heads back to take the last big gulps of cool water. Suddenly we became aware of a mass of live insects wriggling inside our mouths. Rex spit out ants and some long, black colored members of the millipede family. I spit out several earwigs and a small dead snail. At that point we both came very close to losing all our lunch.

Done with imbibing, we packed up and began to walk. We were heading from near S.E. 17th and Tacoma Street to the Close's home at N.E. 34th and Bryce Avenue. In 1931, my Mother and I had lived awhile with Rex's parents on N.E. 35th and Bryce Avenue so he and I knew we were about seven miles from there, much too far to walk. After a short debate we decided to spend a few cents and take the streetcar. Several transfers later we arrived at the home of our friends. Filthy with soot, we were tired but filled with a grand sense of accomplishment. We had planned and successfully completed a difficult task: we had reached our goal without a major mishap.

Rex knocked on the door. Mrs. Close opened it.

"Hi," Rex greeted.

Mrs. Close appeared puzzled. She hadn't seen us for almost eight years. "Yes, can I help you boys?"

Recognizing her hesitation and that she didn't know who we were, Rex spoke. "It's Rex and Gene, we've ju—"!!

"Rex," she broke in on his explanation in mid sentence, "and Gene, what are you doing here?" Opening the screen door she invited, "Come in, come in. Goodness, what a nice surprise!!"

Rex continued. "We just got off a freight train. We rode them from Redding to come and see you."

"Let's get a look at you. My how you both have grown. It's been what, about seven years since you moved to California? Are you hungry? Supper will be ready in about an hour."

Having recently eaten our lunch of lettuce, mayonnaise, cinnamon rolls and various insects, Rex offered, "We're not too hungry."

Mrs. Close surveyed our dirty faces and clothes. "Well, how about a nice bath before supper? Do you have any clean clothes with you?" she glanced at our dirty gunnysacks.

"I guess they're not very clean," I answered

"Let me look, I'll wash them if they need it. We have a spare bedroom and bath upstairs so they will be yours. Oh, I'm so glad to see you! How are your mothers, Hattie and Frances?"

Mrs. Close spoke so fast and with such enthusiasm our answers went unheeded during the mostly one-sided conversation.

"Could you telephone our Grandma Smith and tell her we're here?" I managed to slip the question in.

"Do you know her number?"

"No, I don't know how to use a telephone. We don't have them yet, in Olinda where we live."

"Do you know her full name and address?"

"Yes, that's easy because I write to her a couple of times a month. It's Margaret M. Smith, 1824 South West Market Street."

Mrs. Close located the number in the telephone directory and with one finger demonstrated how to use a rotary dial. Handing me the receiver she said, "It's ringing. Just put this up to your ear and talk into the mouthpiece."

Grandma Smith answered, "Hello."

"This is Gene, Grandma."

"Gene! Where are you?"

"Rex and I are over at the Close's house on N.E. 34th and Bryce. We just got off a freight train we rode here from Redding."

"My land, you shouldn't have done that!" she exclaimed. "It's way too dangerous. Are you all right? How long will you be staying with the Close's?"

"We're fine. We'll probably be staying here a couple of days. We want to catch another freight train and go to Maupin to see where Rex and his folks lived on the Connelly sheep ranch where his Dad used to work."

When told this Grandma Smith gently though firmly said to me she'd have no grandsons of hers ride any more freight trains.

"Gene, when you're done visiting there, call me and your Uncle Harold and I will come and pick you and Rex up. You can stay with me as long as you want."

"O.K. Grandma, I'll call."

Not knowing how to hang up the phone, I handed it to Mrs. Close.

After baths, we spent a lot of time cleaning the sides of the tub, where our bodies had left grease-like black scum. Then, our friend Burt came home, and we spent the evening enjoying conversation typical of 15-year old boys: school, sports, fishing and memories from our years as "back fence" neighbors.

Burt began by asking, "Remember the neighbors living next door to us when we were kids?"

"Sure," Rex answered. "They were the Sweenys, and she was a heavy smoker. She stayed in the house most of the time because she didn't want anyone to know she used tobacco."

For her to smoke was not acceptable in her circle of friends which included our folks—and Mrs. Sweeny sure didn't want them to know.

Burt continued. "Remember the time they had the house painted? In those days that white paint dried real slow. Gene, do you remember what you did just after the painting was finished?"

"Yes I do, but it was you two guys' fault. All of us decided it would be fun to throw a rotten tomato on the wet paint beside the back door. Burt, you found a spoiled and mushy tomato in the garbage and handed it to me. Then we all walked next door. I was only 6 years old, and both of you kept telling me to do it. It was about noon when we stood in the driveway ready to act. You both urged me 'throw the tomato, throw the tomato'. I threw it hard, and it made a noisy 'splat' when it hit. Juice and seeds ran down the wall, instantly mixing with the paint."

Rex laughed, "Remember what happened next? Mrs. Sweeny rushed out and looked at the damage. 'Just look at what you did! My husband will get after you for this!' While she scolded she kept one hand behind her. Then, Gene, you saw the smoke rising in back of her and you said, 'I know, but we can see you're smoking.' Jerking at her dress she spun around and hurried into the house...and we never did hear anything about it from her husband."

"Remember the time we told you about...when Rex and I made a booby trap in the trail that led from the school ground to the street?" I asked. "We dug a shallow hole in the damp sandy soil using a stick and our hands. Then we found a bottle nearby and broke it. We put the shards of glass in the bottom of the hole making sure they stood straight up, then we put a piece of thrown away cardboard over the top. We covered this with a thin layer of sand to make it look just like the rest of the trail. Most of us boys who used the trail went barefoot, and we thought it would be a big surprise if they fell into our trap. But as soon as we got home, seven blocks away, our conscience began to take over. Suddenly, without speaking, Rex and I both ran back to the trail hoping no one had fallen in and been badly cut. We took away the cardboard and quickly covered the glass with a lot of sand to make it harmless. That was one 'joke' we simply could not carry out."

Rex agreed but recalled something else. "Burt, do you remember that many of the streets here were not paved? At the corner of N.E. 35th and Bryce they became a sea of mud when it rained. From our house on 35th, three houses from the corner of Bryce, we could see the cars passing by. Most were Model T Fords each using the same muddy ruts to make the turn onto N.E. 35th. Gene and I found a 3-foot long 2 by 4 and pounded a lot of long nails through it. About two inches of the sharp nails stuck out the opposite side. At the corner we mashed the 2 by 4 into one of the mud ruts, with the sharp nails sticking upward and made sure it was covered by plenty of muddy water unable to be seen. Then we went home. Inside the living room we watched from the large window as a Model T slowly rounded the corner—and ran right over the points of the nails. The tire blew out with a "speeoosh" sound we could hear from where we watched. We saw the man pull over to the side of the road, almost in front of our house and change the tire. For awhile we thought it was funny. But after seeing the man get soaked in the downpour of rain the joke lost its humor. We felt bad though, and when the man left we hurried out and took the 2 by 4 from the rut. We hid it behind the garage and never did that again."

After supper, tired and relaxed we were off to a nice soft bed. In the unaccustomed luxury of crisp, cool, white percale sheets we were quickly asleep.

Two days later Uncle Harold and Grandma took us to her apartment. We stayed there a week. During that time we visited the Battleship Oregon, which was tied up in the Willamette River, close to downtown Portland, southwest of the Burnside

Bridge. Below decks we were fascinated by its unusual triple expansion engine, partially cut away to demonstrate how the same steam was used over and over as it passed through three cylinders, each larger than the other, to drive the propellers.

We rode the old-fashioned trolley car to Council Crest, where we enjoyed the best view of the city and ate the picnic lunch Grandma packed for us. Returning, we got off at the Vista Bridge and sat in the sunshine on one of the cement benches the builders thoughtfully incorporated in the design. Grandma lived only three blocks down the hill from there, on Market Street.

Rex and I were hungry for entertainment. During all the years we lived in Olinda our families were so poor they never had an extra 15 cents to give us for admission to an afternoon movie in Redding. Grandma gave us all the money we needed to see one, and sometimes two, double features a day. I don't remember the name of any, but after a week we had our fill and were ready to move on. Grandma bought us Greyhound tickets to Maupin and gave us extra money for tickets from there to Redding. She didn't ask, and we didn't tell her that we planned to save the money and ride the freight trains from Maupin back to California.

At the Greyhound station, we were treated to the kinds of hugs and kisses only a doting Grandmother can give. Then we were on our way. By mid-morning we arrived in Maupin.

Rex was eager to see the site where, many years before, his dad, Billy, had provided his family a shelter. They had lived about six months in a weatherproof tent, under a large oak tree beside the Deschutes River. Their site was a short distance north of the bridge on the east side of the river. We made our way there. Time had erased almost all signs, but to Rex's delight one very big, rusty nail remained stuck firmly in the tree. Rex knew that was the nail on which his mother, Hattie, had hung her small dressing mirror. It was in the area of the tent used for her and Billy's bedroom many years before. Billy later went to work full-time at the Connelly sheep ranch, and the family moved there with him.

After looking over their old campsite and reliving a lot of good memories, Rex and I walked downriver from town and up the hill toward the sheep ranch, which was situated on hot and dusty Bakeoven Road. At the top of the hill we looked down into Buck Hollow, a deep canyon that opens into the Deschutes River close by. Looking for prey, a pair of red tailed hawks circled high over the depth of the canyon's hot desert like terrain. In the absolute stillness of this mostly uninhabited countryside their distinctive hunting cry, "Kiyeee! Kiyeee!" could be heard for miles. We walked until mid-afternoon. During this time not one vehicle came from either direction. We realized our destination was too far away to walk that late in the day and decided to return to Maupin.

Clouds gathered, thunder barked and lightning flashed across an angry black sky. Starting only as a scatter of large raindrops it soon became obvious that this was going to be a "gully washer", a violent storm typical of an eastern Oregon August. We saw no shelter and were desperate to get into any protected area. Nearby stood the local grain elevator, and we thought it had possibilities. Circling it, we found no unlocked door but did spot an opening about a foot square in the cement foundation. It took a lot of effort but we managed to squeeze through to the inside. We didn't know what to expect, but luck favored us. There was dim light entering through windows high in the walls. A generous blanket of clean, dry straw covered the floor. Just as we got inside a cloudburst of hail and huge raindrops came crashing down. The sky opened, thunder roared and lightening flared. We heard the water rushing outside. Tired from the long hike (undertaken without any food) we made a thick pile of straw, put our clothes-filled gunnysacks on it as pillows, snuggled together for warmth and drifted into fitful slumber.

The next morning we squeezed our way back out the hole and into the world. The weather was warm and dry. In a small cafe, we ordered an inexpensive breakfast of pancakes. Then we were off, to see if Rex's schoolmates, the Green's, still lived nearby.

They did. After everyone had a good time talking about the past, Rex asked, "Do freight trains still run south like they did when I lived here?"

Someone spoke up, "Yes, but instead of several a day, now only one runs out of here every week. Today is when it comes in. It stops to fill the tender with water, then leaves. It gets here around 2:30pm, about twenty minutes from now."

After a brief goodbye, we slung our gunnysacks over our shoulders and hurried to the rail line. The train was taking on water. Once more, we chose a tank car on which to ride.

From Maupin the railroad runs south on the west side of the spectacularly scenic Deschutes River canyon. This section of the line is one of the most beautiful in the United States. Expensive excursions set up especially for railroad buffs now run regularly on it. In 1940 Rex and I had the pleasure to watch this grand scene unfold as we rode the rails at the slow speed of a freight train. We had, at no cost, an unobstructed view. The rapids in the river near Maupin rush white and wild. In other places the water is still, very deep, dark green and mirror smooth. In sun, the sides of the canyon are ablaze with a pallet of color. From the rich dark-brown scab rock rim, color changed to lighter brown rock falls half way down then to the green glow of grasses and low shrubs along the riverbanks. As we rode along, bright sunshine worked its magic.

When the train ran out of the canyon awhile later, one of the best scenes appeared. For a short distance the rails run across flat land then suddenly onto a high trestle spanning a very deep and narrow gorge. As we approached it looked like a giant ax had split the earth. To cross it the train slowed. On the span we had the illusion of being suspended in mid air because both tracks and wheels, unseen below, were narrower than the body of the tank car.

In the bottom of the gorge a creek flowed. Its serpentine course, lined with trees, shrubs and lush wild green grass, contrasted beautifully with the brown, yellow and rust-red hues of the scorched high desert surround. This final magnificent scene was painted for us in an unforgettable manner upon the canvas of nature.

Hours later, now headed home, we entered Klamath Falls. The train stopped and was broken up. Parts were routed east to Alturas, California, others south to Redding. We thought it would be a new adventure to return home by way of Alturas, but my instinct told me that a bum we saw on the train headed in that direction might be a dangerous companion. Rex and I had a heated argument over this. I finally told him he could go back any way he wanted, but I was going back the same way we had come no matter what he did. He agreed to stay with me.

Leaving Klamath Falls that balmy summer night, we wanted to ride outside in the warm air. We chose a flat car hauling extra long, large diameter telephone poles. In 1940, not many loads of these long poles were hauled by rail: only the longest and heaviest were transported in this manner. We thought it would be a novelty to be able to say we rode on the specially made flat car that carried them. A 10-foot square area on the back end of the long rail car, under the ends of the poles, looked ideal. The poles were stacked six deep and eight across on "bunks", racks made of strong, thick timbers, reinforced with steel, that held them about four feet off the flatcar floor. We thought the poles would provide shelter for us while crossing the Siskiyou Mountains.

The train rolled slowly along through the darkness. Passing Mt. Shasta the air remained warm, the night crystal clear. In the black velvet dome of sky myriads of stars looked close enough to touch and so thick they seemed to compete with the Milky Way for space. Almost home, we were content. We lay down pillowing ours head on our gunnysacks of clothes. An expression Uncle Alfred used many times during calm moments, when things in his life were going well, came to my mind.

"God is in his heaven and all is right with the world."

Rex and I had experienced a grand and exciting adventure traveling more than a thousand miles without a major problem. Nowhere during our trip, either on the trains or in the rail yards had we seen one "railroad bull", a man hired to kick bums off the train. Perhaps they understood the hardship and suffering of the many jobless people, financially ravaged by the Depression, who were riding the rails from town to town in search of work. In sympathy, they might have kept out of sight or turned the other way.

The next morning we arrived in Redding, covered with soot and grime, tired and hungry but with heads filled with memories to last a lifetime. Hitchhiking back to Olinda we stopped first at Rex's house where my Mother was visiting her sister, Hattie. Mother saw us walking up the driveway and called out, "Hattie look, here come the boys!!" When I got close enough she gave me a brief hug while admonishing, "Where have you been? I've been worried stiff. I'll bet Rex put you up to whatever you did." As usual she blamed him for any trouble that involved us we both.

All I could think to say was, "The day we left I told Carrol Ulberg to come by and tell you not to worry. Didn't he do that?" I got no answer.

Hattie, a calmer person, giving Rex a hug and squeeze, asked, "Are you boys all right?"

"Yes Mom, we're just tired and kind of hungry and need to go out to the irrigation ditch for a bath. We'll tell you later about where we've been. We had a real good time."

The day after we arrived home we heard that two men riding a south bound freight train out of Redding early the previous afternoon had been crushed to death in Chico, a few miles south. They had been riding on a special flatcar in the shade under a load of long heavy telephone poles that shifted and fell from the bunks onto the flat car floor. Was this the same load of poles we had ridden under all night and early morning the previous day? Because of where and when it happened we felt absolutely sure it was.

Some people think they were born too soon, others that they were born too late. In my enthusiasm and nostalgia I believe I was born at exactly the right time to live during the final banner days of railroading with steam. During my lifetime steam engine technologies reached their peak in development and application. Credit must be given to the steam engineers who, with exceptional ability and skill did everything right...many times under the most difficult conditions. Steep grades, sharp curves, rain snow and ice challenged each man's abilities. They were an unusual breed, possessing an instinctive mechanical feel and an ear for the right sound from each of the massive engines' hundreds of working parts. How engineers, as a team in two leading Malley's, could synchronize the machines' awesome power to firmly tug a long, fully loaded freight train and get it rolling, demonstrated a talent few could duplicate today. Though the cab forward Malley's reached the peak of their excellence, the demise of the great 4-8-8-2's was inevitable with the introduction of the more cost effective and efficient diesel electric units.

Sadly, no one will ever again see the steam driven giants in live action, clouds of black smoke billowing from their stacks while they snarl in defiance at a steep winding grade, their massive power pulling as many as 116 loaded freight cars. Even movie footage is rare. I have hunted extensively but found none showing the configuration of two Malley's pulling and two helpers pushing, such as Rex and I rode north from Redding up the Sacramento River canyon in 1940.

Children standing near the rails today will never smell the steam, lubricants and smoke nor hear the earth shaking, chug, chug, chug, or the clanking of the slides and huge iron rods that turn each Malley's 16 driving wheels. They'll never hear the sharp sound of a full 250-pound head of steam ready to be throttled into the huge pistons to start the train moving. They'll not hear the mixed sounds as a small amount of steam escapes from the many fittings on valves and blowers, nor the whoosh, whoosh, of crossover pumps working hard. Finally, they'll never hear the hiss of air pressure building up as brakes are released, nor the deep clang of the big bronze bell loudly ringing just before the train moves away. Those Living sounds forever lost in time, available now only on recordings and video.

Most of all, they'll never hear the unique music of the six chime whistle used on the earlier model cab-forwards. One Malley alone, pulling a passenger train 75 miles an hour, would slowly begin to whistle. First, a low mellow moan built in intensity until, when fully open, the whistle shattered the air with a note that shouted, "Danger, get clear of the tracks. I am rapidly approaching."

In memory I still hear the echo of that whistle, undulating from a grade crossing in Anderson, six miles east of my home in Olinda. On a quiet moonless night, when all else was silent, it faded away in the distance.

It signaled the end of an era.

❖ SOME HIGH SCHOOL DAYS ❖

In 1941, Cody decided he'd like to try his hand at mining so we moved from Alfred's 11-acre farm in Olinda to the mountains one mile east of Whiskeytown at Poverty Flat. That year my cousin, Rex, and I both went out for high school track. He lived in Olinda and went to Anderson High School. I attended Shasta High School in Redding.

To compete in track required special shoes. To buy new ones wasn't possible because our folks were too poor. Fortunately one of my classmates, Francis Aloysius Jedidiahs Burmingham, bought a brand new pair and sold his perfectly good used shoes to me for $2.00. The shoes, with sharp metal spikes on the soles, have no heels. On my feet they felt strange. Walking in them, only on the ball of each foot, felt like always being on tip- toes.

Rex and I wore the same size. Non-conflicting competition schedules at our schools allowed us each to make use of them when needed. There was only one problem. We lived 25 miles apart that year and had to hitch hike 50 miles round trip if one of us needed to pick them up from the other to use at a track meet.

Chico High School, in 1941, competed with Shasta High in the 440-yard relay race. This race has four runners on a team, each runner carrying the baton during their 110-yard segment. The number three and number four runners are picked for their speed. The coach selected me as runner number three because I ran the one hundred yard dash in just a little over ten seconds, considered fast in those days.

On the field in Chico I noticed that the number three man of the opposing team could not be more than four feet, six inches tall. Looking down at him I smugly thought, "Don't they have anyone better? This dwarf-like kid has no chance against me. Look at his baby-like legs." Relaxed and complacent I thought, "I'll leave this short little guy far behind."

The starting gun barked. Soon our number two man rushed

toward me about two feet ahead of his opponent. Taking the pass of the baton and maintaining our small lead I wasn't worried. I thought, "I'll outdistance this midget sized guy so quickly." Laughing inwardly I quickly changed the baton from my left hand to my right while gaining speed.

Running close behind me the short number three man of the Chico team also took the pass of the baton perfectly. Now came the surprise.

Running about one foot ahead of him I began to lengthen my stride and increase the action of my legs in an effort to cover ground faster. Unbelievably this diminutive runner matched my speed. His leg movements were amazing. As I glanced momentarily they appeared to be working like a pair of mechanically driven trip hammers. Although he took at least two steps to one of mine he continued to remain only a foot behind. Any gain I made he matched and we ran our entire 110 yards keeping the same one-foot interval between us as when we started.

The fastest man on our team ran last. I never felt happier to see a teammate. Trying so hard to outdistance the midget-like runner I became totally exhausted making no progress against the very short kid with the trip hammer legs. The expression, "You can't tell a book by its cover" certainly held true here.

The Shasta High School team won by a few inches only because our number four man ran like a streak. As a result I received my letter in track that year as a member of the winning team.

During the same season Rex, wearing our shared track shoes, had the opportunity to possibly set a record in the northern division of the State in the 440-yard dash. His folks too, were very poor and couldn't afford an essential piece of equipment for him, an athletic supporter. His competition in this meet, held in the State Capitol at Sacramento, were the fastest runners picked from all high schools in northern California.

Running exceptionally well and far in the lead, he suddenly felt an important part of his male anatomy fly out from under his shorts. In full view of thousands of people in the Stadium, the errant organ continued to flap loosely in the air. Rex knew he must quickly make a decision. Should he break his stride, reach down to retrieve and replace the bare organ and risk losing time or continue on and possibly set a record?

He chose to continue running and set the Northern California high school record for the individual 440-yard dash. As far as I've been able to find, the record has never been broken.

Crossing the finish line he received a standing ovation and a very loud cheer. I've asked him at times just what he thought the ovation and loud cheer might have been for.

During high school Rex dated the most beautiful blue-eyed blonde in Olinda, Mildred "Millie" Eberhardt. I dated an equally beautiful blue-eyed brunette, Marian Ulberg (the grocer's daughter). Most of the time we double dated.

On a typical evening we'd pick up the girls and in Rex's 1928 Chevrolet pickup, drive a mile to a rather deep canyon called Telephone Gulch. Here we'd usually build a fire near the creek and sometimes roast marshmallows. We'd take with us several dark green Army blankets, which we'd gotten from Alfred. He had joined the Civilian Conservation Corps and was stationed a few miles north of Redding at Camp Sims, where he helped build hiking trails. On his weekends he brought home a lot of discarded Army issue, olive green, thick wool blankets. Having little damage except perhaps a small tear or a burn from a cigarette, they were excellent to put on the ground three or four deep for protection and comfort.

When darkness came, having roasted and eaten all the marshmallows, we'd snuggle with the girls under the thick blankets beside the crackling fire cuddling, necking and often kissing as normal high school seniors do. Though all four of us were highly hormonally challenged, young and eager, Rex and I never stepped over the line of decency. Sometimes we'd all fall asleep between the blankets and didn't get the girls home until after four o'clock in the morning. When this happened we were afraid the parents wouldn't let us date their daughters again after bringing them home so late. But their folks never denied us. I suspect this was because they were told how we remained gentlemen at all times.

During our high school years Rex and I were inventive. We thought up ways to make our own good times. One day we thought up a devious scheme.

Olinda's dirt roads were slippery, deep muddy ruts in winter and beds of choking red dust in summer. In places they were narrow and unsafe. Every spring after the rainy season ended, two road graders came from Anderson, six miles away. They graded out the winter ruts and for a month everyone enjoyed wonderfully smooth dirt roads. A mile from our homes the narrow road ran for several hundred yards along the north edge of Telephone Gulch, a rather deep canyon. Guardrails had not been placed there to protect cars from accidentally dropping off straight down. Going over the edge in some places on this stretch of road could be fatal. Everyone living in the area knew of the danger here and drove carefully. Rex and I discovered, at the west end of this dangerous area of roadway, a small intersecting ravine where a vehicle could be turned off the road then, in a sort of controlled fall, be driven safely over the side to the bottom of the canyon. A few short manzanita and chapparal bushes, along with some tall Johnson grass, obscured the area. To most people driving by it was not apparent that a car could actually drop off the road at this point and be driven without harm down the steep, chute like, side ravine. Several times Rex and I climbed up and down the drop off to check it for safety. The controlled fall would be about 50 feet and because it leveled off gradually at the bottom, we knew there would be no danger.

Preparing for the joke we removed every large rock and stick that might pose a hazard on the way down. For the place to stay hidden we left standing, at the top, some of the tall Johnson grass and low brush. We choreographed ahead of time exactly what Rex and I would do and say. Late one day we enticed the girls to come with us pretending we were going to take them for a leisurely ride in the cool of evening. The old pickup was open-topped from the windshield back and had only one bench type seat. It held Rex, who was driving and the two girls. In the pickup bed I knelt behind the drivers seat on the padding of the thick wool blankets to protect my knees while holding on to the steel roll bar welded all the way across, above and behind it.

As we drove slowly along the canyon rim close to the very sheer drop off area we acted according to plan. I said, as though in casual conversation, "You know, this part of the road is really dangerous."

Then, a moment later when we'd reached the spot that we had prepared, Rex swung the steering wheel to the left and the pickup jumped the small dirt mound beside the road. The wheels ran over the small brush and tall Johnson grass and we rapidly dropped down the nearly vertical slope. Rex yelled, "Something's gone wrong with the steering." Then he hit the brake pedal, letting his foot slip off and loudly pound the bare wood of the floorboards. He hollered, "The brakes have failed, the brakes have failed" as he pretended to continue fighting a useless steering wheel.

That was my cue to grasp Marian's shoulder with one hand while holding on to the steel roll bar with the other. I shouted "We'll all be killed. Hang on for dear life!!" My words, "hang on", were emphasized so the girls wouldn't be tempted to jump. We smart alecks had thought of everything.

For a few moments we dropped almost in free fall. It was like plunging from the highest point on a roller coaster. The girls screamed, scared out of their wits. To be safe Rex kept yelling, "Hang on, hang on—I think we can make it."

The controlled fall lasted no more than six seconds with a top speed of about 30 miles an hour, and then we were safely at the bottom. But all did not go well. We thought we had pulled a wonderful joke until the girls began to ask questions.

Marian asked, "What went wrong?"

Knowing he always kept the pickup in top mechanical condition Millie questioned accusingly, "How come you ran off the road Rex? What's the matter with the steering?" Getting wide grins from us but no answers both girls got out and said, "We're leaving. We're going to walk home." Rex turned off the engine. He and I couldn't keep from laughing. The girls realized they had been set up and were furious. As they glared at us Millie said sarcastically, "A typical Rex and Gene trick."

Being true gentlemen we apologized and asked them not to be mad at us. "We only did it to make a little fun," I said.

"Blame it on Gene" Rex said to Millie, "He talked me into it."

They finally saw the humor but only half-heartedly forgave us.

We had promised them a leisurely evening drive, but because of two scheming and inventive young boys, things turned out just a little different.

❖ LIFE AT POVERTY FLAT ❖

PART I

From September of 1938 to June of 1939 as a freshman and from September of 1940 to June of 1941, as a junior I attended Anderson High School in Anderson, California and lived six miles to the west in Olinda and rode the school bus daily. From September of 1939 to June of 1940, as a sophomore and again from September of 1941 to June of 1942, as a senior I attended Shasta High school in Redding, California again having to ride a school bus twenty miles each day to and from Poverty Flat where we lived on a gold mining claim. During the two alternating years on the mining claim, in the mountains of the Coast range to the west, I lived with my mother Frances, step dad, Cody and half sister, Myrtle Louise. After Cody came into our lives in 1934 he and Mother soon found common ground and were married. Myrtle Louise arrived in July of 1936 born in Redding.

Unfortunately the placer mining claim produced little more than a tiny bit of gold daily and we constantly existed on the edge of starvation. Twelve people lived in our tiny community, Poverty Flat. Whiskeytown, located one mile west had one combined general store and gasoline station, a few homes and an historic old hotel dating back to the 1850's when people and gold were plentiful here. Despite the fact that no public electric lines existed in our mountainous area, the old hotel had electric lights. They operated from a "direct current" 12-volt generator powered by a gasoline engine. At dusk the engine growled to life and every night at exactly ten o'clock the owner turned it off. In our "tar paper shack" we had only one "Baby Ben" clock, a wind up type. Sometimes it wouldn't get wound and stopped. Living a mile from the hotel we could easily hear the generator's engine echo in the surrounding canyons. When it stopped we knew ten o'clock had arrived and Cody would re-set the clock.

During the years we lived here the major economic depression, which began in 1929 continued. It forced many men to try to make a living looking for gold in the streams of the area. This one man endeavor to gather gold is called "sniping" and those who did it were known as "snipers".

At Poverty Flat Cody staked a claim on a small tributary of Clear creek. To provide a place for us to live he built a "tar paper shack." A simple and inexpensive structure made from rough lumber, it took its name from the walls being covered on the outside with a layer of cheap, heavy, black colored, tar impregnated, waterproof building paper. The tarpaper provided no insulation. Far less costly than wooden siding it was secured to the outer walls of the shack by nailing thin wooden lath over it in vertical rows about a foot apart in a mostly unsuccessful attempt to keep out the freezing drafts of winter.

Beginning late in May or early in June, summer temperature often rose to 118 degrees or more. The black tarpaper on the outside of the shack absorbed and held the heat of the sun causing the living space inside to become almost unbearably hot. Having one narrow door and only two tiny windows, which did not open, a breeze seldom came in. A wood-burning stove used for every day cooking also heated our bath water and "sad irons" that Mother would use to press some of my school clothes. This added to the terrible heat inside. I didn't realize the discomfort I must have caused when I'd say, "Ma, I need a shirt ironed for school tomorrow. We're having an orchestra recital during assembly and I'll be on stage playing the bass violin so I want to look good." She'd never complain but I realize she must have been reluctant to put an extra chunk of firewood in the already hot stove to keep the temperature of the sad irons up when the air outside hovered around 118 degrees and perspiration poured off of her forehead.

In winter the temperature dropped to 15 degrees or less with snow and ice everywhere. During cold snaps the small wood burning stove never kept the inside of the shack comfortably warm so we had to wear stocking caps, sweaters or coats indoors most of the time. Surrounding the shack Cody built a sturdy fence about four feet tall. From the long limbs of trees he made the rails and cut down their trunks to use as the upright posts. It discouraged deer or bear from coming to look for food and break down the door.

The one room shack measured sixteen feet square and held all our needs for living. In one corner stood a double bed for Mother and Cody. Beside it was a small bed for Myrtle Louise, then about 4 years old. Attached to one side of the shack, from scrap lumber, Cody built a six by ten foot unheated lean-to for me to use as a bedroom.   In the corner close to the door inside the main shack sat a small wood-burning stove. Next to it on a waist high bench rested a heavily chipped, granite coated dishpan and a two and a half gallon galvanized, but partly rusted, water pail. In it I carried the water we needed from a spring about 50 feet away. It ran cold in summer yet never froze in winter. After being washed and dried the cooking utensils were placed on two wooden open shelves above the bench. The soapy dishwater, never wasted, Mother had me pour on the two, three-foot square Zinnia patches she planted inside the fence on both sides of the gate. In another corner of the shack sat a table and four chairs. Cody made the chairs from scrap lumber and the branches of small trees. Though primitive, they were very sturdy. The "hand me down" table gave me a place to do my homework assignments for school. On it, after dark, a kerosene-burning lamp provided the only source of light. Kerosene cost 10 cents a gallon but we were so poor it had to be used sparingly.

A foot pumped organ that Mother played well, was our only luxury and took up much of the space against one wall. Our few extra clothes hung on long nails pounded in a short distance on any empty space of every wall. We had no clothes hangers. As a result all my shirts had a bulge just below the neckline, in the back, caused by the head of the big nail that held them when not being worn. We had no pictures and no mirror to hang anywhere.

On the home made bed Cody built for me in the lean-to he put a thin store bought "mattress tick" he filled with straw. There is almost no insulating factor in straw and the winter cold rose easily up through it from below. I wrapped myself tightly in two thin wool flannel blankets every night but in cold weather still shivered constantly. My teeth chattered keeping me awake. I waited eagerly for morning to leave my bedroom and go inside the main shack and be near the stove to get warm. In the cold of winter it was kept burning day and night.

Having no heat in my bedroom, the stress of chilling and Streptococcus germs, many times caused me to have a viciously sore throat. It became so painful I dreaded swallowing. For long periods of time I'd drool in a washcloth or towel. However, Cody had an unusual but quite effective remedy. He'd tear a four-inch square of cloth from a clean but worn out denim work shirt. Using Crisco shortening he made a walnut size ball and rolled it in sugar. With a nail he'd punch a hole half way through it. In the hole he put 10 drops of kerosene then squeezed the top of the Crisco ball shut sealing the kerosene inside. Placing the sweetened ball in the center of the cloth he gathered the four corners and twisted until the ball lay tightly trapped. He secured this with a piece of string and called it a "sugar tit". Holding it in my mouth it melted and relieved much of the pain. The contents, seeping through the cloth, slowly coated the inside of my mouth and throat and the sugar tit became a primitive version of the modern cough drop. From the laundry box he took one of his thick wool "boot socks" and with a large safety pin, secured it around my neck.

He'd say, "Sonny boy, it has to be an unwashed wool sock. A clean one won't work."

Amazingly, in a day or two the sore throat disappeared. However, I wonder if it got better because of his treatment or in spite of it. Many young people my age that came down with such a violently sore throat contracted streptococcal tonsillitis. Sometimes this caused the dreaded, debilitating and sometimes fatal, heart disease, Rheumatic fever. Many who lived were incapacitated for life. Fortunately, perhaps because of Cody's remedy, the dirty wool sock and primitive "sugar tit", I suffered no ill effects.

In summer, when water in the stream became too low for any kind of mining, sometimes Cody traveled to Pondosa, California, about 100 miles east of Poverty Flat, to work for the McCloud Lumber Co. Working as a "timber beast" he could do every job required in the woods. For example, he felled, de-limbed then bucked, that is, cut to specified lengths by hand with a muscle powered "misery whip", a cross cut saw six feet or more long, the huge "old growth" fir and pine trees then in abundant supply. This hazardous job claimed the life of many loggers who were struck by a "widow-maker". A widow maker is a large heavy limb that breaks off of a falling tree and temporarily hangs high up in another next to it. Later in a windstorm, the unattached branch falls unexpectedly, killing the logger working below. Other accidents in the woods were often fatal. If a tree would suddenly split lengthwise while being "topped", part of it could catch on the safety rope or harness and squash the man topping it, in half. Cody was lucky, never having an accident.

While he was away Mother, Myrtle and I remained at Poverty Flat. He'd return every few weeks to see us and pay our grocery bill at Michado's store in Whiskeytown. The logging job provided "a grubstake", money for the following fall when rain brought enough water back to the creek, so Cody could resume his obsessive search for gold.

To keep possession of the claim at least $100.00 worth of work had to be done every year and inspectors could drop in any time unannounced. But the way Cody tore away the stream banks the authorities had little doubt that the work he did was worth a lot more.

With the fall rain Cody returned to the claim and resumed the miserable, backbreaking, wet and often bone chilling work. He had a serious case of "gold fever", always believing he'd soon find what he called, "The Big Deposit". As soon as rain caused the water in the stream to run about a foot deep he began to work in the wet fall season "crevicing." This kind of gold gathering requires only a gold pan and a few specially shaped tools. Cody made them by hand from two-foot lengths of thick, used copper wire, shaping them with a ball peen hammer on a foot long scrap of railroad track he found and used as an anvil. When finished some looked like a spoon, others like a wide, flat letter "L".

Crisscrossing the bare gray granite bedrock on the bottom of the stream were hundreds of cracks of various sizes and depths. In the ones slanting upstream, backward to the flow of water, gold nuggets that were forced to move along downstream by the raging flow in winter, dropped down into the fissures becoming trapped. Working inside an upstream slanting crevice, with the right shaped tool, Cody patiently dug out the deposit of gold bearing "muck" and placed it in the pan. In a quiet back eddy pool of the stream he'd then "pan it out." Today, the often-heard question, "How did things pan out for you?" originated from this miners expression. More than a century old, it relates to a snipers work.

How thrilled Cody and I were to see, glistening in the sunlight, the bright flash of yellow gold as it followed behind the somewhat less heavy black sand when he swirled the water around and around in the pan. "Oh, he's just a flash in the pan", today a pejorative expression, is still alive also having survived from the early days of mining. But the expression originated in a much earlier time. It derived from the misfiring of the old flintlock guns. The powder in the primer pan ignited but the flash failed to travel through the touchhole and set off the charge in the barrel, becoming "just a flash in the pan".

Because of the severe economic depression even the smallest amount of gold in Cody's pan represented a necessity to sustain our lives. However, in spite of many hours of backbreaking work, the mining claim yielded only a meager amount. But Cody refused to give up his dream of striking it rich.

In the fall before the water rose, Cody devised a unique method to remove huge amounts of "overburden." A non-gold bearing layer, this is tons of useless dirt and gravel at times 10 feet or more thick, that lies above the one or two inch layer of gold bearing material which rests right on top of the gray granite bed rock. Not able to afford a bulldozer, he relied on his knowledge of the massive power of water to move the unwanted earth. His "shooter" took the place of a bulldozer and made the stream do all the work.

Cody had only a few basic tools with which to make the shooter, a pick, shovel, bucksaw, hammer, long spikes, an ax and wheelbarrow. First he made a dam of logs, big boulders and fill dirt. About 10 feet high he built it across a narrow part of the creek. He left an open place in the center and from thick planks of rough lumber, he fashioned a frame within the opening. He built an almost waterproof gate that would tilt outward only from the bottom because he suspended it inside the frame using a thick wooden suspension shaft on each side that he placed a little above the centerline. Attached to the top of the gate he built a heavy locking pin and a quick release device, all made from wood. To the pin release, he secured one end of a ten-foot pine pole and to the other end attached an empty, 55-gallon steel drum. The waterproof drum, having both lid and bung sealed tightly in place, acted as a very large float, just like the small one in a modern toilet. With the gate closed and locked and the pin set, water built up behind the dam and the steel drum floated. When the water level reached a point just below the top of the dam, the locking pin at the end of the long pine pole, pulled itself out tripping and opening the shooter gate. A massive surge of water rushed from beneath the gate holding it fully open as the raging torrent, under great pressure, gushed from behind the dam. It scoured clean much of the bedrock downstream carrying away tons of useless overburden. When all the water behind the dam drained out the gate slammed shut, again locking itself. As long as water ran in the creek the cycle continued indefinitely. With the help of a good rainstorm, in a few days all overburden for many yards downstream from the shooter swirled away in the wild rush of the muddy current.

With the light gray granite creek bottom exposed in many places, as the water receded, for a day or two between rainstorms, we "cleaned bedrock". We could pick up the bigger gold nuggets from beneath the now clear water with our fingers. But smaller nuggets and flakes can't be seen even under tiny ripples in slow moving water though it's crystal clear. Because of this Cody made special devices so we'd be able to easily see the bedrock beneath the water.

From the metal body of old discarded three-cell flashlights he removed the dead batteries, bulb, reflector and back end cap. He screwed the flat glass lens back on and sealed all the edges and the on-off switch with "Permatex number 2", thus making a foot long waterproof hollow tube. With the metal flashlight body partially submerged, lens first under the water, the bedrock beneath could easily be seen with no distortion. We picked up the little nuggets and flakes with tweezers and placed them in small white opaque glass containers we found in the Whiskeytown dump, that Cold cream or Mum deodorant came in. We used them for safety reasons because of their "screw on" type lid that never came off unexpectedly which would have allowed the very small amount of gold found daily to be lost.

After cleaning the bedrock Cody would put a sluice box in the creek close to the bank. Using big stones he diverted some of the stream water through it and we'd shovel in the one or two inch layer of gold bearing mud and gravel, called "muck". As the water carried the muck along in the sluice box a series of wooden riffles and some special shaped metal screen, laid over carpet or burlap on the far end, trapped the black sand and the much heavier gold. At the end of the day, with great anticipation, the riffles and screen were taken out of the box and the contents they caught Cody placed in the gold pan. This is called, "the clean up". The expression, "He really cleaned up today on that deal" also originated in the early days of gold mining. It implied a large amount of money had been made in a deal by someone who really had been lucky, just like a sniper who in only one day might have found a lot of gold.

For transportation Cody had an old 1929 Chevrolet. Due to badly worn piston rings, it burned a quart of oil about every 150 miles and from the exhaust pipe poured clouds of blue smoke. With unusual mechanical skill, he kept it running far past its life expectancy. I looked forward to Saturday when he'd take Mother, my half sister, Myrtle and me to Redding to sell the small amount of gold gathered that week. At Dubrowski's jewelry store it brought $35.00 an ounce. Mounted over the street in front of his corner store Mr. Dubrowski had a huge four-sided combination clock and thermometer. Two sides told time, two showed the temperature.

Redding lies in the far northern end of the Sacramento River valley surrounded on three sides by major mountain ranges. To the west the Coast range, to the north the Siskiyou mountains and to the east the Sierra Nevada. As a result, when having no prevailing breeze in summer, the air stagnates and the heat builds oppressively. In Redding, early in June the temperature often rose to 118 degrees. In August at times it climbed to an almost unbearable 121. If a little money remained after buying groceries and other necessities, Cody would ask, "Sonny Boy, how about all of us going across the street to that "sodie fountain" for an ice cold Green River drink?" a brand name popular at that time. Before I could answer Mother, always thrilled in anticipation of a few relaxing moments, would quickly exclaim, "Oh yes, let's do!!"

What a treat the five-cent iced drink provided and for awhile we felt cool and very happy.

But it's easy for a boy 17 years old to have happy moments — unable to anticipate what lies ahead.

❖ LIFE AT POVERTY FLAT ❖
PART II

Seven tarpaper shacks and two heavy-duty all weather tents made up the tiny community of Poverty Flat. My step dad, Cody, my Mother and half sister, Myrtle Louise and I were the only family unit. All the rest were bachelors. I remember some of them.

Roy Sappingfield: In early summer, when the water in the tributary on his mining claim near Clear Creek dried up, Roy left. He went to work picking fruit, strawberries, peaches, apricots and pears in the Sacramento River valley, usually near Red Bluff or Chico. He saved most of his money and used it to grubstake himself the following fall and winter. When rain fell and water returned to the tributary, Roy came back to work his claim. A true "salt of the earth", honest and hard working, he kept life simple. About five feet, nine inches tall, thin, brown haired and with blue eyes that always appeared to be smiling, he looked to be about 45 years old. Cheerful and having a wonderful sense of humor, he laughed a lot. He told me he enjoyed my frequent visits and I enjoyed listening to his vast array of stories.

Roy lived in the smallest tarpaper shack on Poverty Flat, only 10 feet square. In it, built in against a wall was his single bunk bed. A very small wood-burning stove stood in one corner. Beside it a tiny table held a kerosene lamp. He had only one chair. When I visited one of us sat on the bunk and the other on the chair. He said he built the place small so the little stove would have less space to heat, could heat it fast and he'd have to cut less wood. In this way he represented one of our earliest conservationists. With inexpensive caulking he sealed out drafts and managed to weatherproof his shack quite well. Because his shack was always much warmer than ours, in the coldest days of winter I made many excuses to visit him.

While working in the orchards he saved a good-sized

grubstake and with only himself to support, had the luxury of setting his own schedule. As a result he kept "regular hours", as he described them, from nine thirty in the morning until three in the afternoon with every Saturday and Sunday off.

One Saturday he told a story about his younger days when he "rode the rails." In the story he used a phrase that struck me funny and made me laugh so hard I could barely breathe. I also wet my pants. Roy made light of the accident putting me at ease and he too laughed heartily seeing me devastated with glee.

His story began, "As I stood in this boxcar the train started to move. I spotted a fat 'yard bird' coming my way. Well, I just knew that this BIG ASSED BIRD would ----."

The story got no further. A yard bird is a policeman or security agent for the railroads. Having never heard a fat human called a big assed bird before, the description triggered my strange sense of humor. I visualized a fat man covered with Ostrich-like feathers that flapped in the wind as he ran beside the train in an unsuccessful attempt to kick Roy off. When we regained our composure he finished the story. I don't recall how it ended except that he stayed on the train and rode it from Redding to Chico. He enjoyed telling stories and told many more. But this is the only one I partly remember.

Old Russian Louie: Nobody could agree whether Louie was German or Russian and he never told anyone. Short and very muscular, he appeared to be about 70 years old. He had blue eyes, snow white hair and spoke with a guttural accent. Though he lived a half mile away I liked to visit him after dark because he had a two-mantle Coleman lantern that used a special white gasoline as fuel. The mantles glowed brilliantly with an almost white light that I enjoyed much more than the dim yellowish flickering light from our one small kerosene lamp. To have his lantern continue to burn brightly a piston in the base had to be pumped about every half hour to keep the correct amount of air pressure in the fuel tank. Louie practiced safety first with his brilliantly glowing lantern. He hung it with a three-foot length of small chain attached to the ridgepole of his weatherproof tent. He said to hang it with rope would be dangerous because the intense heat rising from its top could cause a rope to catch fire.

A lot of the time Louie was covered with soot. The reason became clear when I first visited him. Into one side of his weatherproof tent jutted a big fallen log. Many years before Louie came to Poverty Flat, a forest fire had burned out the inside of the log and he now used its six foot charcoal covered interior as a dry closet-like place to store clothes and supplies. Of course soot covered everything and he almost always looked like he needed a bath.

Our Old Harry: We called him "ours" because another Harry lived across Clear Creek about two miles downstream. Our Harry lived close to us around a bend of the unimproved dirt road winding through the area. Like Louie, he too lived in a heavy weatherproof tent. He appeared to be about 80 years old. With blue eyes and gray hair, his leather like skin, tan in both summer and winter, had many deep wrinkles. About six feet five inches tall, I believe he was of Norwegian descent.

During the winter of 1940 Cody dropped by to visit him. Seeing no smoke rising from Harry's chimney he stepped inside the cold tent and found no fire in the stove. Harry had died. Pneumonia struck so fast no one knew of his illness. Three days previously when Cody and I stopped to see him he talked, joked, laughed and appeared to be fine except for a slight nagging cough.

E. L. "Mac" McDonald: Everyone for miles around knew Mac. In his 1924 Dodge touring car he'd travel the rough roads near and far visiting friends. A kind and generous man, when I failed to catch the school bus, so I wouldn't miss class, he'd let me use the old Dodge to drive to Redding over the narrow, treacherous, steep mountain highway. With hairpin curves, sharp "S" turns and with no guardrail, the road ran on the edge of the sheer drop-offs of the high cliffs. At age fifteen I didn't have a license to drive. But in 1940 most kids who lived in isolated places like Poverty Flat and Whiskeytown knew how and we drove safely. At that time there were few California Highway Patrol people on the road checking driver's licenses. Most of us learned to drive out of necessity. I learned in Olinda at age nine so I could help on Uncle Alfred's farm. At this time my legs were so short my feet barely could reach the clutch, brake or gas feed of the big old 1926 Buick sedan Cody bought for $10.00. Sometimes my foot slipped off of the brake pedal at a crucial moment during the learning process and I managed to tear out many feet of fence belonging to Uncle Ed Everson, Uncle Frank Moravec and Ev Sayler who, unfortunately, were our neighbors.

Mac's younger brother, Donald, lived near Oakland. Working for the Navy as an electrical engineer he helped developed the top-secret guidance system in WWII for submarines. He visited Mac at Poverty Flat once or twice every year and as youngsters, Donald's interest in science rubbed of on his brother. As a result, Mac had an awesome collection of rocks that could be made to glow brightly under a black light device that Donald made for him. Under it they glistened with a spectacular variety of unusual colors. At Poverty Flat we had no electricity but Mac's brother rigged the black light to work using a converter and the12 volt battery temporarily removed from the old Dodge. How fascinating to see the surface of an ordinary looking rock, when placed under the black light in the dark of night, come alive with brilliant, multi colored flame. I'd spend hours with the collection often running the battery down so far that the next day when put back in the Dodge it wouldn't turn the starter. But Mac always parked the old car on a small rise and being a "stick shift", by turning on the key, putting it in second gear and rolling it down the incline then at the bottom engaging the clutch, it started easily and the battery again became fully charged.

I remember some of the people from Whiskeytown.

The Michado Family: They owned the combined small general store and filling station a mile west of Poverty Flat. The two old-fashioned gasoline pumps, with their ten gallon glass viewing tanks on top, had to be pumped full by hand before each sale. The hoses, made from synthetic butyl rubber, gave off a skunk-like odor that clung stubbornly to hands and clothes and was almost impossible to wash off. Only two grades of gasoline were sold, Regular and Ethyl. Mac's old Dodge ran equally well on either. The only difference I noticed is that regular had a light pink color and cost 14 cents a gallon and ethyl had a deep red color and cost 19 cents.

Behind Michados store on the high bluff overlooking Clear Creek was a hand operated, "pull yourself over" creek crossing device. Used by snipers to get across the gorge from one side of the stream to the other it was a necessity because no bridge existed in this area. Constructed as a strong and heavy wooden box it measured about 6-feet long, 3-feet wide and 18-inches deep. It had room for one person, some groceries, tools and perhaps a gallon of kerosene. Suspended by two pulleys riding on a steel cable running all the way across Clear Creek, the overhead carrier cable was encircled and locked with cable clamps to a steel post driven all the way down to bedrock on each side of the creek. The occupant in the box could slowly pull himself across hand over hand. Even in good weather the crossing was somewhat dangerous. But in the winter rainy season a deep, muddy, frothing torrent often raged violently beneath. No one ever crossed during this time because the wild churning water often rose to within a foot of the bottom of the box and to fall out meant certain death.

The Other Harry: His last name was Burgess. He appeared to be about 65 years old, had deeply tanned skin, black hair and brown eyes. Of mostly Cherokee Indian descent, Harry and my step dad Cody shared this common heritage and were close friends. Harry lived on the other side of Clear Creek about two miles downstream from Whiskeytown using the cable and box to cross over at Michado's store. A veteran of WWI, in France during the conflict, he had been gassed. As a result, part of his mouth had been eaten away and his lungs too were in poor condition. He received a small but steady pension and lived a little better than other gold seeking "snipers" who had no extra income.

In good weather Cody and I rode the cable box together across Clear Creek to visit Harry once or twice a month. High above the gorge wall, on the other side of the creek on the trail to his cabin, a lot of broken bits of sharp, jagged rock lay scattered. This loose granite scree on the trail made my footing unsure and it wasn't enjoyable for me to go on these visits. There was nothing to hold on to and beside the foot wide trail the cliff face dropped straight down hundreds of feet to the huge half submerged boulders in the water below.

Most of the people I knew at Poverty Flat and Whiskeytown died from malnutrition or pneumonia. The cold and dampness in winter could not be overcome with a few blankets and a small wood burning stove. In spite of his physical problems Harry lived to be over 90 in less than ideal conditions in the small shack clinging precariously to the gorge wall high above the waters of Clear Creek.

For a high school boy Poverty Flat provided no entertainment. My chores, cutting wood for the stove and carrying water from the spring, took little time. I enjoyed school but the assigned homework, done by the light of a kerosene lamp, was so easy it presented little or no challenge. As a result visiting with the adult neighbors took up a lot of my time after dark. We couldn't afford a flashlight and batteries and the primitive trails between the shacks located deep in the canyon, on cloudy, moonless nights, could not be seen. A heavy downpour of wind driven rain often made it impossible even to see a hand placed only inches from ones face. To overcome the darkness Cody provided a solution. He made us a simple, effective and practical lighting device. He called it a "doodle bug".

Using a size two, cleanly washed out tomato can, he removed the paper wrapper. Laying it on one side he punched two small holes, about three inches apart, in what now would became the top. Threading some bailing wire through the holes it formed a handle. Wrapping the wire thickly with old-fashioned, black cloth-type friction tape insulated it so the heat from the candle that would later burn inside, would not be transmitted through the wire to our hands. Lighting a fat, two-inch tall candle he dripped a puddle of wax about an inch in diameter onto the side opposite the handle, that now was the bottom of the inner surface of the can, then stood it in this liquid pool and waited a few minutes for the wax to harden. The short candle now stood rigidly upright inside the can ready for use. Because the can had a bright silvery finish on the inside it reflected light quite well. On the darkest night I could use the doodlebug as a flashlight when going to get water, bring in wood for the stove or visit a neighbor. High wind or rain never could put the candle out though the flame jumped and danced as it defied the elements.

In 1940 Cody's Mother came to visit and stayed almost a year. A full blood Cherokee Indian, she had strikingly beautiful features. Her walk and carriage, to me, seemed Queen-like. She spoke softly like the whisper of a gentle breeze. A tiny woman, about five feet tall, she weighed less than 100 pounds. Her waist length black hair showed only a few streaks of gray. Every day she washed and braided it then wrapped it on top of her head like a crown.

Hanging by a rawhide cord around her neck an Asafetida bag rested on her chest. Ornate copper bracelets adorned her ankles, wrists and upper arms. I asked her what purpose the bracelets and anklets served and what the bag contained. She wouldn't tell me what the bag had in it but she did say, "The bracelets and anklets keep my joints from becoming stiff and the things in the bag keep me free from colds and my body well." It worked for her because during her stay, even during winter, she remained spry and active. On the day Cody drove us to Redding in the worn out, smoke belching 1929 Chevrolet to take her to the Greyhound bus depot for the return trip to Oklahoma, she celebrated her 100th birthday.

Cody would often say, "I'm a jack of all trades, and master of none." In truth he did many things well. Proficient as a carpenter, automobile and truck mechanic, placer and hard rock miner, blacksmith, logger and heavy earth moving machinery operator he joined the Navy in 1942. As a Petty Officer First Class with a Sea Bee construction battalion he served in the

South Pacific during WWII operating all types of heavy equipment building and maintaining airfields and harbors.

Over the years he developed silicosis, "hard rock miners disease", from breathing rock dust without wearing a respirator while operating jack hammers and drills in deep underground mines. I can't recall the date but in the late 1930's one of the many hard rock projects where he worked was the Lost Cabin Mine in the Sierra Nevada mountain range near the Aiden summit in California. In addition, he told me that because most employers didn't provide it, he seldom wore breathing protection while operating heavy earth moving machines that threw up clouds of choking dust.

Starting in his early teens and into adulthood, he smoked heavily usually making "roll your own" cigarettes from Bull Durham tobacco that came in a white cloth pouch tied at the top with a yellow drawstring. Once in awhile he'd "splurge" and buy a can of Prince Albert or Half and Half. He always used brown colored "LAX wheat straw" papers with which to roll, what he called "a quirley". I asked him why he didn't use white papers. He said, "Sonny boy, the brown ones are less harmful than the white." Cody is the only person I've ever known who could make a perfect "roll your own" cigarette using only one hand, a fragile cigarette paper and bulk tobacco from a pouch or can. Smoking all his life resulted in a severe case of emphysema. Cody and my Mother split up at the end of WWII. He later re-married and had another family, most of whom I've had the pleasure of meeting.

Cody died alone in a hotel room in San Francisco in 1956 from a combination of emphysema and silicosis. In addition, two bouts of pneumonia contracted while working in the miserably cold conditions trying to find gold in a stream running through Poverty Flat further weakened his lungs. The deadly combination of tobacco smoke, needle sharp quartz rock crystals and pneumonia had ravaged his lungs.

One day in the 1960's, while inspecting the newly cleared area that later would become the bottom of Whiskeytown Lake, three

U.S. Government geologists were driving slowly along on the site that had once been Poverty Flat. One of them noticed an outcropping of white quartz a short distance up a hillside near a flat area by a spring that looked like a place where a structure once may have stood. Curious, they stopped and walked up the hill to examine the white rock formation. With the small hammer, that geologists usually carry, one of them broke off a piece. To his surprise, on the two freshly broken surfaces, glistening brightly in the sun, were web-like threads of pure gold. Geologically, this unique formation exists only where a "pocket" of the precious metal lies within a few feet, enveloped within the quartz, and a pocket almost always contains thousands of dollars worth of treasure.

Many years before, the flat place on the low rise below the outcropping on the hill, actually had been the site of our tarpaper shack. Every day all of us saw the quartz formation jutting from the ground on the hillside about seventy-five feet away from our door. Yet with all his experience and knowledge, Cody never thought of it as a possible site for a pocket of gold.

He died not knowing that during all the years he worked from dawn to dusk, enduring terrible hardship while hoping to "strike it rich", he lived within seventy-five feet of his cherished dream, "The Big Deposit".

In 1963 a line of nine helicopters flew west from Redding airport following Highway 299. Hundreds of people gathered at the newly completed Clear Creek Dam, a Federal water project. At the dam a tall, dark haired man cut a ribbon formally dedicating the structure. The man: President John F. Kennedy. That same day he dedicated, on a hilltop high above the lake, the Whiskeytown-Shasta-Trinity National Recreation Area. From this lofty spot most of Whiskeytown Lake can be seen. Its deep water now covers all the sites, where once a few primitive homes, including mine, made up the tiny community of Poverty Flat.

As the President's helicopter left the dam it passed over the new Whiskeytown cemetery, relocated because of the water rising in the lake. The President didn't know that here rested a humble man whose life, during an earlier time, had touched his.

For it was Cody Stamps and his fellow Sea Bees who constructed and maintained the Navy base at Rendova in the South Pacific from which Ensign Kennedy operated the small ship whose name will be forever remembered in history, the P. T. 109.

Photos & Illustrations: Boyhood

Chores, Winter 1939

Cousin Rex Moravec is swinging the axe. Gene is preparing to carry wood to the house (not seen). In background is Gene's Radio Flyer and the 1926 Buick in which he learned to drive. In front of the Radio Flyer is the cooler Cody designed and built. Narrative: *Olinda* p. 34

Frances Stamps (Curnow)
Mother

This photo was taken in 1943, on the day Gene left for Navy Officer Training.

Harry Curnow
Father

"Dad had been a high climber on construction of the San Francisco-Oakland Bay Bridge, so heights did not bother him. Here, he is standing on the outermost ledge on top of the Assembly Hotel in Seattle, WA. He loved to show me how he could actually RUN all the way around the top of the hotel, even in a strong wind." Narrative: *Skeleton in the Closet*, p. 18.

Cody Stamps
Step Father

"Cody came into our lives when I was 6 years old, in 1931. He was, by birth, half Cherokee Indian. I could not have had a better step dad. In WWII he was a Sea Bee (CB = Construction Battalion) and helped construct the Operations Base at Rendova from which Jack Kennedy (later U.S. President John F. Kennedy) operated the PT 109. During this time Kennedy and Cody were on a first name basis." Narrative: *Life at Poverty Flat*, p. 138-139

Rex's Home in Olinda
Boots in Foreground

Photo taken circa 1939, Rex's dog, Boots, is in the foreground. [From the author: "My dog, Smokey, must have been out after jackrabbits...."]
Narrative: *Boots, Smokey & Adolph* p. 64

Painting of Poverty Flat
by Glenora Curnow

From the author: "Living in Poverty Flat (1939) we were so poor that we could not afford a camera. As a result no photographs of this area or our primitive living conditions exist. But my wife, Glenora, has had fine art training and painted as I "talked the description of the area" to her. She has reproduced it exactly as it looked at that time. I thank her for her excellent contribution, her painting of Poverty Flat, which became the cover illustration for this book."

Cab Forward

In railroad lingo these are referred to as "4-8-8-2's" or "Mountain Malley's." The most powerful steam engine ever built, used on steep grades. The cab in front allowed the engineer and fireman to always be ahead of the smoke when going through long tunnels. Before this cab's invention some engineers and firemen died of smoke and carbon monoxide inhalation. Rex and Gene rode behind this early-style engine in 1940 on a 1,000 mile trip. *The Train Trip*, p. 84.

Picture courtesy of *Smoke in the Canyon: My Steam Days in Dunsmuir* by Dick Murdock.

The Cantera Loop
This image shows a later model forward cab pulling cars through the Cantera Loop. Narrative: *The Train Trip, Part I* p. 93.

Picture courtesy of *Smoke in the Canyon: My Steam Days in Dunsmuir* by Dick Murdock.

Grandma Smith

Pictured here with Gene and Harry Curnow.

"Grandma Smith had one secret. When she and her husband first came to Oregon they were very poor an needed to survive. She opened a 'house of ill repute' on High Street in Baker, OR. She was the owner, hired the 'ladies of the night' and made the money. Grandma Smith moved to Portland, OR and became a respected 'pillar of the community'."

It was she who made it clear 'no grandsons of hers would be riding any more freight trains. Narrative: *The Train Trip, Part II*, p. 105

PART II
WAR

WHAT DID YOU DO IN THE WAR, GRANDPA?

Upon Graduation from Shasta High School in Redding, California on June 10, 1942 at age 17, I moved to Seattle, Washington to live with my dad, Harry and continue my education enrolling at Seattle College. On December 7, 1941 the Japanese had bombed Pearl Harbor and military conscription, "the draft" was established in the United States. All able bodied men, ages 18 through 26, were required to register and be subject to call for military service. By volunteering to join before age 18 I had the option to choose the branch of the military in which I would serve. From someone I heard the expression, "The Army does the work, the Marines get the glory but the Navy gets the pay." Coming from a family in poverty and wanting to be paid the most money possible I joined the Navy.

Enlistment at age 17 required parental permission and my Mother signed for me. In the Judges chamber she sobbed as the papers were notarized on February 4, 1943, four days before my 18th birthday. Tears ran down her face as she said, "I'm afraid you'll be killed."

I wanted to erase such a thought and put her mind at ease so I said, "Hey, don't worry Ma, I'd never let that happen."

Because I currently attended college in Seattle as a pre-medical student, the Navy allowed me to finish the quarter and pre-assigned me to the V-12, officers training program. Scheduled to begin active duty on June 20, 1943, the Navy transferred me to the University of New Mexico in Albuquerque, where I would continue training. With many other pre-medical students in the V-12 program, as a group we lived on campus in the Pi Kappa Alpha fraternity house that had been taken over as housing by the Navy. Though the war continued fraternities were allowed to actively recruit. As did most pre-medical students here, I pledged

Sigma Chi. The Navy required us to live in the Pi Kappa Alpha house, so as Sigma Chi pledges we were quickly taught a short song to denigrate the other fraternity. The first words, sung in normal volume were, "Pi Kappa Alpha, Pi Kappa Alpha, Pi Kappa Alpha—followed by a massive shout of, **HORSE SHIT!!**" It remained an effective ditty because no one dropped Sigma Chi in favor of Pi Kappa Alpha.

In the fraternity house lived a number of "active" Sigma Chi members. As pledges we found ourselves treated nearly as slaves by some. Most active members looked at the pledges with at least a little respect. P.P.M. (Phil) Wiegle did not. A senior in the Engineering school he would soon graduate and become a line officer with the rank of Ensign. Overbearing and greedy, he enjoyed "hazing" the pledges. One hot day in August, having taken enough from him, I devised a scheme to even the score.

On the first floor of the two-story fraternity house stood a Coke machine. Filled to capacity every morning, most of the time during hot weather it soon became empty. With no air conditioning Wiegle and I and about twenty other students, sweated out life on the upper floor. Every night Wiegle sought me out and demanded that I shine his three pair of shoes. If he'd see me drinking an ice cold Coke, he always took it away from me.

On an exceptionally hot evening Wiegle went to get a Coke from the machine downstairs but found it empty. Half an hour later, taunting him, I slowly walked past the open door of his room whistling a tune so he'd be sure to notice me. In one hand, in full view, I held in front of me what appeared to be an almost full bottle of ice cold Coke. He didn't know I had taken about 50 cigarette butts and some light brown liquid shoe polish and mixed them with water in a shallow pan. Squeezing the butts to get additional color from the tobacco I let the brew settle. I then poured the clear light brown liquid that looked to be Coke, into a bottle I had removed from a case of empties downstairs. Fortunately, I had cleared the trick I wanted to play on Wiegle with his skinny room mate and told a lot of other pledges who had been harassed, what I intended to do.

As I walked slowly by his door Wiegle heard me whistling and looked up from his studies. In my hand he saw what he thought to be an almost full bottle of ice cold Coke. Having let cold water run on it a few minutes the bottle became cool to the touch. I didn't dry the outside and the many small beads of moisture remaining on it gave the illusion of cold condensation. Seeing this he jumped up from his desk and ran toward me shouting, "Give me that Coke, pledge!!"

Hesitating purposely I replied, "It's not…"

"Come on pledge, hand it over," he ordered.

Again I hesitated when speaking, "I'm trying to tell you it's not what you…."

"On your knees pledge, put that Coke down or you'll go on report to the fraternity for disobeying the order of an active."

"O.K." I said. Dropping to my knees I placed the wet Coke bottle containing the light brown liquid in front of me. Wiegle scooped it up. As he quickly turned and began to walk back into his room he lifted what he thought to be an ice cold Coke to his lips. Tipping his head far back he eagerly took a huge gulp.

His eyes widened instantly and he almost vomited. Gagging again and again he spit the contents all over the floor. "What the goddamn hell is this?" he roared as he rushed toward me. "Are you trying to poison me? What is this stuff, goddamn it?" Both his big hands were ready to hit me or pull me up off my knees and throw me against the wall. If it hadn't been for his tall skinny roommate I know he'd have beat me senseless. Wiegle weighed about two hundred and twenty five pounds, all of it muscle. I weighed one hundred and twenty pounds, a weakling by comparison.

Grabbing Wiegle from behind in a bear hug, his skinny roommate yelled at me "Get the hell out of here, now!!" Jumping to my feet I ran downstairs and heard Wiegle's roommate shout,

"Give it up, damn it. He's just getting even with you. Remember, if you ever hit a pledge you're out of the fraternity forever."

As Wiegle cooled from his anger I yelled up the stairs, "I tried to tell you twice it wasn't Coke. What's in it is tobacco juice and brown shoe polish. I was going to spit shine your shoes with it later on."

A few days later he saw the humorous side of the joke and laughed. We were together several more months at the University and before I requested and was granted sea duty Wiegle told me he admired my guts and initiative. He also said he thought I'd make a "hell of a good active Sigma Chi member" and that he'd personally recommend me. I felt good about it but never accepted his offer.

It was an unwritten rule that Sigma Chi pledges were to date only Kappa Kappa Gamma girls. They lived in their sorority house a few blocks away. Life in the Navy V-12, officer training program was not all work. With the girls we went on hayrides, picnics and individual dates. As a group we'd sometimes go up in the Sandia Mountains to Cedar Crest or Sandia Park. Among the cool pines we overlooked Kirtland Air Force Base. I don't know how the girls arranged it but on the outings we always rode in the back of a big flat bed truck having five-foot high wooden walls for safety barriers on both sides. A thick layer of straw cushioned our ride if we stretched out on the hard boards of the floor and several unopened bales were used to sit on as we rode. Navy pay was $21.00 a month, but because there were so many of us, when each contributed a few dollars toward expenses, we always had plenty of food and drink. Most of us brought a thick, wool G.I. blanket or two off our bed to sit on while eating in the shade of a friendly fir tree. Later, with stomachs full, each couple would find a cool and secluded place to put the blankets then stretch out on them to rest and relax while enjoying our date.

Starting with the first week of school I dated Connie Spang Ancona, also a pre-medical student. I met her on Monday, the first day of the semester and we were attracted to each other immediately. In Biology class that day every student was given a live frog. The instructor said, "All of you must choose a partner."

Across the lab table I looked at Connie who was looking at me and I asked, "Would you like to be partners?"

Nodding she smiled, "That would be nice."

A pretty blond, five foot two inches tall and a Kappa Kappa Gamma active, as far as my Sigma Chi brothers were concerned they found Connie most acceptable. However, I sensed something wasn't being said when I told them her name. Whenever I mentioned it they reacted, blinking a little with what appeared to be a mixture of surprise and disbelief.

During the experiment on the first day the frogs were to be totally immobilized but not killed. We were to study the organs, tissues and blood flow under several different magnifications of a microscope. Our instructor demonstrated how to "pith the frog" to accomplish the immobilization. He bent its head far forward and inserted a three-inch long, thick, sharp needle through the opening in the back of the skull, the *Foraman Magnum*. Moving and twisting the needle in every direction it destroyed the brain tissue inside the frog's head. The heart and other organs continued to function controlled by the spinal cord and autonomic nervous system. Placing the frog "spread eagle" on its back, in a pan containing an inch thick layer of semi-hard wax, with thumbtacks the instructor pinned down all four legs. Making a shallow incision in the belly wall with a razor sharp scalpel he carefully exposed the still functioning internal organs. We watched fascinated while blood coursed through veins and arteries as the heart continued to beat. Connie couldn't bring herself to pith or cut open the frog and she expressed gratitude when I did it for her.

The following Saturday afternoon Sigma Chi actives and pledges were to have our first picnic. It would be held in the park near downtown Albuquerque and I asked Connie if she'd go with me. To my surprise and delight, without a moment of hesitation she said yes. The Rio Grande River runs through the park but had too much mud and silt in it for swimming. However, the drinking of Ale was encouraged.

This first picnic turned out to be an excuse for the active members to make the pledges get as drunk as possible. Cases of

cold ale were everywhere. Each active picked a pledge and required him to "chug-a-lug" as many bottles of ale as the active
ordered. I don't know how many bottles of ale I drank and remember nothing until waking up about two o'clock in the morning. Fully clothed in my white dress uniform, I lay face down on
the floor in the communal shower on the second floor of the Pi
Kappa Alpha house with cold water running full force over my
clothes, wallet, wrist watch and me. The next day, Sunday, on the
bulletin board someone put up a sheet of paper having on it the
name of every pledge and how each reacted at the "ale party." After the name Curnow appeared this notation: "Says he will get
roaring drunk fast and stay that way longer than anyone else—
and does!!"

Thinking she'd never want to see me again, on Sunday morning reluctant to pick up the phone, I didn't call Connie to find out
how she got home. I was surprised when in class Monday morning she cheerily greeted, "Hi, how do you feel?" After my apology
she said, "It isn't your fault. They forced the pledges to drink too
much. Don't mention it, I understand and it's all right."

During the semester our personal dates became more frequent. In a secluded spot behind thick shrubs close to a decora-
tive fountain we found "our special bench." and each date lasted a
little longer. As we continued to date, in time our hugs and kisses
became intense and her body language more urgent. It didn't
take this normal red-blooded sailor long to realize that soon, on
the campus bench, a new threshold in our relationship could be
crossed.

Late in the semester on what would be the last of our many
dates, she asked me to meet her that evening about 8:30 in front
of a beautiful house located on Regents Row. As we sat on the
curb of the parking strip in front during the cool dusk of evening
she said, "I'd like you to meet my Dad and Mother some time."
She seemed to glow when I told her, "I'd enjoy meeting them.
Where do they live?"

"Right here," she waved toward the large two story red brick
home behind us.

"In a Regent's home?" I asked.

Then I remembered a campus publication I'd seen about Professor Leo Ancona, Chairman of the Physics department who had accepted an "outstanding achievement award" from the military for doing some unique work for them at Alamagordo.

"Is Professor Ancona your Dad? And your Mother, is she Grace Ancona, a member of the Board of Regents?" My questions stumbled out almost on top of each other.

With a little laugh she answered, "Yes they are. You didn't know?"

Shaking my head I said, "I sure didn't."

"Well, that's why I usually tell everyone my name is Connie Spang. I seldom tell anyone like I told you, that my last name is Ancona. You understand don't you?"

It seemed like I heard myself answer from a long distance away, "Yes I do."

Professor Ancona had the reputation for being a no-nonsense, hard to get along with, hot headed Italian and one of the best educators in the field of Physics in the United States at that time. No wonder the active Sigma Chi members who knew her background always seemed a little surprised and appeared to be holding something from me when I told them Connie and I were dating.

Throughout the semester, having heard the stories of "action" in the Pacific told by some of the students that were veterans who had been there and successfully requested admission to officers training in the V-12 program, I couldn't see myself only going to college during the war. Adventure now called and I answered.

On our date a few nights earlier at the secluded bench by the water fountain, Connie didn't know I had requested a transfer to sea duty and it had been granted. Now sitting at curbside in front of her home I told her of my decision and that this would be my last night in Albuquerque. For awhile she remained silent. Then quietly she asked, "You'll write won't you?"

"Sure," I promised.

Glancing at my watch I realized soon it would be ten o'clock time for "lights out" and the door of the Pi Kappa Alpha house would be locked.

For awhile Connie and I stood in the parking strip behind the trunk of a large tree so her parents wouldn't see us hugging and kissing.

I told her, "I'm going to miss you Connie." Just as on the first day when we entered the Biology class together, again our eyes met. Hesitantly she said, "I'll miss you too, but we'll write."

A tear ran slowly down her face before we kissed passionately for the last time. For a moment I had misgivings about my decision to leave Albuquerque.

Connie usually wore a pretty floral print dress. I often told her that she looked just like a walking bouquet of beautiful flowers and that she was the prettiest one of all.

As she walked slowly toward her parent's house a soft evening breeze followed her pressing the silkiness of her dress closely against her body revealing a suggestion of her charms. At her doorstep she turned to wave. I waved back then hurried to the fraternity house.

The next morning at five thirty I boarded the train for San Diego. Departing from the station I realized I had forgotten to ask for her address. But soon I became so involved in an intense new adventure that Albuquerque quickly faded from memory.

I would never see Connie again.

❖ BOOT CAMP ❖

There were some unique moments on the trip from Albuquerque, New Mexico to Los Angeles. As a low priority train ours carried only enlisted Navy personnel. Other passenger trains with high-ranking officers on board and priority freights hauling tanks, trucks, big guns and ammunition, had the right of way. As a result we frequently were pulled onto a siding to let them rush by.

Though crowded, hot and noisy, because all of us were young and adventuresome, most of the time a lot of laughter and horseplay prevailed. One sailor from Georgia could walk on his hands almost as well as on his feet. He'd amuse everyone as he walked up and down the aisle upside down while whistling "Dixie". Near the end of our trip someone bet him a dollar he couldn't do a handstand balancing on the arm rests of two seats on opposite sides across the aisle from each other.

"I can do that easy." He laughed, "Getting your money will be just like takin' candy from a baby." Pulling out his wallet he said "Put your money where your mouth is" and handed a dollar bill to a sailor who offered to hold the bets.

Up he went gripping the outer armrest of a seat on each side of the aisle. For a moment he balanced perfectly. Then the train lurched as a less experienced wartime engineer tested the air brakes before descending a grade. One hand slipped and the acrobat fell from his perch. His mouth hit the sturdy wooden armrest and one center top tooth and two center bottom teeth broke off at the gum line. With the nerve in all three exposed he suffered intense pain and we had no dental help on the train. For him to eat or drink became nearly impossible. No sailor collected a bet and when we arrived in Los Angeles an ambulance took him to the nearest Naval medical facility.

Much of the rail route from Albuquerque to Los Angeles runs across Arizona. The desert here, for the most part, is hot, harsh and unforgiving yet holds a stark beauty. The older Pullman car in which we rode rattled along coupled on close to the end of the train. To "see the engine" as the cars snaked around curves made the trip an adventure. Approaching Kingman, Arizona from our vantage point we could look forward to watch the long train, pulled by only one steam engine puffing columns of black smoke, laboriously drag us around an almost full circle of track. For many young sailors taking their first train ride, this spectacular sight was impressive.

Arriving in Los Angeles we were hustled into the biggest dining room I've ever seen. Located in a building close to the station hundred of chairs waited beside long tables. Real cloth red and white, checkered table coverings gave a touch of hominess and each setting had china plates, metal eating utensils and a full glass of ice water. The meal, provided by the Navy, was served by a lot of volunteer civilians, mostly cheerful middle-aged ladies wearing aprons matching the tablecloths. In serpentine fashion we moved in, sat down and enjoyed our first hot meal in three days, a welcome change from the sandwiches on the train. In a long convoy of Navy buses we headed for our final destination, thirteen weeks Boot Camp on Point Loma in San Diego.

As part of the training cycle, the first few weeks were spent in "detention." This meant we couldn't leave the base or have contact, other than mail, with the outside world. On the base there were many so called "boot camps" and each entered into competition during all aspects of training. At four forty five every morning a bugle blaring reveille crashed into our dreams. It clearly sent the message it's time to "hit the deck". In addition, several "wise guy" recruits always yelled, "Hey, it's time to leggo your cocks and grab your socks."

Life was not pleasant here. At five thirty, assembled outside the barracks, we marched to breakfast. Every morning we were fed, as our main staple, navy beans and reconstituted dehydrated scrambled eggs. We were also offered several dry cereals or cooked oatmeal. On Sunday's we were given bacon, sausage or Spam in addition to the eggs and beans. We always drank coffee, milk, lemonade or water. Rumor said that "Saltpeter", Potassium Nitrate, was added to the lemonade just before being served. This is a chemical that supposedly keeps hot-blooded, hormonally challenged sailors from becoming "wildly horny" during their initial confinement to base. I don't really believe anyone added this to the lemonade that arrived on the base in dehydrated powder form then was reconstituted with water. The fact is it tasted so bad this alone was enough to kill anyone's sex drive.

Calisthenics, marching and drills, carried out for many hours on a huge 20-acre blacktopped field called "the grinder", became the daily routine. We learned "the sixteen count manual of arms" both standing in place and marching in unison carrying a .30-06 Springfield rifle moved into various positions as we moved along. It was a pleasure to watch when done correctly but not easy to learn. At Camp John Paul Jones, our group ranged in height from five feet two inches, Dick Hjermestad, to six feet five inches tall, a Swede I remember only as Andy. To march correctly, for obvious reasons, the group had to be positioned with the shortest people marching in front and the tallest in back. In addition, one person of average height had to be selected to become "the right guide". It is he who determines the final speed of all the marchers.

The first morning on the grinder, the Chief called out, "Anyone here had marching experience? I want someone five feet seven inches tall who knows how to march to step forward and volunteer." I had completed five months of marching experience in the V-12 program at Albuquerque, stood five feet seven and a half inches tall and stepped forward becoming the right guide. Positioned alone at the right hand corner, just one step in front of the entire marching group, I set the pace. Everyone had to adjust to my rhythm and at all times remain one pace behind and to my left as all eight long lines marched in block formation.

During the first weeks of instruction the exasperated Chief frequently yelled, "The guide is right, the guide is right. Now line up on the guide!!" This meant our block formation had a lot of marchers not positioned side by side and front to back in perfectly straight lines in relation to all the others as well as to the right guide. As the weeks passed it became noticeable that the admonition from the Chief became less frequent indicating to everyone we were making progress. All Navy personnel had to learn to march in coordination to assure we'd be able to be moved quickly as a group, from one place to another.

With basic marching learned it became enjoyable to take part in more exotic and spectacular maneuvers. For example, when the Chief called out specific orders, two lines of sailors marched away at a 45 degree angle to the right, two lines 45 degrees to the left and two lines spun around marching to the rear while the last two lines continued forward in the original direction. It made the sailors appear to fan out over the grinder like they had exploded in all directions. When the Chief repeated the orders in exactly the opposite sequence the sailors came back together. When done correctly, without missing a beat, they'd quickly return to the original position and continue to march in block formation going the same direction as when the unusual maneuver began. If correct rhythm is maintained and orders are followed exactly as given, this becomes a perfect example of how effectively giving and receiving orders will work. However, when only one person in any column makes the slightest mistake it results in total disaster for the entire group. Recruits crash into each other at the re-assembly points as the Chief shouts, livid with rage, at such stupidity.

Some sailors were slow to catch on to the rhythm of marching and were held back in Boot Camp a couple of weeks. Placed in "D for dumb" company, they were given intensive marching instruction. Most eventually did learn. However, some were totally uncoordinated and found it impossible to march correctly. They were either discharged or later assigned to desk jobs where marching is not required.

Camp John Paul Jones did so well in competition against all other camps we graduated from detention with top honors and won the Admirals Commendation for special marching. After four weeks we were given our first liberty to go off base and were moved to Camp Farragut, a less restrictive and more modern barracks.

The next few weeks consisted of testing our aptitude for learning. Making specially designed knots in ropes, rowing lifeboats, using radios, learning "dot and dash", Morse code, signal lights and semaphore flag communication to name a few. Training became intense because skills learned here might someday mean life or death for any one of us and maybe our shipmates.

On rare occasions we had a day with nothing scheduled. When this happened we were issued large push brooms with coarse bristles. Arranged side by side in long lines we were to sweep the 20-acre blacktopped grinder. Because of its huge size, sweeping the grinder was, of course, an impossible task to ever finish and typical of a Navy "make work" project to keep us occupied. A lot of grumbling went on about the foolishness of this activity because, on the grinder, there never was anything to sweep off.

All sailors accepted for sea duty are required to know how to swim well. From Boot Camp on Point Loma, in the block formation we had mastered, we were marched as a unit through a residential district of San Diego to the big Natatorium several miles away at Mission bay. As we marched into the complex located beside the ocean, little white-capped waves splashed against a low seawall. Looking to the west across the Pacific I thought, "This water is going to be my home for the next few years." It comforted me and I felt an inner peace. It seemed the ocean whispered a friendly greeting and said I'd be safe sailing on it during one of life's great adventures.

In the huge indoor pool we learned how to remove our uniform under water and convert it into a flotation device. Taking a deep breath and going limp, under the water we'd remove our jumper top and pants in the usual way while floating in any position that gravity placed us. Surprisingly, it's not hard to do if one remains relaxed and unhurried bobbing just below the surface. Coming back to the top, while "treading water", we'd tie a knot on the end of each pants leg. Then, holding the pants at the waistband and flinging the pant legs into the air while at the same time bringing the waist down fast, both pant legs fill with air becoming an efficient floatation device, much like a pair of store bought "water wings". Because the cloth is so tightly woven the air remains in the pant legs almost half an hour and they can be filled as many times as needed using the same method. The Chief warned, "You better learn this real well. Knowing how to do it could save your life if your ship goes down in enemy action."

Next, we each were given a thick, gray, Kapok filled life jacket. With only our swim trunks and the life jacket on, one at a time we climbed 30 feet up to a platform above the deepest end of the pool. Here an instructor showed us how to cross our arms tightly beneath our chin to avoid injury to the neck and head. We then jumped feet first from the platform as though abandoning a sinking ship. Learning this maneuver is a necessity. To jump off incorrectly from the great height of an aircraft carrier or a battleship deck can result in serious injury or death from a broken neck or skull fracture from hitting debris in the water.

To qualify as swimmers ready for sea duty we had to successfully swim under water through a long obstacle course. In the first 50 feet the obstacles were worn out car tires, size six hundred by sixteen. Tethered to the bottom in groups of two, then four and finally six tied together, they made short underwater tunnels through which we were to swim. Almost everyone passed easily through the sets of two but not the sets of four and six. There isn't much room to spare when a normal body goes through a sixteen-inch opening, which is about the same inside diameter as that of a ship's porthole. For unusually fat or big sailors to get through became very difficult. Two lifeguards were stationed at every set of four and six tire groups ready to pull the securing pin, quickly detaching the tires from the bottom of the pool and pull to safety the people who couldn't make it through. Some got stuck and were terribly frightened by their ordeal. As they panicked before being pulled to safety, they gulped down lots of water but no one drowned.

Just before we completed Boot Camp early one morning we were lined up to be given a series of immunizations to protect us from the highly contagious diseases to which we could become exposed overseas. Each of us received nine shots as we "ran the gauntlet" of examining doctors and needle wielding medical corpsmen. Some needle shy individuals fainted while being given the shots. Others passed out right after getting them and some fell over far back in the line even before they got them. As is the case a lot of times, the biggest and meanest sailors fainted more often than the tough little wiry ones. "The bigger they are the harder they fall" proved to be right this day.

We were told that after being immunized many of us would be sick for about a day and a half. By "chow time" at five o'clock that evening, about 75 percent were affected. They remained in their bunks vomiting then retching with dry heaves. Though many ate no supper they still had plenty of stomach contents remaining from lunch to disgorge. It became the duty for those who didn't get sick to rush around with a large bucket to the bunks of those who called out loudly, "Hey, over here, I'm going to puke again." "Unfortunately" I didn't get sick and spent all night and half of the next day with a bucket full of bad smelling vomit which I constantly emptied only to have it quickly re-filled —- over and over.

Only one serious injury occurred during the time I spent in Boot Camp. It happened a week before we were to leave for our first assignment. On "laundry day" we washed our own dungarees, white uniforms, socks and underwear, called "skivvies". In addition we stripped our bunks and, weather permitting, hung all our bedding outside. After washing clothes and hanging them in the sunshine on the outdoor clotheslines we'd sit in the barracks in our shorts, or naked, waiting for them to dry. One sailor climbed to his top bunk and sat down on the bare flat spring assembly to wait. As he sat naked on one side of the bunk, with both legs hanging over the edge of the solid steel frame and his rear end pushing down on the spring assembly, his testicles dropped unnoticed through the now significantly larger opening between the flat spring assembly and the steel outside rail that held it. A lot of heat had build up in the barracks and his "family jewels" hung down much lower than usual dangling below the space between the rigid steel frame of his bunk and the flat spring. The weight of his rear end pushing the flexible spring assembly downward is what caused the large gap to open between the spring and steel frame. He didn't realize a very delicate part of his male anatomy swung in jeopardy beneath him.

Just then the Chief walked in and someone yelled, "Attention!!" The sailor on the top bunk, using both arms, braced himself on the solid steel frame, immediately lifting his rear end off of the edge of the flat spring. As he began his jump to the floor and with the weight of his rear end absent, the usually small space between the steel frame and spring snapped tightly together instantly trapping his scrotal sac and testicles. In mid air he gave a horrible shrieking scream and crashed to the floor where he lay writhing in excruciating pain. As he rose to jump his testicles had been tightly caught in the very tight space below and between the flat spring and steel frame. It nearly tore them off his body resulting in massive trauma and what can only be described as "unbearable gut wrenching agony".

The Chief rushed over. Seeing the massive swelling and deep purple discoloration of the sailor's scrotum caused by massive blood loss from the torn arteries and veins inside, he knew this was a medical emergency.

"Carry on," he shouted as he rushed to the phone to call a base ambulance.

A few days later the rest of us left for new assignments. But one unfortunate sailor remained behind in the hospital, the victim of an unusual accident on a hot day.

❖ CIRCLE OF DESTINY ❖

On October 31, 1943 I arrived at the Naval Training Station on Point Loma in San Diego. Now on the drill field in Boot Camp all of us struggled to learn the "sixteen count manual of arms." Close by at the Naval Air Station at Coronado, advanced student pilots were learning their final skills needed to fly a new aircraft, the Lockheed P-38 Lightning. Formed into two groups of about twenty each with an experienced instructor in each leading plane they flew in separate columns playing "follow the leader". Many times a day they flew above us and we'd hear the throaty roar and shrill screams from the twin engines as the novice pilots rapidly worked the throttles of these newest and very fast fighter planes. The two groups, in serpentine lines, moved in unison and sounded to me, like flights of giant angry bumblebees.

With the lines about a mile or two apart each leader dove toward the other with his students following. At the last moment they were to "peel off" and safely bank away from each other flying in opposite directions.

Again and again we heard them race toward each other. The high-pitched noise engulfed us as each student pilot veered off, rapidly pulling almost straight up out of the shallow dive. During our training we heard the sound so many times we recognized it as normal and seldom looked up. But today our routine was shattered as we witnessed one pilot successfully fight for survival and one tragically fail.

We first heard a loud metallic "bang" at impact, followed by a crunching and grinding noise and a very different sound coming from troubled engines. We knew right away there had been a mid-air collision. One or both student pilots failed to judge speed and distance correctly and for a moment had locked together the wings and part of the fuselage of their planes.

When they separated one plane, still partially controllable and with both engines still running, wobbled and swayed, as the pilot guiding it away from the residential area and out over the bay off Point Loma. Smoke and flame billowed behind. Above the bay the pilot jumped from his crippled plane and his parachute opened. With him safely strapped in the harness beneath, the 'chute drifted down looking like a giant white mushroom. A short time later he splashed safely into the water and a rescue boat soon took him aboard. As we watched the plane, it hit in a distant part of the bay, sending up a huge geyser of spray.

Engrossed in the fate of the plane that dropped into the bay it took a few moments before we noticed what happened to the other. The left engine slowed to a fast idle but the right one continued to run at just a little less than flying speed. This caused the plane to make tight counter-clockwise circles. In the language of pilots, this is a "flat spin".

With each circle it made, the crippled P-38 passed fairly high above us, then the dental building, boiler room with its tall smokestack, the Point Loma Highway and finally a small white house beside a vacant lot in a low-rent residential district just across from the Naval base.

Each time it circled overhead the plane sank lower but the pilot didn't appear. We wondered if he was injured and unconscious. Our fears were temporarily relieved when he suddenly jumped. Opening his parachute very quickly he began to float earthward close beneath the plane. As the pilot drifted lower it looked as though he would come down on a hillside half a mile away in an expensive residential district. Moments later our relief turned to shock as we watched the plane, still spinning, rush toward him. The pilot also saw it and pulled frantically on his parachute shroud lines in a futile attempt to get out of the way. The plane came at him and the rapidly spinning propeller on the right wing ripped into him, cutting his body from the harness and tearing the pilot to shreds before our eyes. Weightless and empty, the remains of both 'chute and harness drifted aimlessly to the ground.

In trance like numbness we witnessed the tragedy. But now a new danger confronted us. The Chief recognized the hazard the plane still presented as it continued to circle, drifting lower and closer each time. He shouted, "Every man for himself. Take cover. Re-assemble here when the plane is down."

As we scattered I thought I should run to the dental building about 100 yards away to alert the people inside. However, time wouldn't allow it. The plane now circled much too low as it came around again. I thought if it crashes on the highway, residential district or dental building a lot of people could be killed. Continuing on its path on the final pass it circled less than 50 feet above us. We could hear the rushing sound of air as it swooped toward the small white private residence located just across the highway from the Naval base. Then it disappeared from our line of sight crashing in a ball of orange flame and black smoke.

In a state of shock we re-assembled. The Chief, who had recently returned from active duty in the Pacific, was visibly shaken. But he rallied us together in the face of tragedy continuing to give instructions that later might save our life in combat. We had just witnessed the reality of death and learned that luck sometimes plays a part in whether we live or die. But now we listened attentively as the Chief reminded us that how we'd do our individual job in an emergency might change the balance on the scales of life and death. The unfortunate pilot had forgotten his survival training. Instead of continuing to let himself fall quickly a much greater distance beneath the plane before pulling the rip-cord he panicked and pulled it too soon causing the circling plane to overtake and strike him.

Even in tragedy miracles happen. When we read the story in the paper the next day it said that the plane crashed, exploded and burned in the only vacant lot remaining beside the crowded, business lined Point Loma Highway, hurting no one.

The only damage was some scorched paint on the little white house beside the empty lot.

❖ HOSPITAL CORPS SCHOOL ❖
AND FIRST STATION

Navy personnel records indicated I completed almost one year as a pre-medical student at Seattle College and the University of New Mexico. As a result, after finishing basic training in Boot Camp, on December 24, 1943, the Navy assigned me to Hospital Corps School located at Balboa Park in San Diego.

Here I came face to face with the intense competition of several hundred students. At our indoctrination meeting we were told that the ten highest scoring people in the class, upon graduation, would earn the rate of Petty Officer and be awarded an eagle and the first red stripe to be worn on the left arm of our uniform. We'd then be called "rated hospital corpsmen", though Pharmacist Mate is the official Navy designation. As an additional incentive we'd be able to choose our first duty station and remain there for at least six months. It could be any Naval medical facility located within the 48 States. We'd also get more pay on the fifth and twentieth of every month.

All Navy hospitals and annexes enjoyed the reputation of being "good duty". They had the best food, cleanest quarters, a regular eight hour shift, "liberty" every night and pretty nurses to work with. This added much to our eagerness to earn the eagle and red stripe to become rated corpsmen.

Upon arrival, conditions at Hospital Corps School left much to be desired. For lack of room in the regular buildings we were housed, in tents in groups of six, in a place we called "Pneumonia Gulch". The tents had no heat and only one 25-watt light bulb hung from the center ridgepole. During the last week in December and first two weeks in January, we endured the cold, damp, and drafty conditions with less than enough blankets to keep us warm at night. But after three weeks we were moved to more comfortable quarters in a heated building.

Settled in our new housing we were required to have a dental checkup. In a large room at the medical dispensary were a dozen or more dental chairs. Each dentist worked as fast as he could. I didn't realize what the Navy dental policy was until I sat in the chair. Quickly examining my teeth the dentist said, "Ya' have several cavities. But don't worry, we'll fix 'um up for ya' real quick like."

I didn't like his grammar or the way he nervously rushed around preparing to drill. The way his hands shook didn't give me much confidence either. Even though he told me not to, I worried anyway — though not about my cavities. He continued, "Ya' know, a lot of corpsmen who go through here get transferred into the Marines."

"Not if I can help it," I thought to myself.

Still speaking he said, "All of ya' who get selected have to take the Marine's training and it's pretty rough. Ya' got to learn to "take it" if ya' get in the Marines so I won't be givin' ya' any anesthetic while I drill. Ya' maybe might feel it just a little."

Feel it a little? What an understatement. I felt it a lot!! Having a low threshold for pain, for me, even a small amount hurts real bad. His old-fashioned, low speed drill burr had no air or water cooling system and felt like it burned into the nerve of each tooth causing blazing white pain. Feeling torture and intense agony, I grasped the handles of the dental chair, squeezed and pulled as the hot burr ground its way relentlessly into the rock hard enamel around my six cavities. I could see a full vial of 2 percent procaine anesthetic resting right in front of me on the dental tray and became very angry.

Two and a half hours later the dentist cheerily announced, "There now, that wasn't so bad for ya' was it?"

Raging inside I thought to myself, "If it's not so bad, you no good son of a bitch, I'd like to drill a few holes in your teeth sometime without anesthetic, especially with the stuff there right in front of you to use." Sweating from the ordeal, I returned to the living quarters, swallowed two Aspirin took a hot shower and without eating supper, went to bed.

But I must give the devil his due. The dentist proved to be very competent. Nearly sixty years later I still have every one of those "six damn fillings, all trouble free."

Striking up friendship with two other students, Nichols and Jennings, we three always studied together. Six days a week, on the grounds of Balboa-park we attended "long winded" lectures five hours a day in the famous and historic Old Globe Theatre. It had been built as an identical replica of the all wood Shakespearean structure in England. Our instructors were Chief pharmacist mates, Navy nurses and Physicians. Some of the subjects taught were, Materia medica, Pharmacology, Minor surgery, War gas and antidotes, General nursing and bandage application plus a host of other technical subjects. We felt sure we'd never be called on to make use of a lot of this specialized information but we had to learn it anyway.

Every day we were given a test consisting of 100 questions. For example, Question: "Name two sternutators (war gasses). How do they affect the human body?" Answer: "Diphenylchlorarsene and Chlorocetaphenone. They cause the lungs to fill with fluid and drown the victim." Question: "In what classification do we find Mustard gas? What is the effect on the human body?" Answer: "It's a vesicant. It causes massive blisters wherever it comes in contact with living human tissue."

Because of the highly technical nature, it was amazing that we could absorb this kind of knowledge and remember it. Every day we were given additional assignments in this and other disciplines, to be read from our books in preparation for the test the next day. Unable to complete the reading before "lights out" at ten o'clock, the only places where lights remained on all night were the toilets. Nichols, Jennings and I studied here night after night, fully clothed against the winter weather, using a "john" for a chair on which to sit. Many times we burned the "midnight oil", not getting to bed until one or two in the morning.

We completed Corps school in six weeks and found it unbelievable how close the scores of the highest top ten who received an eagle and first red stripe were. A short, semi-balding red haired kid had the highest, 99.9 for the six-week course. He answered only one question incorrectly out of a total of 3600. Second highest in the class, I answered only two wrong and earned a score of 99.8. Everyone else scored lower, but the lowest person to get rated scored 98.9, which represented only 11 incorrect answers out of the 3600 asked during our six weeks of training. Unfortunately, neither Nichols nor Jennings made the cut though they studied as hard as they could. After Corps school, I never saw them again.

My score earned the privilege to be stationed anywhere in the United States for at least six months before being eligible for assignment to sea duty in the combat zone. Because "a cute and very desirable person of interest" lived in Santa Clara, about 65 miles south, I asked to be sent to the Mare Island Navy Hospital at Vallejo, California. On February 11, 1944, with fifteen non-rated personnel, I arrived at the facility.

In the receiving office, where we sat with our heavy cold weather "P" coats covering our sleeves where a "rate" would show, a Navy Captain asked the Chief who escorted us, "Any rates among these men?"

"Yes sir, one." Pointing to me the Chief said my name.

Looking over my grades from Hospital Corps School he ordered, "Send him to Imola immediately."

Ten miles north of Vallejo, Imola was a tiny community on the site of the California State Asylum for the Insane. Here an annex to the Mare Island Navy Hospital had been built. All patients were either Navy, Marine or Coast guard personnel suffering from deeply incapacitating psychotic conditions, usually brought on by having seen too much horror in combat and some from being unable to stand the stress of being totally regimented in military service. All rates and classifications were represented. Mental problems have no respect for rank. Patients ranged from the lowest, a seaman second class, to an Admiral whose dress blue uniform and hat rippled with gold braid. But in only pajamas covered by the gray and white striped hospital gown, worn by every patient, they all looked the same and we treated everyone as equal.

Of the many patients I cared for during this tour of duty I recall only two. One was an emaciated Navy kid with the lowest classification, seaman second class. He had deep set, dark circled eye sockets. The grayish pallor of his skin made him look like "warmed over death." A catatonic, he never moved, uttered a sound or looked anyplace on his own accord. He stood, sat or lay for hours in the same position in which he had last been placed. He lived in a "quiet room", a ten by ten locked cell without furnishings. All the walls and floor were thickly padded. To keep him safe he remained naked at all times because catatonics can sometimes become tangled in clothing and choke to death. He slept on the floor and one of us had to change his position every couple of hours so he wouldn't get pneumonia or hypostatic congestion caused when blood "pools in the lungs" due to total inactivity. He couldn't feed himself and all nourishment, in the form of liquefied gruel, had to be force fed by actually pushing the food down his throat with a spoon. In one of our training sessions the resident psychiatrist demonstrated the mental devastation of this case.

Standing the patient beside the podium the doctor fully extended one arm of the young man straight out to the left side of his body at shoulder height. The other he positioned fully extended upward toward the ceiling and rotated the young sailor's face as far as possible to the right side. A normal person can remain in this position only a short time. We were lectured for more than half an hour while he stood immobile as a statue. He never moved his eyes or flinched when the doctor walked silently in behind the young man and slapped two wooden rulers explosively together within an inch of and behind the patient's head. Because he wouldn't speak and give information, the cause of his condition could not be determined.

The other patient, a battle seasoned Marine sergeant, appeared to be about 30 years old. During the fighting on a Pacific island he saw more than his mind could cope with and broke down. His room had one window reinforced with steel bars and heavy gauge wire. Through it, at night he could see the glow from the many outdoor lights in the town of Napa, about a mile away.

Every few nights, while he stood looking out the window he'd start to scream as if warning a friend. Then, obviously he'd re-live the horror of the friend's death.

"George, over here, over here," he'd begin in a whisper. "Quiet or he'll spot you." Then he'd point upward and say, "O.K., now get that one over there." With a great rise of emotion and concern suddenly he'd yell, "George, don't try THAT!! Keep down, keep down, Ssshhh." The sergeant paused a moment as he turned his head from side to side as though looking for something. Then cried out, "Oh God, NO—NO, NO!! Oh George, George." Tears then poured from his eyes as he sobbed and crumpled to the floor in total devastation.

In his rare lucid moments the Marine sergeant told the doctor what happened. In his mind he continued to re-live the death of his best friend George, a sharpshooter mortally wounded, who died in his arms during the invasion of Tarawa. On patrol George, and his best friend the Marine sergeant, had the job to shoot Japanese snipers out of the tops of Palm trees in which they'd often hide to fire on our troops. The Marine sergeant spotted the enemy for George, his sharp shooting friend, by watching for puffs of smoke caused by rounds being fired from Japanese .31 caliber rifles. The psychiatrist told us grief and self-blame broke the sergeant's mind as he re-lived the last moments with his best friend George. It had been caused by his not insisting that George not do "THAT". He also hadn't physically held George down at that last moment, an action which he thought, might have prevented his best friend from doing "THAT". Because it was too painful, the psychiatrist never could get the sergeant to reveal exactly what "THAT" had been. I don't know if the young catatonic Navy man or the Marine sergeant ever recovered after they were transferred by plane from the Navy annex at Imola to the United States Public Health Service Hospital in Fort Worth, Texas.

"The Navy gets the pay" held true during my time at Imola. Every Monday and Thursday, ten of us rated corpsmen and one

Chief went along with the most incapacited patients who were flown from Oakland, California to the Hospital in Fort Worth. We prepared the patients from Imola for the flight by giving them a Peraldehyde, Retention Enema and an intra-muscular injection of Sodium Pentobarbital, each a sleep producing medication. The effect lasted about 18 hours, plenty of time to fly from Oakland to Fort Worth. We flew in the Navy version of the twin engine DC 3, called an R 4 D and always flew two planeloads out together. Each plane carried five corpsmen and 14 immobilized patients. A Chief Pharmacists Mate rode in one of the planes. On Monday he flew with the group from Imola and Thursday with those from the main hospital in Vallejo. Navy Captain, Rand, who piloted the plane in which I always flew, was the millionaire son of the founder of the well known Ingersoll-Rand Company that produced large air compressors and other heavy machinery for the war effort.

At the Oakland airport we unloaded the patients from the Navy ambulances and placed them on board the two waiting aircraft. Inside, still strapped to their stretchers, the patients were tightly secured on tiers of bunks that were solidly attached to the floor and inside fuselage of the plane, making it impossible for anything to move.

One evening after loading the planes I ended up in the wrong one. I always flew with the group of corpsmen from Imola but after loading the patients I found myself in the plane with the corpsmen from the main hospital in Vallejo. Another corpsman, Swan and I had somehow been crossed up while loading patients and we each entered the wrong plane. The engines, already started, were warming up idling noisily. The open doors and self-storing steps of both aircraft were still in the loading position. Realizing the mistake I jumped out of the wrong one and ran as fast as I could over to the door of the one I should have been in. Above the noise of the engines I shouted to the Chief Corpsman who stood in the doorway, "Hey, can I trade planes with Swan who is over here with you? I always make liberty with the guys in here from Imola and I'm over there with those Mare Island guys where Swan belongs." The Chief appeared agitated and short tempered because he wanted to pull the steps up and close the door quickly. But noticing a little hesitation I implored, "Come on Chief."

"Oh hell, O.K.," came his exasperated reply.

The Chief called Swan and told him, "Hurry up and get on over to that other plane." Out of breath from running I gasped, "Thanks" as Swan ran past me, trading planes. The exchange took only a few seconds, but it saved my life.

On the way to Fort Worth we always stopped in Flagstaff, Arizona to check patients, have lunch and refuel the aircraft. After the stop, early in the afternoon both planes took off within less than a minute of each other. Gaining altitude we flew between a familiar set of snow capped landmarks. Pointing a finger the Chief called out, "We're coming up on the San Francisco Peaks." Sitting next to and gazing from a window I watched the other plane flying below and to our right. As I continued looking it began to very slowly make a descending right hand turn. The nose kept dropping steeper and steeper. The pilot made no distress call as the plane slowly, almost lazily "peeled off" crashing with full fuel tanks in a huge ball of flame and black smoke. All on board were killed.

Scared and in disbelief I excitedly yelled to the Chief sitting on the opposite side of the cabin, "Hey, did you see that? Our other plane just crashed into that mountain." As I spoke the door to the cockpit burst open and the co-pilot appeared.

"Men, sit tight and avoid moving around. Our other unit just went down and we're returning to Flagstaff for an inspection. It could be sabotage," he warned. As he spoke Captain Rand already had banked the plane and we were on the way back to the airport.

An extensive and thorough inspection took several hours but the inspectors found nothing. The Chief, deeply affected by the tragedy, knew all the corpsmen from Mare Island, including Swan and had gone on liberty with them many times.

Later, again in the air, I went over to where he sat on a large wooden crate of medical supplies. As he leaned forward with his chin in his hands obviously deep in thought, I said, "Chief, I'm sure lucky you let me come aboard this plane, thanks. I feel awfully bad about Swan too." His chin remained cupped in his hands as he nodded in acknowledgement and we needed no more conversation.

A final board of inquiry never was able to find the cause of the crash.

After unloading the patients in Fort Worth we'd fly on to El Paso, staying overnight at a YMCA that had been taken over by the military. We arrived in mid afternoon and as a group, we'd share a taxi to Juarez, Mexico in search of "recreation". Here we'd have a few cold beers and some of the corpsmen would buy several "fifths" of Waterfill and Frazier whiskey. Used for "medicinal purposes" later back at our assigned station, they cost less than $3.00 each, compared to more than $7.00 in the States. Many corpsmen also took advantage of the low price charged by the beautiful Senoritas, only $2.00, for a relaxing session of "horizontal refreshment". Offered to the hormonally challenged sailors, the Senoritas enticed them by administering to an anatomically specific area, a few short lasting but highly effective, "feely touchy massages" specifically designed to awaken the most basic carnal instincts of any red-blooded male. The sailors figured they were getting a bargain here, because in Tijuana, at The Stockade the same session cost $3.00, a whopping increase of 50%.

Flying back to Oakland from El Paso we always stopped for fuel at Big Springs, Texas. Here, on a different flight, we had another close call. We had just lifted off and the plane's fuel tanks were full. Looking out the window I saw a lot of the 100-octane aviation gasoline pouring from under a gas cap on top of the right wing. Gushing out, the wind caught it, whipping it into a fine spray that poured like heavy fog from the back edge of the wing not far from the red-hot engine exhaust pipe that belched blue flame. Motioning for him to look outside I asked, "Hey Chief, do you think the pilot should be told about this?"

Taking a look at the fuel draining out of the tank he sprang to the locked door of the cockpit. Pounding on it with both fists he yelled, "You've got a real bad fuel leak on the right wing." The co-pilot came out, looked for a moment and rushed back to tell Captain Rand.

Returning quickly to Big Springs, on the ground a mechanic found the fuel cap hadn't been fully turned to the locked position. Just after takeoff it came loose held on only by the safety chain. The pilot told the Chief if he hadn't been told about the gasoline coming out of the tank the plane almost surely would have exploded in flight. He said this probably would have happened either when reaching cruise altitude or prior to landing when, at both times, the fuel mixture to the carburetors is changed. This often causes an imperceptible backfire that would have acted like a spark plug igniting the leaking fuel vapor, blowing the plane from the sky.

There were two major benefits working with mentally disturbed patients in the Mare Island annex at Imola. First, all corpsmen working in any Navy mental hospital were the only enlisted personnel allowed to carry their liberty card at all times. Upon arrival at Imola the head psychiatrist let us know that working with the mentally disturbed is the most difficult assignment a corpsman can be given. Only those with top grades in Hospital Corps School are eligible. He said there may be times when the pressure becomes so intense it could affect us and we ourselves could mentally "snap." Jokingly he explained, "Sometimes these people are enough to drive a person crazy." He also emphasized that if at any time during our eight hour shift we felt like we were "loosing it" to go to the doctor or nurse on duty and say you have to get away from the job. "No matter how short a time you've been on the shift, even if it's been only fifteen or twenty minutes, there will be no questions asked and no explanation will ever be required. As soon as you sign out you'll be free to go," he said. During my time at Imola, not one corpsman left his duty station and abused this privilege.

Another benefit was that we earned a lot of extra "flight pay" because we spent more than a certain minimum number of hours in the air. Most of us who knew we would eventually be assigned to active duty in the combat zone in the Pacific carried some kind of "lucky charm". With my "flight skins", the extra money, I bought a gold ring with a one-quarter carat, flawless D, investment grade diamond set between two slightly smaller ones. Calling it "my lucky diamond ring", I never took it off during the rest of my tour of duty overseas in World War II. When our youngest daughter, Yvonne, married in 1985 I surprised her by having the center stone removed from my ring, adding it to her custom made engagement band and had the two smaller stones mounted on our oldest daughter, Berniece's, black opal pendant. I hope the diamonds will bring them as much good luck as I think they brought me.

❖ SEA DUTY: FIRST ADVENTURE ❖

After serving as a medical corpsman at the annex to the Mare Island Naval Hospital in Imola for six months my request for sea duty was honored. On October 3rd, 1944 I was transferred to Astoria, Oregon to board a brand new ship, the *USS Sanborn, APA 193.* The letters, APA stand for, Attack Personnel, Amphibian. Built at the Kaiser shipyard in Vancouver, Washington and sailed down the Columbia River to Astoria by a Kaiser crew, there the Navy took her over at the commissioning ceremony on October 4th. Under her new Captain, Sydney S. Huguenin, she now officially belonged to the Navy's Pacific fleet.

Designated a C-3 hull, she weighed 10,500 tons. C-3 was a designation that she essentially had the configuration of a "cargo" vessel. However, the ship was modified to provide accommodations for 1,500 troops and some of their less heavy equipment to be used at invasion sites. Most of the time the personnel carried on board were the Marines. However, late in the war we carried some Army personnel. Twenty-four LCVP's, also known as "Higgins boats", were stowed on the main deck. They were our "Landing Craft, Vehicle/Personnel" and each could be used to carry light equipment or as many as thirty-six men to the enemy beaches during an invasion. We also carried on deck four, somewhat larger, LCM's. These were called "Landing Craft, Medium" and could carry a Sherman tank, a big truck or other fairly large equipment to enemy shores.

At the commissioning ceremony I met Byron Alfred Dary, also a rated corpsman and we quickly became best friends. The day after commissioning we sailed about seventy five miles west of Astoria on a totally calm sea while the ship underwent a three-day "shakedown" cruise. During this trial run every piece of equipment was thoroughly tested. Both boilers were brought to maximum working pressure and the propeller run from the lowest to the highest number of revolutions possible to bring the ship to its very fastest emergency rate of travel called "flank speed." It turned out to be one hundred six turns a minute giving the ship a speed of twenty-one knots, about twenty-three miles an hour. During this first cruise the ships crew of four hundred and fifty men, were given intensive instruction about how to conduct their work when on sea duty. The outside decks bristled with armament. The largest gun, a five inch thirty eight stood on the main deck at the very back end of the vessel, the "fantail". Having a special "stop" mechanism for safety reasons, it could only be pointed away from the ship, behind it or to either side. Because of its position, everyone called it "the stinger". It could be used to shoot down high-flying aircraft or to hit surface ships a mile or more away. Seven groups of "quad forties", mounted in "gun tubs" could be used to shoot at incoming aircraft about half a mile away. Ten 20-millimeter guns, used to fire at aircraft as they came close to the ship, made up the rest of our protection. On the shakedown cruise we had only two minor problems. One electricity-producing generator failed and one main propeller shaft bearing overheated. Both were malfunctions easily repaired at sea.

With the successful first cruise finished we were ordered to Seattle to take on provisions. Here we picked up tons of food and other supplies. With both of the ships huge food freezers filled as well as all the dry storage areas, we would be able stay at sea for several months. Before leaving for the combat zone in the Pacific, most of us sailors had never been to sea. For myself as well as many others, the short trip from Astoria to Seattle became a major disaster. My dad Harry, a member of the Merchant Marine, often used the expression, "Never get excited on your first cruise." On the way to Seattle I didn't get excited, but I sure did get seasick. Unfortunately, so did many others.

The open ocean rolled with long, glass smooth, high undulating hills and valleys of water called "ground swell". Each, about twenty-five feet high from bottom to top caused the ship to rock up and down from end to end. Up and down, up and down she went until I became so sick all the lunch down in my stomach suddenly came up.

On the main deck amidships, the sick bay had two fully equipped surgeries, two small isolation rooms, a tiny diet kitchen and the main hospital ward. The hospital area had port holes to let in fresh air and being in the center of the ship, it rocked much less than the fore and aft portions. Located far below decks were three well-equipped first aid stations. On the way to Seattle we practiced the "general quarters" drill. During this time each of us went to an assigned battle station. During the general quarters exercise I joined four other corpsmen and the Chief in number three station located in the prow, the peak nearest the front and deep below decks. It was the place where seasickness always became the worst. In the combat zone general quarters is called whenever enemy submarines, ships or planes become a threat. All corpsman go to their assigned medical areas and all other seamen man the guns, radios and other vital equipment.

As we sailed along on the open ocean, for the first time over the loudspeaker system came the order "Now hear this, general quarters, all hands man your battle station" followed by the announcement, "This is a drill." Then the loud clanging of the emergency bell sounded throughout the ship. Before the drill, feeling only a little nausea, I had been at my regular sea station amidships in the sick bay where the portholes let in fresh air and the rocking and pitching was minimal. But as soon as I entered my general quarters area, the number three first aid station below decks and all the watertight doors were dogged tightly closed, my nausea rapidly increased. There were no portholes here and a less than efficient blower system brought in very little fresh air. As a result my shipmates and I turned green with seasickness.

Up, up, up went the front end of the ship following the smooth roller coaster like rise of the huge ground swell. The pressure of gravity during the upward pushing motion of the ships front end made my body and legs feel like they were made of lead. Then the ship topped out giving relief for a few moments while remaining poised and steady riding the crest of the swell. But now she rapidly went down, down, down, like a fast elevator. In contrast, my body and legs now felt as light as a descending feather and everyone in the aid station became even sicker. Without portholes I couldn't see outside to get a visual check of the horizon and my body talked to me. The nerves in my leg joints and the balance system of the inner ear said, "Without that third point of reference, the horizon seen by your eyes, you will become horribly seasick, so vomit and do it a lot until your stomach is empty. Then continue to retch until nothing comes up and you're so weak you can hardly stand, much less do any work."

The acrid odor coming from the large amount of vomit and with little fresh air in the small, tightly enclosed space, worked a sickening alchemy on everyone except the Chief. Having been at sea before and knowing this would happen he wisely provided several empty five-gallon pails, plenty of white soda crackers and lots of water to combat our "Mal De Mer." The drill lasted only ten minutes but it seemed like forever. That evening, in the best Navy tradition the first time severe seasickness is expected to devastate a new crew, the cooks were ordered to prepare pork chops, dripping with grease, for supper. Soon after the meal a lot of sailors "fed the fish" plenty of good food provided to them by the ship's seasick personnel who hurried to the deck and leaned out over the side rail. That pretty well describes the first of several general quarters drills we experienced in the prow of the ship in first aid station number three.

Early in the morning each day Yeoman William "Bill" Robertson, III, the ships secretary, distributed an eight and a half by 11 sheet of paper to the Chief of each section of enlisted men and to all Officers. This "plan of the day" tells everyone in the crew what the ships movements will be that day, what to do and exactly when to do it as well as what to wear. When tied up to a dock in port, it also tells what time liberty begins for those going ashore and when all personnel must be back on board. My turn came to leave the ship while she provisioned at Pier 91 in Seattle, and I read the plan of the day carefully before going ashore. It clearly stated, "Liberty will end at 0800." This meant I had until eight o'clock the next morning before having to be back on board.

At four o'clock in the afternoon I left the ship and headed for what most normal red-blooded, sailors have in every port. Now, when I phoned her from the dock she told me her parents were visiting in Bremerton and wouldn't be back for three days. In addition, being a newlywed, every day she tracked the whereabouts of her husband, stationed on an icebreaker off the coast of Alaska, by reading the "ship movements column" published daily in the newspaper, the Seattle Post Intelligencer. When she said, "I'll be so glad to see you. I'm so lonesome here by myself. Can you come on out right away"? I thought, "Lady luck sure is smiling on me." As I rode the Greenwood avenue bus to her house I fondly recalled how we first met and had always kept "in touch".

On this evening, we went to dinner, then to "Playland", an amusement park on Aurora Avenue and I returned home with her to spend the night. Trained to always be on time, before going to bed I set the alarm for four thirty in the morning. After breakfast we lingered long together, over that "most important goodbye".

Catching the first bus running that morning on Greenwood Avenue I arrived back at Pier 91 at ten minutes before seven surprised to see the "casting off" crew on the dock making preparations to hoist the gangplank. From about a hundred yards away I yelled, "Hey wait, I've got to get aboard that ship."

"Hurry up," came the curt reply from the Boatswains mate.

Running the rest of the distance I arrived on board a few moments before the gangplank lifted.

Entering the sick bay I asked the Chief, "How come we're taking off an hour early? Won't some people be left behind?"

"No, we were lucky," he said. "All other personnel are on board. You were the only one missing. During the night, orders to the Captain were changed. We're heading out right now for San Pedro."

A few experienced men, "old salts", made up the core crew in each division. But three out of four sailors on board were greenhorns about sea duty and life aboard ship.

Fully loaded with provisions we passed through the Straits of Juan-de-Fuca and steamed southwest until about twenty miles out in open sea then turned due south toward California. By now we were used to the slight roll and the moderate up and down pitch of the ship. In a few days the feeling, as it moved under our feet, created an almost pleasant sensation. Seasickness for almost all the new crew became a thing of the past.

During mid-morning of the second day out, while steaming along using both of our boilers, an inexperienced crewman almost caused the ship to be lost. We were twenty miles off the coast of central California and with no troops or equipment on board the ship rode high in the water. On this gray, stormy day a steady, strong west wind blew and heavy rainsqualls were intermittent. Cruising at seventeen knots, suddenly the ship slowed. Nobody seemed to notice until we coasted to a stop, "dead in the water". In the sick bay where most corpsmen gathered we noticed the lights begin to dim. Then they went out. Something major had happened.

This potential for disaster had been caused by an inexperienced crewmember, working in the engine room, someone in the "black gang" as they are called, who quickly opened a pair of valves much too far letting a rush of cold water into the two boilers that were producing steam. As a result, even though the fire in the boilers continued burning at peak capacity, all the steam was "killed" and the ship bobbed helplessly on the water like a cork.

Without electrical power the radios were dead and we couldn't put out a call to the Coast Guard for help. Drifting and slowly turning end for end, we were being driven by the strong west wind toward shore a few miles away. Captain Huguenin became furious. As he stood on the bridge of his brand new command, beneath him it floated helplessly while he considered the very real danger of it being driven up on the beach and wrecked. He thought about dropping the two anchors to hold the ship in place but the water here was too deep and it would do no good because the anchor chains were too short. All he could do is order the two boilers to continue with maximum burn. With the boilers roaring flame it still would still take hours to build up enough steam to start the turbine that turned the propeller. The generators too had to come up to speed so the lights would come back on and radio communication restored. The Captain ordered the ships whistle blown every fifteen minutes so the crew could follow our progress of regaining steam. At first it didn't make a sound. Gradually, after many tests, it began to make an uninspiring noise much like the "moo" of a sick or dying cow.

As we drifted closer to shore with danger lurking in the form of undersea shoals and rocks, clearly shown on the quartermasters chart to be in the area, the Captain ordered lookouts equipped with battery-operated walkie-talkies to climb to the top of the loading masts to watch for underwater obstacles. However, everyone knew nothing could be done even if one of them saw a hazard that could sink the ship.

It took almost four hours to regain steam, turn the ship in the right direction and get under way. For many it had been a nerve-racking experience. But my Dad's advice, "Never get excited on your first cruise", served me well under stressful circumstances and it became for me a unique, first time seagoing adventure.

Captain Huguenin considered demoting the Chief of the engineering department. Being very fair, he gave only a resounding tongue lashing to the inexperienced young sailor who incorrectly turned the two water inlet valves on the boilers. He didn't demote him because it is always the responsibility of the Chief himself to oversee his men or have someone totally familiar with the task watching at all times.

There were three medical doctors in our crew.

Dr. Collentine, about 25years old and only a short time out of residency was of English and Irish descent. With light almost baby-like skin, he had barely enough whiskers to shave. He specialized in diagnosis and internal medicine.

Dr. Whalen, about 40 years old was of German and American Indian descent. His complexion always looked like he had just completed a great "California" tan. He had exceptionally black whiskers and a terrible case of "five o'clock shadow" all the time. Every whisker looked as coarse as bailing wire. Even after a good shave the blackness of the stubble beneath his skin remained very obvious. This became a source of embarrassment to him and he'd try to cover it every day by dusting large amounts of Mavis talcum powder on his face. He specialized and excelled in surgery.

Dr. Fleishner, about 64 years old was of Jewish descent. Short and balding, he came from New York where he had a lucrative practice in obstetrics and gynecology in mid-town Manhattan. Subject to "the doctors draft" until age sixty-five he had the misfortune to be called for duty at age sixty-three. Though he held the Officers rank of three-stripe Commander, he often socialized with the enlisted corpsmen spending hours in the sick bay talking, reviewing our knowledge, answering medical questions and just "hanging out". On several occasions he made the comment, "I don't know why the Navy put me here ready to go into combat where I might possibly have to treat massive traumatic wounds. I've been an obstetrician and gynecologist for thirty five years and have brought thousands of babies into the world but I've never even lanced a boil, set a bone or done any major surgery." One of the most friendly and compassionate people I've ever met, I believe deep within he must have been very lonesome for his wife and family.

The day after we lost steam off the coast of California the medical department got the first patient requiring confinement to the hospital ward. An hour before finishing the graveyard shift, about five o'clock in the morning, a young sailor named Fred came to the sick bay where I sat at the desk dozing while on duty.

"Hey," he said as he shook my shoulder, "Can you help me?"

Jolted awake I asked "What's wrong"?

"I've got this real bad pain in my right side, down here," he pointed to a spot low on his abdomen, "and it keeps getting worse."

"The doctor will be here for sick call at six o'clock. Do you think if you lie down you can wait about an hour? You'll be first on the list for him to see."

"Sure, it hurts less anyway when I'm on my side curled up."

When Dr. Whalen arrived to conduct sick call he examined Fred and made a tentative diagnosis of appendicitis. Craig Hardegree, our first class rated corpsman and laboratory technician, also arrived and drew a phial of blood from Fred's arm. Making a smear of the blood on a glass slide and staining it, under the microscope it contained twenty seven thousand white blood cells per cubic centimeter instead of the normal nine thousand. This test, along with other symptoms confirmed Dr. Whalen's diagnosis.

By seven o'clock our first surgical procedure began and by eight Fred, minus his infected appendix, lay in bed in the hospital ward waking up from the unpleasant smell of the ether anesthetic.

In WWII, a Navy man who underwent an appendectomy had to remain in bed for seven days. During the following three he could get up and go anyplace so long as a rated corpsman went along to "eyeball" his every move.

As soon as the ship arrived in San Pedro our schedule of liberty began. Fred's turn came on the eighth day after surgery and as his assigned rated corpsman I had to go with him no matter where he went. He chose to go to Tijuana, Mexico. When we arrived there he asked a sailor walking by, "Hey, where's the best whorehouse in town"?

The reply, "Hell, that's an easy question. You just go right down this here street for a couple blocks. You'll see it. It's called the Stockade."

When we arrived Fred lost no time picking out a young and pretty Senorita to accommodate him. Perhaps 5 feet 2 inches tall, she appeared to be about 18 years old. She had a nice smile, lush red lips, sparkling brown eyes and a most attractive figure. During their negotiations he explained to her that because of his recent surgery I had to stay in eyeball view of him at all times and she agreed. In one corner of her room I made myself comfortable in an old but plush chair while Fred eagerly conducted business on the bed.

The room, dimly lighted by one bare fifteen-watt bulb hanging from the ceiling by partially frayed wires, had no windows. Amazingly, the young girl had almost an entire wall made into a shrine, complete with many statues and pictures, dedicated to Jesus and the Virgin Mary. In a corner several devotional candles, each in a red glass holder burned, shedding a soft flickering glow on the walls. The incongruity struck me seeing these things while hearing the rhythmic noise of the bed and the moans and groans of Fred and the young girl who vainly attempted to bring his activity to a successful conclusion. Sitting there I wondered for a moment what in her life made it necessary for such a pretty girl to turn to prostitution, though I suspected poverty had to be a factor.

Suddenly Fred turned to me, "Gene, you've got to leave. I can't finish up here with you in the room." I reminded him my orders were to eyeball him at all times, and I'd get court-martialed if he got hurt. But both he and the girl insisted that I go out in the hall to wait.

Whispering she told me, "When you in here he no comeee, he no comeee. It waste my time. You go, you go." As I left I made sure I closed the door behind me hard enough to be heard.

In the hall a few minutes later Fred, smiling and relaxed, joined me. "O.K., let's get back to the ship," he chuckled. He didn't know that as soon as I closed the door loudly I quietly re-opened it enough to be able to eyeball him, thus keeping my assigned voyeuristic vigil as required by Navy regulations.

Before departing for overseas everyone in the crew had one

more night of liberty. On our last night, my best friend Dary and I planned to go down town in San Pedro. Mistakenly, we got on a train that ran past the town and non-stop on to San Diego. Red in color, it had several cars and used electricity from a catenary wire and wheel high above the tracks. On the trip it ran about ninety miles an hour, which to me seemed too fast. Looking out a window as we sped past a huge junkyard we saw piles of wrecked cars and trucks at least five stories high placed there by the huge crane standing close by. One special stack caught our attention. It consisted only of blue and gray electric trolley cars that used to run in towns of the area on rails in the middle of the street. The city of San Pedro and other communities in the area recently took them out of service and replaced them with rubber tired gasoline driven buses that pulled over to the curb to pick up passengers. The old trolleys had been inexpensive to operate, were efficient and still appeared to be serviceable yet had been discarded in one monstrous heap. Dary and I agreed "such a waste."

In San Diego in a bar downtown we happened to meet Don Street, another corpsman from our ship. "I'm goin' over to Tijuana and get laid. You guys wanna' come along? I hear there are some real gorgeous girls over there at a place called The Stockade." I told him I'd been there a few days ago with Fred and that the information he'd been given about the gorgeous girls was right. Dary and I agreed to go with him.

The Stockade had a nicely appointed, open air Cantina and served very cold Ballentines extra strong, 6 percent export beer. Sitting at a table we began quenching our thirst. Several lovely Senoritas came over asking if they could be of service. After drinking several extra strength beers in less than an hour we were feeling happy and uninhibited. Street saw a beautiful young "hostess" who attracted his attention.

"Hey guys, look at that. Man, she sure looks good to me." He called her to the table and quickly made a deal. As they walked arm in arm toward her room, over his shoulder he called out cheerfully, "See you soon, and I'll be a lot more relaxed." Dary and I ordered another beer and nursed it along. Fifteen minutes later Street returned and gave a detailed report about the many and varied talents the beautiful Senorita demonstrated for him.

"Boy, I'll remember THAT for a long time. Geeze, you guys should try her. She'll give you something you've never had before." Hearing this last combination of "buzz words" in my slightly alcoholic fog I thought of a joke I once heard.

"Hey Street, did you ever hear this one?" I asked. Not waiting for his reply I continued. "There were two old sailors walking on Bourbon Street in New Orleans one evening. From a balcony a young lady of the night called down. Hey boys, come on up and I'll give you something you've never had before."

One old sailor turned to the other, "Geeze, ain't that a shame. The poor girl—she must have leprosy." Street and Dary gave an approving chuckle.

The young girl Street chose earlier approached again. In great detail she told Dary and me about the many varied and wonderful pleasures of the flesh she could provide for only $3.00. Having just heard an enthusiastic first hand account from Street coupled with the effect of the extra strong 6 percent beer and knowing there would be no more liberty before heading for the combat zone and because she smelled so nice while looking so beautiful, I soon entered her room for a rendezvous.

Dary and Street were waiting at the table when I returned and now Dary went with her to accomplish the task she laid before him. Relaxed and "feeling no pain", as soon as Dary returned we headed back for San Diego and found a bar that had great ambiance with good music played by a live band. Here we ordered mixed drinks. Their effect, coupled with that of the 6 percent beer we drank at the Stockade, hit us with a vengeance.

We became melancholy because this would be our last liberty in the States and we got roaring drunk. Unbelievably drunk!! So drunk we could hardly walk or find our way to the station to catch the same red colored train to take us back to San Pedro. Only because of some miracle we caught the last one. It seemed like everyone else also caught this last tightly packed, overcrowded train. With standing room only, in a drunken fog, for me the ride became a nightmare. I think the driver either wanted to get home in a hurry or he ran late because of waiting longer than usual at the station in San Diego for stragglers. In any event, someone told me later, he drove the train nearly one hundred miles an hour. It swayed crazily, rattled and creaked roaring into the night so fast I had to sink to the floor. I couldn't stand up even when holding on to the edge of a seat. Riding on the floor, to me it felt like the train surly would de-rail and leap off into space. Back at the station in San Pedro, I was one sailor eager and more than ready to get off. The biggest reason for wanting to leave quickly is, because of the confined space, while I lay crumpled on the floor, I became nauseated and vomited all over myself and on the legs of the uniforms and into the shoes of at least two markedly disturbed fellow sailors.

The next night, under cover of darkness in a convoy of fifteen ships, we left San Pedro heading for Honolulu.

Byron Dary, my best friend, came from a wealthy family. They lived in an exclusive neighborhood on Lake Geneva in Darien, Wisconsin. He and I were transferred to the *APA 193* at Astoria, Oregon at the same time and stood at attention together during the ships commissioning ceremony. He told me that before joining this crew he had made the initial invasion of Normandy, landing on Omaha beach with Eisenhower's forces on D-day, June 6, 1944, giving medical attention to injured Navy personnel. Although Omaha beach sustained the most casualties of the invasion and many people around him were being killed or wounded, he never got a scratch. He made his way onto the beach accompanied by a Navy physician. At one point, as they were being pounded by the deadly German 88 cannons located on the cliffs above, they both dropped to the sand keeping their heads down. As they lay there waiting for the shelling to slow or stop Dary heard a "thump" and a short gasp next to him. A few moments later when he looked he could see the doctor had been killed instantly. A four-foot length of jagged metal falling from the sky had torn through his chest like a spear, pinning him to the sand of Omaha beach.

As we left San Pedro that night Dary and I stood together at the rail of the ship watching the harbor lights and others of the surrounding area blink out one by one as the curvature of the earth obscured them. For a long time he remained silent, looking straight ahead over the water as though reminiscing. Then he turned to me and quietly said, "Gene, I'm never going to see the lights of those fair shores again." Turning quickly from the rail he waved, "Goodnight, see you in the morning."

❖ ON THE WAY TO WAR ❖

On the way to Honolulu, at sea we enjoyed perfect weather. The gun crews used this opportunity for target practice using live ammunition. A special ship in the convoy carried radio controlled, "drone" airplanes. Launched and flown past our ship, each time from a different direction and at various altitudes, the "quad 40" gun crews manning each of the seven battle stations, tried to shoot them down. It proved to be much needed practice. As they tried to gain experience for use in future enemy action not one of the 40-millimeter guns registered a hit.

In addition, a two-engine plane sent from the Miramar Naval Air Station in San Diego flew quite low over us. Trailing far behind was a long target made of heavy white canvas used for the 20-millimeter gun crews to shoot at. Their bullets were dipped in various colored wax. When one hit the white cloth the wax melted and the color rubbed off as the bullet passed through. Each crew's ammunition had a different color so if a target was hit it could easily be determined which gun scored. When the tow plane returned to Miramar, the number of holes and the colors were recorded and the results radioed back to our ship. After the first practice run above the *APA 193*, only five holes ringed with color-coded wax were recorded. Though thousands of rounds of 20-millimeter ammunition were fired, all five hits were the same color–scored by one "lucky" gunner.

To give the 5-inch gun crew practice, a DDE, a destroyer escort ship, towed a surface target slowly across the water about two thousand yards away as our crew fired shell after shell. Every projectile missed. However, they didn't miss everything. A greenhorn on the gun crew "cut the fuse", that is, set the timer on the tip of one projectile too short causing it to explode with a huge puff of greasy looking black smoke only a few feet after leaving the barrel. Our "fantail", the back end of the ship, received a shower of shrapnel and two crewmen were slightly wounded in the legs and feet. This could be called the Navy version of "shooting yourself in the foot." Fortunately, the wounds were minor and after first aid and bandaging everyone, including one wiser and more careful fuse cutter, returned to "the stinger" for more target practice.

Continuing to steam toward Hawaii, in the sick bay things became routine. Each morning at six o'clock ships personnel having medical complaints, were checked by a physician. Other than the few shrapnel wounds, the complaints usually included sore throat, cough, rash, headache and constipation.

However, two days before we arrived in Honolulu things became far from routine. Don Street didn't come to see the doctor that morning. Instead, acting secretive and sneaky he came to the medical laboratory later in the day to see Craig Hardegree, our first class corpsman and lab technician. Street, also a knowledgeable rated corpsman, worried about a small sore that, during the past few days, gradually appeared on his penis. The lesion he showed to Hardegree had a crater-like center and raised edges that were red and irritated. In the crater lay a tiny drop of crystal clear, semi-sticky fluid.

I had the duty that day in the sick bay. Hardegree called me to the lab a short distance down the passageway to look at the sore. Nodding toward Street he said, "Curnow, if he has what I think he has you'll have to 'write him up'. It also means he'll get a bad conduct discharge if I'm right." As we three stood just outside the lab door, each an experienced and rated corpsman, we suspected the worst and Street became visibly distressed.

In the lab Hardegree lit an alcohol-burning lamp. To the microscope he attached the Darkfield adapter and prepared a clean glass slide. He then passed a small platinum wire loop through the alcohol flame until it glowed red and became sterile. Letting it cool a few moments he drew it through the clear liquid of the lesion gathering some to smear on the slide.

Hardegree, a six foot four tall, gentle Texan always spoke softly. A good Southern Baptist, he had completed three years as a pre-medical student at Texas Christian University and he never swore or used bad language. Bending over the microscope he looked at the slide and jumped back like he'd been hit with a sledgehammer. Then he loudly uttered two words, instantly giving away the diagnosis. The words were, "Chick-uun sheee-it!!" Turning toward us he continued, "Street, you've got primary syphilis. Geeze, I feel like I've been pole axed."

Embarrassed by his outburst Hardegree quietly said, "Lookee at this you guys." Street looked then I looked. Brilliantly back lighted like tiny silver barber poles rotating on a field of black velvet while dancing around and around beneath the lens of the microscope, were thousands of spirochetes, Treponema Palidum. Street obviously had contracted it at the Stockade in Tijuana from the beautiful Senorita Dary, Street and I had each paid $3.00 for a few moments of pleasure. The same one he spoke of so enthusiastically and perhaps prophetically when he told us two things "She can give you something you've never had before" and "I'll remember THAT for a long time." On both counts, he was right.

I asked Street if he'd used one of the condoms in the prophylactic kit we were offered when we went on our last liberty in Tijuana. He said, "Hell no. Using one of them damn things is like washing your feet with your socks on."

"Didn't you take a wet prophy when we got back to the ship?"

"Naw, I was too tired. Besides, that young girl looked so clean and her perfume smelled so good I figured she wouldn't have V.D."

Street knew on our last liberty I too had a rendezvous with the same girl. "Did you use a condom?" he asked.

"Of course, why do you think I took the kit along?"

My mind went back a long time ago to Boot Camp. Before we were allowed to go on our first liberty after 13 weeks of confinement, we were shown a movie. Its name, "She may look clean, BUT, V.D!!" The film drilled into us to always pick up, carry and use the prophylactic kit provided at no charge to all sailors leaving a ship or the gate of a Navy base on the way to town. Each kit contained two Trojan brand condoms, a small tube of mercuric oxide ointment to prevent *Lymphogranuloma Venerum* and a washcloth wet with a solution of non-stinging, "tamed" Iodine with which to wash away various other germs. These kits were provided at the quarterdeck of the *USS Sanborn* and everybody was urged to take one before going down the gangplank on liberty. I did, and I used it. Street did not and would pay a terrible price.

That afternoon I made, in triplicate, the report, "Active syphilis on Board" and the following morning at sick call handed a copy to the doctor on duty and delivered one to the Executive Officer, Mr. Schwartz. The third copy went into Street's medical record, his H-8. Confined to one of the ship's isolation wards he spent the rest of the trip to Hawaii alone except for someone bringing him meals and medication. Dr. Collentine started an intravenous drip of *Salvorsan*, Ehrlich's "Silver Bullet" (also called Preparation 606). Unfortunately, this medication is extremely destructive to flesh causing extreme pain, disfiguration and sloughing if even a small amount gets out of the vein while being administered. The flesh dies, rots and falls off within only a day or two exposing tendons, large arteries, veins and bone at the site of the accidental spill under the injection site. By the time we arrived in Honolulu two days later, Street's median cubital vein in both elbows had leaked and the inside of the joints became visible and were nearly destroyed. In addition, the Navy doesn't look kindly on anyone who contracts syphilis in wartime. The penalty is a Bad Conduct Discharge, a BCD. After the war no G.I. Bill, low cost life insurance, housing or business loans or 10 point Civil Service job preference would be given a sailor with a BCD.

As I watched Street leave the ship, despondent and remorseful accompanied by two burley Shore Patrol personnel I thought to myself, "Street, you should have washed your feet with your socks on." Taken to the Navy hospital in Honolulu, no one on board our ship ever heard from him.

The built in radio system on the *USS Sanborn*, to which we listened for news and entertainment, picked up both short wave and standard broadcast. Far at sea, only short wave could be received. In 1944 the quality of it left much to be desired. It sounded like a rainstorm echoing and swooshing over and over again, fast then slowly, as though it came from the bottom of an empty 50-gallon steel drum. Two days before arriving in Honolulu the radioman switched the sound system to "standard broadcast". Beautiful, clear sounding Hawaiian music drifted throughout the ship and the deep, mellow voice of an announcer intoned, "You are listening to KGU, Honolulu." An hour later the radioman switched to another station, KGMB. What a thrill forty eight hours later to see Diamond Head gradually seem to rise out of the sea as we approached Oahu. I could hardly wait to swim at world famous Waikiki beach but Dary wanted to go to a movie that day so I went to the beach by myself. I found the water here warm, shallow and almost as flat as a lake. Wading out for at least a quarter of a mile it came up only to my belly button. It seemed far enough and to return to shore I dropped in and began to swim on my back. Watching the cotton like clouds drifting above in the blue of the Hawaiian sky and thrilled by my good fortune to be swimming at Waikiki, at this time without a care in the world I back-paddled lazily toward shore.

One afternoon while crossing the main street, Kalakaua Avenue, coming toward me I saw someone I'd been with in boot camp in San Diego. Of Armenian descent, I always thought he had a strange sounding last name, Shekerjian.

"Curnow, what are you doing here?" he greeted. I asked him the same thing.

"I'm a film processor. The Navy has taken over Kodak of Hawaii and that's where I work. How'd you like to see some of the movies using the new color film the Navy cameramen have now?"

At the Kodak building we sat in a dimly lighted room as he ran two, one hundred foot reels of sixteen-millimeter film in color but without sound. The combat film showed the invasion by the Marines at Tarawa. Uncensored and never shown to the public, it was graphic, gruesome and horrible. It showed individual Marines equipped with flamethrowers and hand grenades, drive Japanese soldiers from underground bunkers then shower them with the hell fire of Napalm, jellied gasoline or blow them to bits with grenades. As the enemy soldiers dropped to the ground writhing in agony, obviously being burned alive, their mouths were open wide as they screamed, silent on the screen, in searing agony. The moment they quit moving another Marine stepped forward and shot each one in the head with a .45 caliber automatic pistol. Some hearts were continuing to beat and geysers of bright red blood gushed from the bullet holes blasted in their skulls. In vivid color, it became almost unbearable to watch. In silence I hoped I'd never be exposed to such horrible conditions in combat.

In 1944 there were only two hotels on Waikiki beach. The famous, pink colored Royal Hawaiian and the one made with white stucco, the Moana. Late one morning as I walked up the front steps of the Moana, down the steps at the same moment stepped my Uncle, Captain Joe Smith.

My dad Harry's younger Brother, he was one of United Air Lines most experienced pilots and on loan to the Military Air Transport Command (MATS), for the duration of the war. He flew the C-87, a cargo-carrying version of the four-engine Lockheed B-24 Liberator bomber. Stripped of guns and bomb racks and all other military equipment, his route was from Mills field in South San Francisco to Brisbane, Australia. He carried critical supplies for General MacArthur and his staff prior to the island hopping sweep up the Pacific and on to victory in Japan. After the war Joe told me that some of the "critical supplies" came in cases of 12 and had names like "Chivas Regal" in the purple flannel sack with the gold colored drawstring on top and "Haig and Haig" in the pinch bottle. "Of course the big brass and their top aids needed to have the finest Bourbon or Scotch in order to do their best work to win the war."

On the way to and from Australia, one of the places Joe

stopped overnight to rest and have the plane serviced and refueled was Honolulu. After lunch he took me to see his room. One of the best in the hotel at that time, a corner room on the third floor, it overlooked Waikiki beach.

"How much does this room cost?"

"It's $6.00 a night."

On the small lamp table beside the bed I noticed a book, *Island in the Sky*, I think the author was Ernie Gann, a personal friend of Joe's. Joe told me he read some of it every night before going to sleep. This impressed me and showed the dedication he had for his job. Even though at this time he held the number two place among all living airline pilots in the world for number of hours in the air, (Hamilton Lee, also a United Airlines pilot held first place). Joe still read stories about airplanes.

Both of us were in the military, subject to be sent for duty anywhere in the world. So before we said goodbye I asked, "Joe, what do you think the odds were for you and me to meet at this moment in time, in this place in the world, on the steps of one of only three hotels in this city?"

Shaking his head he smiled, "Pretty slim Gene, pretty slim."

During our stay in Honolulu, on liberty my best friend Dary and I sometimes walked several miles to the residential areas. Here Hawaiian people still lived in grass shacks, many near the smaller beaches a few miles from Waikiki. If we heard music coming from inside we'd stop to listen. Many times the people would see us, come out and invite us into the yard where we'd sit and enjoy their singing.

Dary was a music enthusiast. "You know, these are the true and original songs of Hawaii we're hearing. It's not like that stuff on the radio or in the bars downtown. I never thought I'd ever be so lucky and get to hear anything like this."

Every home had at least two people singing and many homes had only two musicians playing. One picked the guitar and one strummed the ukulele. Sometimes we'd get lucky and there'd be three players, two guitars and a ukulele. The ukulele always played the melody and guitars filled in the background with richly sounding runs and chords. For the most part the rhythm was slow and the singer's voices blended with melody and countermelody. These people were happy Hawaiians playing music and singing songs while leisurely enjoying life.

On December 22nd we were ordered to the Island of Maui to take on board some of the two thousand five hundred men and part of their equipment, a contingent of the 4th Marine Division. There were no docking facilities available from which to load so the men and all their equipment were brought from the shore to the ship on large motorized barges called "lighters". Waves and swells, about fifteen feet high made it very difficult and dangerous to get anything aboard the ship that day. The big barges raised and lowered, rapidly following the motion of each wave. When a person thought something would be "here" it suddenly moved to "there", far above or below where it had been moments before. To keep our APA from being damaged large "fenders", made from worn out tires wound with thick rope, were placed between the ship and the barge.

One of our deck gang put a fender, suspended by a long rope, over the side and began adjusting it to be sure it hung in the right place to give protection beneath the overhang of the afterdeck. Leaning out he extended his right arm downward to pull on the rope and correctly align the fender. Just then the barge came rushing up and his arm was caught between its rail and the hull of the ship. Severed instantly between his elbow and shoulder, the lifeless arm dropped into the water below. At that moment for him the war ended. A hell of a way to get one but it proved to be his "going home" wound. Ironically, because his wound was not caused by enemy action he was not eligible to be awarded a Purple Heart medal.

Fully loaded with some of the Marines from the 4th division and their equipment the *APA 193* remained in the harbor at Lahina three more days. The troops stayed on board but as members of the ships crew we were granted liberty. In WWII the Navy emphasized two expressions for all personnel and every sailor and Marine was to pay full attention to them. They were, "Loose lips sink ships" and "The slip of a lip can sink a ship."

Imagine the anger, surprise and dismay Dary and I felt when we walked into the lobby of the Pioneer hotel in Lahina one afternoon. Hanging on the wall was a large map of the Pacific. Someone had stuck a big red headed pin in it piercing an island in the volcano group called Iwo Jima. With a string they tied a piece of cardboard to the pin and on it wrote, "The next invasion for the 4th Marine Division." Almost at the same moment we both exclaimed, "How the hell could any son of a bitch be such a goddamned fool and put this up for everybody, including spies, to see?"

We were angry, we were bitter and we had a right to be. We thought of tearing the map and pin off the wall but were afraid we'd get in trouble and possibly be demoted and loose our rate so we left without doing anything.

With the Marines on board we headed for Saipan, an island in the Marianas group that U.S. forces invaded on June 13, 1944 and had taken. Here we disembarked the members of the 4th Division but kept their equipment on board.

We remained at anchor, "hanging on the hook", in the harbor for fifty-six days experiencing humidity and boredom while waiting for orders. Every day we were encouraged to go swimming along side the ship for exercise so we'd stay physically fit. The crew lowered the gangplank making it easy for us to enter the water. Jumping from the main deck, about three stories high was dangerous and forbidden, but a few daredevils did it anyway. Three Higgins boats were put in the water and several lengthy rope "lifelines", fitted with cork floats were strung out behind them. If anyone got tired and needed a little help he could signal a Higgins boat by waving one hand high above his head then grab a rope when the boat came by and be towed back to the gangplank to rest. The constant speed of the current always pulled us seaward and we were unable to make any headway swimming against it to return to the ship. As a result, the Higgins boats worked like busy mother hens as they again and again returned swimmers to the gangplank or the area beside the ship. It amazed me how easy it was to swim in the added buoyancy of salty ocean water. With very little effort I thought I could stay afloat almost forever. Thousands of sailors from the many other ships in the harbor also swam daily and no one ever reported seeing a shark.

Given liberty every third day we'd be taken in one of the boats to the recreation area on the island. Other Marines earlier had put up a large Quonset hut here thickly insulated with shredded Redwood bark. They added a large capacity refrigeration unit to keep it very cold inside and hundreds of cases of Coca Cola and beer were stored in it. Near it they poured a big slab of cement over which they placed a patio cover for shade. Chairs and tables with cheerfully colored large beach umbrellas were also provided. Each of us were given two cans of ice cold beer, Ballentines 6 percent export and a frosty Coca Cola in the original old-fashioned clear glass bottle that in those days held only six ounces. Dary always drank his two beers and the Coke. I drank only Coke and traded my beer to others to get two extra Colas. We weren't supposed to, but I took the two extras back to the ship hidden in the medical bag I had to carry in the war zone even when off duty. As Dary and I walked toward the dock to catch the boat and return to the APA, a short distance ahead on the trail we noticed two sailors approaching each other from opposite directions. One had just got off a boat and was heading for liberty. Totally sober, he walked toward the recreation area. The other had just come off liberty and was headed back to the dock to return to his ship. Talking loudly to himself, he was "roaring drunk", staggering almost aimlessly along the path toward the dock. A big, tall, raw-boned kid, we decided he must be from Texas by listening to his drawl. We wondered how he could get enough of the rationed beer to be so drunk. The sailor walking silently up the path was smaller. They approached each other and slowed. Neither surrendered an inch. The surface on each side of the sand path was made of the same semi-soft material and nothing would be either gained or lost by momentarily stepping off from it. About a foot from each other they stopped. The sober sailor got ready to speak. The raw boned Texan clenched a massive right hand. Then he threw an uppercut that could have floored a mule. His victim seemed to lift a foot into the air as the up-rushing punch landed squarely on his jaw and he landed unconscious off to one side of the path. The drunken aggressor slurred, "That there's fouh nothin', ya see. So juss you watch out." He then staggered on his way in an alcoholic fog continuing to mumble. How he got enough beer to get roaring drunk is still a mystery.

❖ THE REALITY OF WAR AND FIRST BLOOD ❖

On board the *APA 193* at anchor in the harbor at Saipan on February 8, 1945, I had my twentieth birthday. Sometimes while on duty in the sick bay I'd write a letter home. When writing that night I realized that twice during 1945 if the day, month and year were written using only their numbers they would line up, all in consecutive order. The dates were, 1-23-45 for January 23rd and 12-3-45 for December 3rd.

Most evenings when not on duty I'd go into the dental office next to the sick bay where the dental assistant, Bill Swanberg hung out. From Montana, and married, he had graduated from Law school. But as a conscientious objector, he wouldn't accept a commission because as an officer he'd be required to carry a gun. For this reason he volunteered to join the Navy and become a non-combatant medical corpsman and a technician in the dental department. He enjoyed playing chess and his game board folded and locked together when not in use. If anything interrupted our game, with it closed every piece in play would remain securely in place. For those not expert, chess is a slow game and since we both were in this category we did well together.

On board the ship the sick bay had a refrigerator with a small freezer compartment that made ice cubes. On the evenings when we'd play the game, though it was not allowed, one of us would "liberate" a couple of trays full and take them to the dental office. Here Swanberg would empty the ice into the small sink to cover my two Cokes and his one can of beer. In the oppressive heat and humidity the ice cold drinks were a welcome treat. In her letters, Swanberg's wife always included the daily column about chess cut from the Helena, Montana newspaper. It included illustrations and the position of the chessmen and a theoretical problem that, for example, might state: "Checkmate in six moves." We'd try again and again to figure which moves to use. Most of the time we failed but had a lot of fun trying which lessened the monotony of our bleak existence. Fortunately, on the exact reverse side of the newspaper clipping the solution to the chess problem always appeared. When we'd finally give up, turn it over and look at it we'd feel a little stupid because neither of us had thought of the six correct moves. A game could last for weeks because we'd play several hours then close the board locking the chessmen in place enabling us to continue the same game later. It provided many hours of relaxation but neither Swanberg nor I became good at it.

Day and night the heat and humidity on board the ship, as we lay at anchor in the harbor at Saipan, were stifling. The ship had no air conditioning and the fans inside the ductwork brought in only the ambient air from the deck area. For the sailors whose bunks were deep inside the hull, rest was almost impossible. The Captain allowed some to sleep "topside", on deck as long as all bedding was returned to our bunks by five o'clock in the morning. Twice a week, Monday and Thursday, we were required to remove the cover and drape the bare mattress over the ships rail in the hot sun attempting to dry it out. This became a waste of time because, even in the sunshine, the humidity allowed very little moisture to evaporate. As a result we slept on damp, moldy smelling bedding for the fifty-six days we remained in the harbor.

Saipan and Tinian next to it, had huge airfields. Hundreds of the newest Boeing, four engine B-29 super fortresses were stationed here and many more were about two hundred miles south on Guam. At raid time the planes from Guam joined those from Saipan and Tinian. From their rendezvous point directly over us, with full bomb loads they roared away each to supposedly hit Tokyo or other cities in Japan. Many of us outside on deck stood watching in awe. At various altitudes and in "V" shaped formation, to me they looked like gaggles of giant thundering geese. Whenever a one thousand-plane flight came over, because of the way they were "stacked" at different altitudes, the sun above our ship became almost blotted out and for a few moments we stood in the relative coolness of their shadow. As we watched and admired them, "scuttlebutt", the ships gossip, said that some were not going to Japan. A short time later we would find this to be true.

Uncle Joe's mother, Grandma Smith wrote that he now flew

the four engine C-54 airplane bringing supplies to Saipan. One day Dary and I hitch hiked to the airfield to see if Joe might be scheduled to come in. We just missed him. His plane had been unloaded fifteen minutes before we arrived and he had taken off to return to the Philippines. But, just like when we met in Honolulu, having come so close to seeing him again here in the war zone, made this a small world.

After anchoring for fifty-four days orders came to bring back on board the Marines of the Fourth Division we brought to Saipan from Maui. Then on February 17, 1945 we left the harbor to join a large convoy steaming north. There were APA's, 10,500 ton Attack Personnel Amphibians, that carried Marines and some of the lighter equipment while AKA's, 12,000 ton Attack Cargo Amphibians carried their larger equipment. There were also oil tankers, destroyers, submarine tenders and many other types of support vessels. Along the way we rendezvoused with hundreds of ships from Guam, Hawaii, Ulithi, the Philippines and the west coast of the United States. The red headed pin, with the cardboard sign dangling from it by a string, stuck in the map of the Pacific that Dary and I saw and had angered us in the lobby of the Pioneer hotel in Lahina, proved correct. "Iwo Jima" in fact became "the next invasion for the 4th Marine Division." Many of the B-29's in the one thousand plane raids we saw over Saipan were diverted to bomb the island every day for seventy-two days hoping to minimize Japanese resistance or even cause them to surrender soon after we'd come ashore. General Howland M. Smith, the Marine General in charge of the invasion, thought the Island would be "secured" in ten days.

To sharpen and speed the response of the ships crew, so orders would be carried out almost without thinking, general quarters drills came often on the two-day northbound trip. Always a surprise, they generally fell into the category of being a nuisance. When hearing the ships loud speaker system blare, "Now hear this. General quarters. All hands man your battle station" followed by, "this is a drill" and the loud clanging of the warning bell, we'd usually walk lazily toward our assigned area. The life belts of the corpsmen on duty were stowed on top of the foul weather gear locker in the wide hallway outside of the sick bay. Each had the name of the owner stenciled clearly on it in bold, black, waterproof letters. The first thing we'd do walking past the locker on our way to our battle station was pick up our belt and snap it snugly around our waist. It could be inflated by mouth through a rubber tube or by pressing together two small levers that punctured a pair of replaceable compressed carbon dioxide gas cylinders. These new type life belts, when inflated, could easily keep the head of any size man above water.

Steaming north, time and again we heard the voice make the same announcement until it became routine and meant nothing. But things got different about ten o'clock in the morning of February 18th.The voice once more blared throughout the ship, "Now hear this, General quarters. All hands man your battle station", this time followed very loudly and most urgently by the clearly emphasized words. "THIS IS NO DRILL. I REPEAT, THIS IS NOT A DRILL!!"

It took only a moment for everyone to suddenly become hyper energized. Our lazy walk instantly changed to a run and everyone's eyes widened with apprehension. All unnecessary chatter stopped as we rushed grim faced to our station. In the excitement someone grabbed the Chief's life belt. When he reached for it expecting it would be in the usual place, it was missing and there were no extras.

The cause of the authentic general quarters command came because a sailor on board a destroyer in the convoy had picked up on his Sonar set, the "pinging" sound bouncing back to him off of the iron hull an enemy submarine. Destroyers and destroyer escorts raced like hounds after a fox trying to pinpoint its location, but it escaped.

The combination of excitement and fright brought home to each of us, for the first time, that we were participants in a real shooting and killing war. When the "all clear" sounded the corpsmen and the Chief all returned to the sick bay. Looking around at everyone he bellowed, "Who the hell took my life belt?"

Keith, one of the corpsmen had it and embarrassed, held it

toward the Chief. Trying to explain he said, "I'm sorry Chief, but after the drill we just had before this one I left my belt in my sleeping compartment and that's three decks below. When I heard the words **"this is not a drill"** I knew I didn't have time to go get it so I panicked and grabbed yours as I ran past the locker."

Giving Keith a well-deserved tongue lashing the Chief asked, "What if we'd been torpedoed and had to go overboard? Do you realize a life belt might be the only thing that could save a man?" He continued, "Keith, I'll give you this one because it's your first time at sea. But don't you ever pull such a stupid trick again."

That afternoon the Chief, a prudent man, made himself a one-foot square plaque from some hardwood he found in the carpenter shop and coated it with white weatherproof enamel. After it dried, on it he stenciled in large upper case letters using black waterproof ink, "LIKE HELL IT'S YOURS. PUT IT BACK." He signed it, Chief Moore. Over these words he applied two coats of clear, waterproof, spar varnish. Then, with a small chain through a metal loop, he hooked the plaque to his lifebelt where it remained for the duration of the war.

In darkness, at four o'clock in the morning on February 19, 1945, reveille sounded. After getting dressed everyone on board was given an unusually good breakfast, steak and eggs. There was no limit on how many steaks each person could have and I saw a lot of sailors and Marines eat as many as three. Everyone knew this was the morning of the invasion. For some the meal was just an unusually good breakfast. For many, it would be their last. After eating Dary and I went out on deck where we saw huge flashes of light and heard deep rumbling sounds coming from the area of Iwo Jima, the island ahead. As our ship continued the approach we saw the Battleship *USS Missouri BB 63*, the largest and newest of the Iowa Class, firing her 16-inch guns for the first time, in anger. She fired salvo after salvo, each consisting of three one-ton high explosive shells against the well-fortified Japanese positions at the base of Mt. Suribachi on the south end of the island. Every time she'd fire a salvo, the "kick" moved the battleship sideways 45 feet.

As our APA came closer, in the dim light before dawn, our eyes easily followed the red-hot shells arcing gracefully toward their targets hitting with explosions that shook both the earth and surrounding water. One salvo hit either an ammunition or fuel dump. Jagged tongues and billows of brilliant orange and yellow flame shot in all directions. Some, almost as high as the mountain, lit the sky. It looked as though the most massive 4th of July fireworks in the world exploded in front us.

Later, in daylight, our eyes were still able to follow the projectiles fired from the other battleships in the area. But now each salvo looked to me like three fat black bumblebees flying side by side in the air arcing toward their goal.

Close to the island our ship slowed, stopped and dropped anchor not far behind the battleship *USS Iowa*, BB 62. She stood off the center of the island on the east side lobbing hundreds of shells that shredded the beach where we would go ashore a few hours later. Roaming close to shore, special ships, equipped with massive arrays of five inch rocket launchers also pounded the full length of the beach and the first few hundred yards inland, with thousands of rounds of high explosives in an effort to destroy as much resistance as possible.

Nothing about the invasion of Iwo Jima would be easy. To coordinate the unloading of the Marines of the invasion force from the many Attack Transports became a monumental task. The choppy, wind whipped water had swells of eight to ten feet. Many Marines and combat corpsmen climbing down the debarkation nets draped over the sides of the APA's, had trouble getting into the Higgins boats waiting alongside. The Coxswains who drove these invasion craft tried to hold them as steady as possible next to the ship. But as the waves rose and fell a lot of men getting ready to step away from the net and into the boat found it had quickly dropped out from under them. Some fell eight feet or more carrying a full battle pack on their back suffering major sprains and bruises. Broken arms and legs were not uncommon. As a result they were taken to the beach already wounded. Later in the day they would return, perhaps in a boat full of fellow Marines, the wounded and dying, who were being brought to the medical facilities on board the many APA's, AKA's and one fully equipped hospital ship.

Circling near the Attack Transports and Attack Cargo ships after eight o'clock in the morning, hundreds of Higgins boats loaded with Marines and their own corpsmen got the signal to set off for the assigned beach areas. A lot of the APA's had 35 or more corpsmen on board. On the day before the landing our group was asked if anyone would like to "get his feet wet" by volunteering to go in on the invasion with the Marines. We'd be called "roving corpsmen." Not attached to any group we could go anywhere on the Island we were needed. Four volunteered but I only remember the name of Byron A. Dary, my best friend. The destination for the Marines in the boat I was in was "Blue beach, number two", the most northerly beach on the east side of the Island and the one closest to the strategically located Japanese held "rock quarry".

The persistent and undulating throb of the twin Gray Marine Diesel engines, combined with the noise of the waves slapping against the wooden hull and the continuous shower of wind blown spray engulfing us from above then collecting as water beneath the baffles under our feet, made many almost unaware of enemy shells exploding in the water. But when one hit very close, with the characteristic sound and "jarring thump" and a heavier shower of spray, we realized we were under fire. Only the Coxswain standing in the control box could really "see it all".

In our boat we had a young Navy Lieutenant JG, scornfully called "a ninety day wonder". He had never been in combat. Wanting to see the action from a good vantage point, he climbed up on to the rear platform. He stood there keeping his balance by holding on to something while he surveyed the situation. He looked kind of like the picture in the history books showing Washington crossing the Delaware.

Our Coxswain, who had been in combat said to him, "Sir, you'd better take cover it's a little dangerous here." For some unknown reason the Lieutenant was wearing his soft Officers cap. "Sir," the Coxswain said again, "You should wear a helmet. I have an extra," motioning to where it hung in the control box.

"That's O.K. Coxswain," the Lieutenant called out above the throaty roar of the engines. "I'll be all right."

They were his last words. A second or two later an explosive projectile, perhaps a mortar round, hit him. It must have been a dead center shot that perhaps struck the large bone of his hip, sternum or spine. A Marine with us said he thought they were the only ones dense enough when hit to cause a mortar round to explode. One moment the Lieutenant was standing there and the next we heard a sharp and loud, slightly muffled, "bang". Those who were looking toward the back of the boat, saw a mass of thick red mist erupt that contained within it various sized chunks of flesh, internal organs, cloth and bone as he almost disintegrated and instantly disappeared blown backward off the boat. The Coxswain ducked too late to avoid being bathed by a spray of blood, flesh and some small shell fragments. He wasn't badly wounded and continued to drive the boat, which he slowed for only a moment. Looking back he told us all he saw were bits of clothing, a lot of red foam and some flesh floating on the white chop of the wind whipped waves. The Lieutenants cloth cap had landed right side up. Filled with an air pocket, on the water it floated aimlessly. As the Coxswain brought the boat back up to speed continuing toward the island. One Marine said, "This could be a sign that on this island we're going to run into some really awful bad luck." His words were prophetic.

The boat, full to capacity with men, had little room inside for anyone to move. Right behind me stood an unusually big Marine that looked to be about six foot five and perhaps weighing 250 pounds. Having heard him talking I knew he had seen combat. The Marine standing in back of him yelled, "Hey Doc, how's about changing places with me so's I can shoot the shit with my buddy standing there in front of you?"

I nodded yes and with difficulty we squeezed past each other and the big Marine while trading places. Only moments later a loud slamming, crashing combination of noises ripped the air as a jagged hole appeared, torn through the right hand side of the wooden hull. A two-foot long chunk of flat steel about six inches wide and half an inch thick come through like a big knife blade cutting the Marine, who had just traded places with me, almost in half as it whipsawed crossways through his chest. Miraculously it hit no one else. Without a sound and with the metal shard still sticking out one side of his body he crumpled to the floor, killed instantly. Almost all his blood poured quickly from him. Mixed with the water in the bottom of the boat, while it continued to rock, gallons of crimson sloshed back and forth beneath the lower baffles. Nearly all of us were so scared we could hardly speak. Several Marines vomited. After shaking off an immobilizing fear, I tried to move forward to see if I could help. "It's no use Doc, he's gone," the big Marine now positioned in front of me covered my chest with one big hand and pushed me back. Those of us making our first invasion suddenly realized that we were in a "play for keeps" deadly, shooting war.

Heading for the island that morning 80 percent of the Marines in the Fourth Division were replacements. Only 20 percent knew what we were in for. With the fresh blood of two casualties covering nearly everything, everyone in the boat knew the jarring fear of combat and grim reality of war.

❖ ON THE BEACH WITH THE FIRST WAVE ❖

Iwo Jima had to be taken. There were two good airfields on the island. In the hands of the Japanese, they were packed with fighter planes creating a major hazard, shooting down B-29's flying in tight formation to and from cities in Japan. In addition, the time required for the big bombers from Saipan, Tinian and Guam, to stay in the air, eleven to thirteen hours, resulted in engine and other mechanical failure causing many to crash at sea with loss of both plane and crew.

The Island, about half way between the main targets in Japan and the U.S. bomber bases far to the south, could become a "safe haven" for many bombers crippled by anti-aircraft fire over Japan, and by fighters on Iwo Jima, as well as those having engine and other mechanical trouble from the long journey. For these reasons General Curtis Le May, in charge of the bomber command in the Pacific, wanted it taken.

Everyone in the invasion force knew his request was reasonable, especially those of us who saw many crippled planes returning from participation in the one thousand plane raids, limp back to the airfields on Saipan, as we lay at anchor.

There were those with large holes in the fuselage, wings and tail caused by either anti-aircraft fire from the defenders of the cities in Japan or from the fighter planes based on Iwo Jima that ravaged them, both going to their targets in Japan and on the way back to their base. We also saw many with mechanical trouble having one or two engines stopped and their propellers "feathered". Struggling to reach the end of the runway and safety, one or both of the other two engines might trail smoke or backfire, delivering less than normal power. Some pilots lost control of their plane only a few hundred feet before they were to touch down, crashed and burned. Many times everyone in the crew was killed. Every time a flight returned we'd see pillars of black smoke rise from fires near or on the airfields on both Saipan and Tinian fed by the remaining fuel from the planes that "didn't make it".

Although B-29's and B-24's bombed Iwo Jima steadily for seventy two days before we arrived, Japanese resistance proved to be the most deadly of any invasion in the Pacific during WWII up to that time. Mt. Suribachi at the south end of the island stood like a fortress bristling with mortars and big guns. Many of them rode on rails inside tunnels protected by almost impenetrable doors of steel and concrete. On wheels and tracks, they could be rolled out and fired then quickly pulled back into the tunnel as the huge doors closed. The massive doors, set at various angles, made many of the bombs from our planes and the shells from the big guns of our ships almost useless as they glanced off when they hit exploding with little effect. Anticipating the invasion, the Japanese had accurately "pre-targeted" every inch of the landing beaches using more than two hundred big guns and twenty blockhouses located on the high ground of Mt. Suribachi in the south and "The rock quarry" to the north. Though of higher ground, parts of the quarry area were not readily visible from Blue beach number two. However, like Mt. Suribachi, it also had big guns that were able to hit almost anyplace on the approximately two and a half mile long landing area on the east side of the island.

More than thirteen hundred ships made up the invasion fleet forming a huge semi-circle that extended out to sea for seven miles east of the island. I wondered what the defenders thought that morning when they saw this armada approach, the largest array of ships ever assembled anywhere on earth up to that time. Under the command of Admiral Spruance, who earlier in the war had won the most important battle in the Pacific at Midway, sixteen aircraft carriers and eight battleships with their escorts of cruisers and destroyers arrived at Iwo Jima two days ahead of us firing thousands of shells of every size. Planes from his carriers dropped tons of bombs aiding the effort to "soften up the island". Unfortunately, because of the superb Japanese defenses, his attack did little damage.

Between eight thirty and nine o'clock on the morning of February 19, 1945 our Higgins boat ran straight in bottoming perfectly on the black volcanic sand of Red Beach which was south of our objective, Blue Beach Number 2. The coxswain dropped the front ramp open and we poured out rushing over and past the Marine who still lay where he died, slumped in the crimson pool of seawater and his own blood. Other Higgins boats "broached", that is, turned sideways in the surf while attempting to bottom in, front end first, onto the beach. When their front ramps opened the men had to jump into cold water as much as five to eight feet deep, then struggle to the beach several yards away. In the constant pounding surf, this was not an easy task carrying a rifle, extra ammunition, C rations, hand grenades and full battle pack. Many drowned.

On landing, our group headed to our assignment, Blue Beach 2, the most northern objective and the closest to the heavily fortified rock quarry. All beaches on the more than two-mile landing area were designated in code by color and number. Starting from the south, closest to Mt. Suribachi and progressing northward, were Green Beach, Red Beach 1, Red Beach 2, Yellow Beach 1, Yellow Beach 2, Blue Beach 1 and Blue Beach 2. All beaches soon became a jumble of equipment, piles of supplies and always more and more men. During the first half hour or more we were met with only sporadic fire as the cunning Japanese allowed many more Marines and tons of supplies to come ashore.

Not far from our area on Blue Beach, were several pillboxes. On the way in to the island we were warned by Marines who had combat experience, not to go near them because Japanese soldiers could still be alive and hiding inside. In our Higgins boat we had a kid from Louisiana. His last name was Peckinpah. An apprentice Navy coxswain, a boat driver, he volunteered to come in with us hoping to get some "hands on" operating experience to help him become rated and earn his eagle and first red stripe. Only five feet two inches tall, but well muscled, he had a baby face and no whiskers at all. As soon as we were on the island he had offered to come along with us to help establish a foothold on Blue beach number two.

Though under age, nobody at the recruiting office in Louisiana questioned him when he lied in order to join the Navy. With the rest of us, he too heard the warning to stay out of unsecured pillboxes. But being young and eager, during the first half hour or more on the beach, because we were taking only moderate enemy fire, he said he wanted to go in one to see if he could find a samurai sword on a dead enemy soldier. Over protests from several combat wise Marines he crept over to a pillbox and went in. A short time later screaming, "Help. Oh God, help me!!" he staggered out an appalling sight.

Inside four Japanese soldiers were alive and hiding. When he entered they grabbed him, stripped off his clothing from the waist down then cut him wide open all the way across his belly disemboweling him. Then they shoved him out of the pillbox. Still screaming while gushing both blood and bowel contents from his massive wound, with both hands and forearms he tried to hold on to the dangling intestines hanging out of him. A few steps from us he fell forward, rolled over on his back gasping and staring at the sky in shock. Bending over him as he quickly lost consciousness I knew nothing could be done to help. While he lay on the sand weakening rapidly from loss of blood he called out three times, "Momma, momma, momma," then silently died. He was only fifteen.

On the way in on the boat and at Blue beach, the Marines took a liking to Peckinpah. Being very young, it seemed to me that he appeared to them as kind of an innocent "mascot" and his death made them intensely angry. As soon as it became obvious to those grouped around that he had died several Marines shouted, "Let's fix those yella' sons-a-bitches." Two grabbed "Bangalore torpedoes", a tube like device that fires an explosive projectile. Under protective cover fire from the rifles of several others each Marine shoved the barrel of the torpedo into an opening in the pillbox. A Marine with a flamethrower moved toward the front opening and called out. "If those bastards try coming out of there I'll fry their ass good."

As soon as the Bangalore torpedoes were fired, devastating the inside, the Marine with the flamethrower charged the entrance spewing Napalm in front of him. Two of the four

Japanese soldiers, thrown to the floor by the explosions, were semi-conscious. The other two were dead. The man with the flamethrower entered only part way pouring blazing fire on all four until they were reduced to unrecognizable cinders.

After someone called, "all clear" I later looked inside. The sickening odor of recently burned human flesh combined with the volcanic "rotten egg", sulfur-like smell of the island almost made me vomit. Seeing the destruction and charred remains of what had recently been four soldiers I don't know why, but I thought of the gruesome Navy combat films that Shekerjian had shown me in Honolulu at Kodak of Hawaii. I also thought of the saying, "An eye for an eye, a tooth for a tooth and a life for a life." The life of Peckinpah was avenged— four times.

About half an hour later, when thousands men in the first waves were ashore, as the expression goes, "all hell broke loose". We were totally pinned down by a horrendous barrage of enemy fire. The seventy two day bombing by the Air Force, ineffective against the defenses on Mt. Suribachi at the south, also caused little damage to the thick concrete and steel doors set at various angles at the mouth of the tunnels on the north end of the island, the rock quarry. As a result, the enemy holding the high ground on both ends of the island, lobbed shells and mortar rounds on us at will. Through slits in the cave doors they fired their Nambu machine guns with deadly accuracy. Wounded and dying Marines accumulated in ever-larger numbers. By nightfall of the first day, on Blue Beach Number 2 we had nearly two thousand casualties. There were those with severe head wounds who would soon die. Some had penetrating chest wounds so bad that as I leaned over them I heard air gurgling through the blood, skin and muscle tissue as it sucked in and out of the wounds and collapsing either one or both lungs. Most of these died. Many had arms or legs broken or blown off.

The cry, "corpsman, corpsman" came all too often. Making my way from one to another I'd treat the least wounded first by applying sulfanilamide powder, put a gauze square over it then wrap it with enough tape to be sure the wound remained securely covered. Next, if I'd find no more minor injuries and someone had a compound fracture of the lower arm and blood was gushing from a severed artery I'd tie a tourniquet on the upper arm to stop the bleeding then put sulfanilamide on the exposed bone and tissue then cover his wound with a large padded bandage having four "ties" that held it as firmly in place as possible. For pain I'd inject a Syrette of morphine into the muscle of the other arm and with a special grease pencil write on his forehead: MS 1415. This told the next medical people who saw him what time he was first treated and given morphine, (2:15 PM), so they would know when to continue. Most Marines with this kind of wound survived.

In WWII the Navy taught all corpsmen this: During enemy action your job at all times is **"to keep as many men at as many guns as possible."** This means that those least hurt will be given help immediately while those severely wounded must wait. Many of them will die. A Marine with a small cut on his arm is to be treated right away. One with an arm or leg blown off and bleeding badly, even though right beside you, is not to be looked at until later when all those with minor wounds are treated and returned to duty firing a weapon." At Hospital Corps School in San Diego this concept bothered me terribly. But as a practical matter in war, it was absolutely correct as I so quickly realized beginning on the first day of the invasion.

To provide light at night, battleships, cruisers and destroyers standing off shore continuously shot "star shells" above us. Each had a small parachute attached causing it to drift down slowly. The shells provided about the same amount of eerie flickering light as that seen at early dawn on a cloudy day. Coupled with many shades of gray by the color of the volcanic debris of the island, to me it looked almost unreal. Everything seemed to exist in shadowy silhouette against the Stygian landscape.

The invasion was under the command of Marine General Howland M. "Howling Mad" Smith who thought that the light at night from the star shells would prevent the Japanese from making "Banzi" counterattacks. During the first few nights some Japanese banded together in an attempt to overrun the positions of the Marines. But their efforts usually failed. Many tried to sneak in individually. Some were successful but most were killed.

In daylight during the first few days of the invasion, dive-bombers from the aircraft carriers screamed in dropping bombs on pillboxes that overlooked the beaches. The steel and concrete doors of the tunnels concealing the large artillery were also pounded. Many of the planes made long strafing runs. Every fifth round, a "tracer" trailing flame and smoke, enabled the pilot to clearly see where his bullets hit. I saw an unusual and tragic accident happen to one pilot. As he dove at the north end of the island in the area of the rock quarry, while making his strafing run, perhaps his bullets hit a steel door placed at an unusual angle or it may have been some rocks. From the ground they bounced at a long angle, zipping back skyward. The pilot didn't realize what was happening and "shot himself down" as he flew into and through his own bullets and tracers. Too low to bail out, we watched as he died when his crippled plane crashed, disintegrating in billowing flames and black smoke.

Some of us rated corpsmen from the ship I was on had volunteered to go ashore. We were among a group of thirty-six I knew to be in the area of Blue Beach Number 2. I don't remember the names of the others but my best friend, Byron Dary and I were two. Because he and I were volunteers, or "roving corpsmen" we were not assigned to any specific place or group of Marines and due to the large number being killed or wounded, we could go wherever we were needed. For three days the intense action continued as our artillery and that of the enemy traded volley after volley while the Marines very slowly gained ground. Nights were the worst. We were afraid to sleep because the Japanese continually tried to sneak among us to wreak deadly consequences. Sleep deprivation resulted in many being less efficient doing our job.

On the morning of the fourth day after a difficult climb, Marines with rifles, flame-throwers and satchel charges arrived at the top of Mt. Suribachi. Here, on a short pole, they put up a small flag that was barely visible from anywhere on the island. Then a few Marines were sent down the mountain to get a much larger flag. After they returned they secured it to a long pole, salvaged with difficulty from under some debris in the area. Six people then grasped it and the man closest to the bottom end of the pole set it solidly in a large pile of rock and the wind whipped flag started going up. During the few moments it took to be raised Mr. Rosenthal of the Associated Press, who was rather short in stature, had balanced himself precariously on top of some rocks, and snapped his award-winning picture. Within moments the big flag stood tall and a strong southerly wind caused it to be vigorously whipped northward above the heads of the six Marines.

Then, at that moment, to me, it sounded like the whistle of every ship in the area blew as loud as possible. A continuous roar, penetrating and deep, shook the inside of our bodies then seemed to continue to shimmer and remain hanging in the air. Several Marines looked around to see what all the noise was about. One happened to look toward the top of Mt. Suribachi and I heard him shout, "Hey, lookie there, we've took that mountain and raised the flag." Moments later he took a bullet through the heart and died.

The feeling of emotion I felt seeing the flag waving cannot be described. We've all heard the expression "It was the most gut wrenching event in my life." This remains mine. Almost all of us were so deeply moved at that moment we began to cry and laugh at the same time.

I feel privileged to have witnessed this bit of history while doing my job helping wounded Marines and continue to have deeply mixed emotions whenever I see the event either in a photograph or replica. One of those who raised the large flag was a combat corpsman attached to the Marines. But because I was a volunteer "roving corpsman" he and I never met.

❖ THE QUICK AND THE DEAD ❖

Near Blue Beach Number 2, all corpsmen were overwhelmed caring for the massive number of wounded and dying. Our front moved inland only short distances at a time as we continued to take heavy enemy fire. The type of shelling, "enfilading fire", was extremely deadly because it came from both ends of the line at the same time. During a particularly bad barrage on the afternoon of the fourth day we were pinned down. We hugged the ground in depressions and craters, hardly anyone one moved. Dary, a short distance away was hit but didn't cry out, perhaps having temporarily lost consciousness.

A Marine near him, squirmed the few yards over on his belly, "Hey Doc, that other corpsman over there he just got hit and he's real bad. One side's about gone. I don't think he's gonna' make it." I nodded an acknowledgement and wanted to go and see if anything could be done but the intense shelling wouldn't permit it.

In Hospital Corps School our instructors emphasized, "During an impossible situation stay down. Remember, a dead corpsman can't help anybody." The shelling continued to rage for about fifteen minutes more then lessened a little. As I crawled the short distance over to see how bad his wounds were Dary weakly called, "Get Doctor Collentine, get Doctor Collentine," then was silent. He had been almost ripped in half, torn upward from his hips to his chest. His left eye was missing and there were puncture wounds all over his left side. I knew he was dead and crouched low next him. I became almost paralyzed by the intense feeling that I would be next to die and only remember saying, "Oh shit Dary, oh shit, goddamn it." Then, shaking with fear I lay beside him and cried uncontrollably.

Later, before Graves Registration personnel took him away, I identified myself to them as his best friend. They gave me his wallet, High School class ring, watch and the gold identification bracelet his parents gave him when he joined the Navy. When I returned to the ship six days later I put everything in a box and mailed it to his home. I enclosed a long letter telling his folks about the good times he and I had since we first became friends in Astoria, Oregon. They wrote back and invited me to visit them at Lake Geneva in Darien, Wisconsin if I ever got out that way. I deeply regret never having had the opportunity.

In the afternoon of the tenth day I returned to the *APA 193*. The ordeal for me on the island, which in such a short time took an unusually large number of lives, came to an end. Of the thirty-six corpsmen that I knew about who went in on Blue Beach Number 2, six of us came out alive and three were wounded. Of the 2500 Marines in the Regimental Combat Team of the 4th Division, many transported to the island by the *USS Sanborn,* only eighty-eight survived and a lot of them were wounded. Marines fighting on Blue Beach Number 2 suffered the most casualties in the shortest time and received the dubious honor of becoming the reason for the island to be named "Bloody Iwo." On Iwo Jima the 4th Marine Division, for all practical purposes, was wiped out and has never been remanned.

Day and night without rest, for the next six days on board the ship, we cared for the wounded that were brought to us almost every hour. All medical personnel worked to the point of exhaustion taking only a ten to fifteen minute nap every few hours. We became so tired we hated hearing the loudspeakers make the announcement, "Now hear this. Prepare to receive wounded at davit number four, port side, aft." This meant even more work and long nights of sleep deprivation. Working on the many horribly wounded for so many hours without rest, overwhelming exhaustion twisted my reasoning. The emotional toll caused me to almost resent taking on board so many wounded and foolishly, to blame them for their own misfortune.

About nine o'clock one night we received another twenty casualties. For lack of space in the ships hospital area, they were placed--remaining on their stretchers--in the officer's ward room on dining tables that were pushed together. As Dr. Whalen looked them over he pointed to the ones with minor wounds he wanted to see first so they could be quickly treated and returned to combat.

As another corpsman and I walked to the operating room bringing two of the less wounded patients from the wardroom to the doctor for treatment, we passed by a young sailor lying on a stretcher on a table. He didn't move and with both eyes swollen shut, he couldn't see. But I could tell he heard us talking because as we came close he called out.

"Please, please will you help me sit up? I know I'll be O.K. if you'll just help me sit up." Over and over he kept pleading for us to help him sit up.

For a moment I stopped to look. He had a ghastly head wound. A bullet passed all the way through entering at the right temple and going out the left. He didn't die instantly because the shot passed inside just behind the bone of his forehead partially destroying the two frontal lobes of his brain, much of which protruded out each side of his head through curly, blood soaked, black hair. He couldn't move because the rest of his brain had swollen from the trauma. I had seen enough head wounds to know he had no chance for survival. Every time we passed him escorting other slightly wounded patients to the operating room he'd continue to call.

"Please, oh please help me sit up. I know I'll live if you'll help me sit up." As we left the wardroom he kept pleading.

About half an hour later, when I could spare a few minutes I returned alone to see him. He was dead. But in my mind I could still hear him say, "Please, please, won't someone help me sit up. I know I'll be O.K. if you'll just please help me sit up." Wiping away a lot of tears I slowly returned to the operating room to help.

Even in this hellish place, at times humor could be found. One big Marine had an entire buttock muscle, one of his "buns", sliced off by shrapnel. He told us he picked it out of the volcanic sand and held it tightly to his chest to keep it warm and protected. He said he thought if he kept it warm enough maybe it could be sewed back on. When the combat corpsman on the island found him and told him this couldn't be done he still insisted on keeping it close to him. No explanation by a mere corpsman could convince him it wouldn't grow back if sewed on by a "real doctor". He got the chance to hear about the futility of his idea from Dr. Whalen who firmly but gently told him he had to give it up. As the Marine handed the doctor "the left cheek of his ass", with good humor he said, "You know, when I get home some people will ask to see the scar where I got wounded. So I guess I'll just have to drop my pants and show 'em."

Another even bigger Marine with blond hair bleached by the Iowa sun, had a wisecrack about everything. He had been hit by an unusual chunk of shrapnel, the entire nose cone of a Japanese mortar round, that broke off from the rest of the shell. When it struck it fractured his right arm just above the elbow. Traveling downward it entered his abdominal cavity ripping holes in his intestines and continuing down and across his body ended up breaking the bone in his left thigh. Finally, it lodged as a big lump, just under the skin above his left knee. The impact of the shell apparently threw him violently down a steep slope breaking his right hip. After treating the least wounded first to return them to duty the doctors, though extremely tired, worked on him for hours. They set his arm, repaired the holes in his intestines, set his leg and put him in a full body cast to keep his hip immobile. The cast weighed at least fifty pounds and incorporated three steel rods with which to carry him. Without the cast he probably weighed two hundred and fifty pounds, with it, over three hundred. Dr. Whalen saved the nose cone as a souvenir for the Marine and incorporated it solidly in the front of the body cast leaving it stick out of the Plaster of Paris like a huge steel belly button that the blond wisecracking guy from Iowa treasured. He said, "I guess I wasn't born with a big enough belly button so now I had to get plastic surgery and get this one put in." In spite of serious and painful wounds his cheer and good humor never left and he inspired all of us daily.

Another patient, a short, stocky and well-muscled Marine, came aboard having both sightless eyes dangling down his face out of their sockets. A bullet had passed from one side to the other just behind them blowing both completely out. Severely damaged, they couldn't be saved. One of the doctors cut them off and sutured the lids closed. The next morning when the young man awoke he sat up in bed and said loudly, but with good cheer,

"Hey, I can't see it but it sure as hell smells like bacon and eggs. Boy I'm really hungry!!" Hearing this I fed him first.

Several days later, with more than three hundred wounded on board, we received orders to pass them to a much faster ship that would take them to the Navy hospital in Honolulu. The transfer, using a Stokes stretcher, a deep wire basket rigged to pulleys and lines high above the water, took almost all day. A large brightly lighted red cross had been rigged on each side and another on the top deck of this other ship making it easily identifiable, day and night, as a non-combatant, mercy vessel.

That night, having no more wounded on board, most of us slept at least ten hours. But the next day when we got up we heard deeply disturbing news. Just after midnight, as the brightly lighted ship sped toward Pearl Harbor she was sunk. There were no survivors. Before going down, the radioman sent an SOS and said the ship had been hit with three torpedoes. Very fast destroyers tried to locate the enemy submarine but it wasn't found.

All of us remembered the many hundreds of hours of work done for the patients beginning from when they came on board the APA 193 until they were transferred off. We talked about the feeding of the many Marines who always needed the help of a corpsman, the hundreds of shots given of the newest antibiotic called Penicillin that had such a peculiar odor, the I.V. injections, blood transfusions and the changing of bandages day and night along with the catheters and the making of Wangenstien sets to keep injured stomachs empty while they healed. But mostly we thought of the stories told to us by the wounded, their dreams and plans that now would never happen.

I especially remembered the patients who showed unusual courage. The wise cracking farm boy from Iowa in a full body cast, with its fake belly button. He was unable to move. The stocky kid, though blinded, calling loudly for the bacon and eggs and the one who, in the conflict had "his ass blown off". Each envisioned himself going home and each had his dream shattered when hearing, if only for a moment, the torpedoes smash with horrendous explosions into the ship taking them on a one way journey to the ocean depths.

In the large "walk in" type deep freezer of the *APA 193*, designed by the builder to store perishable food, five dead Marines were stowed. They were the most seriously wounded who died before they could be taken aboard the faster ship. We were to bury them at sea the following evening. The ceremony is unforgettable.

In preparation a four by eight sheet of new plywood is selected. A piece of brand new white canvas, a little larger in size is put over it on which the deceased is placed. A heavy five inch thirty eight projectile is placed below the knees between the lower legs of the man. The legs, with the projectile, are lashed securely together with rope and the white canvas is then drawn tightly around the dead Marine, in the manner prescribed by the Navy. Sewn shut with unbreakable sail twine, it forms a cocoon that now rests on the new plywood sheet. At the rail of the ship each shrouded body is placed under an American flag. The flag is attached to the plywood only at the top end. Over the loudspeakers the Captain announces that at sunset, a burial at sea service will be held. All personnel not on duty are encouraged to attend. Those on duty are asked to maintain silence until the ceremony is finished. The ship's speed is reduced to slow.

On the evening of the day after a Japanese submarine sank the faster ship, the bodies of the five Marines, each in a canvas cocoon and on the sheet of plywood, lay under a flag at the rail of the *APA 193*. The Catholic priest, Father Frank and the Protestant minister, Reverend Vierling, in their colorful vestments, conducted an individual service for the dead of each faith. The last thing done by those present is to sing the hymn, "Eternal Father Strong to Save". All Navy personnel learn it during basic training. In boot camp, where it is almost a requirement that we sing, it is mouthed by most as rote. This is not the case when five men who died from wounds sustained during enemy action lie before you ready to be dropped over the side of a ship into the ocean.

The spectacularly beautiful gold and purple Pacific sunset, added to the moment its haunting ambiance, reminding me there would be no more sunsets seen by the men beneath the flags. In boot camp when we sang the hymn during church services on Sunday, no reality of war and death were attached to it. After all, we were the young lions, teen aged and invincible. Death was not on our agenda. But on the gently swaying deck of the USS Sanborn, the stark reality and silence of death lay in front of us.

The last words of the song, "Lord, hear us as we cry to thee for those in peril on the sea," drifted slowly away in the warm evening air. At the top of each of the five plywood sheets two sailors in dress uniform, one on each side, stood at attention beside the flag covered body. Both clergymen nod and the boards, all at the same moment, are tipped to a nearly upright position allowing the five to drop as one. The swishing sound the canvas cocoons make as they slide down the plywood and out from under the flag is followed by a few seconds of silence as the dead hurl feet first, weighted down by the heavy projectile, into the eternal sea. Then a splash and all becomes quiet. From the loudspeakers the finality of a trumpet sounding "taps" fills the twilight. The service has ended.

The ship resumes speed. Over the loud speaker the Captain announces, "Carry on."

As the ship steamed south we were located almost over the same spot where the much faster vessel sank the night before. Here the five Marines we buried at sea joined others in one of the deepest places in the Pacific Ocean, five miles down in the bottom of the Mariana trench, an eternal resting place for brave young men.

❖ THE MISFORTUNES OF WAR ❖

Of all land-based weapons used by either side during the battle for Iwo Jima our flame throwing tanks were the most horribly destructive. At the tip of their large gun muzzle a nozzle and an ignition source were fitted. Behind each tank a steel container filled with several hundred gallons of jellied gasoline, called "Napalm" trailed. Most of us found it both fascinating and terrible to watch them in action.

Against a Japanese stronghold the tank driver aimed the weapon and fired engulfing everything in yellow, roaring flame. Because of Napalm's stickiness it couldn't be wiped off or the fire put out. A unique roaring noise combined with an extremely high pitched, ear shattering, scratching squeal, heard at times for more than a mile, accompanied each graceful arc of flaming death.

Almost everyone has heard the expression, "She screamed like a Banshee", an old woman in Scottish lore that would moan and wail loudly foretelling death, came to mind every time I heard a flame throwing tank in action. The roaring scream was caused by the high vacuum needed first to suck the sticky Napalm from the container behind the tank, followed by the even higher pressure that sent it through a hydraulic line to the nozzle at the end of the gun barrel where it exited. I don't know how the vacuum and pressure were created but with tremendous force the Napalm raced from the nozzle and ignited, engulfing the enemy as far as a hundred yards or more away, in fire. It's one of the sounds of war, once heard, that cannot be forgotten.

The film Shekerjian showed me in Honolulu was nothing compared with seeing Napalm used against groups of the live enemy and the horror it caused. On Iwo Jima witnessing the real thing, the sight of Japanese soldiers burning alive as they ran from their hiding places, the unbelievable screams wrenched with excruciating pain from their throats, the smell of burning human flesh together with the "rotten egg" odor of the Island's sulfur gasses were all far worse than any film could depict.

Fat, greenish colored flies covered the many enemy dead, casualties of our artillery, mortars, bombs, rifle and machine gun fire as well as the flaming Napalm. Bulldozers were used to gouge trenches in the volcanic earth in which to dispose of them. Whole bodies and parts of bodies of the Japanese were piled in a common grave. Tank trucks sprayed hundreds of gallons of diesel fuel on them. Then a flame-throwing tank, positioned at one end of the trench, shot a massive arc of flame that ignited the fuel incinerating all to cinders. Finally, bulldozers covered the remains with volcanic rock, sand and debris. No attempt to identify any of them took place.

Another sound a corpsman will always remember is that of someone next to him being hit by machine gun fire. First a "splattering" sound is heard, as though someone is rapidly clapping hands together or slapping them against their own thighs. After a momentary pause the exact rhythm of that machine gun, firing in the distance, sometimes will be heard.

The surface of Iwo Jima is made up of volcanic debris thrown out long ago from Mt. Suribachi located at the southern tip. Loose and sand-like, it's soil readily absorbs sound. The bullets impacting the man would arrive a moment earlier than the sound of the gun. The fact that a fatal bullet always strikes a moment before the sound from the gun that fires it accounts for the expression used by combat veterans, "You'll never hear the one with your name on it."

One aspect of the conflict on Iwo Jima is seldom mentioned. The composition of the volcanic ash ranged from an almost hard surface to powder a foot or more deep. Many Marines were hit and momentarily stunned by the impact yet sustained a very survivable wound. But with a heavy pack on their back and because they fell forward, temporarily unconscious, many suffocated and died with their face buried in less than two inches of powder-like volcanic ash.

Steaming south we received orders to divert to Leyte, Lingayen, Zamboanga, Samar, Mindanao and lastly to Cebu, all in the Philippines. In Cebu we picked up a group of Army personnel, members of a tank battalion. All through the war the soldiers had been driving Grant tanks but were recently given the new and improved Sherman. We were to take them and the newer tanks to Guam.

Among the men in the tank battalion were two "very best friends." Because of their time in combat plus the overall number of months in the service, each had more than the "93 points" required to be eligible for immediate discharge. They did not have to make the trip to Guam but agreed to go and help load and off-load the new Sherman's. On the dock the tanks to be moved were lined up in a long row. Every time one was hoisted on board our ship, all the tanks behind it had to be driven several feet forward and placed in position so the next one could be picked up by our loading boom.

During the day the slow work went well. At four o'clock in the afternoon I came on duty in the sick bay on the main deck. Half an hour later a soldier rushed in yelling. "Come quick Doc, come quick!! Someone out there where they're loading the tanks has been hurt real bad."

I grabbed the first aid bag, followed the soldier and rushed down the gangplank. On the dock a man with a massive traumatic wound lay fully conscious. He had stepped between two tanks to urinate when suddenly the Sherman in front of him, getting ready to move ahead for loading, had been put in reverse gear by mistake. As it jerked backward it trapped the soldier between its own set of hard rubber treads and the treads of the one behind. After they collided, the treads of the moving tank continued to grind in reverse against those of the one in back with the soldier crushed between them being torn apart. Ripped almost in half as far up as his belly button, his entrails spilled down toward his knees. Nearly all the flesh had been pulled from both legs in a massive avulsion and every bone was shattered. Sharp and jagged pieces poked out from what had been his legs.

A soldier sitting on the planks of the dock cradled the wounded man's head and chest in his lap while talking to him. Positioned on his back the injured man asked, "How bad have I been hurt?" and kept saying, "Hold me up a little higher so I can see—I can't feel my legs."

Trained in trauma care I knew he'd go into irreversible shock almost immediately if he saw his wounds. I whispered to the soldier holding the man, "Don't let him look. He'll die from shock. Do you understand? Don't let him look"!! I emphasized the last sentence. The helper lowered the head of the wounded man backward a little more, tilting it further toward the sky. For distraction he continued to make small talk. I could do nothing but inject the mangled soldier with a Syrette of Morphine to ease his pain and with a grease pencil write on his forehead, "MS 1645", military time for 4:45 PM

Two more corpsmen closely followed by Dr. Collentine brought a "Stokes" stretcher down the gangplank. I'd never heard the doctor cuss even during the horrors of Iwo Jima. But as he turned to run back up the gangplank to the surgery wash room to "scrub up" he exclaimed, "Good God, get this man to the surgery room right now!!"

The injured man, placed on the stretcher and covered by a blanket, remained conscious. Many of his blood vessels retracted and much of the bleeding stopped. He continued to talk to the people who helped carry the stretcher to the surgery room. Dr. Collentine had scrubbed up and Dr. Whalen, who had been called to help, was in the process. Placed on the operating table a corpsman positioned a wire arch several inches above and all the way across the soldier's chest. Draped over this a white sheet prevented him from being able to look downward to see his injury.

Meanwhile several corpsmen cut away the remainder of his torn clothing carefully separating the bits of cloth intertwined with a lot of grossly mangled flesh. At one point the injured man called out, "Hey Doctor, be sure and save my 'family jewels', you know, my balls. I'm getting married just as soon as I get home. My best friend and I already have a double wedding planned."

As Doctors Collentine and Whalen worked our first class corpsman, Craig Hardegree, found a volunteer with type O, Rh negative universal type blood and started a direct donor to patient transfusion. In addition, through intravenous lines inserted in each arm, physiological saline solution, five percent glucose in saline, pentnucleotides and plasma flowed. Dr. Fleishner arrived and saw how bad the injuries were. Because of his experience at Iwo Jima, now an experienced trauma surgeon, without scrubbing up he inserted a large 18-gauge needle into the right subclavian vein of the soldier through which he started another unit of plasma. However, a negative trade off occurred with the administration of so much life saving fluid. The markedly lowered blood pressure of the soldier now increased to normal. As a result, most of the vessels that originally pulled back and closed from the fall in blood pressure as he first lost blood on the dock, reopened as normal pressure began to return. With each ragged tear the doctors tied off in the badly injured arteries and veins of the soldier, because of the now increasing pressure, a new hole blew out in another weakened or partially torn place. Sometimes only an inch or less further up the leg from the last, this allowed significant blood loss to continue. When the doctors saw the nearly colorless fluid spurting from the arteries and welling up from the torn veins was almost nothing but plasma and other blood extenders having few oxygen carrying red blood cells in it, they knew their efforts probably would be futile, yet they continued to work.

The soldier asked for a drink of water and Dr. Collentine nodded for me to go ahead and give it. I don't know how it happened, but as I raised his head while holding the glass of water close to him and placing the curved glass straw to his lips, someone brushed past, hitting the wire holder causing the white sheet hanging on it to fall away. Before it could be replaced the soldier looked down at what had been the lower half of his body. For a moment his eyes widened then his head dropped heavily back on the operating table and he died. Loosing the soldier was a major disappointment but no one could have anticipated what happened next.

As the primary surgeon on the case Dr. Collentine looked in the soldier's wallet to find the address of his next of kin so he could write them a letter. Among the photographs in the wallet was one of the newly dead soldier standing beside a buddy of his, each arm-in-arm with a beautiful girl. The person who had mistakenly put the Sherman tank in reverse on the dock and backed it against the injured soldier was the other man in the picture. Writing, found on the back of the photograph, said it had been taken at home in Chicago where they already had their double wedding planned.

No one knew or paid any attention to the soldier standing in the passageway of the sick bay looking through the large double doors that remained open to the operating room. Curious people always looked in. Doctors or corpsmen never thought anything about it. But the moment Dr. Collentine snapped off his rubber gloves and said, "Sorry fellas, we've lost him," a cry that could only be caused by primordial anguish, ripped through the area from the throat of the stranger. He was the injured man's best friend, the other person in the picture Dr. Collentine found in the dead soldiers wallet and who had accidentally put the tank in reverse.

Spinning around he ran down the gangplank and over to a Jeep. He bashed his head against the windshield with so much force it shattered the glass. Continuing to scream unintelligible sentences he sobbed uncontrollably. His head and face were soon swollen and blood soaked. Several soldiers tried to stop him as he tore out masses of hair dripping with blood leaving only underlying flesh and bone. He picked up one of the larger shards of glass and tried to slash his own throat. He wanted to die. His grief became so desperate and uncontrollable that it took six soldiers to restrain him.

After they were finally able to place him in a straight jacket, we sedated and tied him down on a bunk in one of the isolation wards on board our ship. A broken man, he remained with us for two days until a plane came to transport him to Tripler Army Hospital in Honolulu.

We were told the accident was caused by the fact that the tank drivers were totally familiar with the gearshift pattern in the old Grant model tanks they drove for years but the shift pattern of the newer Sherman was different. In the place where the shift lever would be set for slow forward in the Grant, in the Sherman this position was fast reverse, causing one of the tragic misfortunes of war.

❖ A LETTER FROM STEVE ❖

From the time he arrived on board the *USS Sanborn, APA 193* at its commissioning in Astoria, Oregon, Steve Travnick said he would beat the system and "get the hell out of this chicken shit outfit" if he ever thought he might be called for combat duty.

"You'll never see me risking my life in no combat on some damn island with the Marines" he gloated.

Partially trained but still a non-rated corpsman, Steve said he joined the hospital corps because he figured it would be "soft duty".

"The way I look at it," he said, "If I can be stationed at a Navy hospital on shore or aboard a nice ship sailing in U.S. waters, that will be O.K. But if I think I'm going to be called for combat duty I'll put in right away for a medical discharge claiming pain and distress caused by my flat feet."

The truth is he did have flat feet but many of us corpsmen thought they were the result of him being overweight. In addition, he had such weak muscle tone in them, when he walked on a dry surface with wet feet his footprints showed he actually had no arch. He also knew this "wet foot test" was the way Navy doctors determined if one really had flat feet.

Steve stood six feet tall and in my opinion was a corpulent, flabby, lazy, boorish, loudmouthed kid of Polish descent from Chicago. He constantly tried to shirk duty and always complained to the doctors on the ship that his back, legs and feet hurt.

Almost every day, from the time we went on our three day shakedown cruise several hundred miles off of Astoria until we later left Seattle fully provisioned knowing we'd soon be going into the combat zone in the Pacific, at six o'clock in the morning he'd appear at "sick call". He'd always complain of pain and distress in his feet. During his early training as a corpsman he realized, to his own advantage, that a complaint of flat feet associated with pain and distress in his legs and back, when entered into his medical record would be a legitimate reason to be granted a discharge. But all of us corpsmen knew he lied about his feet because he laughed and joked about it many times telling us he had no trouble with them at all. "But the dumb doctors don't know that and I'll beat them at their own game, you just watch," he bragged.

By the time we arrived in Honolulu, heading for the combat zone, he had all three doctors on board convinced he had incapacitating pain and distress and Dr. Fleishner transferred Steve to the Navy hospital there for observation. I think this was done because the doctors simply became sick and tired of hearing Steve complain almost every day.

Steve never returned to the ship and since we didn't hear from him we assumed he had either been given a medical discharge or "light duty" on shore. One thing is certain, every person in the medical department on the Sanborn was happy to be rid of him.

For those of us in the combat zone or close to the front on land or at sea, mail service proved to be excellent. For example, while at sea sailing in convoy on the way to the invasion of Iwo Jima, a fast destroyer sent from Honolulu caught up with our ship to deliver twenty huge canvas bags of mail. Using lines and pulleys rigged between the two ships, high above the water they were transferred to us as we continued, steaming northward.

On land mail service was equally good. At Cebu in the Philippines, where the soldier who had been crushed between two Sherman tanks died on the operating table, over the loudspeaker of our ship an announcement came, "Now hear this. Mail call will commence immediately on the starboard quarterdeck." Twenty-five bags of this "precious cargo" had been delivered on board. On the quarterdeck everyone eagerly milled around "Robbie", the ship's yeoman, as he called out the names of those who had mail. After being distributed the men of each division usually went either to their duty area or their bunk to read it. With enthusiasm and good feeling many shared with friends, parts or all of letters from Dads and Moms, wives and girlfriends.

Mail usually comforted us — but not always.

[Author's disclaimer: In the course of writing this book of personal memories it has been my goal and commitment to communicate the truth even if it requires the high price of being painful.

One particular place this commitment was put to a test is in the following letter from Steve. The invasion of Iwo Jima was a bloody battle: of the 2,500 Marines and 36 Corpsmen deployed in our area of Blue Beach, only 88 Marines and 6 Corpsmen survived, after only 10 days of combat.

Steve's coarse and ill-mannered response to the sacrifice for our country and its survival is written exactly in the language he used. His vulgar and insensitive words angered us deeply. If the following letter offends any reader, I offer a most humble apology. It is with deepest regret if I have conveyed that offense.]

Among the mail Craig Hardegree received that evening was a large brown manila envelope with no return name or address on it. After reading all his other letters he opened the large envelope. When he looked inside he could hardly believe what he saw.

"Hey, lookie here guys," he said in his soft Texas drawl. "Doesn't this beat all?"

In his hand he held the eight and a half by eleven glossy black and white photograph of Steve Travnick in a brand new looking civilian suit sitting at a table in a nightclub. In the background on the table were a lot of partially empty whiskey and mixer bottles. Two glasses, half full of booze, were in the foreground. In his hand Steve held a mixed drink up high as if proposing a toast. On his right knee sat a scantily clad blonde and on his left sat a brunette with even less clothing. Each girl had an arm around Steve's neck and they were both cheek to cheek with him. On the bottom of the photograph in big bold letters Steve wrote, "Turn the picture over boys!" When Hardegree turned the photo over and read the writing on the back, it became obvious by the bitterness in his voice that he had mixed emotions.

"Ya'll, just listen to this," he drawled in his Texas lingo. "This here's what Steve wrote. 'Hi guys, *Semper Fi*. Hooray for me and fuck you. I've got mine, how the hell are you doing?'" Signed, Steve.

Below the signature, in one corner appeared the name and address of the nightclub on Cicero Avenue in Chicago where the picture had been taken.

For a moment we were at a loss for words. Then someone exploded.

"Why that no good son of a bitch!" Another said, "I'd like to cut his nuts out so's he couldn't do no good with those babes he's with." The last comment I remember is, "If I had a .45 that would shoot that far I'd put a slug right between that pig fucker's eyes."

Steve did beat the system. But here at Cebu, in the mail he "rubbed it in" at a most inappropriate time because this was the evening of the day all three of our doctors and the rest of the medical staff had just finished working for hours on the soldier who died after accidentally being crushed out on the dock by a Sherman tank driven by his best friend.

❖ NERVE WRACKING DUTY ❖

At Guam, after off-loading the Sherman tanks and army personnel we brought from Cebu, without cargo or passengers aboard we returned to Honolulu. Remaining here for a week we were fully re-provisioned. Every second day we relaxed and enjoyed liberty. During the first of only two times we left the ship Swanberg, and I spent the entire day at the beach on Waikiki swimming, resting on the sand, hoping to spot a beautiful young lady or two. We had no such luck because the beach seethed with mostly male military personnel. The second time, in town we found a small bar that had good music. Slowly nursing our beer we simply relaxed and listened for hours. After what we'd been through and seen, these were golden days.

Ordered to Maui, we again took aboard a unit of Marines. Soon we were sailing northward in a vast new convoy. In fact it now became the largest collection of ships ever to be seen in the Pacific. Because of its size, more than 1600 ships, it will remain as one of the events in naval history that will never be repeated. Rumor told us that we were on the way to participate in the invasion of the mainland of Japan. However, after being at sea a few days our "sealed orders" were opened. They said some of the ships in the convoy were to be used as 'decoys' to lure out from her safe harbor in Japan, the largest battleship in the world, the Yamato and her support group.

The *USS Sanborn, APA 193* had been chosen to be one of the decoys. We couldn't believe that our relatively slow, fully loaded personnel carrying Attack Transport, one of many, along with a number of the slightly larger, fully loaded and equally slow cargo carrying AKA's, were chosen to do this. However, the slow and loaded APA's and AKA's did in fact look like an invasion force heading for Japan. The strategy: Lure the Yamato with her big guns out to intercept us so that planes from a "fast carrier task force" could move in and sink her. As the biggest battleship in the world she remained a major threat to all Allied forces at sea. Her huge 18.1 inch guns, the largest ever produced for a seagoing vessel, could shoot farther and more accurately than the 16 inch rifles on our very best "Iowa class" battleships which included those on the brand new *USS Missouri, BB 63*. For this reason Admiral Halsey wanted the Yamato sunk along with as many other ships in her battle group as possible. Planes from his aircraft carriers were to over fly and protect us at all times and if they saw the Yamato and the rest of the Japanese fleet move in our direction we'd be ordered to reverse course and retreat at flank speed. We were told that before they could catch and sink us, all the Japanese ships would be sunk by bombs from the planes from Halsey's "fast carrier" group.

Only 260 miles from Japan we continued to steam north, getting very nervous. At this distance we were easily within range of the deadly Kamikaze suicide planes and we never saw one fighter plane from any of the aircraft carriers said to be protecting us.

The Japanese secret code had been broken long ago, before the battle of Midway, and we finally learned from our radioman that our decoy mission was a success. The Yamato and her escorting force were getting under way, heading in our direction. Much to our relief we were ordered to turn around and join up with the original convoy to participate in the invasion of Okinawa. The next day we heard the Yamato had been sunk along with several of her escorting battle group.

My days spent on station in the sick bay were routine and usually intensely boring. The personnel we carried were encouraged to come to Navy sick call held at six o'clock every morning. Doing this could prevent a minor problem from becoming worse.

One morning a man came to the sick bay complaining of constipation. He said he hadn't emptied his bowels for six days and that he felt "a distressing sensation of fullness inside." Two of most common problem dealt with at sick call were, headache and constipation.

Dr. Collentine turned to me, "Gene, give him a Triple H Enema." During all of my hospital corps training and refresher courses I'd never heard of this so I asked for clarification.

"Oh," he said, "it stands for High, Hot and a Hell of a lot." Seeing my look of surprise, he chuckled with great self-satisfaction.

In the privacy of the hospital ward toilet the man undressed from the waist down as I filled the two-quart, white enamelware enema can, with warm water. In it I added a generous amount of solution of green soap for maximum lubrication. Slathered its full length with Vaseline I substituted a three-foot long flexible red rubber catheter, about as big around as my thumb, instead of using the hard, black three-inch plastic tip. I then inserted it almost the entire length before opening the hose clamp to let the slippery liquid from the enema can run in. As he moaned, groaned hollered and cussed, the warm, soap-slippery water poured in far above the blockage. I had him wait on hands and knees, head and chest close to the floor, for as long as he could stand it. What happened next, to say the least, brought great relief. Massive amounts of gas rumbled forth in long steady bursts from the man followed by lots of smaller intermittent passages that varied in both their high and low pitched sound and length of time. After a few moments a final rush of gurgling wet, bubbly noise preceded the release of one large mass of the offending impacted material. It remained mostly in one chunk as it dropped into the pot with a loud splash and a thud. Then the man blurted, "Geeze Doc, on the way out that stuff felt like it could have been a baseball bat covered with spikes." After half filling the toilet with a small mountain of much softer debris, he said, "I sure do feel better. Thanks."

The reason so many of the troops we carried suffered from headache and constipation was due to a change in diet and lack of both exercise and water intake. Headache is common with constipation and the tension that accompanied the altered routine while on board the ship was also a big factor.

However, for this patient who left the sick bay about seven

pounds lighter, his triple "H" enema was a "resounding" success because he had left every last bit of his problem behind. However, the unfortunate ship's plumber who had to spend a lot of hours unplugging the toilet pipes, throughout a very long distance, expressed a much different point of view.

The next morning another Marine, reporting for sick call, said his "piles" were really hurting, bad. Dr. Fleishner prescribed a half hour "sitz" bath twice daily and that a tube of Nupricainal ointment be dispensed to be applied liberally on the offending area after each bath. A Navy sitz bath consists of having the patient sit in a small tub of very warm to almost hot water for thirty minutes. This relieves pain, itching and a lot of swelling of the protruding hemorrhoids and usually brings much relief.

That evening he returned to the sick bay for his second sitz bath. While sitting in the water he noticed an old guitar nearby owned by one of the corpsmen. A cheap instrument, it had a warped neck and some of the frets were out of line. Cracked in several places, it wasn't much more than a piece of junk. Motioning to it the man asked, "Do you play it?"

"No" I said, "it belongs to Keith. He's from Arkansas and he's carried that old thing with him ever since we were commissioned in Astoria, Oregon a long time ago. It's not any good. Keith tries to play it but it doesn't have much of a tone."

"Do you think he'd mind if I'd try it?"

Reaching to get the guitar from the top of the bunk I handed it to him saying, "Go ahead, he won't mind."

The man almost caressed the old beat up instrument. He turned it in all directions examining every detail. By the way he handled it he obviously knew plenty about guitars. After tuning it he began to play.

Unbelievably beautiful sounds echoed throughout the sick bay. Enlisted men and officers stopped and looked in to see who was playing the live music. They saw a man, naked from the waist down, sitting on a lower bunk in a small tub of water playing both the bass accompaniment and the melody of some of the best sounding guitar music many of us had ever heard. Without the aid of guitar picks, with his thumb he played the rhythm strokes on the two bass strings and with three fingers played every note of the melody using the other four strings. Some of the songs I remember hearing are, The Steel Guitar Rag, Frankie and Johnnie, The Wreck of the Old Ninety Seven, That Silver Haired Daddy of Mine and Yellow Bird as well as many similar country-western songs that were popular during that time. He played steadily for about 20 minutes before stopping.

"One more, one more," the request came in unison from two-dozen fascinated listeners.

"O.K., I'll do just one more — how's about Nola, anybody know that one?" he asked.

Without waiting for an answer he re-adjusted the tuning of the old guitar then began to play. "Nola" is a song to be played fairly fast and is technically difficult. But he strummed each bass rhythm note perfectly and every treble melody note flawlessly. When he finished he put the battered old instrument on the bunk beside himself. Hoots, yells and the clapping of two-dozen pairs of hands, including those of our executive officer, Mr. Schwartz, a full three stripe navy commander, gave the man a rousing ovation.

"Well thank you," the soldier said smiling. "Right now I've got to be gettin' outta here. Water's gettin' cold."

After everyone left I asked, "Where did you learn to play like that?"

"Oh, down in Tennesee. We have an old Model T Ford flat bed truck — you know, the kind with the Ruxtel axel, a chain drive and solid rubber tires? A friend of mine who knows a lot about electricity rigged up a circuit off it for us boys so our amplifiers would work. We all get together come a' Saturday night and we just mosey through town playin' away. Sometimes they'd be a parade and we'd be asked to be in it."

I said, "Your playing sure sounds good and you make it look so easy."

"Waal," he drawled, "I been at it awhile."

When he finished drying off and got dressed I recorded his name, which I do not remember, in the sick bay log.

As he played song after song it seemed to me like we were "somewhere else." Melody drifted everywhere, engulfing us as a cool and gentle breeze. There was no war here. His unusual talent altered a few moments in time allowing those listening to forget the raw danger all of us realized that soon we might again possibly face.

❖ OKINAWA AND AFTERMATH ❖

We arrived at Okinawa on April 1, 1945 April fools day, Easter Sunday and "Love day", the code name for the invasion. All fell on the same date. As always, when making a landing we were wakened earlier than usual to make preparations for going ashore. At dawn, as we steamed toward our objective we were positioned second from the front in a line of twenty-two ships made up of troop carrying APA's and the heavy equipment support units, the AKA's.

The leading ship, also an APA loaded with troops, carried the Senior Captain in command of our flotilla. To avoid Kamikaze planes as well as enemy submarines, when given a signal all 22 ships zigzagged in unison to the left or right. After a short time they again steamed in a straight line. To confuse the enemy, we always used an entirely different time sequence. Approaching close to the island, we were to enter a massive smoke screen we'd use for safety and shelter. Put in place by destroyers in an attempt to hide our group from the enemy the smoke lay more than a mile away.

Suddenly, out of the semi-darkness of dawn a twin engine Japanese "Betty" bomber, a Kamikaze loaded with high explosives, slammed into the leading APA. Hitting just below the water line it blew a massive hole in the side of the ship. A lot of the Marines, already gathered on deck, were carrying heavy backpacks waiting to climb down the debarkation nets. When the plane hit and exploded many were blown overboard. In the water they struggled to stay afloat. Many were unsuccessful.

Huge amounts of water gushed into the crippled APA. The Captain ordered his battered ship veered to one side out of formation to let the rest of the group continue toward the safety of the smokescreen. Command of the force of now only twenty-one ships passed to our Captain, Sydney S. Huguenin who took over the lead position in *APA 193*.

In the water close to us a gruesome scene unfolded. The Sanborn had been steaming behind and directly in line with the lead ship. Looking down to the water, in the new light of dawn, we saw men thrashing around attempting to stay afloat. We heard their screams of terror and cries for help as our ship continued on course steaming right through them. Many used arms to push and legs to kick against the ship in an attempt to get away from the hull as we moved past. For almost all of them this attempt to save their own life was futile. Watching, many of us on deck trembled with shock and emotion. Someone yelled in anger, "Why the hell don't we stop and lower a goddamn lifeboat?" There was no answer as we continued forward through the sea littered with dead, dying and struggling young men. From along our ship's sides the large propeller rapidly sucked the water backward and underneath. About three quarters of the way toward the rear of the ship the sucking action became extremely strong. So strong that many men were drawn under and pulled through the spinning propeller blades. The water behind the ship became red with blood. Bodies, parts of bodies, clothing and personal belongings boiled to the surface in the crimson wake. We couldn't stop and risk collision with the other ships in our group because it could result in even a greater loss of life. The men in the water were expendable and no attempt was made to rescue them. This was our only first hand experience with a suicide plane.

Later, we saw many other ships, hit by Kamikazes, burn and sink. Among those hit but not sunk was the battleship *New Mexico*. As soon as it became daylight a Kamikaze dove into her. A huge, perfectly shaped white smoke ring rose immediately from where the plane bored in. To me it looked as though some giant had been smoking a big cigarette and blew a massive ring. Rising slowly and gracefully it remained suspended and unbroken for about two minutes. I didn't know then, but found out later, that my dad Harry, a civilian cook on a merchant marine ship carrying ammunition and aviation gasoline for the invasion of Okinawa, was on the deck of his ship that morning only a mile or two from our convoy. He too saw the *New Mexico* get hit and after this he never saw her fire her guns again.

Because Okinawa was only about two hundred miles from the mainland of Japan the people in charge of this invasion thought that men and women of all ages, as well as children, would put up massive resistance and for us to counter this would require the largest force ever assembled.

About eight o'clock in the morning, now behind the protective cover of the smoke screen, we climbed down the debarkation nets into the Higgins boats. Circling in the water near the ship we waited for the order to head for the beach. Supporting the invasion this day were more than sixteen hundred ships. Some came from as close as the Philippines, others from as far as Seattle. We saw the huge flashes of flame and billows of smoke from the guns of our battleships, among them once more, the *USS Missouri, BB 63*. This would be her second and last action firing her guns in anger in WWII. Our lookouts counted nine heavy and three light cruisers and twenty-three destroyers joining in to rake the beach with high explosive shells. The unrelenting roar of the big guns seemed to actually penetrate our body. The intensity pained our ears and pounded our insides with a heavy jarring sensation. It was frightening even though we knew the roaring pandemonium invading our senses came from "friendly fire". At Okinawa during the pre-invasion barrage, our fighting ships placed on their targets the largest tonnage of shells ever fired from the sea.

The order came to deploy the landing craft to the beaches. On the way we met little enemy resistance. Here, so close to Japan, we were told it might be even worse than we experienced on Iwo Jima. To our surprise this didn't happen and in the boat our mood soared. We began to laugh, joke and even play "grab ass" the way happy troops often do. Grab ass is also known as "giving a wedgie or brownie". When done properly the victim's clothing, outside pants and inside shorts together, are firmly grasped from behind and jerked upward and forward very fast and real hard. The idea is to cause the underclothing to be pulled upward and gather very tightly between the "buns" of the victim. Many times this causes a highly embarrassing discoloration to be deposited on the shorts. The degree of success is directionally proportional to the size and stickiness of the offensive brown stain. I heard one

Marine say, "Hell, it don't matter, that stain is only rust from my iron constitution."

Just before nine o'clock in the morning each of the Higgins boats ran aground on an assigned beach. When the ramp lowered we jumped out crouched, then scattered. Though taking no enemy fire we remained very cautious for awhile then began to walk inland. Except for hearing some mortar rounds "crunching" in the distance and a few rifle shots from some enemy snipers, who were soon "eliminated", the entire operation the first day seemed almost like an exercise instead of the invasion of an enemy island.

As a medical corpsman I carried twenty-four, two-ounce bottles of hundred-proof apricot Brandy. Made in Santa Clara, California it had the reputation of being some of the very best. Before leaving the ship, as a "roving corpsman" my orders were, if casualties are light or non-existent I should go no further than the edge of the airfield with the troops before returning to the APA. Since there were only a few minor wounds, arriving at the destination I still had most of my bandages, sulfa powder, tape, Syrettes of morphine and most importantly, all twenty-four bottles of Brandy.

Sitting on the ground near the airfield with a group of 10 men, one veteran of past combat, knowing that corpsmen carried this delicious potion, came over and squatted beside me.

Trying to sound real friendly as if he were half kidding he asked, "Hey Doc, you got any of that there Brandy with you?"

I told him, "I've got all of it. But you know it can only be used for medical purposes, like pain or shock."

"By God Doc, I've got this hangnail here that's been giving me fits of pain. Does that count?" he chuckled halfheartedly.

Another man entering himself into the conversation, leaned toward me, "Yeah, I nicked myself shaving this morning before we left the ship, lost some blood too. Besides, I've got a couple of real bad ingrown hairs here on my neck. Talk about pain Doc. I think I'm about ready to go into shock."

Eight others were starting to crowd in as the pair of pitchmen spoke and by seeing the look in everyone's eyes I knew they each wanted to hear the three-letter word—"yes".

Looking at them for a moment I knew from past experience that everyone here would give his life for me as I would for them and quickly planned a surprise.

Their eager faces fell and they drew back a little when I said emphatically, "You know damn well without a good medical reason I can't give you any of this Brandy."

Making up a story I said, "I suppose you know, I do have to take all the stuff out of my bag and count it before going back to the ship. Now if I forget to put the Brandy back in the bag and you find it scattered around on the ground I suppose you'll pick it up and put it to good use for the relief of pain caused by that near fatal hang nail, your razor nick with blood loss, ingrown hairs and shock plus all the mental agony the rest of you probably are suffering from."

Seeing my wide grin their joy was noisily accompanied by quick yips, yells and outbursts of laughter. You'd think I gave them the world as I tipped my open medical bag on one side letting all 24 bottles roll slowly out—onto a poncho, that like magic, suddenly appeared on the ground under them to protect the bottles from breaking.

Eight of the men got two bottles. To be fair, together they decided that the two who made the biggest "pitch" would each get four.

Walking away to return to the ship, from a short distance I looked over my shoulder and watched as they waved, gave the "thumbs up" gesture and slowly drank the Brandy. Perhaps, for some, this may have been among their last moments of pleasure in this world.

Back on board the ship, because the initial landing had been so easy, I wondered if we might make it away from this island having few, if any casualties. When I mentioned it to one pessimistic sailor he offered his opinion, "Don't count on it Doc."

That afternoon the sky darkened. A massive buildup of black clouds appeared and gale force wind began to blow. Rain gushed in torrents from the angry sky. The Navy weatherman on our ship said he'd never seen a "low" as deep and intense as the one now building. Over the ship's loudspeakers he announced, "Now hear this, all hands make preparation for the ship to withstand severe weather conditions." This is the way regulations required him to officially announce it. But talking personally with the crew he'd say, "We're sure as hell gonna' see some real bad weather for at least the next three days." His prediction would be one of the biggest understatements I heard during the entire war.

The next morning it became evident that anywhere within sight of land was not the place for a ship to be. Howling wind, racing inland at more than 150 miles an hour pushed the water of the ocean ahead of it onto shore and waves here, on land, rose to a height of more than fifty feet. All ships in the area were ordered to quickly "put out to sea" taking them as far from land as possible. Our Captain ordered both boilers "lit off" and for the engine room crew to provide emergency "flank speed" as soon as possible making the propeller turn 106 times a minute, the maximum. At sea we encountered waves towering nearly 100 feet high. The ship rode up one side of a massive wall of water then slid down the other. Crashing to the bottom of the trough, the foredeck disappeared beneath the next wave blasting a spectacular cloud of spray skyward as high as the superstructure. "Lifelines" were rigged along all decks exposed to the weather to keep anyone having to go outside from being washed overboard. We each had individual body ropes with a strong metal snap ring securely attached to one end to be attached to any one of the heavy lifelines if we needed to go out on deck. All watertight doors and portholes were dogged shut. For 72 hours the storm raged. Every time the ship rose to the crest of a giant wave and began to slide down the other side, the stern came completely out of the water. The propeller, spinning rapidly in mid air, shuddered so violently it made the ship feel like it would shake itself to pieces. A few ships, upon reaching the top of a massive wave, broke in half sustaining many casualties.

At 106 turns, if in calm water we would be making headway of twenty-one knots, a little more than 23 miles an hour. But in the storm we were making headway of only two knots away from shore as the ship struggled against the ocean current and gale-force wind while Captain and crew fought to keep it from being driven backward, run aground and destroyed by the crushing force of the ocean.

As the ship battled the savage sea one more danger constantly lurked. The Sanborn, a 10,500 ton, class C-3 hull ship, had been designed to list to either side no more than a maximum of 45 degrees when empty, as we were now, and be able to right itself. In the wheelhouse the crew steering the ship watched apprehensively as the built in "tilt-meter" swung back and forth each time the Sanborn rocked from side to side. In the wild anger of the roiling sea, all eyes in that area nervously checked and re-checked the instrument.

Suddenly the ship listed sharply to one side and "lay over" wallowing in an unusually deep "cross trough". Everyone felt it. All sailors on board quit breathing for a moment. Everyone stopped talking. For what seemed like an eternity the ship remained heeled over to one side. It felt like it would never right itself. Then it began to shudder and very slowly come upright. According to the tilt-meter that recorded the event we took a 47-degree list and only by a miracle recovered.

For two more days the wind of the typhoon howled. The blackness of the water reflected that of the sky. When it was over, on the beaches of Okinawa lay hundreds of dead, washed overboard when their smaller, underpowered ships were not able to success-fully fight the raging storm. These ships made it only a short distance out to sea before being blown back. Grounded high on shore they were broken apart by the power of the immense surf. As the pessimist had said a few days earlier, "Don't count on the invasion of this island not taking its toll in lives."

Photographs I obtained illegally from a sailor on the Sanborn who had a camera, show ships, supplies and dead men washed up on shore in the aftermath of the typhoon. Though we were forbidden to take pictures he did it anyway. How did I get some of them? You might say that medical corpsmen at times also became wheeler-dealers. On board ship we had absolute control of "the goodies" including the wonderful 100-proof apricot brandy. In addition there were almost unlimited gallons of pure medical grade drinkable 190-proof ethyl alcohol stored in the sick bay. We could successfully negotiate for just about anything.

❖ A "SHELLBACK" REMEMBERS ❖

Orders came sending us to Noumea, New Caledonia. Here we would take aboard a load of heavy, thick walled steamfitter's pipe to be transported to the town of Otaru on Japans northern most Island, Hokkaido.

New Caledonia is located northeast of Australia and south of the equator. Navy crewmen who have not crossed this imaginary line are called "pollywogs". During the first crossing they must be initiated by "King Neptune" into "The Ancient Order of the Deep". King Neptune is always an "old salt", an experienced seaman who has crossed the equator at least once and usually many times. Having sailed over it on some earlier trip and is "initiated", he is called a "shellback".

On most Navy ships the initiation to become a shellback is far from pleasant. Limited only by the sadistic imagination of members of The Ancient Order of the Deep, the tradition certainly is memorable. On the Sanborn the carpentry department built an oversized casket. In the lid, at chest level, they cut a hole four inches in diameter. Waiting for initiation day it lay on the hot steel deck. During the last four days before crossing the equator all used coffee grounds, potato peels, left over food, cooking grease, slop and other garbage from the mess hall were dumped into it. Because of the intense equatorial heat and high humidity everything quickly became well rotted. By the fourth day it could only be called putrescent. The casket and its contents were now ready.

On initiation day two muscular shellbacks "helpfully" placed the reluctant pollywog into the casket and closed the lid. Another shellback slipped the nozzle of the ships high pressure fire hose into the four inch opening and turned it on full force sending clouds of sloppy wet, rotten, stinking, putrefied garbage mixed with piles of used coffee grounds, throughout the casket. The blast of extremely high-pressure seawater combined with the smell of putrefaction made it nearly impossible for the person inside to breathe. After a few minutes the initiate, sometimes half conscious from lack of air, was removed from the casket and led to a small stage nearby. Here a shellback waited beside a five-gallon pail filled with "graphite grease". He'd smear the black, sticky substance generously on every area of the pollywogs body where hair grew. This included head, armpits, chest and the extremely sensitive external areas of the reproductive and intestinal tract. Graphite grease is impossible to wash off with soap and water. The only way it can be removed is to flush it with generous amounts of gasoline, kerosene, mineral spirits or a carbon tetrachloride based solvent, all of which sting badly when applied to the "most sensitive" hair covered areas of the male. After initiation every pollywog knew first hand how a stray dog that has been "turpentined" must feel when this liquid is generously applied to its anal opening. It stings so badly the unwelcome animal usually runs away yelping loudly in pain and never returns.

Finally, looking toward the stern of the ship, we were shown a plank extending outward over the ocean. Then we were blindfolded and told because we were such downright no good subjects here in King Neptune's realm, we would have to "walk the plank" and be reported as being lost at sea.

With all the yelling, confusion and mistreatment going on a pollywog, perhaps only semi-conscious and fresh out of the casket full of putrid garbage, easily could be led to believe that the bunch of drunken shellbacks just may do something so stupid as to accidentally drop someone over the side.

I might have thought this somewhat more than most because I knew exactly how many cases of two-ounce bottles of the delicious 100-proof Santa Clara Apricot Brandy we personnel of the sick bay furnished to the shellbacks for the occasion. Putting it mildly, we all were "feeling no pain". In addition all pollywogs were reminded several times of the large schools of man-eating, great white sharks living in the warm waters here close to the equator not far from Australia.

None of the initiates knew that during the previous night

ships carpenters, boatswains and sail-makers rigged up a large canvas swimming pool. Filled with seawater and suspended in a frame beneath the overhanging ships stern, it couldn't be seen from where we stood on deck. A rope ladder hanging into the pool provided access back to the ship.

Blindfolds in place we were led to the plank and without warning, several drunken, screaming, cursing shellbacks shoved each pollywog off, one at a time, where we dropped 10 feet into the pool. The short drop seemed to last forever and because we could then taste the salty water we thought we must actually be in the ocean and frightening thoughts about man-eating sharks immediately came to mind. Two shellbacks, waiting in the pool, jammed us with long handled brooms having stiff bristles covered with a thin rubber sheathing while yelling, "Shark, shark!!" Still blindfolded I thought this must be the previous guy I saw from a distance get pushed off the plank, who got his blindfold off and on seeing some sharks shouted a warning. In my imagination the stiff rubber-covered bristles felt a lot like teeth.

Thus, on June 10, 1945, on an official Navy mission southward in west longitude, and latitude of 00 degrees, 00 minutes and 00 seconds, I crossed the equator properly frightened and became a shellback.

On board one of the other ships traveling with us, as we crossed the equator things did not go well. Their electricians rigged up an official looking metal trident for King Neptune to carry. Wired to an electric circuit it was supposed to give a mild shock when touched to the body of a pollywog. But something went tragically wrong. The first six sailors in the group were waiting to be inducted into the Ancient Order of the Deep. All in a row and tightly pressed together they wore only white under-shorts and stood barefoot in shallow running water used to cool the steel deck. When King Neptune touched one of them with the electrified trident and closed the switch instead of a tiny charge of current, a massive jolt surged through. King Neptune, standing off of the deck on a dry raised platform, wearing rubber soled thongs, felt enough of a shock to realize something had gone wrong. Frightened, he failed to switch off the electricity and dropped the massively charged trident into the water where the six sailors stood.

It took too long for an electrician to get below decks to the generator room and cut off the current. The six sailors fell to the deck together. Writhing in the shallow puddle, all were killed by electrocution. These men had survived some of the worst battles of the war and to die like this was a terrible twist of fate.

Great beauty could be seen and great sadness could be felt this far south in the Pacific. Usually the water remained totally calm and crystal clear. Sailing on its surface felt like gliding noiselessly along on a sheet of glass. Near Guadalcanal, one evening just before sundown, we sailed across a part of the ocean called "Iron Bottom Sound." Many Japanese and some American ships, sunk earlier in WWII, littered the sea floor. The water, though 50 to 100 feet deep, was so clear that while resting on the bottom they appeared to be only a few feet beneath our ship. Most were tipped onto one side. However, a few remained resting on their keel looking like sunken toys in the bottom of a huge bathtub. For many in our crew this eerie and ghostly sight brought to mind that many dead seamen remained in them, trapped forever.

I remembered that much earlier in the war when stationed in the Psychiatric Unit at Imola, California, an Admiral came to the facility to question us. He said there had been a battle off Guadalcanal on a very dark night. In the confusion two of our Cruisers, the Astoria and the Vincennes, had sank each other. Another U.S. ship also was involved, the Quincy. The Admiral wanted to know if we had any hospital personnel or survivors from either ship that were eye witnesses to this action because the Navy was trying to find the cause of this tragic event. Unfortunately, we had no one on staff or anyone in our care that saw it. The truth of exactly what happened that night has never been resolved to everyone's satisfaction and probably never will be.

During the day I'd sometimes go out on deck to watch the

hundreds of flying fish, using their pectoral fins as wings, glide above the water beside the ship. They flew as high as ten feet and as fast as the ship, about seventeen knots, or nineteen miles an hour. Generally their colors were a combination of red and white. Fun to watch, some sustained flight for almost thirty feet.

At night I'd look over the rail and see a beautiful greenish-blue florescence, glowing in the water like thousands of tiny colored fires following alongside. Behind, in the wake churned up by the propeller, the florescence became spectacular. It was caused from disturbing the millions of light emitting organisms in the water as the ship passed through them.

Visible only from south of the equator the constellation Southern Cross appeared nightly in the velvet blackness of the sky. Standing at the rail I'd sometimes think, "How peaceful and quiet everything is here." I wished my best friend Dary, who was killed on Iwo Jima, could have enjoyed this serenity and I was grateful for the darkness that hid sadness and tears.

On the way to New Caledonia we stopped at Tulagi located in the Florida Islands. It lies about twenty-five miles east of Guadalcanal, at the southern end of the strategic waterway known, during WWII, as "the slot". Although the weather was blistering hot, here it rained frequently. When a sudden squall hit the hot steel deck of the Sanborn it caused steam to become so thick when walking and looking down we couldn't see anything below our knees. But as quickly as the rain came it stopped. After experiencing this a few times, during a squall most of us didn't bother to take shelter. When the sun re-appeared we'd be totally dry within a short time and the few extra moments of coolness our wet clothes provided were most welcome in the oppressive equatorial humidity and heat.

At Tulagi, during WWII the only fatality among all of us growing up together in Olinda, happened. William "Clack" Crow joined the Marines early in the war and duty brought him to this part of the world. Thirty minutes before the main invasion of Guadalcanal he accompanied a contingent of men sent to capture Tulagi. His unit, out gunned and out manned, faced a much larger force than intelligence had reported to be on this tiny island. That morning on the beach of a small cove called "Maggott Bay" Clack, and many others, died. The place got its name because after the battle hundreds of dead Marines were left for days to rot in the water or on the sandy beach. Before they could be retrieved, in the terrible heat and with so many flies around, the bodies quickly became heavily infested with millions of maggots. I've heard it said that graves registration personnel never again saw such a ghastly sight during the entire war.

At Tulagi we were given liberty. Someone from home wrote and told me where Clack had been killed and I made my way to where it happened. Standing alone on the sand of the cove I recalled an incident from many years ago involving Clack.

At the grade school in Olinda during lunch hour four of us boys, including Clack, were having fun jumping from a tabletop located a short distance inside the equipment shed and then catch a cross rafter located a few feet above the open doorway. Catching it we'd swing a few moments, hollering like Tarzan, then drop two or three feet to the ground, run back, get in line, climb back on the table and do it all over again. On one jump Clack misjudged, jumped too high and missed catching the rafter with his hands. Instead both forearms hit it flipping him over backward. In mid air he extended one arm behind himself in an effort to lessen the impact of the fall. As he hit the ground the lower end of both bones of the wrist snapped and he sustained a "silver fork" fracture. This made the arm look like it had an extra joint in it just above the wrist. Someone yelled, "Hey everybody, come see this. It looks like Clack broke his arm." Everyone gathered around him curious to see the strange shape close to his wrist. After he let us all have a look at it, Clack walked nonchalantly into the schoolhouse and calmly said to our teacher, "Mrs. Jordan, I think I just broke my arm." Questioning him she found he wasn't in pain and told him to sit out on the porch and wait.

Ulbergs' grocery and feed store was located about a hundred yards from the school and Emil Ulberg was head of the school board. As a result, Clack enjoyed the 12-mile ride to Redding in Mr. Ulberg's brand new shiny black Buick Roadmaster and Dr. Kay set the arm that healed perfectly. On the other hand Mrs. Jordan seemed kind of nervous and on edge while teaching the rest of the afternoon.

Standing alone on the sand of the cove at Tulagi, on the small beach of Maggott Bay where Clack died, with mixed emotion I thought of this incident that happened so long ago and felt sadness.

❖ TRIP HOME AT WAR'S END ❖

For many aboard the Sanborn the entrance to the harbor at Noumea, New Caledonia appeared too narrow for the ship to go through. It looked like anything afloat bigger than a large rowboat couldn't get in. Just as it approached the entrance, the ship also had to make what appeared to be an impossible 90-degree turn. Standing on the prow I watched the harbormaster thread the ship past the clearly visible, massive underwater rocks and jagged reefs. Often within less than ten feet on each side of the hull, as we skimmed past it looked like we'd surely hit one that would rip the ship open and we'd perhaps sink. I didn't think the Sanborn, the 10,500- ton Attack Transport could pass through this small channel. But at the last moment the harbormaster guided the ship in a tight left turn and we glided between the high bluffs on each side, safely into port.

Ever since Dary was killed I always went on liberty with Swanberg. Noumea had no theaters or USO but it did have a huge PX. As we entered, close to the doorway we were amazed to see thousands of packages of Wrigley's chewing gum in a massive heap. Within a stabilizing enclosure, at least fifteen feet across and four feet high, it was piled to almost overflowing. We couldn't believe that much chewing gum existed in the world and servicemen in uniform could take all they wanted at no charge.

There were two houses in town where "pseudo affection", and I'm sure real infection, could be obtained. One had the name, "The Pink House", the other, "The White House." Both opened at three o'clock in the afternoon, about an hour before liberty cards for the Navy and Marines and passes for the Army were issued. A lot of comparing went on between the servicemen who participated in the "fleeting pleasures of the flesh" the occupants of the houses offered. Each claimed the girls in the one he always visited were superior in the knowledge of how to use their many and varied carnal talents. Swanberg and I were often urged to "just go and try one out". Seeing what syphilis did to Street after he contracted it at the Stockade in Tijuana, the night before we sailed from the United States for the war zone, neither Swanberg nor I had any urge to compare the talents of anyone from either house.

There were only three bars in Noumea. They were, "The New York", "The California" and "The "Montana". Two of the owners must have had good business sense. They obviously knew the States of California and New York were the most populated and that the name visible outside their bar would attract lots of homesick servicemen. On the other hand, just what the owner of the Montana Bar was thinking when he named his establishment we never figured out. But because it was always quiet Swanberg and I visited it several times to drink one or two bottles of cold beer. There were never more than six other servicemen inside and how the owner remained in business with so few dropping by remains a mystery.

It took more than a week to take on a load of thick walled steam-fitters pipe and when we were scheduled to leave New Caledonia we almost didn't. The extra weight of the pipe caused the ship to ride deeper in the water than usual.

A tug brought us away from the dock and left us in the middle of the small harbor. Captain Huguenin signaled the engine room, "slow-ahead". The blades of the propeller began to turn and each one dug deeply into the muddy harbor bottom. The ship shuddered as clouds of silt and muck welled up in the water behind. The Captain quickly gave the order, "all stop." Stepping outside the wheelhouse high above the main deck he called down to a local resident in a small boat along side asking if he knew whether the harbor got any deeper in the direction we were heading. The man in the boat said it did. With the propeller turning slowly each blade again struck the harbor bottom bumping and jarring the ship. For a short distance it continued to suck up and churn out a torrent of mud and silt. A machinist mate told us if the propeller hit bottom hard enough this could strip the gears inside the turbine or break the main shaft. Worrying all the way we finally made it out to the open ocean.

Our destination; Otaru, Japan, located on Hokkaido Island just north of Honshu across the ten mile wide Tsugaru Strait.

For weeks we steamed north. The weather slowly changed from oppressive equatorial heat and humidity to the pleasant coolness of the northern hemisphere. In Wakayama we made our first stop. A small city on the southeast part of Honshu, the main island of Japan, it hadn't been bombed. It had the nickname, "the glass city" because close to the waterfront dock it had a large, though long unused, plate glass manufacturing plant.

Built on a hillside, public transportation was provided by a typical old-fashioned streetcar, a real "Toonerville Trolley" that took electric power from an overhead wire through a single catanary wheel fitted on the end of a long spring loaded pole above the car. A rope trailing from the pole was used, exactly like those on the old "streetcars" in America, to re-position the contact wheel on the electrified wire above if it came off on a sharp turn or because it rolled incorrectly, while under power, "sparking" through an overhead switch.

The ancient trolley ran from the waterfront area, by way of many switchbacks, up a long steep grade to the business section at the top. Given liberty, everyone wanted to buy a souvenir to represent the first time we set foot in now defeated Japan. An old Japanese man operating the nearly worn out rickety conveyance, insisted we pay nothing to ride. At the top of the hill the partially malfunctioning brakes jolted us to an abrupt stop. Swanberg and I went into a nearby business house. Some sailors we met earlier on the dock told us that in this store bolts of beautiful silk were a great buy.

As we came through the doorway several young Japanese girls smiled and bowed but did not speak. Neatly arranged on tables were hundreds of bolts of gorgeous silk shimmering in every hue. After looking at the outstanding display I told Swanberg I'd like to buy two bolts of the white glistening cloth.

Approaching the young girl I considered the prettiest in the store I gestured toward the tables with their profusion of color and blurted out, "Want silk, want silk. OK?" Before she could reply I continued to babble using stilted language. "How much yen for silk?" I asked.

To me, my question sounded like it could have been Davy Crockett talking with the Indians and I suspect, as it turned out, it also must have sounded the same to the pretty young girl.

She smiled showing beautiful straight white teeth. Obviously amused, with a gentle voice and using perfect English she calmly replied, "Oh, that's a great buy. Each bolt is for sale today for just ten yen."

Foolishly I once more blurted out, "Where did you learn to speak English so good?"

Continuing to smile, obviously enjoying our encounter she said, "I'm a graduate in Business Administration from the University of California at Berkeley. My Father and Mother had a large ranch near Sacramento. I came to Japan during the last week in November of 1941 to visit my Grandparents. When war broke out the Japanese government wouldn't let me go home, so here I am." Her dark brown eyes sparkled noticing that I hung intently on her every word.

I liked her right away and blame raging pent up male hormones for keeping me talking such a long time. She was so cheerful, enthusiastic and so American and I had just spent months at sea as well as on foreign soil without seeing anyone this pretty.

Because she indeed was an American it seemed natural, when the thought crossed my mind, to ask her for a date. Taking Swanberg aside I asked if he thought it would be O.K. His law school trained mind advised against it. "A gang of young Japs might resent seeing you with one of their own, jump you and kill you." Reluctantly I dropped the idea but did buy two bolts of white silk. Many years later after I married my wife, Glenora, from the bolts she made beautiful sheer silk drapes that graced our home for many years on N.E. Alameda St. in Portland, Oregon.

We continued on to Yokohama. Here devastation from

incendiary bombs was total. The damage had been caused by some of the one thousand plane raids of B 29's we watched fly overhead earlier in the war as we sweltered in the heat for 56 days while "hanging on the hook" in the harbor at Saipan.

During liberty Swanberg and I walked around for a couple of hours among the wreckage of this once great metropolis. We didn't see one Japanese citizen. The city, like a shattered corpse, lay abandoned.

Leaving Yokohama we steamed toward the northern end of Honshu. As we began to pass through the east end of Tsugaru Strait we saw the white smokestacks of the sugar mill in the town of Hakodate, located north of Honshu on Hokkaido. At that time the tallest in the world, from our vantage point looking north while sailing in the narrow, ten-mile wide Strait, they appeared to pierce the sky.

Half way through the Strait we diverted south into Mutsu Bay docking at Aomori. One of the most northern cities on Honshu, it had been totally leveled by firebombs dropped from the B-29's. Except for a large bank vault, made from steel and concrete and the entrance to an old cemetery, having a "Gate of Heaven" fashioned from wrought iron, not one thing remained standing. In an incendiary bomb firestorm, Aomori vanished from the face of the earth.

Piled neatly on the dock were hundreds of brand new .31 caliber Japanese rifles. Their semi-polished stocks, perhaps made from cherry wood, were a dull red color that looked like velvet. Each rifle had the Lotus blossom design deeply stamped into the blued steel of the breech. Everyone on the ship wanted one but Captain Huguenin was reluctant. However, after our executive officer, Commander Schwartz and first officer Lieutenant Gray "talked with him" awhile they reported the Captain said, "Oh, what the hell, give one to each member of the crew."

We learned later that about an hour before the two senior officers met with the Captain, our first class corpsman, Craig Hardegree, had been seen providing Mr. Schwartz with two cases, 48 two ounce bottles, of 100 proof apricot brandy. After some speculation and laughter as to whether this had any bearing on the ultimate decision by the Captain, we corpsmen discretely dropped the subject.

I don't know how but after getting it home the rifle has been lost.

A few days later we arrived in the harbor at Otaru on Hokkaido and began to unload the heavy cargo of pipe. As when loading in Noumea it took almost a week. During this time we were allowed to go on liberty. We were told when we were in Yokohama by sailors who had already been to Otaru, that a bar of soap, a carton of Lucky Strike cigarettes and Baby Ruth or Milky Way candy bars were worth a lot more than the United States Military issued "script" that replaced Japanese Yen. However, orders given by Captain Huguenin said that no one was to take these items ashore. It was illegal to take anything bought from the ship's PX onto Japanese soil and all personnel leaving on liberty would be subject to search. But I knew that almost all sailors were both devious and inventive.

Inside the top of our cold weather dress blue hat we could tape several single packs of cigarettes. Another two cartons were easily taken from the ship, one taped just below the knee to each leg. With the lower end of the carton secured against the inner leg inside the top of a sock and the upper end wrapped with tape just below the knee, in our bellbottom trousers they couldn't be detected by the deck officer as we saluted the flag on the fantail and left the ship.

Soap and candy bars, small but heavier, required special handling. A little slit, just big enough to put the candy and soap through, had to be cut in the top near the shoulder of the inner lining of our cold weather pea coat. If cut in the bottom the contraband could slide downward inside the lining and might fall out in front of the officer of the deck as we left the ship. The truth is that every officer, including Commander Schwartz went ashore carrying these trade items. As a result, the possibility of being searched fell to zero.

No one slowed as he stepped from the quarterdeck and with

one smooth motion saluted the flag at the stern of the ship and in seconds descended the gangplank. Would a Lieutenant Junior grade, the lowest of the deck officers, even though he knew the orders existed, so much as even think of requiring a three stripe, full Commander to undergo a search? If contraband items were found on him, would the lowly young deck officer confiscate it and "write up" our three-stripe Commander? Never!! Navy politics and the "good old boy" network, created by what we had been through together, simply didn't allow a search to happen to any one going ashore from the Sanborn. But Captain Huguenin had to issue the order and place it in the ship's log as some "C.Y.A" (cover your ass) insurance for himself.

Otaru, like Wakayama, had not been bombed. But the conditions of abject poverty, such as little food, fuel and lack of almost all other supplies, devastated the people. For example, to move around in their community they either walked or rode poorly maintained bicycles that had no oil on the chain or grease in the wheel or pedal crank bearings. All squeaked loudly and constantly when in use. I don't recall seeing one car running during the time we were there though many were at curbside thickly covered with dust. From disuse, most tires were flat or nearly so.

Swanberg and I walked toward the business section where a few stores with very little to sell were open. On the way to town we came upon what proved for us to be rare treasures.

In a small "Mom and Pop" business conducted in a private home, the owners had brought out for sale their authentic family ceremonial robes. Handmade from very heavy silk, on them they had thick appliqué of large dragons and many other designs made from gold and silver metallic thread. Each robe blazed with color and was offered in both men and women's styles. They had large square "sleeve pockets" that dangled between the wrist and elbow. In addition, they had beautifully hand-sewn sashes complete with intricate tassels on either end, made from the same gold and silver metallic thread. They were breathtaking!!

Pointing to the robes I asked an older lady who stood near, "How many Yen?"

With a deeply wrinkled face, weathered skin and a thatch of unkempt gray hair, the woman looked to be at least 85 years old as did the man standing next to her. They smiled and bowed from the waist, in the typical custom of older Japanese, then pointed to the robes shaking their heads "No". Taking out our wallets Swanberg and I again pointed to the robes, then turned our fingers toward our money. We could tell they understood we wanted to buy the garments, but by shaking their heads at our occupation issue yen and indicating by moving their hands in a pushing motion, we knew we should put it back.

The old man gestured pretending to light a cigarette. Holding two fingers of one hand to his lips as though smoking he nodded, "Yes". We knew he meant, "Do you have cigarettes?" Then the old lady smiled and pretended to be washing her hands. Despite the total language barrier Swanberg and I easily understood. Leaning toward the man I pointed to the beautiful vermilion robe. Bending down, from inside a trouser leg I removed the tape and brought out a full carton of Lucky Strike cigarettes, the ones that came in the original green package with the red ball on the side. The man quickly took the brightly colored robe from the hanger and shook his head "yes" at least a dozen times. Obviously hooked on nicotine, as he handed me the robe he smiled widely. His open mouth showed pyorrhea infected, shrinking gums and exposed roots. Most of his deeply pitted decay blackened snags that once were teeth, badly needed repair.

I took off my "lumpy" pea coat and put it as flat as possible on a small table. From it I slid out from the slit at the top of the lining, four bars of Navy issue saltwater soap, the kind that lathers equally well in fresh or salt water. Extending them toward the grizzled old lady I pointed to the white robe. She saw the remaining bulges in the lining of my coat and realized there were other things inside. A good businesswoman she hesitated. Backing away a few steps she touched the white robe nodding "Yes" while pointing to the remaining bulges in the coat.

Swanberg said, "Besides the soap you better offer her something else or you won't get the white one."

I took his advice and slid out a Milky Way. Still not bringing the robe she stepped hesitantly toward me. This time she beamed a smile showing her own dental disaster as I slipped out a second candy bar, a Baby Ruth. Her head nodded "yes" many times as she stepped over to remove the stunning white robe from the hanger. While I put my pea coat on she wrapped both robes in some yellowed newspaper and tied the package with strips of old cloth.

After going through a similar bargaining routine Swanberg bought an electric blue robe for himself and for his wife a soft pink colored one. We had made a coup. I found out later because of the authenticity, that is, no brand name labels and made by hand, they were each worth about one thousand dollars when I had mine appraised in 1955. They now would be priceless.

On board the Sanborn I managed to keep the rifle, robes and bolts of silk safe and brought them home. My Mother kept them for me for several years. After Glenora and I were married in 1948 I got the robes back and on special occasions, we'd wear them. They were so comfortable and the heavy, cool silk felt good against our bare skin. Sadly, as with the Japanese .31 caliber rifle, they too became lost.

After the war I sometimes thought of the two old Japanese people who, for economic reasons or perhaps survival, traded their treasured family ceremonial robes for a pittance. A carton of cigarettes cost me $1.25 each. A bar of soap cost ten cents and candy bars were a nickel.

The war had not been their idea. They harmed no one. Yet, through no fault of their own, these older citizens suffered terrible hardship.

Carrying our treasured robes, in town we entered a three-story department store. Here I bought a small statue, made from fired ceramic, of a green dragon on whose back rides a princess dressed in a white flowing robe carrying a mace of office. The sales lady, who spoke some English, told me it represents the victory of pureness and peace over the distress and hardship of war. This statue remains in my den at home.

From Hokkaido we were ordered to return to the United States where the Sanborn would be put in dry dock in San Diego for repair. Upon arrival in the Golden State, in typical 80-degree weather under a cloudless sky, we were greeted at dockside by a band on a raised platform playing rousing music.

In front of the band stood an absolutely gorgeous young blonde, scantily clad in a very tight, blue "short shorts" bottom, at least several sizes too small. With every move hundreds of sequins on her uniform glistened in the sunlight as she sang. Her equally scanty halter-top reflected thousands of sparkling sunbeams from the matching sequined cloth that, with little success, tried to contain her heaving bosom as she sweetly crooned the question, "Why not take all of me?"

Hundreds of us who lined the ship's rail as the tugboats slowly pushed the Sanborn the last few feet toward the dock, sure as hell would have "taken all of her" if we could have approached anywhere near. To make matters worse, as she slowly rotated time after time we'd clearly see every one of the perfectly defined hills and valleys of her delightfully curved and scantily clad body that held the very highest interest for all of us fantasizing, girl starved, sailors. I found it hard (oops! A Freudian slip), as did many sailors who tightly pressed themselves against the rail of the ship, to believe that anyone would torture returning servicemen this way.

As if to compensate for our misery, we were treated to a humorous incident. While the ship was being tied up, out on the dock a sailor from another ship stood directly in front of the raised bandstand looking up in awe at the gorgeous blond. He became mesmerized as the band played while she sang, turned and gyrated. In one hand he held a fresh donut and in the other a newly opened quart of ice-cold milk provided by the Red Cross. Standing bug-eyed he intensely watched every movement of her extremely tight uniform as it faithfully followed even the smallest indentation and rise of each outstandingly gorgeous curve of her body. At the moment she breathlessly crooned the final words of the song, "So why not take all of me?" he let out a loud raucous groan heard by everyone near. Then quickly brushing off his hat with one forearm he slowly poured the entire quart of ice-cold milk over his head.

After sailing on the Pacific more than 62,000 miles, for me the war was over.

❖ HOME IS THE SAILOR ❖

On November 28, 1945, having seen continuous duty in the Pacific for almost a year the *USS Sanborn APA 193* arrived in San Diego, California. Here she would be placed in dry dock to make repairs and repaint all surfaces that had long remained beneath the water line.

All personnel with the required ninety-three or more "points" were eligible for discharge and we were told to pack all extra clothes and personal belongings in our sea bag. While doing this, the opportunity presented itself to easily "liberate" a wealth of valuable items. Portable typewriters, calculators and sets of tiny, precision medical instruments could easily be wrapped inside clothes and concealed. "Amazingly" from the ships PX, the entire supply of low cost cigarettes, which we were absolutely forbidden to take off of the ship, suddenly became totally depleted.

I was tempted to wrap inside of some clothing a couple of microscopes, including the one Hardegree used on our way to Hawaii to confirm the diagnosis that Street had contracted primary syphilis in Tijuana, before we left the United States. I also wanted to "liberate" many other surgical instruments, as well as dozens of syringes and hypodermic needles of every size, all of which were brand new in their original boxes.

Of exceptional interest: state of the art instruments used for eye surgery. There were very small scissors, precision ground and very sharp, scalpels and extra blades, retractors and needle holders. In addition, there were tiny needles pre-threaded with suture as fine as human hair, used to repair the smallest small blood vessels. I planned to take advantage of the G.I. Bill and return to college as a pre-med student. Thinking ahead, I thought these items could be of future value.

Over the public address system came an announcement, "The sea bags of all personnel leaving the ship will be subject to inspection before being transferred to the dock and shipped home."

Obviously a scare tactic, this never happened. Instead, all bags were quickly tossed, one on top of the other into a huge rope sling, winched over the side and thrown into a waiting American Express truck for shipment to the address appearing on the attached destination tag.

Raised until age 17 as a Seventh Day Adventist, a denomination which strongly teaches that one should live by the Ten Commandments as much as is humanly possible, somehow I couldn't bring myself to steal. Two factors caused me to reject the urge. A "still small voice", the eighth Commandment whispered within me, "Thou shalt not steal." It then continued with a verse from the Bible, "Be sure your sin will find you out." What deterred me least was the announcement from the loudspeaker of the ship's public address system.

At the end of the first week in December, with the ship in dry dock, I saluted the Officer of the Deck and handed him the copy of my 33-day pre-discharge leave papers and picture identification card.

"Permission to leave the ship, Sir."

Returning the salute and glancing at the documents he replied, "Permission granted Curnow. I see you're mustering out. Good luck and well done."

"Thank you Sir," I replied

At the top of the gangplank, with deeply mixed emotions of both joy and sadness, I turned to the American flag. As if to wave goodbye, it fluttered in a light breeze above the afterdeck. Looking at it and what I could see of the rest of the superstructure, for the last time I quickly raised my right hand giving the required salute to the flag as I had so often done before. Descending the gangplank tears dimmed my eyes. On the dock I turned to look at the ship one more time. "Well Sanborn, you've been a good ship. You gave us a great ride under some harrowing circumstances and you brought almost everyone home. I wish you well." Turning away I wiped my eyes several more times before heading for the Greyhound bus station.

With some of the $100.00 mustering out pay I bought a one-way ticket to Redding, California, the town nearest to Olinda. Here I'd first visit my Cousin Rex and some High School buddies and later my special girlfriend from High School, Marian Ulberg who now lived in Redding.

Telephones in every home were not available in Olinda, a very rural community, so I hitchhiked the 12 miles to get there. In my dress blue uniform, I had no trouble getting a ride. Tailor made in Honolulu it had my expert rifleman insignia on the lower left sleeve just above the wrist. With both a red cross and a chevron of red beneath a blazing white American eagle just above the elbow, these identified me as a rated, Navy Medical Corpsman. Pinned high on my chest on the left side of my tunic were my "theater of war" bars one having two stars indicating the number of enemy actions in which I participated.

The first car that approached stopped and an older couple from Red Bluff drove 12 miles out of their way to take me to the front gate of Rex's home in Olinda.

He had recently returned from serving with the Army in Greenland.

His oldest brother, Bud, also had recently returned from Army service. He had the distinction to be selected to serve as "honor guard" at the ceremonies in San Francisco that brought about the formation of the United Nations. This special assignment was given to only a few soldiers.

Seeing me thank the old couple and get out of the car Rex walked down the driveway to meet me at the gate. The country road, still nothing but dirt and red dust, put up a choking cloud that drifted over us as the car moved away. Though we hadn't been together for several years we greeted each other, as we always did, unemotionally and matter of fact as though we had parted only a day or two before.

"Boy, you've gained a little weight," Rex said

"Not much. I weighed 119 pounds when I joined up and now I'm 147. How about you? You gain or lose any?"

"Nope, I'm about the same, 160 or so."

"You got any clothes I can wear? I'd sure like to get out of this uniform."

"Sure, plenty. We're about the same size now so they'll fit O.K."

When his mother, Hattie, saw Rex and me strolling toward the house she hurried to the door.

"Gene, Gene," she greeted with a hug. "It's so good to have all you kids home. How are you?"

"I'm fine and I can smell something real good cooking."

"You're just in time. I have a double batch of chocolate chip cookies in the oven and a big frying pan on the stove full of those extra thick hamburgers smothered in mushrooms and onion gravy I make from deer meat and beef. I know how well you like both of those."

When able I asked, "Well, how is my 'young old' Auntie?"

"Now that every one of you boys are home safe, I'm just fine," she smiled.

Rex's mother, Hattie, was my favorite Aunt. Because Rex and I were only seven weeks apart in age I spent as much time at his house as I did at mine and Hattie also considered me to be "one of her kids". She jokingly named Rex and me "The Gold Dust Twins." Rex and I grew up in the California sun where in summer the temperature often rose to 116 and sometimes as hot as 121 degrees. Our normally light colored hair would bleach almost platinum blonde and our very white skin became so tanned it looked like brown leather. She got the idea for our nickname from the boxes that contained the very popular powdered soap she used for washing clothes. Called "Gold Dust", on the box it had a picture of two very clean, deep brown Negro twins with bleached blonde hair. Beneath them was the caption, "the gold dust twins".

Even when she reached the age of 80 she continued to have a sense of humor, a youthful spirit and a zest for life that few her age still knew. She looked forward, always planning for the future never living in self-pity or dwelling on the tragedy of loosing her husband in an automobile accident early in her life. To me my 'young old Auntie', as I jokingly called her, remained to the end, ever young.

The day after I arrived in Olinda Rex suggested we get together with two friends, Kenny Rassmussen and Piffer Smith who also recently returned from military service. With Rex and I in his 1928 modified Chevrolet pickup and Kenny and Piffer in Kenney's 1929 Ford coupe we drove to Anderson, a small town six miles east of Olinda. At Deusenchans drug store Rex bought a "fifth" of whiskey. To save money he selected Johnny Walker, Red Label, a cheap, almost "rot gut" brand that felt, when swallowed without a mixer, like liquid fire burning all the way from mouth to stomach. Rex made the observation, "you know, after the first swallow your mouth, throat and stomach become totally numb. The result is, the rest goes down feeling just as smooth as an expensive brand." He was right and we were going to use it to celebrate our safe return home.

After driving south to Red Bluff, we headed west on Gas Point Road driving 45 miles into the beautiful mountains of the Coast Range. Two miles past the tiny town of Beegum, on the road fresh December snow became too deep for us to continue. We got out, threw snowballs, took snapshots —- and drank a lot of toasts to various things. As the alcohol in our blood increased so did the silliness of the toasts.

"I'd like to toast to your shoestrings," Piffer slurred.

Finding it difficult to stand, I sat on the running board of the 28 Chevrolet and mumbled, "O.K., I'll toast to your left thumbnail."

Rex and Kenny, bleary eyed and swaying on their feet, agreed we should drink to "all those hundreds of cold little lizards hibernating under the snow."

Soon we were happy and "roaring drunk" but we didn't care. We were home, out of military service and comfortable to be once more in familiar surroundings. We also were grateful to have returned alive, not disfigured or with major wounds, after having actively been in harm's way.

Many veterans that saw combat, when they arrived home, avoided girl friends and stayed drunk in an attempt to forget, or at least dull, their very unpleasant memories. I too did this. Thus, began almost a month that Rex and I stayed drunk every night and most days.

Rex's brother Bud let us use his car, a well kept 1936 Chevrolet four door sedan he bought brand new for $695.00. It was the only car in the family having legal and current license plates. On Saturday nights we'd sometimes use it to go to a dance in Cottonwood, a small town 15 miles south of Anderson. Wearing my tailor made dress blue uniform with the colorful insignia, combat ribbons and stars, I had no trouble attracting a number of young ladies. I'd choose a pretty one who seemed to be the most receptive and Rex would choose one of interest to him. With them in the car we'd leave the dance and drive a few miles out of town to some remote spot on a country road. Here in the moonlight, in the wonderful presence of some far outstretched limbs beneath a white oak tree, we'd soon be doing that which in youth came naturally.

Other nights we'd drive to Redding, sit in a bar until closing time listening to music while downing drink after drink. I'd usually drive back to Olinda because most of the time Rex wasn't able to sit up behind the steering wheel. On the way home he'd usually vomit several times.

One night he became what can only be described as "outrageously drunk". The nausea hit him about three o'clock in the morning when we were out in the country driving home on the seldom-used dirt road between Anderson and Olinda.

"Pull over Gene, I'm going to puke," he said. I stopped the car. Rex, got out and half falling weaved and stumbled about 50 feet from the road to get behind a telephone pole. I heard him retch and spit, while bringing up everything.

When he came back to the car, with a thick tongue I asked, "What I want to know is how come you went all the way over behind that telephone pole to throw up?"

"Well I sure didn't want anyone to see me," he slurred.

In spite of our drunkenness this ridiculous answer hit both of us funny. Even in our alcoholic fog, it was obvious that no one in his right mind would be on the deserted road at this hour.

Screaming with nonsensical laughter Rex vomited some more. From laughing so hard I wet my pants. To protect the cloth upholstery, while sitting on a folded up gunnysack we found in the trunk, in soaked pants I drove the rest of the way home.

Right after lunch on the last Sunday before leaving Olinda for Bremerton, Washington to receive my Honorable Discharge, Bud let Rex and me use his car to go to Redding to visit Marian Ulberg, my special girl friend through High School. Rex waited in the car. Marian's Mother answered the knock on the door and I greeted her with my usual, "Hi Mrs. Ulberg."

"Oh Gene!!" she burst out. "My conscience grief, (Mrs. Ulberg always used this expression when she got excited and nobody I knew could explain why she said it or what it meant), it's so good to see you. Come in. I'll tell Marian you're here." She called, "Marian, Marian, Gene's here." Turning to me in one breath she asked, "How have you been? Are you hungry? Marian got your letters and she let us read some of them." Pointing to the sofa she invited, "Here, sit down."

Because of the way she had urged me to come in the house on Sundays to read the funny papers during the eleven years I lived in Olinda and how she always called for Marian to come and visit with me whenever I'd accept the invitation, it became obvious that Mrs. Ulberg had more than a little interest in seeing that her daughter Marian and I would eventually marry.

When Marian entered the living room her smiling blue eyes met mine and I felt like a jolt of electricity hit me. She quickly came over and sat by me, pressing very close.

"Well, I'll leave you two together to talk." After saying that, Mrs. Ulberg went into the kitchen.

Though we often wrote letters I hadn't seen Marian for almost four years. She was even prettier than I remembered. I felt out of place for a moment and a little bashful. But she snuggled closely and as we talked the feeling vanished. Soon it seemed like we were continuing our lives from where we left off.

As soon as Mrs. Ulberg left the room, Marian and I turned to each other. After hesitating the briefest moment we were wrapped in each other's arms in a long lasting bear hug. After several "special kisses" no doubt remained and body language told me our relationship had quickly become re-established.

Finally I asked, "Would you like to go out later this afternoon?" Rex has a date with Margaret Rush and we're going up to Shasta Dam. Could you come with us?" My words seemed to tumble out too fast. Then I added jokingly, "Rex wants to see how all the cement he packed down with that big vibrator machine when he worked on the dam has held up."

Marian's receptiveness both pleased and startled me.

She spoke excitedly. "Yes, this afternoon would be fine. What time?"

"About four o'clock. Would that be all right?"

"Sure, I'll be ready."

"We have to go," I said. "Bud needs the car awhile this afternoon."

"See you later." We squeezed hands as I began moving toward the door. "Say goodbye to your Mom for me." Crossing the big screened in "sleeping porch" I headed for the car. Before air conditioning in homes became common many people had a full-length, enclosed porch on the front of their house. In hot weather, such as 116 degrees or more that was common in Redding, screens in frames enclosed the porch. Here people could "beat the heat" and sleep comfortably. In cold weather the screens were removed and glass in frames were taken from storage and put in.

About two weeks earlier Rex and I had found a secluded place off of Highway 99 near Red Bluff. Thirty five miles south of Redding, its only access was an abandoned, poorly marked, rutted road. Here we spent one of our many days of drunken binges laughing, crying and talking over childhood memories while pouring an entire fifth of cheap Johnny Walker, Red Label whisky down our anesthetized throats. In addition, we decided this would be an excellent place to bring our dates in the future.

That afternoon, after picking up Margaret, we drove to Redding to get Marian. On the way we stopped at a small grocery store where Rex, who was not yet twenty-one but who looked the oldest, bought a pint of Orange Gin. Having been drunk on it before, we knew it went down smoothly even without mixer.

"This would be a good drink to give girls," Rex observed.

"Sure would," I agreed. "And we should always keep in mind that candy may be dandy but liquor sure is quicker?" I added.

With the girls, late in the afternoon we drove to Shasta Dam, took pictures and enjoyed the spectacular scenery of the Siskiyou Mountains and the Sacramento River.

Driving toward Red Bluff with Margaret and Marian and the pint of Orange Gin, now in darkness, Rex found the abandoned old road. He drove slowly to the secluded place located in a thick stand of manzanita and Sagebrush half a mile off of Highway 99. The night air of December was cool but crystal clear. Stars, looking close enough to touch glittered on the black velvet background of the sky. They twinkled brilliantly as the bright silvery orb of a friendly moon slowly moved westward overhead across the heavens. With the car's engine and heater turned off it quickly became cool enough to encourage Rex and Margaret in the front seat and Marian and me in the back to enjoy the warmth we felt snuggling closely in silent embrace while the pleasant tasting Orange Gin, drank straight from the bottle, removed a lot of inhibitions.

At 1:30 AM, we drove back to Olinda. Rex took Margaret to

her door and lingered awhile saying goodnight. Then he drove to Marian's house in Redding arriving there at 2:30 A.M

"Can you come in awhile?" she whispered.

Rex, in the front seat, overheard. The shadow of a smile crossed his face as he nodded a silent yes.

Marian quietly opened the door to the full-length front porch. On the far end her sister Eunice and brother Carroll were in bed asleep. She grasped my hand and guided me to the opposite end where we sat down on her bed. She pulled the comforter part way down exposing white pillow slips. Longing kisses made time stand still. Gently she lay down. Like a shadow in the now pale yellow light of the setting moon, her long dark hair cascaded against the whiteness of the pillow. Silently she beckoned me to lie with her.

"What if they wake up?" I glanced toward the other end of the porch.

"Please," she urged. "They won't wake up."

Again and again we kissed. She was irresistible. Her eyes closed and her lips slowly parted. She breathed deeply. Leaning down I buried my face in her lightly perfumed hair.

As it sank in slowly deeper and deeper between two uplifted mounds of a saddle in the mountains of the Coast Range, the brilliant light now fading, the moon completed its mission and softly disappeared.

The next day Rex drove me to the Greyhound Bus station in Redding where I bought a one-way ticket to Seattle on my way to the Navy base at Bremerton, to be discharged.

After serving his tour of duty in Greenland with the Army Corps of Engineers, Rex returned home. Five years later he married Millie, his High School sweetheart. They moved six miles from Olinda to Anderson and had three sons. Taking advantage of the G.I. Bill, Rex attended the California College of Arts and

Crafts in Oakland and earned a four-year degree, Bachelor of Arts in Art Education. Continuing on, he earned a special secondary degree in the same field. For his life's work he returned to Anderson and for 25 years taught all aspects in the field of fine art. Before retiring he rose to the position of Head of Department at Enterprise High school, a few miles from Redding.

One of his students was Sam Bucher who became famous for his concept of the world famous "Precious Moments" figurines. When Sam entered High school as a freshman, Rex saw an unusual talent in this young man and mentored him for the next four years. Sam later sold the rights to the figurines to Hallmark who paid him the highest price for anything they ever bought, making Sam a multi-millionaire.

I returned from duty as a Navy Medical Corpsman associated with the Marines in the Pacific and spent all but three of my 33-day mustering out leave in Olinda. Now, at age 20, I dated Marian, my special high school girlfriend. As in times past we got along wonderfully well, as though we'd never been separated for almost four years. But we dated only that one time because the following day I got a letter from my Dad, now a member of the Boeing Security Force in Seattle. He said I could come live with him and it would cost me nothing just like after graduating from High school. But this time I'd have the G.I. Bill and could return to Seattle College, that later became Seattle University, the largest Catholic school west of the Mississippi. It sounded like a golden opportunity, and the next day I left California.

All my life it's seemed strange, but upon arriving in Seattle I felt like a massive steel door slammed shut behind me, almost erasing from memory some of my life and some of the people I knew growing up in California.

Two years later Marian married someone else and moved to Florida. I've never seen or heard from her again.

Photos & Illustrations: War

Harry & Gene Curnow, 1944

Gene was stationed at Imola as a "Rated Corpsman," taking care of the "shell shocked" (WWI description) and the "Battle Fatigued" (WWII description). These are descriptions for the condition today known as Post Traumatic Stress Disorder (PTSD). See *Hospital Corps School and First Station*, p. 169. Photo courtesy of the author's personal collection.

USS Missouri BB-63

Seen firing her first shots in anger at an enemy,. Iwo Jima is visible in the background, with Mt. Suribachi directly beyond the ship.   The *U.S.S. Missouri* is shown in position, firing salvos of 9 one-ton shells from each of her three 16-inch gun turrets.   Each salvo pushed the ship sideways 45 feet. The BB-63 was the last of the "Iowa Class" battleships made.   Photo courtesy of the author's personal collection.

Capt. Sydney S. Huguenin.

In command of the *USS Sanborn*. Shown at Iwo Jima during the landing of Marines at Iwo Jima, February 19, 1945. See *Okinawa and Aftermath*, p. 246. Photo courtesy of the author's personal collection.

Raising of the U.S. Flag at Iwo Jima

This flag is shown going up correctly, flying over the heads of the Marines. The author watched from a distance as the flag was raised. Photo from newspaper archives. See *Okinawa and Aftermath*, p. 246

War Memorials
Summit of Mt. Suribadri

Memorials to those who gave their life.

This and the Iwo Jima Cemetary photo were taken at the author's request in late 1946 by Bob Kiesel, a WWII pilot who later flew a C-46 cargo plane in the Pacific area and would land at Iwo Jima to refuel. Photo credit of author's personal collection.

Cemetery at Iwo Jima

In Memory of Byron Dary

"Byron Dary, my best friend, rests here."

Byron was from Lake Geneva and Darian, WI. He was a Navy Corpsman associated with the 4th Marine Division fighting on Iwo Jima. Dary was blown in half by a large mortar round during the first few days of the battle." Narrative: pp. 182-224. Photo by Bob Kiesel, 1946. Courtesy of the author's personal collection.

Home
1946

Pictured are four of Anderson, California's sons, home from WWII. From left-to-right: Differ, Kenny, Rex and Gene. Notice the old 1928 Chevrolet pickup that had been cut down from a 4-door sedan: a pickup was needed on the small farm. Photo courtesy of the author's personal collection.

30 Days

"Rex and I had 30 days of total drunkenness to celebrate our survival of WWII."

Rex then used the G.I. Bill to get a Bachelors and Master's in Fine Art. He taught art in high school, where he recognized one of his students, Sam Butcher, as very talented. Rex took Sam under his wing and mentored him. Sam went on to produce the "Precious Moments" figurines. Under Rex's guidance, Sam sold the rights to Hallmark Corporation. Sam built a theme park in Carthage, Missouri, where people can view every figurine and stay overnight. As one walks into one of the main buildings in the park there is a massive replica of an old fashioned curio. At the top are the words "This Park is Dedicated to my Teacher, Mr. Rex Moravec." Photo courtesy of the author's personal collection.

WWII Veterans
Shasta Dam

Rex quit high school in his sophomore year to work at Shasta Dam, running a large vibrator that made sure none of the newly poured cement had air spaces in it. In this photo, Rex (left) and Gene (right) had recently returned from active duty in WWII. Photo courtesy of the author's personal collection.

Marian Ulberg & Gene Curnow

High School sweethearts on a date, after the war, at Shasta Dam, December, 1945. Marian and Gene shared the same birth date and time: Feb. 8, 1925 at 3:30pm. See *Hungry Boys* and *Some High School Days.* Photo courtesy of the author's personal collection.

PART III
CIVILIAN LIFE

❖ BACK TO WORK AND A NEW FRIEND, KEN ❖

At the Navy Separation Center in Bremerton, Washington on January 10, 1946, I received a "Battleship" discharge. This document, also called an Honorable Discharge, has in the heading a picture of a battleship slicing through the sea under full steam.

From Bremerton I hitchhiked to Tacoma where I'd try to adjust to civilian life while living with Mother's sister, Aunt Helen and Mother who was now separated from Cody.

For more than three years in the military, every hour of my life had been written in an outline on a single sheet of paper Called "The Plan of the Day". Distributed early every morning it told us exactly what to do, when to do it and even what to wear for the next 24 hours. This regimentation had stifled and dulled my mind, weakening the ability to make decisions or plan anything for myself. When it was no longer there, I felt apprehensive, without initiative and abandoned. I had no idea of how to look for work, nor did I have the incentive to find any.

There were two more months of $100 mustering out payments. But then the "free money" ran out and to survive I was forced to make a decision. I bought a newspaper and turned to the "help wanted" ads. The first one I saw read, "Machinist wanted. Apply in person at I.W. Johnson Engineering Co., east end of the 11th Street Bridge." The next day I had the job.

The I.W. Johnson Engineering Co. made equipment for the many sawmills in the Tacoma area. I told John, the personnel manager, I worked nearly a year as a machinist helper for Western Gear in Seattle before being called for active military service. In addition I told him that in high school I learned how to use the powerful Oxy-acetylene cutting torch and burning equipment used to cut through and make shapes from very heavy sheet steel. Because I knew how to do this he hired me. The pay would be 99 cents an hour.

Fred, the foreman, put me in the assembly department where

I used the cutting torch to burn through the thick steel making the shapes that would become a machine used in a sawmill called a "re saw". Twelve saws are lined up inside this machine, each able to slide from side to side on a common spinning shaft within the steel box. In the sawmill, after a workman sets each saw by hand into various positions, wide slabs of lumber coming from the primary band saw run through the re-saw and are simultaneously cut into 2x4's, 1x6's or any combination of sizes.

Two weeks later John told me that Mr. Johnson, the owner of the company, wanted me to work in the main office. In this new capacity I "wore many hats" becoming the company secretary, typing all outgoing letters, serving as file clerk and junior accountant, keeping track of accounts receivable and payable using a double entry ledger system and being the company timekeeper. I also worked as "back up" truck driver when the regular man called in sick or went out of town on a job. With it I'd pick up for repair, or deliver for replacement, parts from various sawmills in and around Tacoma. Because the I.W. Johnson Co. could make or repair every part of any sawmill the job was never boring.

Once or twice a month I'd borrow Aunt Helen's old 1935 Dodge and drive to Seattle to visit my Dad. During one visit he asked, "When do you think you'll be going back to College like I suggested in my letter?"

I hesitated, "I don't know. Right now I've got a pretty good job in Tacoma."

With gentle persuasion Dad continued, "I hear Western Gear is looking for anyone with gear cutting experience. You worked there almost a year and learned to run a lot of the machines before you were called for active duty. I think more than likely you'd get on right away. You could live with me, rent free like before the war, work swing or graveyard shift and if you wanted, go to school during the day. You know, you risked your life for the G.I. Bill and really should take advantage of it. It's the opportunity of a lifetime."

Because of my continuing mind crippling inability to make a major decision and few if any minor ones on my own, his excellent advice went unheeded. I always put off anything suggesting change. "Procrastination is the thief of time" could have been tattooed on my forehead.

When I visited Dad a month or more later he told me that Western Gear paid $1.25 an hour on the day shift and a bonus of 10% for swing and 15% for graveyard shifts. This represented at least 25 cents an hour more than I.W. Johnson, a non union shop, paid. It is said, "money talks", and calculating at least a $2.00 a day increase at Western Gear, this would add a minimum of $50.00 a month more than I now made. I accepted Dad's offer and in the early summer of 1946 moved back to live with him in Seattle.

While growing up in California, Dad continued to live in Seattle and because he had no fear of height, made his living as a roofer. When WWII broke out he went to work for Boeing in the security department. During the last year and a half of the war he worked as a cook for the Alaska Steamship Lines. During this time he made many trips to the Pacific in ships that carried full loads of ammunition and aviation gasoline. He told me that the substantial "hazardous duty" pay was why he volunteered for this.

After the war he continued to work for the Alaska Steamship Lines and had moved from 9th and Madison to a better apartment in the "crows nest", the top floor, of the Frye Hotel at third and Yesler Way close to downtown Seattle. The hotel provided laundry and maid service. Close by, a small "mom and pop" restaurant served excellent low cost meals. With Dad at sea, sometimes for three or four months at a time, because of the hotel services and the restaurant, for me his absence now posed no problem.

For $5.00 I bought from Aunt Helen her 1935 Dodge. It provided far better convenience than the Seattle Transit System offered.

After "settling in" with Dad for a couple of days I applied for work at Western Gear. Hired the same day, this time as an experienced machinists helper and gear cutter, I had a job with an excellent income. A 100 % union shop, swing shift paid $1.37 and the graveyard shift paid $1.44 an hour. To earn extra money I chose to work the graveyard shift. Saturday paid double time, $2.88 and Sunday and holidays paid triple time, $4.32. The shop did so much business, for weeks in a row I often worked both Saturday and Sunday. During this time my only pleasure and relaxation came every Wednesday when I deposited my substantial check in the bank.

During WWII, by 1946, because of military contracts, Western Gear grew to be the largest and most diversified gear cutting shop in the west with branches in California and Texas. During my total time of nearly eight years with the company the smallest gears I ever cut were used by both the Sweden Freezer Co., in the manufacture of their ice cream making machines and by the Pfluger Fishing Reel Co. They were so little I could put six of them on my thumbnail. The largest were giants weighing twenty-one tons each. Made in 1949 for A. O. Smith, Ltd. they would be used to open and close floodgates in a dam on the Yangtze River in China.

They were so big that no machine existed in the United States that could cut them. But Mr. Tom Bannan, owner of Western Gear and a mechanical engineer designed and built the special machine on which to mount these "gear blanks" in order to cut the teeth. Because of their great size only one tooth at a time could be made using a "forming cutter" system, which he also designed. After each tooth was completed the gear blank had to be rotated a short distance moving it to exactly the correct place where the next immense tooth would be formed. Rotating the gear blank was done using a "dividing head", a device attached to the mandrel and rotation table on which the massive gear was mounted and rested securely. The rotation formula for the dividing head was, 19 full turns plus five extra holes to advance the gear blank the correct distance to the exact position for cutting the next tooth.

We worked 24 hours a day in three shifts to cut the monsters. Oscar Howell, with 28 years experience, worked days. Bill Wamhoff, with 24 years experience, worked swing shift. Both worked under supervision. With less than four years experience by 1949, I worked the graveyard shift —- alone and without supervision.

If any of us went past or failed to advance the dividing head by even one hole when moving it to cut the next tooth, the huge gear would be ruined costing Western Gear thousands of dollars in penalties and very likely, the loss of the highly lucrative contract.

For 41 years after this event the thought nagged me. Why did Curley Rogers, the dour and rather unfriendly shop foreman, and Mr. Bannan, the owner of the company, select me, who had less than four years of "cutting time" experience, work without supervision to cut the most massive and expensive gears the shop ever handled?

Forty-one years later I would find out.

At age 17, upon graduation from Shasta Union High School in Redding, California, at my dad, Harry's suggestion I moved to Seattle, Washington to live with him. His apartment, at that time, was in the Assembly Hotel at ninth and Madison. From here I could walk the few blocks to Seattle College, (later to become Seattle University) located at Broadway and Madison where I'd go to school. At this time Dad was still a member of the Boeing Aircraft Security Division in charge of the Hunt Warehouse at 12th and Madison. Here Boeing kept thousands of parts used for making the B-17 heavy bomber. Knowing the "right people" he was able to get me a job at the warehouse driving a small forklift called a "jitney". With it I loaded trucks with the parts called for by the main Boeing plant located south of town. The job paid 72 cents an hour for working the graveyard shift. Dad paid my tuition and during the day I attended Seattle College conveniently located only two blocks from the warehouse.

Some work history is offered here for clarification.

Not satisfied with the low wages I became interested when hearing that a company, Western Gear Works, was hiring. They paid 93 cents an hour, for me a substantial increase, for anyone who could read micrometers, dial indicators and run lathes or any kind of metal working machine. Having taken two years of machine shop instruction in High School I could do all this. In addition I did brass welding and knew how to use high-powered Oxy acetylene torch equipment to cut through thick sheet steel. So when I got off work for Boeing one Friday morning I cut my first class at College and walked the short distance to Western Gear at 417 Ninth Avenue South at Jackson Street. Herb Dobbs, the personnel manager said he didn't have an opening for a machinist helper just then but did have a job for an "oiler" at the same rate of pay. He expected a number of jobs for helpers would open up soon and if I was working there, with my knowledge of machines and instruments, I'd have first chance at one. Accepting Mr. Dobbs' offer, after I finished work on the graveyard shift for Boeing Friday night, that same Saturday morning I quit Boeing. The following Monday afternoon, after finishing my regular daytime classes at Seattle College, I went to work on the swing shift at Western Gear Works. As an oiler I'd keep all the glass viewing reservoirs filled and the drip-rate set correctly on the many different gear cutting machines running on my shift.

In the northwest corner of the huge gear shop, that covered two entire city blocks, was a machine that cut gears of moderately large size. Operated by a young man six foot three, about 20 years old and of Danish descent, Kenneth Paul Hansen, "K. P." or Ken, as he wanted to be called, always wore a greasy, gray colored skullcap at work. He scowled a lot and usually had a two or three day growth of scraggily whiskers. To me he looked like a criminal and I was afraid to go over to his machine and oil it because he looked so mean. Though scared of him, that first afternoon on the job I somehow got up enough courage to go fill the oil reservoirs on his machine and set the drip. However, because of his sour look, his was the last machine I serviced on my circuit.

But as I approached he leaned away from his work to introduce himself. Extending his hand "Hi, I'm Ken Hansen," he said pleasantly.

Surprised by his friendliness, we shook hands. "I'm Gene Curnow. I'll be keeping your machine oiled."

"That'll be fine. Hey, it's nearly lunch time, want to eat with me?"

Relieved by his openness I answered, "Sure, I'll meet you at the benches in the heat treat room if that's O.K."

During lunch we talked about fixing up old cars, sports people, family and flying. Ken, a pilot, had a license with a rating to carry passengers. He was impressed when I told him my uncle, Joe Smith, was a Captain who flew for United Airlines and that Joe held the world record for number of hours in the air for airline pilots of his young age, more than 31,000 hours at age 55.

After the last gulp of coffee Ken asked, "Would you like to go flying with me this Sunday? A friend of mine owns a plane, a two place, side-by side control, all aluminum Stinson. He lets me use it whenever I want. We could fly over the farm in Kent where my folks live."

"O.K. If I don't have to work that day it sounds good to me."

He continued, "With both sets of controls working together side by side, you could hold on to them lightly and get the feel of their response in flight. Then after you get used to the sensation of the controls I'll let you fly it yourself."

"Isn't it hard to learn?"

"No, it's easy once you're in the air. Taking off isn't too bad. But landing can be a little wild, especially if a fairly strong wind is coming at you from the side. All you need to do while you're in the air is look out the windows at the underside of the wings and keep them level by watching the horizon on both sides."

On Sunday morning we met at Boeing field. At the hanger for private planes he signed the Stinson out and checked it carefully. In the office he filed a flight plan and we were soon flying toward Kent. As we neared the farm Ken said, "I'm going to buzz the house. I do it whenever I fly over. My folks and anyone visiting always come out in the yard and wave. It's a lot of fun."

Flying over the farm Ken opened the throttle and put the plane in a steep dive. Down we sped, engine roaring as the propeller slapped the air. The downward ride was tolerable but as soon as Ken pulled back on the controls to regain altitude my stomach objected and I became airsick.

"I hate to tell you this," I gasped, "But I can't take the coming back up of this buzzing stuff. It's going to make me vomit and I don't see anything to catch it in."

"Gee, I'm sorry," he answered. "Do you think you'll be O.K. if I just fly over low and dip the wings as we leave?"

"Sure. It's not the fast down but only the fast up part that my stomach can't take."

Dipping the wings didn't bother me as we left, skimming over the house and barn. Then, slowly gaining altitude, we turned west to fly over Puget Sound near Redondo Beach. Ken, a cautious pilot, showed me how he always kept a lookout for a possible place to land in case of engine failure.

"One of the first things my flight instructor taught is, if the engine quits always be prepared. He told me he'd have a place spotted at all times and enough altitude to be able to glide there and make a dead stick landing. There's an unused road over here on the left, you can lean forward and see it. Then there's good old Highway 99 just below. But having quite a few cars on it I'd use it only as a last resort. On the way down I'd watch out for telephone and electric lines. I only have to look at which way the poles are set and I can tell the direction the wires run. We'll be over water in a couple of minutes. What I'm going to do before we get there is climb higher so I could glide back to that old road, land on the beach or even put us down in shallow water if I have to." I told him I was impressed by his idea of safety. "My instructor had a saying that I keep in mind. It went like this: There are a lot of old pilots and there are a lot of bold pilots, but there aren't any old bold pilots. That's why I'm so cautious."

After climbing smoothly we leveled off and I felt a little better. During the entire flight I kept my hands and feet lightly on the controls and felt confident when Ken said, "Here, go ahead, try it awhile."

I pulled up and let down, sort of like a Porpoise swims. Using the foot pedals and giving the engine almost full throttle, I made a climbing turn, a Chandelle, then a "peeling off" descent before bringing the Stinson back to altitude and level flight. I discovered that as long as I had my hands on the controls while using them to make the plane to move up or down, bank to turn right or left or change speed, my airsickness didn't get worse and the rest of the flight was tolerable.

It had been fun but I felt glad when we arrived back at the hanger. Ken cut the ignition. The engine stopped. I opened the door on my side of the plane, stepped out—and promptly threw up.

❖ THE HYPOCHONDRIAC ❖

To prevent monotony, as our gear cutting machines seemed to endlessly cut away small amounts of metal while forming a gear tooth, sometimes one of us would think up a "practical joke". They'd give us a few laughs and brought out our sense of humor. We were never mean-spirited or hurt anyone with the jokes, but designed them to be like the "sight gags" of the early silent movies.

If anyone could be known by the expression "He's the salt of the earth", it was Randy. He had a good word to say about everyone and always would lend a hand when needed without being asked. A fellow gear-cutting machinist, he worked with me on the swing shift at Western Gear and was the worst hypochondriac I ever had the misfortune to know. Month in and month out he'd itemize every ache and pain to anyone who would listen. One of his most frequent complaints was, "I have this really bad headache."

For weeks I tried to think of a way to stop him from taking so much time at work complaining to a captive audience. Finally I formed a plan that included the use of some methylene blue pills that Dad had left over from when he had a minor bladder irritation. When I told the plan to the others in the shop they were delighted.

For several nights Randy complained of a bad headache. I asked him if they were frequent though I knew his answer would be yes. Appearing to listen intently and be greatly interested in helping I set him up. Continuing to question Randy and rope him in, a few nights later I asked, "How often do you have these bad headaches?"

He answered, "Almost every day."

"How many days in a row do you have them?"

"I've had this one now for about a month."

Randy knew I was a second year Pre Med student at Seattle University and listened closely when I explained what his condition might be.

"Do you urinate often?" I asked.

"I guess about as much as anyone."

"Have you noticed any blood or other discoloration in your urine associated with the headaches?" I planned ahead to use the two words, blood and discoloration and in a strong voice, emphasized both because I knew physicians often used them and the words would set off within him a massive alarm of potential danger.

"Has there been a color-change such as to a greenish blue?" I continued.

"No, there's been no greenish-blue. What would that mean if I'd see some?"

Earlier in my plan I made up a medically sounding name for a non-existent disease and now used it.

"Well, from what I've read in medical text books and seeing some cases in the Navy Medical Corps, if your urine turns greenish-blue after you've had a headache for about 30 days it means you probably have Tri Butyl Kidney Degeneration. There is no cure. You'll die within 72 hours after you first see the color. It's a horribly painful and agonizing death." I emphasized the word death.

"Geeze, it must be a really bad disease!!" he exclaimed.

"Yea, they think it's caused by one of them rapidly mutating viruses. Antibiotics won't touch it. By the way, I just remembered, I've got some excellent headache pills in my lunch pail. I got them at Bartell's Drug Store this morning. They're something new and are supposed to stop a headache within two or three hours. You're welcome to try a couple to see if they'll do any good."

"Sure, I'll try anything," he said.

I gave him two of the shiny white Methylene Blue tablets, each about the size of an Aspirin. At the drinking fountain I watched carefully as he washed them down. Within an hour or less the result would be a brilliant greenish-blue discoloration of his urine and I made sure everyone in the shop knew about it.

He had been completely set up and I knew Randy would panic seeing the bright color change next time he emptied his bladder.

The swinging bat wing doors to the urinal could be seen from everywhere in the shop. After telling everyone that Randy had swallowed the pills all of us watched for him to enter.

A worried look on his face told me I'd spread my propaganda well. After he swallowed the pills my last words to him were, "I sure hope you don't have that fatal viral disease, Tri Butyl Kidney Degeneration."

"Yea, so do I," he mumbled.

Less than an hour passed before Randy approached the urinal. In great anticipation we waited. We didn't have to wait long.

Slamming the urinal doors wide open, obviously in great distress, he rushed out. Distorted with fright, his face seemed to have taken on a grayish color.

He hurried over to where I pretended to be closely watching the twin cutter heads of my Sykes machine work their way through steel, cutting an in line herring-bone pattern of teeth in a gear blank. In a low shaking voice he said, "Something's wrong. I've got bright greenish-blue piss, just like you told me about. Do you think I'll die? Do you think I've got that kidney disease?"

By this time several of the shop crew gathered around. Oscar Howell asked loud enough for everyone to hear.

"What's wrong Randy, you don't look so very good."

"I don't know. My piss is a greenish-blue color. I might have a fatal kidney disease. Gene here knows the name of it."

After this statement we couldn't hold back the laughter. As we roared Randy realized he'd been the victim of a joke.

He glowered, "You bastard Gene, did those pills you gave me make my piss turn that greenish-blue color?"

"Yes, but they're harmless" I assured him. "It's a medicine called Methylene Blue. It's made to soothe the bladder. It can't hurt you. As a matter of fact it's good for you."

Randy must have learned something from this experience because from then on the complaints to his co-workers became few and far between.

❖ THE BOMBER ❖

Dick Mullethaler, a 6-foot 3-inch, 250-pound muscular out-doorsman, came from Montana to work at Western Gear in Seattle. He was an excellent gear cutting machinist, but somewhat unsophisticated. He drove an older Ford V-8 car with a flat head, 85 horsepower engine. One Monday evening at work he told me he thought the carburetor wasn't working right.

"The old girl sputters and jerks along sometimes backfiring for half a block, then she runs O.K."

In my devious mind a plan formed of how to play a practical joke on him using the information about loud explosions coming from the tail pipe and I brought the rest of the machinists in on it.

On the swing shift lunch break at 7:00 PM Dick always ate lunch in his car. His friend Charlie ate with him while they listened to the radio. This pattern of regularity would be a deciding factor of how well the scheme worked.

Tuesday evening, acting excited, I questioned Dick, "Hey, did you read in the Seattle Times about the 85 horsepower Ford V-8 engines all over the United States having terrible explosions?"

"No, I didn't see it. What did it say?"

"It said many faulty carburetors overflow and some cars even explode like a rocket. Before the people can get the doors open they died in the massive fireball. Sure sounds dangerous to me. I'm surprised you didn't see it in the paper. I think the story was somewhere in the second section."

Planting the seed of worry in Dick's mind I chuckled to myself.

Then on Wednesday evening I asked casually, "How's the car running?"

"Oh, about the same," he said.

"Boy, I'd sure get rid of that potential killer," I admonished. "I just got a letter from my cousin Rex in Redding, California. He sent me a clipping from their newspaper, The Redding Record. It said two Ford V-8's, just like yours, blew up there during the past week and both drivers were killed. One was a man and one a lady. They couldn't be rescued because of the sheets of flame and black smoke pouring from the cars. The paper said the gasoline fire instantly roared out of control just like a blow torch." I used the name of my cousin, Rex who lived in Redding and the name of the newspaper there to add a substantial touch of authenticity to the deception.

Dick looked apprehensive and told me he'd just have to take the chance because he didn't have enough money right now to re-build the carburetor.

"As soon as I can afford it I sure am going to fix it. I know it might be kind of dangerous."

I reminded him, "Don't wait too long. You could be blown to bits or burned beyond recognition."

Close to the Frye Hotel where my Dad and I lived was a novelty store. Having browsed in it I knew they sold the large, combined smoke and noise bombs that could easily be attached with their pair of small wires, to the spark plugs of a car. As soon as the car started, the electricity from the spark plug wire would set off the bomb. Producing a raging scream they also poured out massive gushers of thick black smoke that billowed from under the car as well as from every seam in the hood and every other opening in the engine compartment.

Thursday I visited the novelty store and told the owner my plan. I asked, "How many bombs do you think I'll need?"

"Oh man, one will be more than enough. Those things are outrageous."

"No," I said, "I want to put three on this guy's engine."

"Well, they're going to scream something terrible and put out an awful lot of the thickest black smoke you'll ever see. It could almost scare a guy to death because they're each so noisy and powerful. Sometimes the Police or Fire Department gets called when just a single one of those babies go off."

"Just what I want," I smiled.

I punched the time clock at 3:27 on Friday afternoon and put the three bombs, carried in a brown paper sack, in my locker. I said hello to Dick as I caught up with him on the way to our machines and asked, "Hey, did you fix that car yet?"

"No, but maybe this weekend if I have enough bucks left over."

"Don't put it off any longer than you have to. I'd sure hate to have you blown up and burned beyond recognition just because you waited too long," I repeated the same earlier phony warning words to keep them uppermost in his mind.

"I know, I've got it on my 'to do' list for tomorrow if we don't have to work overtime. I've told Charlie about the danger and he said he'd help me."

After working for three hours, at 6:30 I asked Oscar to watch my machines a few minutes and went upstairs to my locker. Removing the brown paper sack I hurried out the side door. As usual, a few yards away on Jackson Street, Dick's car sat parked and unlocked beside the shop. Opening the hood I quickly wired two bombs to the spark plugs on the driver's side of the engine and one to the plugs on the passenger side. Making sure the connections were tight, I closed the hood and returned to the shop.

During the next half hour, before lunch break, I told everyone the three bombs were attached. Dick and Charlie remained oblivious to the scheme.

Holding to their routine, at 7:00 o'clock they left the shop heading for the car. To keep the battery from running down Dick always started the engine and let it idle keeping the generator running as they ate lunch while listening to the radio. In August, the sun remained shining during our lunch break so from our hiding places we could see everything. Some of us hid behind a corner of the shop and a few behind partially closed windows inside the locker room only ten feet from the car. On the rooftop others had a birds-eye view.

In the car the two men opened their lunch buckets. Each took out a sandwich. Dick reached in his pocket for the key, slipped it in the ignition and pressed the starter.

As the spark plugs fired in sequence, from each of the three bombs came a horrendous, ear-shattering scream that ripped the air, one right after the other. Clouds of black smoke rapidly boiled out from under the car almost totally engulfing it while also pouring out of each seam in the hood and every other opening from which it could escape. The terrifying, screaming wail from the bombs continued for more than half a minute and the dense black smoke roiled skyward. For a moment, from my hiding place around the corner of the building a few feet away from the front of the car I could see Dick and Charlie inside. The instant that the bombs went off I saw their looks turn to sheer terror. With eyes bulging and for a moment not moving a muscle, they appeared frozen. Realizing they had to get out of the car, my warnings for the last four days of death by fire and explosion undoubtedly crossed their minds as their arms began to uselessly flail the air. Bits of bread, pickle, tomato and lettuce and other sandwich making material, splattered against the inside of the windshield as they dropped their food and each wildly fought to find a door handle. With a leap they flew through the air from the car doors. Charlie landed in a heap on the sidewalk, jumped to his feet, ran and ducked behind another car parked about 20 feet behind. Dick catapulted out the door on the drivers side into a traffic lane and was almost hit by a Seattle Transit System electric trolley bus. The driver swerved sharply to miss hitting Dick and avoid what he must have thought to be a car on fire, but he didn't stop. For those of us watching, chaotic laughter reigned.

When the screaming and smoke of the bombs stopped Dick and Charlie realized when all of us came from our hiding places laughing and pointing fingers at them, that they were "had". The men on the roof gave loud horselaughs. Those in the locker room opened the windows wide and called, "Hey, what's the matter Dick, your car explode?"

I stood near Oscar, who was still laughing. Patting me on the back he said, "You sure pulled that one off good." Hearing this Dick walked over and towered above me.

"Gene," he said, "you little son of a bitch, you set me up for this didn't you? I'm going to get you one of these days, you just wait and see."

Because of our size difference, fortunately for me, he never did.

PART IV
LOVE

❖ BLIND DATE ❖

While working at Western Gear, Ken Hansen and I soon became good friends. On weekends if we didn't have to work sometimes we'd go on an adventure. He owned a 1936 Ford V-8 coupe and had restored it to mint condition. Painted baby blue the color complimented the large amount of bright chrome. The car, a classic, looked and ran better than the day it came from the factory. Sometimes we'd go for a scenic drive heading eastward, often crossing the Cascade Mountains to Ellensburg, Yakima or Lake Chelan.

On one occasion, early in winter, we drove to Mt. Rainier. On our way up the mountain, beside the winding and narrow road, walls of hard packed snow at least 10 feet high, towered on both sides. Ken didn't have tire chains for the little coupe so we couldn't go to Paradise Lodge high on the mountain, but only as far as the road had been cleared by a snowplow that, many times, opened just one lane. Ken wanted to turn around but the narrow single lane and solid snow bank on each side made it impossible. We were forced to continue on. The gasoline gauge indicated very little fuel remained in the tank. With it running low we realized we could be in danger. We hadn't brought along warm coats or hats and weren't prepared to be out in the bitter cold of the mountain.

The heater in the car provided warmth from the running engine while driving but if we'd run out of gas and were stranded we could freeze. Finally, as we rounded a bend, to our relief we saw a wide spot cleared by the snowplow. To turn around here would be easy. Close to the high snow bank on our left, an old Model-A Ford truck sat parked. By the logo on the door and license plates we saw it belonged to the State of Washington, Highway Division.

For emergencies, in the trunk of the car, Ken carried a two-gallon gasoline can and a siphon hose. After parking the car we went over to the old truck. Through a side window we could easily see the gasoline gauge in the center of the dashboard. It read over half full. Because there are no locks on gas tank caps of older Model-A Ford trucks it presented a golden opportunity.

"Do you think we should take a couple of gallons so we don't run out before we get to the station at the bottom of the mountain?" Ken asked.

"I think we should. We'd be in real serious trouble running out of gas in this weather."

Opening the trunk of the coupe Ken took out the gasoline can and the siphon hose. As he approached the Model-A truck he said, "You listen for cars. If you hear one coming just call out and I'll run back and put this stuff in the trunk. It'll look like we're just up here enjoying the scenery."

It seemed to take forever to fill the two-gallon can. The old thin, almost rotted, red rubber siphon hose had been salvaged long ago from a worn out combination enema, douche and hot water bottle. In several places kinks, small cracks and flattened areas in the deteriorating hose greatly slowed the passage of the gasoline adding to our apprehension.

At last the job was done. Ken replaced the truck's gas cap and with all evidence of our illegal adventure out of sight we breathed much easier.

At the Standard Station at the base of the mountain, he filled our gas tank, something that should have been done before attempting to drive to the lodge. This emergency was the only time on our many trips we ever "liberated" gasoline.

When we got home Ken threw the old worn out red, cracked, partially rotted, kinked and flattened rubber hose in the garbage and replaced it with a brand new white one from another combination enema, douche and hot water bottle—just in case!!

One evening at work on our lunch break Ken asked, "How would you like to go on a blind date? Twila, the girl I go roller-skating with, has a friend, Glenora, who sometimes comes with her to the rink in Renton. I've never met her but Twila said Glennie, as she likes to be called, doesn't have a steady boyfriend and that she's a really nice girl. Twila says she's about five foot three, just the right height for you."

"I don't know if I'd want to" I answered. "I've never been on a blind date. What if she turns out to be fat and sloppy, a real dog?"

"Oh no, Twila says she's really pretty. Flowing brown hair, blue eyes, good manners, has a nice laugh and is cheerful all the time. I think she weighs about 115 pounds. From what Twila told me I think you'd probably like her."

The description of Glennie did interest me so I asked,

"When would this date be?"

"Twila thinks it would be nice to go up to Paradise Lodge on Mt. Rainier on Easter Sunday. I'm keeping Andy Drotning's brand new Mercury convertible for him in my garage while he's in Alaska on a commercial fishing boat. He wants me to put some miles on it every few weeks so we'll use his car. How about it, would you like to go?"

Reluctantly I agreed and told Ken to let Twila know I'd come along and that she could tell Glennie.

About nine o'clock Easter Sunday morning, April 6, 1947, in Andy's brand new convertible, Ken, Twila and I arrived in front of Glennie's apartment house at 715 1st Avenue West, at the foot of Queen Anne hill. Ken sounded the horn and she appeared at the window of the third floor apartment. Twila leaned out of the car and called, "Hi, we're here."

Waving, Glennie answered, "I'll be right down."

Soon, from the door of the apartment building I saw a beautiful girl, bundled against the cold in a pink, sheared wool coat, approach the car. On the coat she wore a pin with a design of pink and yellow roses that perfectly matched her earrings.

At the car door Twila introduced us.

"Glennie, this is Gene. He works at Western Gear with Ken.

Gene, meet Glennie."

Her skin without blemish and her makeup flawless, she looked so pretty I thought, "She could become a movie star." Awestruck and wide-eyed at her beauty I could barely say, "Hi." Her blue eyes smiled as she got in the back seat with me. Still in awe and shy, I scooted as far from her as possible to my side of the car. Apparently sensing my uneasiness, she too stayed away as far as she could.

But to my surprise, as we traveled along, conversation between us came easily. We talked about where we were born, school, food we liked and our jobs. She said she worked at the United States Court House for the Department of Justice in the Office of the United States Attorney, Mr. Dennis, arranging and preparing the Court Docket for the next day's legal action. I told her I had attended Seattle College for almost a year before WWII, was a veteran and saw action with the Marines in the Pacific. She told me she recently had dated a Marine Lieutenant a couple of times who was stationed on the *USS Missouri* now docked about three miles away at Pier 91.

I thought, "With such a responsible job in a major Federal Office and dating a Marine Lieutenant she must be a lot older than she looks. She has to be at least 26 and I'm only 22." In my mind this was all the more reason to stay on my own side of the seat. I thought, "What a total waste of time, this date sure isn't going anywhere."

We stopped in Puyallup for a hamburger and milkshake. Her manners were superb. In a soft, soothing voice she said please and thank you whenever proper. I thought, "This girl sure comes from a high class family. She really knows etiquette." My mind drifted back to my painfully humble beginnings living at Poverty Flat one mile east of Whiskeytown in California. My stepfather, Cody, was a "Sniper" who prospected for gold but had little or no success. As a family, many times close to starving to death, we were among the poorest of the poor. It seemed that the beautiful girl sitting on the other side of the back seat and I, were worlds apart.

By noon we arrived at Paradise Lodge. On the way up the long, narrow road we were greeted by spectacular scenery. Evergreen trees pushed their spires far into the bright blue sky. The pleasantly refreshing fragrance of their balsam drifted into the car. Shaded by tall trees, lush ferns, Trillium and low growing shrubs, their wind blown leaves still covered with dancing droplets of persistent overnight dew, grew thickly from the dampness of the forest floor. Glistening slime trails of the many large greenish-yellow banana slugs crossed each other or merged on the wetness of the ground as shiny intersecting paths, perhaps to end in some secret rendezvous. Standing near the road a few dead snags, trunks weathered to a silvery sheen, added interest and character to the scene. Beside the road, several small streams babbled happily as we passed. Narada Falls churned frothy white plunging over a wide basalt cliff. At every "scenic turnout" we stopped to take pictures.

At the end of the road, beside the parking lot of the Lodge, tables and benches stood in a picnic area. Several galvanized sheet metal garbage cans here were chained to trees. Piles of snow, glistening in the sunshine, remained nearby. As soon as Ken parked the car Twila scurried out, hid behind a bush and made snowballs. She ran from her hiding place and threw one at him just as he got out. It missed, but to protect himself, he took the lid off of one of the garbage cans and held it in front of him, using it as a shield.

"Come on Glennie, throw some at Gene," Twila laughed.

Following Ken's lead, I removed a garbage can lid just in time to protect myself from an avalanche of snow thrown by both girls.

After exploring the Lodge, we walked on a trail outside for a short distance to look across a narrow valley at a permanent glacier on one flank of the mountain. Inside the ice were a series of spectacular caves but our light shoes didn't permit us to go and explore them. But from where we stood we were able to see the glistening light blue color of the glacier ice just inside the large entrance of the caves. It contrasted beautifully with the gray rock scree, the snowfields and dark blue sky.

After a late lunch at the Lodge, about five o'clock we began the drive down the long crooked road back to Longmire, the entrance to Mt. Rainier National Park. Tired, and cold because the heater in the car wasn't warm yet, Twila snuggled close to Ken. She saw Glennie and me in the back seat still sitting far apart.

"Hey," she teased, "It's a lot warmer if you sit close together."

Glennie smiled and moved a little toward the center of the seat. After some hesitation I did too. As she nestled her head on my shoulder I put my arm around her. It felt good. The aroma of her perfume was so pleasant and on my shoulder she seemed at ease, almost asleep.

Stopping in Puyallup once more, this time we had a hamburger and a cup of coffee before continuing homeward.

At Glennie's apartment Ken said, "If we don't have to work maybe we could get together again next weekend." Twila echoed the suggestion.

Feeling the undertow I silently nodded, O.K.

Glennie turned to me, "Why don't you take my phone number and call me Thursday. By then I'll know whether I can go out."

As she wrote the number on a slip of paper, GA for Garfield—-4856 and handed it to me I said, "O.K., I'll call you at exactly seven fifteen Thursday evening during lunch break. I'm working swing shift and lunch is seven to seven thirty."

In her soft, refined voice she said, "Thanks everyone. I had a real good time and a lot of fun. It's been nice to meet you, Gene." Almost sounding like a very direct question she added, "Maybe I'll see you later??"

At the apartment house door she turned to wave, "Thanks again," she called and disappeared inside.

❖ MT. ST. HELENS, SPIRIT LAKE ❖
AND AN OLD DODGE

Glennie and I had been dating for five months. In the fall we arranged a double date with Ken and Twila. We would drive in the old Dodge to Harry Truman's Lodge beside Spirit Lake at the foot of Mt. St. Helens, a little over 100 miles south of Seattle.

Early in the afternoon, after checking in, we rented a motorboat to tour the mirror-like surface of the lake. Covered with snow half way down its flanks, the big mountain loomed. At the east end of the lake, a waterfall rushed noisily over an escarpment in an old basalt streambed. A pleasant aroma of dampness and fresh pine filled the air. After several hours on the water, as the sun hung low in the autumn sky, we returned the boat to the dock. Still feeling strong, before returning to the Lodge, we took time to climb a short distance up the mountain to marvel at the spectacular view of the lake, thick conifer forests and snow-capped peaks of the Cascade Mountains.

After a hearty dinner, we were more than ready to rest. Ken and I had a room adjoining the one Twila and Glennie used. On the wall, because Twila understood it, Ken tapped out the message "good night, sleep tight" in Morse code. Exhausted from the activity of the day, surrounded by an almost palpable sound of silence in the mountain wilderness, soon we were asleep.

About five thirty the next morning Ken knocked on the wall to wake the girls. After we showered and dressed we met them downstairs in the dining room and had breakfast. Bacon and eggs, home made baking powder biscuits, still hot from the oven and covered with butter and honey along with the aromatic coffee readied us for a morning walk. On one of many well-maintained trails near the lake, in the stillness of the autumn air, a sharp chill persisted. The warmer forest floor and lake surface caused a two foot thick, "ground fog" to form above both our path and the water in the lake. We could hardly see our feet beneath the billowing, gossamer-like layer and it seemed like we were floating on the trail instead of walking. Under a canopy the fresh aroma from stately evergreens mingled with the morning dampness. After exploring several of the longer trails after lunch we started back to Seattle. The old Dodge ran well on our way to the lake. But on the way home, it began to lose power. Clouds of blue smoke erupted behind us. Cars following had to slow so drivers could see the road. From our exhaust came a rhythmic, hiss, hiss, hiss as thick smoke belched from the tailpipe to rise in the pristine air.

"What do you think is wrong?" I asked Ken as I slowed on the narrow road looking for a safe place to turn off.

"It's either a blown head gasket or a hole burned in the top of one of the pistons. Is the water temperature running hot? I can't see from here in the back seat."

"No, the heat gauge says normal, but we're sure pumping a lot of oil from someplace. Look at all that smoke back there."

"Well, if the water isn't too hot it's probably a hole in the top of a piston. Oil splashes up through the hole and burns with the fuel causing the cloud of smoke. It won't hurt anything. It'll just suck up and use a lot more oil. You better stop and check the level as soon as you can. We should go in at the first gas station we come to and get a few extra quarts so we can add and keep the level topped off."

Stopped at the roadside we found the oil down only a pint so knew we were in no danger of burning out the bearings or for the engine to seize. At the first gas station we bought eight quarts of oil hoping the old car would burn no more than this the rest of the way home. Adding some about every 20 miles we continued on, like a smoking "Chariot of Fire", successfully to our destination.

With the car in need of repair, the following week I walked the two miles to work from the Frye Hotel, at 3rd and Yesler Way to Western Gear, at 417-9th Avenue South at Jackson Street.

On the weekend, at his home at 45th and Aurora, Ken and I

removed the head and oil pan from the cars engine. As he predicted, a hole had burned in a piston, on the top of number five. Fortunately, it didn't damage the cylinder wall.

We replaced the damaged piston and with the pan off, put in a new set of rod and main bearings. Back together, the old engine ran perfectly.

I kept the car another year and had no mechanical problems. However, during the unusually cold winter of 1948, because I hadn't put enough antifreeze in the radiator, the water in the engine froze and cracked the block, causing a bad leak. By this time two tires were nearly worn out. New ones were expensive and hard to get after WWII so I bought two used casings. Ken cut the metal beads from one of the old casings and put the remaining rubber skeleton inside one of the less worn tires that would be kept on the car. This formed in the old tire a continuous "boot". We twisted gunnysacks and old bath towels tightly into rolls and wrapped them with thick string to keep them from coming apart. They looked like thick cloth sausages as we placed them inside the heavy makeshift boot in the worn tire where an inner tube should have been. Mounted back on the rim it held up the weight of the car as if it had an inner tube full of air inside. We also inserted a fake valve stem through the hole in the wheel rim so the tire looked fully inflated, though it had no air in it at all.

Into the radiator, to stop the leak, we poured double the amount of "Silver Solder" that the manufacturer suggested. This product is made to stop small to medium size leaks in engine blocks and cooling systems. We had the idea, "if a little does a little good then a lot will do a lot of good". In this case it worked.

In 1948, after WWII, new cars were almost impossible to obtain and any used car having an engine that ran brought a premium price. Ken and I washed, waxed and spruced up the old Dodge and took it to the Westlake Chevrolet used car lot. As a salesman approached we pretended to be interested, looking to buy a car.

Having seen us drive up, without removing the lighted

cigarette from his lips, he sounded arrogant. "Hi, looking for a replacement for the old Dodge?" For some reason I disliked the man immediately. His attitude, body movements and language all seemed to say he knew he had a couple of suckers here, babes in the woods that he could easily "rip off."

I said, "I'm thinking of getting something a little better but I don't see anything here I like right now."

"Well, would you consider selling your car outright? I'll give you $500.00 cash. You can always buy something later."

Ken and I knew the salesman was attempting to cheat us. Even an old pile of junk, as long as the engine sounded good, sold for no less than $1,000.00. Ken and I, of course, knew the Dodge was nothing but a pile of junk with a badly cracked block and one totally ruined tire. But because the engine we rebuilt not long ago sounded so good, the salesman was "taken in". As the eager man turned away for a moment, Ken nodded, "yes" to me.

"I guess I could sell it." As an inducement I added, "I sure wish you had something here I liked."

The man appeared delighted to be buying the Dodge for $500.00 then acted like he didn't care whether I bought a replacement or not.

He seemed to sneer condescendingly saying, "That's O.K., you'll find something later." A crooked smile crossed his face as he filled his lungs to capacity with tobacco smoke. With half closed eyes and head tilted toward the sky he lazily blew it out.

He seemed delighted at his good fortune to get a car in good running condition for only $500.00. He, of course, expected to quickly re-sell it for at least two or three times as much.

Before leaving home, I put on my most tattered work clothes so I'd look poor to make the salesman think I'd be an easy mark. Hoping to sell the worthless piece of junk at the used car lot I had the title in the glove box. I quickly took it out, placed it on the hood, dated and signed it over to Westlake Chevrolet.

From his pocket the salesman took out a roll of money. With

obvious disdain he peeled off a $500.00 bill. Grasping it between his thumb and forefinger, both heavily stained with nicotine, he flipped it toward me as I handed him the keys.

Ken and I lost no time getting out of sight hurrying around the corner to where his car sat parked. On the way home we stopped at a bank where I changed the big bill into smaller denominations. Once in awhile the worm turns. Ken and I had out slicked the slicker.

❖ PLAY THE MUSIC, RING THEM BELLS ❖

Ken and Twila, Glennie and I, double dated several times after we first met on Easter Sunday in 1947. On our third date, with Ken driving my 1935 Dodge he stopped to buy two small bottles of 7 UP. From home he brought, in a picnic cooler, ice, plastic cups and a pint of Chablis wine. He said he'd recently learned how to make "7 UP wine coolers."

"I'm going to take us to the park down by the shore at the south end of Lake Washington. I'll mix the wine coolers and you'll get a real taste treat."

At the park Twila took four cups from the picnic cooler and put a couple of cubes of ice in each. Ken filled them with a mixture of half wine and half 7 UP. Both girls told him to put only a small amount of wine in their drinks. After the first taste all agreed the mixture made both the wine and the 7 UP taste better. However, because the girls were so conservative, Ken and I drank most of it.

Finishing the drink, parked in a spot where colorful lights from the opposite shore danced playfully on the water, the scene reminded me of the song, "Harbor Lights". As normal young people on a date usually do, in the front seat Ken and Twila soon were necking. Glennie and I in the back seat, not sitting very close, only held hands.

Ken turned toward us and noticed we weren't necking and knew this was our third date. Earlier in the week Twila phoned him and said Glennie told her she liked Gene a lot. At work I told Ken I did enjoy dating Glennie but that I thought she was too old and far too high class for me. I could hardly believe it when he told me she was 18 and would have her 19th birthday on May 23rd.

Glennie and I knew from information relayed to us by our "go between's", that we liked each other. When we were together we felt at ease and were starting to have that nice feeling of "belonging". Learning she was only 18 added a new dimension.

Leaning over the back of the front seat Ken asked, "How come you two are sitting so far apart?"

"We're O.K." I told him.

"No you're not O.K. You two get closer."

Twila joked, "She won't bite you Gene."

Glennie and I moved slowly toward the center of the back seat until our shoulders touched.

"Now look into each others eyes," Ken commanded.

As soon as we did he leaned into the back seat. Taking Glennie's head and mine, each in one of his big hands, he slowly pushed us together.

As our lips touched for the first time I heard music and bells. Glennie said later she did too. The delightful experience made me want to make it last and I hesitated as long as I dared. Not backing off for several moments after Ken took his hands away I prolonged the magical event.

"Now don't you forget how that's done," he chuckled.

So far, we never have. (In January of 2007 it's been 59 years.)

Because I worked swing shift at the gear shop, I had the opportunity to meet Glennie at noon during her lunch break. On clear days we'd sit in the sun on the marble seats outside the big glass door of the United States Court House where she worked. One day near the end of May, 1947 she asked, "When do you plan to go back to college? You have the G.I. Bill so tuition will be free. It's such a great opportunity."

Months ago Dad asked the same question. When Glennie asked, because of my continuing inability to make decisions, as usual I made what I thought would sound like a logical excuse, to put it off.

"Maybe next year, I'd like to keep working awhile and save some money first."

By the expression on her face I could tell she felt disappointment but she didn't pursue the matter.

Glennie and I now dated almost every weekend when I didn't have to work overtime. With her gentle encouragement, tiny bits of indecision ever so slowly began to be pushed aside. Though dating her was very pleasant, social life for me never became a priority. I found it so comfortable to have the regimentation of my job where someone else assumed the responsibility for shaping my days.

A few weeks later she again brought up the subject of school.

"Why wait to go back to College? It will put you behind a year in what you want to accomplish in life. The sooner you get started the sooner you'll get into medical school, graduate and begin practice."

She always presented the suggestion with such logic I could find no reasonable answer not to act on what she said. Yet I resisted, making excuse after excuse not to return to school.

"Why don't you go to Seattle College tomorrow and talk to someone about registering for the summer quarter?"

Using the unspoken excuse to keep from taking action I thought to myself, "this suggestion sure sounds pushy. After all, we've known each other less than three months."

Yet I knew she had my best interest at heart and was absolutely right, but offered her a weak and illogical answer:

"I don't know if I can live on the G.I. Bill," I whined. "It pays only $90.00 a month and I sure make a lot more than that at the gear shop."

"What about the 52-50 deal the Government has for veterans who are unemployed? They'll give you $50.00 a week for 52 weeks. That's $200.00 a month and with the $90.00 from the G.I. Bill, that's almost as much as you make without overtime."

Her totally logical reasoning compelled me to visit Seattle College the next day to talk about the possibility of registering for the summer quarter. But because of the comfort I felt working at Western Gear with the regimentation of having to punch the clock every day at the same time, returning to school represented a major shift in lifestyle that everything within me resisted.

A sign over the door at the far end of the hall read, Office of the Registrar. I didn't want to enter and almost resented Glennie for talking me into being here. Walking slowly I used every excuse to stop. Though not thirsty, I paused at a fountain to get a drink. At all bulletin boards in the hallway I stopped, reading everything. For a long time I admired the paintings and other art work on the walls. I did everything I could think of to stay out of the office.

The young lady behind the counter greeted, "How may I help you?"

"Thank you," I said. "I'd like to know what I have to do to register for the summer quarter. I'm a veteran and have the G.I. Bill."

"Do you have previous college credits?"

"Yes, in 1942 before leaving for active duty in the Navy I was a student here."

"Did you attend any other college while in the service?"

"Yes, I had a semester at the University of New Mexico in the V 12, Officers Training Program. I later requested and was granted duty at sea."

"Have you attended any more schools?"

"I completed the six week Navy Hospital Corps School at Balboa Park in San Diego, California." Bragging a little I added, "I graduated second highest in a class of 420 and immediately was awarded the classification of Petty Officer, becoming a rated Pharmacists Mate in the Navy medical corps."

"That won't count toward college credit but your time at the University of New Mexico will. The first thing you have to do is send a request to Albuquerque for your transcript. When it arrives, bring it in for evaluation. You'll be credited with all the completed courses and we'll enroll you. What was your major?"

"Pre-med with my major in chemistry."

"Will you be continuing in pre-med?"

"Yes."

"All right, I'll check our records for the date in 1942 that you matriculated and have the forms ready when you bring in your other credits."

Leaving the office I felt a very delicate whisper of confidence in the ability to guide my own destiny, a feeling long suppressed during military service.

That evening from work I phoned Glennie to tell her.

"I'm so happy for you," she bubbled. "When does summer quarter begin?"

"I don't know. I have to send for my transcript from the University of New Mexico. As soon as Seattle College has it I'll be told when to start."

Her enthusiasm reinforced the new, but fragile feeling, of self-confidence.

"I have to work overtime both days this weekend so I won't be able to see you. The shop has a rush order for some special gears."

"Will you call me every evening on your lunch break?"

"I sure will, at 7:15 just like always."

As I answered her, in my voice I realized I could hear the smallest echo of accomplishment coupled with a new enthusiasm and I liked it.

❖ DAY OF DECISION ❖

When I next saw Glennie she asked again if I'd enrolled at Seattle College. She knew I went to see about it and that the school needed my transcript from the University of New Mexico before I could be admitted.

"Have you sent for it?"

"Not yet."

"You said you were going to more than two weeks ago. You really should have done it right away," she admonished softly.

From the way she looked and her comment I knew I had disappointed her and felt remorse. However, the reason I put it off stemmed from the continuing inability to take decisive action for my own good. The effect of intense regimentation during WWII remained with me. I didn't think I put things off intentionally, yet without knowing it, I did. Procrastination became my way of life.

"Every day, you're not in class, you loose valuable time and I think you know it. You surely don't want to wait until fall to start. Send for your transcript and go register," Glennie urged.

"O.K." I promised, "I'll send for it today."

Several more days passed before sending for the transcript. When it finally came I tossed it unopened on the desk in the apartment.

When I phoned Glennie from work I didn't tell her it arrived and lay on my desk. I shouldn't have kept this information from her and regretted having done so. I knew something had to be done about returning to college. If I didn't, I thought Glennie would gradually refuse to go out with me and I enjoyed her companionship so much I knew I must take positive action soon. Her urging for me to take charge of my life worked, though ever so slowly.

After a weekend date on Monday I phoned Glennie from work. "The transcript, it's here." Wanting to minimize my guilt and neglect I didn't tell her it arrived days ago.

"Great!!" she exclaimed. You can go tomorrow and register for class."

I must emphasize once more how abnormal and oppressive the devastating inertia, that is the inability to act on my own, became during the years the Navy told me specifically what to do every minute of my life, twenty four hours a day. It seemed my brain had shut down, no longer generating original thoughts or ideas that would be advantageous for me. Now, with Glennie's gentle encouragement and welcome presence in my life, for the first time since being discharged from the service I could see a glimmer of normalcy return.

Transcript in hand I arrived at the Office of the Registrar at Seattle College. Smiling, the same young lady who helped me previously came forward.

"Hi," I greeted, "I'm Gene Curnow. A while back I came to see you about registering for the summer quarter on the G.I. Bill." Handing her the envelope from the University of New Mexico I said, "Here's the transcript you wanted."

"Thanks. Oh yes, I remember you."

Looking briefly at the transcript she asked, "Would you like to register today?"

Feeling greatly troubled by having to make this decision right away I shrugged lethargically, "I guess so."

"Fine, I'll get the forms. Fill them out and bring them back when you've finished. By the way," she added, glancing at the calendar, "To be able to enroll for the summer quarter they must be here no later than tomorrow afternoon at five o'clock. Not much time I know and there are a lot of questions. But if you put your mind to it I'm sure you'll make it."

She didn't realize how close to the reality of my disability her words, "if you put your mind to it", came. Thousands of veterans who returned from military action and saw frontline combat suffered from lethargy, indecision and devastating memories in the form of "flashbacks". Over the years the condition has had many names. Some were, Shellshock, Combat fatigue, Clinical depression and most recently Post Traumatic Stress Disorder, (PTSD). Recognized by the Veterans Administration as "Service Connected" veterans suffering from it may be granted compensation.

That evening from work I phoned Glennie. I told her I'd been to Seattle College that day, handed in the transcript and been given a bunch of forms with lots of questions to answer before I could enroll. I also let her know they had to be completed and returned to the college by the next day.

"Registration ends at five o'clock in the afternoon tomorrow. I have to be at work by three thirty so that leaves very little time."

Negative thinking within assured me I'd never get the forms filled out, delivered to school and arrive at work on time. Even while thinking these thoughts I realized I now used them to bring about inaction to cause self-fulfilling defeat.

Before ending our conversation on the phone Glennie encouraged me, "I know you can get them filled out on time. I'll be so proud of you when you tell me tomorrow evening that the paperwork is done and handed in."

The next morning I got up two hours earlier than usual to fill out form after form. On and on went the questions, page after page on both sides of the paper. Many times I'd nearly go into rage at the stupidity of the person who designed the form. For example, "List all your work history beginning with the present progressing backward to the earliest. Include the beginning and ending dates of every job no matter how long you worked." At that point the moron who made the form provided a single blank line about a half-inch long. The next question, "Are you married?" required only "yes" or "no". But the blank line provided stretched nearly six inches, across almost the entire width of the form.

I thought, "How stupid can the son of a bitch who designed this mess be? Doesn't even one or two of his brain cells work?"

About one-thirty in the afternoon, after hours of writing, all forms were completed. Weary, I wanted to take a nap. But I knew if I did I'd never get to school, back to the Frye Hotel, pick up my lunch and have something to eat before walking to work and arrive there by three-thirty.

Forced to make a major decision, I struggled with the alternatives. Should I lie down and forget about returning to college this quarter or take the paperwork to school on time today?

I could hear Glennie telling me how proud she'd be when I delivered the forms and registered for class. For her to be proud of me suddenly became more important than rest.

It was far more than difficult, but I made the decision and took the completed forms to school. After hurrying from place to place, to get everything done, when I flipped the lever of the time clock that afternoon, the imprint on my card read 3:29 PM.

Glennie had become a significant factor in my life —with one minute to spare!!

❖ SCHOOL DAYS AT SEATTLE UNIVERSITY ❖

In June of 1942, soon after I graduated from High School in California, my Dad wrote to me from Seattle offering to let me live with him and attend Seattle College located only a few blocks from where he lived. He also said he would pay my tuition and living expenses. I eagerly accepted. When I returned from WWII he made the same offer and I moved in with him again.

In 1947, Seattle College was the largest Catholic College west of the Mississippi River. On May 28, 1948 it became Seattle University. Operated under the auspices of The Society of Jesus (SJ), most of the instructors were Ordained Priests of the Jesuit Order, also called "The Teaching Order." In addition, many held advanced degrees in a variety of disciplines, e.g., B.Sc., M.Sc., PhD and M.D.

Four instructors remain clearly in my memory.

Fr. HOWARD PERONTEAU, S.J.

During my sophomore year I took a class in ethics taught by Fr. Peronteau. In addition to being a full-time Professor, he was also a practicing Priest. Because he'd tell stories on himself, which endeared him to his students, his interesting lectures were filled with both humor and knowledge. He told one funny story about the time he worked alone in church late one Saturday night setting up the Altar for Mass the next day. As he carefully placed the candles, Bible and other items in their precise places he said his mind slowly went blank. Having made the set up so often he had no need to think. Without thought he continued his task. All at once he found himself doing a little song and dance. As his lengthy black garment swirled around his ankles and the tasseled rope belt around his middle flailed the air as he danced, he loudly sang the old Rudy Valle song, "Yes sir, she's my baby. No sir, don't mean maybe. Yes sir, she's my baby nooowww!!" "Without realizing it," he told us, "I sang the song over and over as I continued to dance and set up for Mass. After awhile I heard myself. Though the song had a catchy tune and a nice rhythm it certainly wasn't appropriate for the occasion."

The point he made is that one can, at times, do a very routine task without thinking and also do a second thing, in this case an inappropriate song and dance, which may be in no way related to the primary work. The subconscious mind will allow a person to do two specific acts correctly while being totally unaware of doing either.

To his students Fr. Peronteau's lectures were a joy. He demonstrated how a Priest, a devout Christian, can be overwhelmingly human, tell stories on himself, teach a course in ethics and still have a wonderful sense of humor, laughing at his own foibles.

Fr. Peronteau died in 1949. In tribute to a life spent serving humanity, a memorial to him stands on the southeast corner of the Seattle University campus quadrangle.

Fr. JAMES McGOLDRICK, S.J.

In addition to being a Priest, Fr. McGoldrick held a B.A, M.A. and PhD in Educational Psychology. During my junior year I took his advanced course in this field. Several of his lectures centered on the power of the mind.

"The mind has the ability to make us sick or keep us well, even under adverse circumstances. It also can, at times, produce remarkable and visible physical change in the body."

In class one day before giving the lecture he asked for a volunteer willing to endure a small amount of pain in order to demonstrate the power of the mind. Bernie Bergman, the volunteer, was asked to step out in the hall so he couldn't hear. In the classroom we were told that Bernie would be hypnotized. Then, in a trance he'd be told a lighted cigarette would be touched twice to the inside of his bare forearm. Fr. McGoldrick explained, "I will touch him very gently twice with the rubber eraser of a common lead pencil and as you watch you will see demonstrated the mind's amazing power."

Returning to the classroom Bernie sat on a chair at the front facing the class. Fr. McGoldrick said to him. "Are you willing for me to hypnotize you for a class demonstration?"

"Yes."

As hypnotic suggestions were quietly intoned Bernie's eyes closed and he appeared to be in a dreamlike state. When asked if he felt well and if he could hear he answered, "Yes."

Then Fr. McGoldrick said, "Bernie, I'm going to touch your bare forearm twice with a lighted cigarette. Do you understand?"

Again, Bernie said, "Yes."

"Each time the lighted cigarette touches your bare skin, for a moment it will cause a small amount of pain. Do you think you can accept it?"

Once again Bernie answered, "Yes."

About two inches apart the rubber eraser on the end of the pencil was momentarily touched to Bernie's forearm. Both times he winced as though feeling a little pain.

Fr. McGoldrick spoke soothingly, "Bernie, I promise no harm will come to you." Bernie's eyes remained closed and he appeared to be at ease.

Within moments the two spots on his forearm started to get very red. In a little over one minute, two water filled blisters began to appear. As each student came forward to closely examine the blisters all were in awe.

Fr. McGoldrick now told Bernie, "I'm going to bring you out of the hypnotic state and you'll be feeling good. You will have a little pain in your forearm. You won't recall anything that just happened. When I finish counting, you'll be wide awake—1 2 3."

Bernie opened his eyes and adjusted himself upright in the chair.

"How do you feel?" Fr. McGoldrick asked.

"I'm fine," but pointing to his forearm he said, "I have a couple of places on this arm that sting a little. It looks like I have a couple of blisters."

He was right. They were brought about because Bernie's mind responded with an immediate physical manifestation to the psychological power of suggestion.

Continuing his lectures, the following week another demonstration of the mind's power took place, this time with a young lady volunteer.

On a small low table, next to a chair in front of the class, Fr. McGoldrick placed a deep basin of water. In it floated a large amount of finely crushed ice, pure slush and extremely cold.

"What I will do," he explained, "is first have you put your hand all the way up to the wrist, in the ice water. I want you to keep it there as long as you can stand it while I keep track of the time. Soon the cold will become so intensely painful you will be forced to take it out. When you can no longer stand it, go ahead and remove your hand from the water and I'll make a note of the elapsed time.

"I'll then hypnotize you and again tell you to put your hand in the ice water all the way to the wrist. But this time, under hypnosis, I will give the suggestion that the water is now pleasantly warm and we'll see how long you can keep it in the basin. Even though I've already told you this is going to happen, the class and you will find how the power of suggestion, under hypnosis, will overcome your conscious reasoning. Let's begin now by having you first place your hand in the ice water. Please leave it there as long as possible."

Fully awake she followed the instructions. In a little less than two minutes, with her hand in distress from the low temperature, she had to remove it from the numbingly cold slush.

Fr. McGoldrick then hypnotized her and told her to again place her hand in the water. This time he assured her it was warm and would feel pleasant. Six minutes passed and at intervals he instructed, "Swirl the nice warm water around with your hand. Does it feel warm enough?"

"Yes," she answered.

After another minute other inquiries were made. "Do you think you could keep your hand in this warm water all day?"

Again she said, "Yes."

"Do you have any distress or unpleasant feeling in your hand?"

This time she answered, "No."

At the end of seven minutes, Fr. McGoldrick told her to remove her hand from the water then took her out of the hypnotic state.

"How do you feel?" he asked.

"I'm fine but my hand feels sort of numb and really cold."

His demonstrations, using class members in an active role, made his classes unforgettable.

Fr. McGoldrick died in 1983 at age 88 but he continues to live on in the memory of his many fascinated students.

Fr. FRANK, S.J.

For my major in the Pre Med course at Seattle University, I chose chemistry. To earn a Bachelors Degree required more than 90 credit hours. In my senior year the final course, Physiological Chemistry, proved to be very labor intensive. "P Chem", as it's called, requires long hours in the laboratory doing "hands on" experiments. Each student must follow precisely the instructions from a lab manual, complete every experiment and hand in the results on time.

Unable to work a full shift at Western Gear and finish the time consuming lab requirements, Glennie suggested that I ask Mr. Tom Bannan, owner of the machine shop, if I could work half time on the afternoon swing shift, from 3:30 to 7:30 during school days Monday through Friday.

At our meeting I told him, "I'm a senior in Pre Med at Seattle University. Physiological Chemistry, the final course I need to complete the credit hours needed for my degree, requires a great deal of time spent in the laboratory. I can't continue school if I don't find an extra four hours a day to finish the experiments."

He listened attentively. "Gene, I've never let anyone work only half a shift in the shop during the many years I've been in business. But I'm going to make an exception for you. Yes, you can work the first four hours of the swing shift on school days. However, on week ends, if you are asked to put in overtime I'll expect you to be here."

I agreed with his proposal and thanked him for his consideration. Seated behind his large polished oak desk, leaning back in the overstuffed chair, thickly padded with soft black, rolled and button tufted leather, as I walked toward the door to leave his office he called, "Good luck with your studies. I think Seattle University is a great school."

"Yes Sir, it is, and thanks again."

Sometimes the experiments in P Chem were so complex I didn't finish until two o'clock in the morning. Afterward all the equipment such as micro pipettes, mini test tubes, burettes and beakers used to get the results, had to be thoroughly cleaned. They were very small and getting them perfectly clean required a lot of time. Glennie didn't work Saturdays, so on Friday nights she'd come to the lab to keep me company and help clean the equipment.

One student, Fr. Frank, a Priest, took P Chem with me. About 30 years old he too was a senior in Pre Med. He would later go on to St. Louis University and earn an M.D. degree.

In addition to his intelligence, as do most Jesuit Priests I've known, he had a wonderful sense of humor. Late one Friday night Glennie and I, with Fr. Frank, after finishing a long and exhausting experiment, were cleaning the equipment. About 1:30 in the morning, with sleep long overdue, he broke the monotony of our task by telling a great story.

"A young couple had a baby boy, now nearly a year old. On his birthday they thought they'd give the child a test and perhaps be able to determine what the future held for their son. While he sat in his high chair they placed in front of him on the tray, a Bible, a fifty-dollar bill and a two-ounce shot glass full of expensive whiskey. The idea being that if he reached for the Bible he might become a "man of the cloth." If he picked up the fifty-dollar bill perhaps he'd become a man in high finance. But if he reached for the large shot of expensive whiskey he'd probably end up a drunkard.

With everything in place the couple eagerly waited to see which object their son would choose. The anxious parents waited while the baby gazed at the three items.

Suddenly he picked up the fifty-dollar bill, stuffed it in his diaper, grabbed the big shot glass of expensive whiskey, drank it down in one gulp and picking up the Bible, began to leaf through it.

Horrified the parents threw their hands in the air and covered their faces in dismay. Oh no, they cried, not a Jesuit Priest!!"

With his gentle nature and ability to laugh and tell jokes that reflected, with good humor on his own calling, I'm sure Fr. Frank became a most successful person in his life's work.

DR. FINE

Several of the instructors at Seattle University were not Catholics or Priests. Dr. Fine was Jewish and an outstanding practicing physician. During my senior year I took his course, "Human Anatomy and Physiology."

He taught the course by dividing the human body into its various systems and we studied each separately. When he'd introduce a new system, during the course of the first lecture he'd speak for 35 minutes then call a class member to the blackboard at the front of the room and have the student draw, with colored chalk, as much of the anatomy as the person could recall from having previously read the assigned text. Dr. Fine would correct any errors in the drawing and answer questions.

After finishing the digestive, skeletal and muscle systems, on a Monday we started the new week studying the male reproductive system. On the first day he lectured the usual 35 minutes. Then, standing at the front of the class waving his index finger, he finally pointed at Betty McGillicutty, a senior and one of the most beautiful girls in school. Immensely popular and intelligent, every year she made the Honor Roll.

Called from the back of the room she seemed almost to glide as she stepped to the blackboard. The eyes of every male student were glued to the lithe movements of her stunningly gorgeous figure that, as she walked, undulated beneath her perfectly fitted tailor made clothing. We had a saying on campus, "if any male didn't turn his head to watch her walk by he was either blind, had less than one male hormone in his entire bloodstream or was already dead."

Dr. Fine instructed, "Miss McGillicutty, please draw in color, the major external components of the male reproductive system."

Without hesitation she picked up a piece of pink chalk. First she drew the scrotal sac containing the two testicles. Then, using light-brown chalk, she crosshatched it indicating many wrinkles, hairs and fine lines. Next she drew the penis, again using the pink chalk.

When finished, the drawing was, for the most part, anatomically correct right down to the slightly darker red color at the end of the male organ, the glans, compared with its shaft. But most notable is the fact that she drew it larger than life size—and in full erection.

Dr. Fine, an excellent instructor, thanked her for her effort then gave his critique'.

"You did very well Miss McGillicutty. There is only one small anatomical error. In all male primates, human or animal, one testicle always hangs lower in the scrotum making it look a little lopsided." Pointing to her drawing, he continued, "Your illustration shows the male organ in a state of high arousal. Generally speaking, in medical texts, you'll find the penis usually is shown flaccid, that is to say, in a state of rest. Other than this, you've done a very good job."

As Dr. Fine spoke to Miss McGillicutty about "a high state of arousal," every male student in the class and most of the females, were ready to explode with laughter. Then a young fellow seated at the back of the room, spoke in a loud, exaggerated stage whisper so everyone would hear. "What did you expect Dr. Fine? After all, that's probably the only way she's ever seen one."

Dr. Fine had one more thing to say. A slight smile crossed his face. "All right, that's enough. Class dismissed."

❖ RETURN TO COLLEGE ❖
WITH MY BRIDE

Back in College, I had to prepare homework for the following day. In addition I returned to work at Western Gear on the "swing" shift. This schedule became very difficult. Arriving at school at eight o'clock in the morning I'd attend classes until two in the afternoon then drive back to the apartment in the Frye Hotel. After changing into work clothes, at my desk I'd attempt to get some homework done for school the next day. Hurrying to the "Mom and Pop" restaurant close by, I ate and picked up the lunch they always had ready for me to take to work.

Driving to the machine shop, about a mile away, I'd punch in on the time clock a few minutes before three thirty. At 11:35 I punched out, drove to the apartment, took a bath and got ready for bed. If not too tired, I'd prepare as much schoolwork as I could to turn in the next day. Getting up at six thirty in the morning or sooner, I'd dress for school, have breakfast and drive to college. In the parked car before classes began, I completed any unfinished assignment.

By carrying seventeen to twenty-one credit hours every quarter, while working a full shift at the shop and taking no summer vacation, with this "killer schedule" I earned a four-year Bachelor of Science degree in Chemistry in 2 years, 11 months and 29 nine days.

During this hectic time Glennie and I talked on the phone only a few minutes each evening starting at seven fifteen during my lunch break. We'd date on weekends if I didn't work overtime or have a lot of schoolwork to complete. Fortunately for my paycheck, but not my social life, I worked most Saturdays at double time and a lot of Sundays at triple time.

Western Gear paid their personnel every Wednesday. When I had a seven day pay period and saw the fat paycheck of $120.56 I didn't mind at all paying Union Dues of $5.00 a month to the International Association of Machinists, Hope Lodge Number 25 that made it possible. Including the $90.00 a month allowance from the G.I. Bill, I had a job, at age twenty-two, that paid "a man's wages", $572.24 a month. A better paycheck by far than many older men had in 1947.

Working so much overtime wasn't conducive to dating. Many times Glennie and I saw each other only once or twice a month. Yet somehow, the phone calls at seven fifteen every evening sustained our steadily growing relationship. Once in awhile we'd still double date with Ken and Twila. But more and more we dated as a twosome.

Glennie and I enjoyed natural things. Many were free and abundantly available in Seattle and the Puget Sound area. For example, she'd make a picnic lunch and we'd drive to a museum, then go on to a waterfall, lake or park and eat. Just being together is what mattered.

One adventure stands out. The basement of a building close to Pioneer Square housed a "medical museum". Never having been to it, as a Pre Med student, I thought it might be of interest because a practicing physician owned it. He wanted to alert people about how disastrous the disease syphilis can be. Lining the walls were full size cardboard cutouts in color, of naked male and female figures. The cutouts showed the effects of all three stages of the disease on the external and internal anatomy. In large color photographs, below the cutouts, ravages of the primary, secondary and tertiary phases of the disease on the skin and internal organs were shown. Most vivid were pictures of people who suffered from the tertiary and usually fatal, form. These graphically depicted the victims suffering locomotor ataxia, a devastating condition of the central nervous system causing violent spasms and jerking motions making normal walking impossible. However, most of the people with tertiary syphilis died from the spontaneous rupture of the main artery leaving the heart, The Arch of the Aorta, from a hole eaten through it by the causative organism, Treponema pallidum.

The ugly exhibits in the museum were in several large clear glass jars. Filled with thousands of "foreskins", also called "prepuces", they had been surgically removed from the penises of many men who were patients of the physician. For the most part they looked dry, gray and shriveled, but a few on the top layer were somewhat pink and seemed to look quite fresh. From then on, I made sure of exactly what kind of a museum Glennie and I entered.

When I finished the summer quarter at school Glennie continued to be most encouraging. She lost no time making sure I registered to return in the fall. During the summer quarter, the first time I returned to college after the war, I earned good grades and felt we were drawing closer. The comfortable feeling we both now enjoyed when together was more than just a steady date with someone with a car and a good paying job. I also found out from Twila that after Glennie and I dated only twice she told the Marine Lieutenant she had dated before our blind date that she wasn't going to go out with him anymore. Of course, this gave a massive boost to my self-confidence.

In July of 1947 we began to discuss the possibility of marriage. I said I didn't want this responsibility before becoming a senior, in about two and a half years. At that time I'd know whether or not, after going through the devastating war in the Pacific, I could still study and retain information well enough to be able to earn a bachelors degree in chemistry. Glennie agreed marriage would be a big step, one that should be considered carefully. With this in mind we set a tentative date for June of 1950. But from then on, almost every time we dated she'd suggest an earlier time.

"What about right after you finish the junior year?" she asked. Though reluctant, I agreed.

Things began to transpire at an ever-faster pace. On our next date she accepted the diamond ring I offered. We were officially engaged.

Glennie and I were extremely happy with the thought of being married. But it quickly became obvious that her Mother was not. Valma Murray, a hard working, career oriented single parent and manager of the Lowman-Hanford Co. that later was bought by J. K. Gill of Portland, Oregon, counted among her personal friends many of the "right people" in Seattle. Among them were Eddie Vine, owner of the exclusive stationery and writing instrument shop, Eddie Bauer, owner of the Outdoor Store and Victoria and Mark Colby, a multi-millionaire industrialist dealing in heavy machinery and steel. Outwardly Valma appeared to accept the idea that her 20 year old Daughter was engaged to a struggling Pre Med student whose parents were of considerably less than even modest means. Inwardly she disapproved and in no uncertain terms. I realized just how much she objected one evening when visiting Glennie at her Mother's apartment.

With the door of the bathroom closed she and Glennie were inside talking. As I went past to go pick up the newspaper being delivered out in the hallway of the apartment, through the bathroom door I heard Valma say, "You aren't really going to marry that bull headed German are you?"

Glennie answered emphatically, "Yes, I sure am!!"

Her Mother quickly admonished, "Well, it will never last."

I picked up the newspaper and quickly returned to the living room. Having secretly heard Glennie stand up to her Mother and pointedly tell her she had every intention of marrying me, I felt great.

A week or two later, on a Sunday, Glennie and I, her Mother and my dad, Harry, drove about 20 miles south of Seattle on old Highway 99 to a popular restaurant called, "The Farm." Dad was happy and surprised when we told him Glennie and I were engaged. Obviously delighted he said, "You sure couldn't get a nicer girl." Dad had finished half a dozen drinks within a short time so I hoped it wasn't the booze talking, though I knew his opinion of Glennie was entirely correct.

Still remembering Valma's disparaging remark about me that came from behind the bathroom door in her apartment not long ago, I felt sure she still didn't approve. Having social connections with Seattle's "upper crust", undoubtedly she thought her only child, a very beautiful young girl, could "do better." But at our engagement dinner she made a startling and pleasant announcement.

The small diamond I gave Glennie weighed only one fourth of a carat. But she wore it proudly, never complained or put pressure on me by saying some of her friends had bigger stones. Over dessert and coffee Valma said, "Kids, I have a personal friend, Mr. Green, who owns one of the best diamond and jewelry stores in town. A few days ago I spoke with him and asked how big a diamond he'd let me have for the same cost as the one Glennie now has. He said I could have a much nicer one, a three quarter carat, 58-facet brilliant cut solitaire with a couple of tiny flaws that nobody would ever see without a microscope. This diamond is going to be my gift to you both."

Earlier I told Glennie I had the option to return the small diamond within 30 days for a full refund. She mentioned it in casual conversation with her Mother who in turn secretly contacted Mr. Green and arranged to get one from him three times the size for the same price. A few days later with Glennie wearing the beautiful new solitaire, to me her Mother looked a lot better.

On a date early in December of 1947 Glennie asked, "What do you think of the idea of being married in January during your Christmas and New Year school break? I've resigned from the United States District Attorney's Office because they wanted to send me to Olympia. I have a new job lined up with the Mayflower Insurance Company. Mother's hair dresser Vera, has a small apartment in back of her beauty shop that we can rent for $25.00 a month. The electricity, phone and garbage pick up is included. We'd only have to pay for oil to heat with and to cook. There's a nice refrigerator in the apartment and we can use it too."

Stunned, overwhelmed and flattered all at the same time, I found the opportunity for a little humor.

I asked Glennie, "Do you remember how at first you agreed we'd wait to be married until June of 1950 when I'd be a graduating senior? Then you came up with the idea that it might be all right to tie the knot a year earlier. Later on you thought maybe this last Thanksgiving would work out. Now you're saying next month? This has to be the fastest in my life I've ever seen two and a half years shrink to about six months." Glennie only smiled and said nothing.

"O.K." I conceded. "What day next month?"

Saturday night at 8:30, on January 9, 1948, in the small University Lutheran Church in Seattle, Washington, Glennie and I were married. More than 200 guests attended which meant standing room only for some. Most were personal friends of Glennie's Mother and represented Seattle's finest, such as Eddie Vine, Mark and Victoria Colby and Eddie Bauer.

Glennie's gown of heavy Cathedral Satin was outstanding. Victoria Colby, the wife of Mark Colby the industrialist, loaned Glennie an exquisite full-length trailing veil of French Chantilly lace. Topped with a tiara encrusted with dazzling diamonds, each one had been mounted individually in a bed of daisy shaped blue and white seed pearls. The Colby's had it custom made for their Daughter who had been married a few months earlier. This became the "something borrowed" required by all brides. I rented the mandatory Tuxedo and must say we did make a good-looking couple. Glennie's dad, George, "gave the bride away." My mother, Frances, and Glennie's mother, Valma, stood by looking pleased.

My dad, Harry, who still worked for the Alaska Steamship Company, was in New York on a ship being loaded with cargo. Taking time off, several days earlier he boarded a train bound for Seattle planning to be at the ceremony. Unfortunately, one of the worst snowstorms to ever hit Montana helplessly stalled it for three days in massive drifts near Helena. He missed the event by one day arriving in Seattle on the tenth, just in time to board another train a few hours later and return to New York.

Ken Hansen, who I first met at Western Gear, became our best friend. He had pushed Glennie's head and mine together on our third date that resulted in our first kiss in the back seat of the old 1935 Dodge. He served as Best Man. Twila his girl friend, served as Maid of Honor.

Of all the cards we received congratulating us only one remains treasured in our memory. Given to us by Ken's Brother, Bob Hansen, instead of expressing joy it read, "With My Deepest Sympathy For You In The Hour Of Your Great Loss." Because it's the only one Glennie and I remember who the sender was and what the card says, I guess whatever Bob wanted to impart, he succeeded.

We spent our one night honeymoon on the 13th floor of the Olympic Hotel in downtown Seattle. The next day we drove to Snoqualmie Falls to watch the roaring water and spray of winter's cascade pour a muddy torrent over the edge dropping to the ice bound pool below. The following day Glennie went back to work and I went back to school and to work.

Throughout my life the number 13 has been associated with major good fortune. Having Glennie with me, it has continued ever since our one night honeymoon, on the 13th floor of the Olympic Hotel, in the room with walls enfolding us gently in a color of soft powder puff blue.

❖ HIGH HOPES—DASHED ❖

With the Pre Medical course at Seattle University completed in August of 1950 and a degree, Bachelor of Science in Chemistry in hand, the next step was to make application to Medical Schools. My advisor at Seattle University suggested, "You should select three of the best. I'd say Harvard, Stanford and Creighton." Looking at my records he calculated, "You still have enough time left on the G.I. Bill to take you half way through your third year of medical training. When you reach that point if you have good grades, you'll have no trouble getting adequate loans. There are many sources from which students in medical school who are juniors and seniors can easily obtain enough money with which to finish training and later, as an intern, you'll be paid a small wage."

It sounded great. I felt on my way to be able to provide "the good life" for Glennie and the children we planned to have.

With great anticipation I mailed the requests for application forms. Many WWII veterans were eligible for higher education on the G.I. Bill and I expected with so many applicants the schools wouldn't be in a hurry to send them. This was not the case. Within a few weeks the forms from all three schools arrived. I filled them out, provided a transcript of my grades and a copy of my degree. In a short cover letter I told each school why I wanted to attend.

"Here is something laughable ," I told Glennie. "I'm blowing the same smoke at each of the three medical schools. The cover letter telling the registrar why I consider their school to be my best choice is exactly the same except for the name and address."

It took several months before replies to the applications arrived. Finished with college I asked Mr. Herb Dobbs, Personnel manager of Western Gear, if I could work full time on the graveyard shift, 11:30 PM until 7:00 AM because it paid a 15% bonus.

"No problem Gene, we can use you on any shift. Oh yes, congratulations on getting your degree." He paused a moment as if in thought. "Will you be going on to medical school as you've planned?"

I don't know what I detected in his voice or demeanor, but I knew instinctively that his question was more than polite conversation. I sensed he had a definite but hidden reason for asking. Forty years later, in Indian Wells, California, an event would prove my strange feeling about his question had been justified.

Now working full-time on the graveyard shift I was happy to earn the 15% bonus. Glennie too worked full time during the day at the Mayflower Insurance Co. Because we paid no rent living at a veterinary hospital, we had an excellent income. I told Dr. Ehmer I had to give up the free apartment and my job as his night attendant because of my full-time graveyard shift work schedule at Western Gear. He agreed that the job of night attendant was more suitable for a young single person not working full time and we parted the best of friends.

Glennie and I rented a brand new modern duplex at 916 N.W. 56th. She loved the shiny stove, refrigerator, glistening oak floors and the aroma of newness. Because we were used to paying no rent, $75.00 a month, at first, seemed high. However, with my advancement to "Gear Cutting Specialist" at Western Gear, by myself I now made a "man's wages". Many married men working with me earning the same amount of money, owned a house and a new car. Most had a wife who didn't need to work and two or three children, all easily supported on the same wages I brought home. Glennie's pay simply became a bonus.

Months went by with no answer from the three medical schools. We enjoyed "the good life" which accompanied our above average income. We had sold the worn out 1935 Dodge for $500.00 and for $900.00 bought a 1939 Nash. We ate out frequently, went to movies or attended live plays at The Theatre in the Round at the University of Washington and every Saturday night played Canasta with a circle of friends. The life of a well-paid gear cutting machinist had its rewards. Getting no answer from the medical schools their importance faded as we lived happily in nice surroundings and put money in the bank

"Congratulations," the letter began. "You have been accepted to the Harvard School of Medicine. Classes begin on September 20, 1951. Please complete the enclosed Personal History form and return it as soon as possible with your letter of intent."

Glennie and I had the classic reaction of "mixed emotions". I said "Getting this letter now while we're living so well is kind of like a guy would feel watching his nosey Mother in Law drive off a 10,000 foot cliff in his brand new Cadillac convertible. What do you think we should do?"

"Why don't you wait until tomorrow to fill out the form, keep it a few days so we can think it over slowly and calmly before sending it back."

The next day as I again read it I saw a major requirement, previously overlooked in our excitement. It was one with which we could not comply. The lower part of the last page in somewhat smaller print under the heading, Financial Resources said, "In addition to the G.I. Bill, the student must have available in a personal account, or a letter of promise from another source, stating that $25,000.00 is available immediately on demand as needed."

I read it over several times to be sure I understood exactly what it meant. I thought the G.I. Bill would pay for all books, tuition and equipment and send us a check every month just as it did at Seattle University. We knew the Government money wouldn't be enough to live on in Boston and Glennie had agreed previously that she'd go to work if I were accepted to Harvard. However, the requirement to have this much extra money available, in addition to the G.I. Bill, for us was impossible. An explanation accompanied the request to have the $25,000.00 available.

"We must be assured of the financial well being of new

students. Should one have to withdraw for financial reasons, it would vacate a spot in which a student with financial means could have continued."

The Harvard faculty was absolutely right. Though very disappointed, I understood and agreed with their reasoning.

Holding out hope I said to Glennie, "We still have a chance. Maybe the other two schools won't require any additional funds." This was not the case. Within two weeks, letters of acceptance arrived from Creighton and Stanford Universities and each had a stipulation requiring that $25,000.00 be available. It was a devastating blow.

From the time I became a senior at Shasta High School in Redding, California, to earn a degree so that "Dr." would replace "Mr." in front of my name almost became an obsession. The ultimate goal in my life was to become a physician. But now facing reality I thought, "After all the planning, work and hardship both Glennie and I went through to earn my pre-medical degree in Chemistry, it's not going to happen. I'll have to remain a gear-cutting machinist as my life's work and forgo a career in medicine."

A few days later Glennie said, "What would you think of the idea of applying to the Veterinary Medical School at Pullman? You've worked for Dr. Ehmer and maybe he'd write you a letter of recommendation. With a degree in veterinary medicine you'll still get the title of doctor in front of your name like you've always wanted." Her suggestion, as usual, made a lot of sense.

Dr. Ehmer, in 1936 a graduate of Washington State College School of Veterinary Medicine, became famous and wealthy by inventing the "Ehmer, external fixation bone pinning system" used by veterinarians all over the world. Rather than giving it to the IRS he contributed substantial amounts of money to the veterinary medical school, was a personal friend of the Dean and also of Glennie's family.

The more I thought about a degree in veterinary medicine, the better I liked it. I knew Dr. Ehmer made a far greater income than I'd ever make even as a journeyman machinist. He belonged to the exclusive Rainier Club, Englewood Golf Club as well as contributing to many charities. I realized if I'd go into the profession, I too would make a much better than average living for my wife and children. Money was not, however, the only factor in this decision. While working for Dr. Ehmer I also developed a genuine desire to help sick or injured pets.

On a Friday afternoon I made the phone call. "Dr. Ehmer, this is Gene. Can I have a little of your time one of these days to talk about an important matter?"

"What about tomorrow after two o'clock? We close at noon here at the office and you can have as much time as it takes. Can you fill me in a little on what you'd like to talk about?"

"Yes, I'd like to explore the possibility of going to veterinary medical school at WSC.

His voice rose perceptibly. "Oh, great, I'll be glad to help you."

I took the letters from the three prestigious schools to show Dr. Ehmer I'd been accepted. I explained, "I cannot guarantee to have the extra money each of them requires so medical school is out of the question. Do you think I could get into the veterinary medical school without having any more money than the G.I. bill provides? I know that getting into veterinary school is very difficult." I continued, "One study I read recently, conducted by the Bank of America in San Francisco, found it's nineteen times harder to get into a veterinary medical school than a human medical school." Then I said, "I think the person who wrote the report had a great sense of humor because one of his comments was, 'some veterinary medical students consider medical students in the human field to be the rejects from veterinary medical schools.'"

Chuckling at this humor Dr. Ehmer suggested, "Why don't you write and get an application. It will state whether additional money is needed for tuition, instruments and books. Before you send in the completed application I'll write a letter of recommendation you can enclose and we'll see what can be done to get you admitted. In your cover letter you should mention that you've worked for me as my night attendant and have helped weekends with restraint of the pets while I treated them. It also wouldn't hurt to mention your years of experience as a rated Navy Medical Corpsman taking care of the wounded while on active duty associated with the Marines in the Pacific."

"It's not what you know but who you know" that sometimes can make a significant difference in the life of a person. I'd heard that expression many times. What happened next is a classic example.

I filled out the newly arrived veterinary medical school application and phoned Dr. Ehmer asking him to write the letter of recommendation. Picking it up the following day I thanked him for his help.

"I hope it will do the trick for you Gene, you'd be good for the profession."

His letter wasn't sealed and back at our duplex I read it to Glennie.

To the Dean
College of Veterinary Medicine
WSC, Pullman, Washington.
Dear Dr. Stone

This letter will introduce Eugene Curnow who has worked as my night attendant, medical and surgical assistant for almost a year.

I have found him to be an outstanding employee. He learns quickly, is honest and readily accepts new concepts.

I would consider it a personal favor if you can find a spot for him in the class starting September 21, 1951.

E. A. Ehmer, DVM.

In 1951, the number of WWII veterans taking advantage of the education benefits offered by the G.I. Bill, reached an all time high. Eighteen hundred students applied that year to the veterinary medical school in Pullman competing for the fifty available openings. Many had two advanced degrees and outstanding grades. I had only one degree and a 3.2 grade point average, good but not spectacular. It soon became obvious to me how politics, large amounts of money contributed and the "good old boy" system can come together to work wonders. Without Dr. Ehmer's letter requesting "A personal favor" from Dean Stone, as I would find out later, I would not have been accepted.

The return letter from the veterinary medical school informed me of the date an aptitude test would be given in Pullman and that I must reply within seven days whether or not I would attend. The answer, of course, was yes.

Glennie and I decided it would be wise for me to fly to Pullman rather than make the long tiring drive. Inland Empire Airlines, a very small carrier, operated with a limited number of old WWII surplus DC-3 aircraft. The one-way trip from Seattle to Pullman cost $27.00

On Wednesday, the day before the test, I boarded the plane and showing my ticket to the Steward told him, "I'm going to Pullman." He nodded his acknowledgement. There were only five passengers on the flight. I wondered how the owners could make enough money to provide aviation fuel or routine maintenance work on the instruments, airframes or engines. How could they pay the pilots? The flight was very smooth and in spite of my concern I drifted off to sleep.

The Steward shook me awake, "Here we are," he announced brightly.

I looked out the window and on a sign above a small building saw the words, "BOISE AIRPORT."

"Is this Pullman?" I asked.

"No, this is Boise. It's as far as we go."

"I'm supposed to be taken to Pullman. I mentioned this when I boarded," I said as I again handed him my ticket.

"Wait a minute." He hurried to the cockpit where the pilot and co-pilot were doing paperwork. The pilot came to the cabin with my ticket in his hand.

"Somebody goofed," he said. "Your ticket is for Pullman so we'll just have to get back in the air and take you there." The only passenger now on board, I dozed all the way. That night, for $3.00, I stayed in the Washington Hotel, the best in town. Well rested, in the morning I looked forward to the eight-hour test. It consisted of long paragraphs with lots of medical terminology describing varied and unusual conditions found in anatomy, physiology and chemistry of the many domestic animals. We were to read the text then answer the questions based on the subject matter. A lot of "veterinary medical jargon" was totally foreign to us all. Even with a background in the Navy in human medicine, physiology and anatomy, for me the test was a challenge. Every section of the test had a time limit making everyone work under constant pressure. Most of the applicants I talked with afterward said they doubted whether they passed. I felt the same.

Our best friend, Ken Hansen offered to drive to Pullman and be there by the time the test was finished on Thursday afternoon. He had a brand new Chevrolet convertible, baby blue in color with a white top. He brought Glennie and his girl friend, Twila, with him for the ride back to Seattle.

On the way home, the secondary highway heading north out of Pullman, in 1951 followed the many undulations characteristic of the Palouse country. We'd travel up a short rise then down a small hill, like a giant roller coaster for mile after mile past nothing but vast fields of wheat. There were many "No passing zones" because drivers, oncoming from either direction, couldn't see each other.

Suddenly as we topped a rise, in front of us just off the road, were two wrecked cars, one at each side. Clouds of dust from the accident that had just happened hung in the air. Ken stopped his car safely off the road and told the girls to stay in it. We ran to see if we could help. One car, crumpled but upright in the ditch, held only the woman driver. With gray hair she appeared to be about 65 years old. She could speak, but injured and bloody, she didn't move. The other was driven by a deeply tanned, black haired man. He appeared to be in his forties. He had passed us at a high rate of speed only a short time before. As he sped by Ken said, "That guy is going way too fast for the kind of road we're on. He could end up in the ditch or crash into someone."

As Ken predicted, he hit another car and badly injured an innocent victim. After the impact his car left the road and slammed into a utility pole. Hitting on the driver's side it wrapped itself almost all the way around. The unconscious man was crushed. The steering wheel broke off and the bare metal column had been driven deeply into his chest. Blood and froth gushed from his mouth every time he involuntarily tried to breathe. His clothing and flesh above the right knee were torn away exposing almost the full length of his thighbone. The lower end of it had been driven completely through the dashboard. Starting to clot, pools of blood thickly covered the floor. Ken and I looked in the car and counted eight empty beer cans on the floor and two on the mangled seat beside him. Two full cans, still in the carton, were at his feet. On the floor of the back seat lay an empty carton of twenty-four. Though I had been a Navy Medical Corpsman and wanted to help, I knew in a case this serious and with nothing to work with, I shouldn't touch this horribly injured man.

Called by the people in a farmhouse close to the accident, it took awhile for an ambulance to arrive. But before he could be freed from the wreckage holding him tightly entombed, the man died.

The injured woman was alive when the ambulance crew freed her. Though we looked in the Spokane newspaper the next day for information we never found out if she survived.

That night we stayed in beautiful rustic cabins in a pine scented grove of high timber. It was so quiet Ken and I could hardly sleep. I guess girls are different because they said it was the best sleep they had for a long time.

On the way back to Seattle the next day we took the opportunity to enjoy a guided tour of Grand Coulee Dam and continue on to see Dry Falls and finally Soap Lake.

A letter came from the veterinary medical school in less than two weeks, "You have passed the aptitude test and we are pleased to inform you that you have been accepted to the College of Veterinary Medicine. Classes will begin on September 26, 1951. Please register on September 24th in Bohler gym. If applicable please request married student housing in South Fairway at least two weeks in advance. Rent for a two-bedroom unit is $32.00 a month. A two-month rental deposit in advance is required. You may request beds, desks, tables and chairs that will be provided at no charge. Upon receipt of your deposit, an apartment number will be assigned and the key mailed to you."

Glennie and I were delighted. That evening we celebrated on the waterfront having an oyster feed at Seattle's famous restaurant on Alaska Way, "Ivar's Acres of Clams".

It had been a difficult and convoluted journey. Now a challenging, new and exciting phase of life lay ahead.

Photos & Illustrations: Civilian Life & Love

Gene and Harry Curnow
Seattle, WA

Harry is dressed for work at Boeing. During WWII, he was second in command for Boeing's Security Division. Gene is dressed for school at Seattle University.

Western Gear, Seattle

Above, Gene is inspecting a finished, in-line herringbone gear. He worked at Western Gear before the War and whenever possible throughout his years at Seattle University. The above photo was taken in 1954. Narrative begins on p. 299.

Kenneth Hansen

Our very best friend and a co-worker at Western Gear. His girlfriend, Twila, was a friend of Glenora, who became my wife. It was with Ken and Twila that Glenora and I went on the "blind date" to Mt. Rainier and threw snowballs at each other. Ken too, was a well dressed young man and took the idea of white sidewall shoes from me. Ken became the "Best Man" at our wedding and a Seattle Police Officer.

Glenora M. Murray

"This is the girl, at 18, who I met on a 'blind date' Easter Sunday, 1947. I thought I had no chance with this refined, beautiful young lady...but as it turned out, I did. We married on January 9, 1948."

On the Road to Paradise
Easter Sunday, 1947

Gene stands on the Ford fender to illustrate the 15' of snow along roads to Paradise, on Mt. Rainier. Narrative: *Blind Date*, p. 318

PART V
VETERINARY SCHOOL
& PRACTICE

❖ THE TURNING POINT ❖

In April of 1951 both Glennie and I were working full time and with my overtime we saved enough money to buy a house. By the end of July my Aunt Barbara Smith, a realtor, found one on the north end of Seattle's Magnolia district, 2805 West Elmore Street, high on a hill overlooking the Ballard area and the Government Locks. At night, far below in the distance, rows of street lights sparkled brilliantly like diamond necklaces. We had no trouble qualifying for a conventional mortgage loan and within 30 days enjoyed the first time thrill of moving from rented housing to a home of our own. The house payment, which included principle, fire insurance and interest on the 20-year loan, resulted in a monthly charge of $57.00, exactly the opposite set of numbers we paid to rent the duplex.

Glennie was eight and a half months pregnant with our first child so to help out, her Mother gave up her apartment in the Queen Ann district and moved with us to the new house. She continued to live there for the next four years while we were in Pullman, paying the $57.00 a month mortgage as rent.

We sold our 1939 Nash and Glennie's uncle, Harry Jacobson, gave us his beautiful four-door 1941 Chrysler New Yorker, a much better, bigger and more reliable car with a "flat head, straight eight" engine under the hood. For my solo trip to Pullman we loaded it with as many household things as could be packed in. Almost all the passenger side of the front seat and the entire back seat area we filled all the way to the roof. No room remained in the car's tightly packed trunk. To save money I bought two pounds of ground horsemeat at a market that sold it for human consumption. With it Glennie made two thick, juicy hamburger-like sandwiches for me to eat during the long drive. Glennie would have our first child in less than two weeks and wanted to stay in Seattle to be near her Obstetrician and Gynecologist, Drs. Rutherford and Banks. Because Glennie's Mother lived with us, she could help during the final two weeks of pregnancy.

Our plans were that as soon as we knew for sure that the baby was "on the way", I'd return and be at Glennie's side for the birth. Dr. Rutherford, a Harvard medical school graduate, far ahead of his time, encouraged the husband to participate and be in the delivery room with the wife to hold her hand and talk with her during the birth. Most Obstetricians and hospitals in 1951 wouldn't let a husband near the delivery room. We felt fortunate knowing we'd to be able to be together so I could encourage Glennie as she presented us with our first baby.

In late September I left Seattle to begin my veterinary medical education in Pullman. At four o'clock that afternoon Glennie asked me what I'd like to eat before I left.

"I'd really enjoy a nice 'breakfast supper', you know, bacon and eggs, pan fried potatoes and lots of strong coffee. The 'one for the road' will be another cup of coffee to keep me awake."

I could tell she didn't want me to go without her. But she kept up a good front as she prepared the food. I didn't want to be this far away with the baby coming so soon but had no choice. I tried not to show it, but I felt like I was abandoning her at a crucial time.

The fully loaded car sat ready at curbside. Holding hands Glennie and I walked slowly to it in silence. Before opening the door I put my arms around her. For long moments we hugged and kissed. A tear ran down her uplifted face.

"I sure wish you didn't have to go," she said.

"I know, so do I. But it's only for about two weeks and I'll be back. Call me as soon as your water breaks. I'll get someone at school to give me their phone number and when you call they can give me the message."

Adding some humor so we wouldn't feel quite so bad, I said," Well, next time we hug and squeeze standing up we won't have to stand almost sideways like this because of that big bulge you've got out front."

"Well, you caused it you know," her eyes sparkled as she laughed.

After a final parting kiss I told her I'd call as soon as I got to Pullman.

"Drive carefully," she called while waving her hand.

At six o'clock on Sunday evening I left Seattle. Driving all night I stopped only once, in Ellensburg, for gasoline. It cost nineteen cents a gallon. At four o'clock in the morning, exhausted and hungry, I arrived at the top of a grade on the outskirts of Pullman. Parking the car safely, far off the highway on a wide shoulder, I opened the brown paper bag and eagerly took out one of the horsemeat hamburgers. Now a soggy mass, all of the moisture had soaked into the bread. I'd never tasted horsemeat and though famished, I hesitated. However, hunger won prompting me to take one bite.

It was my first and last. The meat, cold and lean, tasted nothing like beef. The idea of eating the flesh from the same animal as the gentle old mare, "Dixie", that I remembered walking behind as a young boy while plowing on my Uncle Alfred's small ranch near Redding, California, revolted me. Unable to chew or swallow any of it I rolled the window down and spit it vigorously onto the ground.

Frustrated, tired and still hungry I rolled the window up, pulled a pillow from the back seat of the overloaded car and placed it against the side of our old desk top model, black faced, pull button Zenith radio that occupied the passenger side of the front seat. Stretched out sideways I drifted off immediately to four hours of sleep. Having driven almost ten hours and traveling hundreds of miles, without knowing it, I became "inertiaized." As a result, a few moments before I fully woke, I thought I'd fallen asleep at the wheel because it felt to me like the car was still moving along at highway speed. The noise of traffic passing by on the road nearby reinforced the feeling. Suddenly, in panic, I lurched upright slamming my foot on the brake pedal as both hands clutched and tugged at the steering wheel. With eyes now fully open I looked out the windshield. I quickly realized, to my embarrassment, that I had stopped earlier far off the road and remained safely parked.

In daylight the little town of Pullman dominated by large, unique and mostly red brick buildings on the Washington State College campus, lay about two miles in the distance at the bottom of a grade. Driving downhill toward the campus no green vegetation greeted me. Everything looked dry and dead compared with the still colorfully blooming roses, lush green lawns, other flowers, shrubs and tall evergreens all with their unique scent that surrounded our nice home in Seattle. The scene here depressed me. I missed Glennie. Hunger gnawed at my stomach. In town I stopped at the Safeway store and bought a pound of bacon, a loaf of bread and a dozen eggs before continuing on to find the assigned housing unit on campus. Successful in my search I reluctantly unlocked the door and stepped inside. A dim, morgue like interior, greeted me. The blinds were pulled down and most of the pre-requested furniture, provided by the school, lay on the floor in the middle of a tiny living room. To make matters worse the walls were painted an ugly battleship gray using cheap war surplus paint. Unassembled bed frames, box springs and mattresses leaned against one wall.

Having eaten nothing and with only the pillow, that night I slept in my clothes on the bare mattress without blankets. Early the following morning, after finally finding the two-burner hot plate among all the things in the car, I made breakfast of half a pound of bacon, four eggs and bread washed down with water. From a pay phone I called Glennie to tell her how horrible this place seemed. "I don't think it's worth it for you to have to endure four years in this setting. It's even worse than terrible!! You know, I can keep working as a gear-cutting machinist and retire at age sixty-five. I make excellent union wages now as a Specialist and I'll be a Journeyman soon with an even bigger paycheck. We own a nice home and for you and the baby to come here to live in such primitive conditions is unthinkable when we have such a good alternative. I haven't pulled the blinds in the apartment up and it's so gloomy. Besides, what if I flunk out in the last year or two? I don't know if I can complete a medical education," my self-doubt left over from after WWII began to re-surface.

I'm sure Glennie could hear it in my voice and knew how sorry I felt for myself being alone. I wanted so badly to take the easy way out of this new endeavor and made a final try to persuade her to agree. "The car isn't unpacked. I could turn around and drive home as soon as I hang up."

She listened patiently to the complaints, and my desperate attempts to have her accept the idea. Then she answered.

"No, you've always wanted to have doctor replace the word mister in front of your name. You successfully completed college, earned good grades and have your degree in chemistry. This is a major achievement because getting a degree in chemistry isn't easy. It shows me you will do well in veterinary medical school. After all, Harvard, Stanford and Creighton, when they accepted you, all bet you would be successful. The only thing that kept you from attending one of them is money. So why don't you go back to the apartment, pull up the blinds, set up the beds, arrange the furniture and unpack the car. For lunch go to a restaurant and eat a well balanced meal. Eating a lot of bacon, four eggs and half a loaf of dry bread all at one time is not what you should do. After lunch find the Readers Digest you took along then sit down the rest of the afternoon and read some stories. Later, go out and eat supper, come back to the apartment and go to bed early. When you get up tomorrow you'll feel like registering for class. I want you to promise you'll do this."

Back at the apartment I pulled up the blinds letting the daylight in which raised my spirits a little. Looking out the small window I saw a large common area surrounded by many apartments. They were old United States Army WWII surplus four and six unit buildings still painted their original and most unappealing color, military olive drab. The grass in the common area was dry and brown. It looked like an ocean of dead straw.

Hesitation about staying here washed over me and the inability for me to make decisions for my own good reawakened. What path shall I follow? Will it be worth the effort? Can I pass the courses? Maybe I'll be a failure and be pitied, even laughed at by my relatives. I imagined hearing them whisper, "Too bad about Gene. He couldn't make it in veterinary medical school you know, he flunked out. I feel so sorry for Glennie and the baby."

I also knew Aunt Josie would say with smug satisfaction, "I could have told you Gene didn't have what it takes to complete a medical education."

With no enthusiasm I arranged the furniture, unpacked the car and in the evening went to town for supper, bought more groceries then went to bed early. In the morning, refreshed, I showered and after a good breakfast using the newly bought food, my outlook markedly improved. Glennie's voice kept echoing, "Go and register as scheduled on Tuesday. I know you'll successfully complete the four years."

❖ FIRST BORN ❖

Glennie wanted me with her in the delivery room for the birth of our first child. So after class, October 8, 1951 I drove from Pullman back to Seattle. Our obstetrician Dr. Rutherford, a Harvard medical school graduate, encouraged husbands to share the birthing process. In 1951 for a hospital to let a husband remain with his wife during this important event was rare but under Dr. Rutherford's guidance, the Virginia Mason Hospital became the only one in Seattle, at that time, to allow it.

As soon as he diagnosed pregnancy, every Wednesday evening he schooled husbands and more than strongly suggested that we attend the movies he made showing actual births. Viewed in his office, in both color and sound, they were extremely vivid. Blood poured as the camera showed the doctor in close up make an episiotomy, also called "the five o'clock incision". Using a razor sharp scalpel this cut enlarges the outer opening of the birth canal to ease delivery of the baby. The moans and cries of pain from the Mother could be clearly heard. Dr. Rutherford said he believed he must show the graphic films and insist that husbands attend them, to be sure that in the delivery room the husband wouldn't faint as he watched his own child be born.

While changing reels, chocolate chip cookies and milk were served. One evening as a film continued, an especially large amount of blood and amniotic fluid gushed like a river from the episiotomy as the razor sharp scalpel sank deeply into sensitive flesh. A young man in the front row, close to the projection screen, couldn't stand it. He jumped up, ran out the door and vomited. As he continued to retch outside Dr. Rutherford, with his wonderful sense of humor observed, "I guess he's one who won't be in the delivery room. He just lost his cookies."

On October 10, 1951, at 3:27 in the afternoon, our first child, Berniece Lynn arrived. Glennie made arrangements in advance to have induced labor so I could be with her. This is usually done only when a mother is within a week or less of normal term. An injection of Pitocin is given causing uterine contractions to start and the baby soon is born the normal way. Glennie was given a caudal block to reduce the pain of labor, permitting her to remain awake. Sitting at her side in the delivery room I stroked her forehead and whispered encouragement. The attending nurse and her assistant told Glennie again and again, "Breathe deeply, squeeze and push down as hard as you can." It seemed like a long time but when the doctor's work was finished we first heard a small sputter then a howling cry suddenly burst forth from this tiny person. One thing, greatly in evidence, this child had a very good set of lungs.

Dr. Rutherford knew I was attending veterinary medical school and took me aside to show how he thoroughly examines the amniotic sac and placenta, the afterbirth, after delivery to be sure none is left in the uterus that could cause infection and sterility. The human "discoid" placenta looks like a pancake. During pregnancy it furnishes to the baby, by way of the umbilical cord, everything needed. At the veterinary medical school I recently watched a mare give birth and said to the doctor, "That looks a lot like the shape of the placenta I saw last week from a mare after she gave birth to her colt."

Again his sense of humor came through, "Yes, it's similar but smaller. But you better not ever let your wife hear you call her the old nag." I left Glennie and our new baby in the hospital and the next day, proud and happy, returned to Pullman.

Arriving home in Seattle for a three week Christmas break I found both Mother and baby doing fairly well. For the return trip to Pullman early in January, we bought a small car bed I put in the back seat in which the baby would ride. We also bought a stainless steel "hot cup" that attached to the steering column. A wire plugged into the cigarette lighter heated it. With some water in the bottom, as we drove along, it efficiently warmed the bottle of baby formula.

Glennie didn't want to use artificial formula but circumstances made it necessary. For the first two weeks she breast-fed. Being "well endowed", (Zoftick, a la Dolly Parton), she was happy knowing she'd have plenty of nourishment for our Daughter. But Glennie had very fair and sensitive skin and when she left the hospital her doctor provided some salve meant to strengthen the "milk faucet" areas. But it worked too well, eventually causing hardening, cracking and bleeding. Infection set in and her temperature rose to 104 degrees. As a result Glennie had to have antibiotic shots. She also had to take pills to stop the production of milk.

On this trip, now in the dead of winter, when it came time to heat the bottle we realized neither of us remembered to bring along any water to put in the cup and in the sparsely populated area of eastern Washington we were miles from a town or service station. Our hungry baby, with lungs like leather, cried louder and louder with every passing mile. At the top of Saddle Mountain grade I saw an ice covered puddle beside the road and pulled over. Breaking the ice I scooped some of the cold muddy water into the cup and in the car it soon heated the formula bottle just as well as clean water. As soon as her stomach was full, Bee, as we nicknamed her, went back to sleep.

In Pullman we didn't have an electric clothes dryer. Because the baby used cloth diapers Glennie had to wash every day. Placed on the clothesline outdoors, the laundry would only partially dry in the severe winter temperature that fell as low as thirty degrees below zero. Outside, in less than half an hour it froze solid. But with the ice on the outer surface of the fabric most of it could easily be removed by swatting the clothes and diapers a few times with a two-foot length of flat board. With every stroke ice crystals fell in glistening clouds to the ground instantly ridding it of most of the remaining water. To complete the drying process Glennie brought the wash inside and put it in the living room. Using a wooden fold away clothes drying rack she stood it, as close as safety permitted, near the small oil fired space heater. High up in each of two corners of the room I built shelves. On each I put a small electric fan to blow the heat downward from the ceiling, across the area of the clothes rack. On the floor, beneath the still semi frozen diapers and clothes on the wooden rack and at least a foot from any cloth, Glennie put an electric, fan-forced heater turning it on to its maximum power. This jury-rigged drying process became, in winter, a very time consuming daily chore.

The heat in the apartment came from a primitive oil fired "stove". Made from a three and a half foot length of six-inch diameter thick walled iron pipe standing upright this had heavy mesh screen set four inches away from and encircling it to provide protection against us touching the very hot pipe and being burned. A bottom cover had been welded on and an oil line attached to a regulator, led inside. Even with the regulator set on high flow with maximum flame burning and both small oscillating fans on the shelves in the corners close to the ceiling running at full speed, the apartment remained so cold in winter that every older type single glazed window became covered inside with an inch thick sheet of ice. The cause was excess moisture from cooking, showering and the daily drying of clothes and diapers inside the apartment.

The outer walls of the apartment and the ceiling had no insulation and inside the temperature dropped so low Glennie had to bundle Bee in a snowsuit that remained on day and night during the coldest part of winter. Of course, during this severe weather, we too wore extra clothes.

The school furnished an old-fashioned icebox in which to keep perishable food. Inexpensive blocks of ice, delivered twice a week, gradually melted and the water ran into a large drip pan underneath. It had to be emptied every evening or would overflow. Several times I forgot and on mornings after I should have emptied it our kitchen floor became water soaked. However, most of the water ran down one wall into the apartment below. But fortunately Alva Roberts, another veterinary student lived there. No harm came to his personal property so he laughed it off, "No problem Gene," he said. "We've all forgot to empty the pan since we're not used to these primitive old ice boxes and having to get rid of the water every day. By the way, you two sure have a good baby. We seldom hear her cry during the day and never at night."

Berniece, our new baby, had no problem with colic or sleep.

She'd remain perfectly content in the five-foot square, padded playpen all day. She'd coo and make other sounds of contentment as Glennie washed clothes, cooked, wrote a letter or rested. Fortunately our baby slept soundly all night, allowing her mother and I to do the same. After another classmate living across the hall from us complained that his child, when she was the same age as Bee, had kept him and his wife awake almost every night crying, he said, "Yours is a really good baby and you are very lucky. But much of that luck is because your wife keeps the baby well fed and her diaper dry and clean so she never has a moment of discomfort."

In what appeared to be an afterthought he remarked, "You sure have a good wife too, not everyone does you know." As he spoke I noticed some remorse and sadness in his voice. A short time after graduation he and his wife were divorced.

❖ A CLOSE CALL ❖

The freshman and sophomore years in veterinary medical school are spent absorbing vast amounts of basic knowledge, gross anatomy being the most difficult. Many species have major differences and remembering them all is not easy considering the vast number of creatures living on land, under the sea and in the air having medical and surgical problems veterinarians must be able to recognize, to be able to diagnose quickly and how to resolve. For example, all cattle have three extra bones, located in the heart. Pigs have one extra, the *os rostri* in the end of the snout. Canines have two in back of each knee, the *fabella*, and one located inside the length of the penis. One member of our class, as we were dissecting the dog and memorizing the anatomy, as soon as he found that bone, made the pithy observation, "a dog's life may not be so bad after all."

Horses do not have a gall bladder. To remember this we learned this expression, "If you hold a horse up by the gall bladder, its eyes will fall out." This "no-brainer" was very helpful in the learning process and all of us in the anatomy class needed all the help we could get. Studying skeletal structure we also used many word associations, called "mental crutches", making some difficult anatomical sequences easy to recall. For example, to quickly bring to memory the names of the eight bones in the wrist in their correct sequence, in two rows of four each in many domestic animals as well as all primates including man, one only needs to think of the first letter of each word in this slightly risque' sentence. "**N**ever **L**ower **T**illie's **P**ants, **M**other **M**ight **C**ome **H**ome." The first letter of each word in this sentence represents the sequence and names of the bones. They are: *Navicular, Lunate, Triangular, Pisaform, Greater Multangular, Lesser Multangular, Captate* and *Hamate.*

This sentence is also good advice to young veterinary medical students, most of whom have gallons of blood laced with raging hormones, racing through their veins.

It is my hope that the reader will understand how "easy" it is to obtain a veterinary medical education. It may seem all one has to learn and remember of the vast amount of knowledge that will be required at any instant in practice, is something about gall bladders in horses and bones in unusual places in cows, pigs and dogs. Then lastly, bringing up the rear, are Tillie's pants. I'll admit, perhaps they could become a significant part of it.

Other courses, Bacteriology, Pharmacology, Hematology, Microscopic Anatomy and Parasitology, held many challenges for everyone during the freshman and sophomore years because most have difficult names in Latin, a subject I flunked in high school. But in veterinary medical school the names, for some unknown reason, became easy to remember. During the first two years the only problem was the plethora of work and the vast number of hours required to read and remember the literally thousands of unusual names, every one in Latin. For example, in Parasitology, *Eutrombiculus Alfreduggesi*, (the red chigger mite of Oklahoma) and *Macrocanthorynchus Hirudinaceous*, (the thorny headed worm of swine), are only two of hundreds that must be recalled instantly to pass a State Board Examination. We also learned the names in English, of all parasites common to each animal, reptile, bird, fish and many exotics in addition to the correct medication and dosage needed to eradicate them. In addition we learned which parasites are transmitted from animals to man, cause disease epidemics and how to prevent or contain them when this happens. The Black Death that killed 66 percent of the people in Europe during one outbreak is a classic example of an epidemic caused by a bacterium (*Pasturella Pestis*) living in parasites (fleas living on wharf rats) that bite people.

It became routine to study from 6:00 o'clock in the morning until midnight and I considered myself lucky to have such a quiet baby who never cried or fussed at night. In my mind Pullman transformed itself into a foreign land with an entirely different language and different customs. So many facts had to be memorized in only four years and retained for instant recall to earn the degree, Doctor of Veterinary Medicine.

I seldom found time to be together with Glennie and baby Bee. During the four years of veterinary medical school Glennie and I went to only two movies, *Shane*, with Alan Ladd and a 3-D event in which we wore special colored glasses to be able to see the frightening effect of firebrands that seemed to be hurled out above us in the audience. We never went out to eat in a restaurant.

As juniors we began the two-year clinics phase doing "hands on" surgeries. Divided into teams of four, each group was assigned a dog. Ours, a large black female Labrador we named "Queenie." We took extremely good care of her because she was ours alone and had to remain alive for the entire year.

To be absolutely sure of all procedures before ever working on Queenie we learned the different ways of suturing by stitching two pieces of cloth together correctly, giving intramuscular shots by putting the needle through the peel of a fresh orange and for intravenous injections we practiced on rubber tubing filled with colored water to be sure we were inside the "vein". In addition we viewed films of every operation we were to do before we did it. We also had Dr. Ott, head professor of small animal medicine and surgery close by, always watching. He made no suggestions, would answer any of our questions but required us to make every decision and do all the work. Lastly, the day before we did any operation we were given a printed outline, the "modus operandi" to study, complete with pictures and diagrams. As our guide we used The Hand Book of Surgery by Markowitz, an M.D., a leading surgeon in the human field. Though his text is a primer of surgery in man, since all surgical principles are exactly the same the book is also used in the veterinary medical field. All steps from the skin incision to the final closure had to be meticulously followed. Having had a full year as freshmen, dissecting an embalmed horse, cow and dog, we were fully aware of Queenie's every anatomical feature.

Our team consisted of Loren Brown, Bill Armfield, Bill Blackmore and me. On subsequent days we'd rotate the tasks to be performed. On Monday, for example the schedule could be, Blackmore, surgeon, Brown, anesthetist, Curnow, instruments scrub and surgery assistant and Armfield, read and explain to us as we worked, the 'modus operandi', the method of doing the operation, from our guide book. On Monday we might do a total ovario hysterectomy, (spay). The next day it could be a spleenectomy, (spleen removal). This operation is commonly done on an emergency basis in veterinary practice to save a pet that has been hit by a car and has a ruptured and badly hemorrhaging spleen that can be fatal.

On successive days we'd rotate one spot. By the fourth day everyone on the team had held each position. This allowed all of us to become familiar with every aspect of surgery. The same routine continued for the entire nine months during both our junior and senior year. As a result we had almost two years of actual surgical practice before graduation and made few mistakes during our one-year internship when we became licensed, associated with and working for a practicing veterinarian.

On the first day of our junior year when we were given Queenie, Dr. Ott, head of the department in small animal medicine and surgery, told us, "If your dog dies during any surgical procedure, no matter who is at fault, your entire team flunks and will be required to repeat the junior year putting you twelve months behind for graduation. Some surgery will not be easy and requires skillful hand-eye coordination. For example, intestinal anastomosis, the re-attaching of two ends of a severed intestine in a kitten or a puppy making sure the inside remains open for the passage of bowel contents. However, if each of you read the instructions the night before and pay careful attention to the text, every dog will be alive and well at year's end. To prevent mistakes during surgical procedures you should each closely watch even the smallest detail and continually monitor each others work."

We took this advice seriously because during our first two years of instruction we heard of third and fourth year students whose animal had died. They were flunked by Dr. Ott, and had to repeat the entire year.

In our third year now, everyone on our team felt more than confident. We had the attitude, "Nothing bad will ever happen to THIS team!! After all, we each were experienced having worked for a veterinarian in a dog and cat hospital before coming to veterinary medical school. We felt sorry for the poor souls who had no previous experience. To us surgery class will be a breeze."

A breeze! How wrong could we be?

The surgery scheduled on this day was to simply place a stainless steel intermedullary pin within the shaft of a femur in a broken right hind leg. The X-Ray showed the fracture to be a simple transverse break. During the year we did many difficult surgeries successfully and had confidence in our skill. As we worked we horsed around, gossiped, laughed and told jokes. Our smug attitude: "Any idiot having our knowledge and experience can do a simple bone pinning procedure", and for the most part this was true.

Today however, Dr. Ott caught us off guard. We would be introduced to and use an unfamiliar medication with which to relax muscle. We each read the instructions the night before about its use and how it reacts physiologically. It's name, Curare!! The inhabitants of the Amazon jungle place this extract, in crude form, on the tips of their blowgun darts used to kill animals for food. This medication, when used in surgery, causes skeletal muscle to become extremely relaxed making it much easier to align the two ends of a fractured bone. However, it can also relax the muscle of the diaphragm that regulates spontaneous breathing. For this reason it must be administered with utmost caution to prevent respiratory arrest.

As the anesthetist this day I gave the usual intravenous Sodium Pentathol according to the calculated dose and soon our patient slept peacefully. Blackmore, the text reader, cautioned us for a moment about the Curare. I failed to listen carefully and injected it, assuming incorrectly it would act as other muscle relaxants we used in the past. While continuing to work and joke Armfield interjected, "Hey Gene is she breathing?" Quickly I compressed her chest to determine if a rise and fall could be felt. No movement!! I knew instantly we had on the table a dead or potentially dying dog. The three others on the team knew it too and that it was my fault.

I reached into my surgical gown for the antidote. In nervous haste the ampoule of Physostigmine slipped from my fingers several times and dropped back into my pocket. An eternity seemed to pass before I got it out — then promptly dropped it onto the wooden floor. Luckily, it didn't break. Finally I got it drawn into a syringe and injected. The rest of the team began checking the pupils for reaction to light, doing chest compressions to bring air in and out of the lungs and monitoring the heart. These proved inadequate. Brown said, "Gene, you've got to give 'mouth to mouth' or we're going to loose her." The thought of me causing the others and myself to have to repeat the junior year was uppermost in my mind and I didn't care what I had to do to keep Queenie alive.

Clasping her jaws together I put the big black wet nose in my mouth and blew. Her chest rose and fell easily, indicating an unobstructed airway.

"We have a strong heart beat," Brown called out. "Keep breathing for her."

I continued to huff and puff air into the cold black nose. "In goes the good air out goes the bad" the rhythm ran through my mind. I hoped it would be the correct 18 to 24 times a minute. Five minutes passed but it seemed a lot longer. Suddenly Queenie heaved a sigh and with an explosive sneeze, blew gobs of slimy mucous from her nasal chambers into my mouth. I gagged and spit in distress as three classmates, with great relief, laughed long and loud.

During the crisis Dr. Ott moved toward our surgery table but remained silent offering no advice. When Queenie finally started to breathe normally he made his assessment.

"Well fellas, you've learned that because of a small oversight, even a routine procedure can go seriously wrong. Because one of you had the antidote against Curare in your pocket and didn't have to run over to the Pharmacy to get it, shows that as a team you did your research, anticipated a possible emergency and were ready for it when it happened. Your dog certainly would have died if one of you would have had to go after the Physostigmine and you know what that would mean. All told though, you handled the problem well. But be assured, this is only the first of many close calls you'll experience during your practice years." Feeling great relief, but still shaken we felt Dr. Ott had given us a compliment, and our morale soared.

After a lot more spitting while wiping the rest of the dog's nasal contents from my chin, I asked Blackmore for a stick of gum to counteract the taste and odor.

"I really shouldn't give you any, but under the circumstances——." His voice trailed off as he grinned and handed me a much appreciated stick of Wrigley's Double Mint.

When final grades came out, our surgery team and two others were awarded A's for the entire year. This was a proud moment of accomplishment and I could hardly wait to get home that evening after class to share it with Glennie.

❖ THE CITY KID IN THE SENIOR YEAR ❖

As seniors, we were exposed in the clinical setting at veterinary school as well as in the "out call" service away from school, to the practice of Large Animal Medicine and Surgery.

Ranchers for miles around took advantage of the low cost treatment at the school and brought in every kind of sick farm animal. In addition, owners of racehorses brought them to us from the track in Spokane. Most were Thoroughbreds. With their high-strung nature these animals were very difficult to work with. Many owners, skittish like their horses, wouldn't let us "cast", that is lay their animal on the ground and restrain it with ropes so that comprehensive examination or work could be done with relative safety for both students and patient.

Everything had to be done for them in the standing position. X-rays, samples of blood from the jugular vein, minor surgery and suturing under local anesthetic and shoeing all were done with the horse standing. Even castrating a stallion had to be done with the animal upright. Though we'd tightly "sideline" them with ropes in a box stall, against a strong fence or place them in a stanchion made from sturdy iron pipe for restraint, almost always at least two "chain twitches" were needed to keep them from trying to break away.

A twitch has a handle cut from inch and a half round hickory stock three feet long and fitted with a loop about twelve inches in diameter made from smoothly polished stainless steel chain, firmly fixed to one end of the strong wooden shaft. The chain loop is placed to encircle the soft tissue at the end of the horse's nose then the handle is slowly twisted causing the twitch to tighten firmly. It results in a little discomfort but makes the horse stand still yet causes no injury and is an absolute must for safety. To restrain mean, frightened or fractious and uncooperative horses, additional twitches sometimes had be placed at the base of one or both ears to stop the animal from fighting those of us trying to administer helpful treatment. As students, we were never happy to see a Thoroughbred arrive at the large animal clinic for evaluation or treatment.

Since the day I was knocked off of Fats Johnson's old "crow-hopping" plow plug, being hit by a low branch that stuck out sideways from an oak tree while riding her in the Olinda schoolyard one noon hour, I've been afraid of horses. Even though I love the look and admire these beautiful creatures, many years later in veterinary medical school, the fear resurfaced. Dr. Kuhen, the Large Animal professor, knew of my phobia, that I came from a big city, Seattle, and that upon graduation I planned to go into "companion animal practice", dogs and cats only. But he went out of his way in a genuine attempt to resolve my fear. He honestly thought he was doing me a favor by selecting me to work on some of the nearly uncontrollable racehorses as well as the huge work animals we called "plugs". This was a favor I certainly never wanted or thought I needed.

Early in the senior year one afternoon we were in the corral with a huge Percheron workhorse to be cast, that is placed on his side on the ground, as a demonstration of how to prepare a fully grown stallion to be "gelded" (castrated). Dr. Kuhen, using a single 50-foot length of rope, demonstrated how to make a "casting harness" that could easily be used anywhere to gently bring any horse to the ground.

Shaping the rope properly is a difficult and involved procedure. To prevent the horse from choking, the rope must be formed exactly right to prevent it from slipping and tightening after being placed around the neck. Both free ends are trailed off toward the back end of the horse then curved, first to the inside then around behind the pasterns, the area just above the hind hoofs and out to each side. When correctly set the two free ends, now placed just above and behind the rear hoofs, are slowly pulled forward by people helping. When done correctly, this causes the horse to gently sink to the ground on its haunches where it is easily pushed or simply rolls over to one side. A figure of eight tie is made with one end of the trailing rope and wrapped around the leg that is not under the body. The leg beneath the body is held firmly in place by the weight of the horse. It is now totally restrained.

This sounds like a fairly easy task but is extremely difficult for a novice. Once more trying to allay my fear and maybe demonstrate that it couldn't be done by anyone that had no experience with a rope, Dr. Kuhen picked the city kid to be first to make the attempt.

"O.K. Gene," he said, "get a couple classmates to hold the trailing ends of the rope. Go ahead and make the harness as I've demonstrated, get the ends set around the pasterns, up behind the back hoofs and bring him down." As he spoke, Dr. Kuhen undid the demonstration harness he just made, laying the rope out in its original fifty-foot length. For help I picked Ken Creer and Jim Dowe, the strongest students in the class.

I'd never seen or heard of a casting harness made from rope before that day. Up to this point the big horse did not fully cooperate, prancing in place and tossing his head. I expected a low grade plus a lot of embarrassment because several "cowboy types" in the class, who lived all their life on ranches, nodded knowingly at each other indicating they knew exactly how to do this. Well, I sure didn't.

Reluctantly I picked up one end of the rope and doubled it end for end on itself. In spite of great uncertainty, as best I could remember, I twisted and formed the double loop in the center. Only seeing it done once, I worried. Is it a right or left hand turn now? Which end do I pull tight first? Is that double loop in the center big enough for the horses head and neck? Will it slip and choke off his air? In my mind I fielded a more important question. How will this monster strike and kill me, with his front hoofs or his rear ones? Faking it while trying to look relaxed and like I knew what I was doing, I slowly and methodically shaped the rope into a harness.

When finished I picked up the double center loop and shaking with fear, walked over to the huge plow horse. Speaking softly to him I placed the loop over his head. After patting him reassuringly I slipped it down the neck to his shoulders. Surprisingly, he never moved now except to flip a fly or two from one ear and roll a big brown and white eyeball suspiciously toward me. I thought, "Boy, what luck, he's quieted down. Now what comes next? Oh yes, just put the two loose ends on the inside aspect first, then around the top and behind the rear hoofs and have Ken and Jim pull the rope toward the front of the big horse."

As they slowly but steadily drew the rope toward themselves, to my amazement and I'm sure to that of Dr. Kuhen and the rest of the class, the huge and previously uncooperative beast, slowly and without a fight, sank to the ground and toppled onto his side. I hurried over, took one end of the rope from Ken and quickly wrapped a figure of eight tie over the exposed free leg locking it firmly in place. The big work stallion now rested in exactly the correct position for castration.

I had lucked out, doing it perfectly. I felt so elated as soon as I had the figure of eight tie firmly in place that I threw my hands up and jumped back yelling like a cowboy at a Rodeo who just completed a six second calf roping, "How's that for time judge?"

Always a gentleman, Dr. Kuhen gave a nice compliment and a lot of encouragement when he said, "Now guys, that's the way it should be done—who's next?"

I am absolutely positive never again in my lifetime could I fashion a casting harness from a single 50-foot length of rope and bring a huge stallion to the ground. My one successful attempt, with the help of Ken and Jim, can only be attributed to "sheer dumb luck."

In 1955 during our senior year we did an experiment that brought worldwide attention to the Large Animal Clinic at Washington State College. Up to this time little had been established about the physiology, at the cellular level, of the digestive process in cattle. Dr. Kuhen suggested we might be able to place a "window to the stomach" in one side of a cow and through it, see digestion take place as well as safely and painlessly remove samples for analysis.

Just in front of the prominence of the hipbone on the left side, Dr. Kuhen made an opening eight inches in diameter that penetrated all the way through the abdominal wall and into the rumen. With the hole permanently sewn open a three eights inch thick plate of clear Lucite plastic was made to fit in it and sutured snugly in place. Through this "window", the action of the rumen could easily be seen. A three-inch opening with a cork in it gave access to the contents within. Dipped out with a long handled ladle, digesting material could be easily removed for study in the laboratory.

Contrary to the popular misconception, cattle do not have four stomachs. They have only one, divided into four separate chambers, each having a specific function. In addition, they get no nourishment at all from anything they eat, such as alfalfa, oats, clover etc. They do in fact take in and swallow this material that consists mostly of cellulose. It feeds the billions and billions of bacteria harbored within the first and largest chamber of the stomach, called "the *rumen*". Here the contents are temporarily stored and partially broken down by masses of "good bugs", but is still too rough and coarse to continue on to the next chamber. When the rumen becomes filled with roughage, the cow, usually lying down, begins to peacefully "chew her cud", (ruminate). As the cow rests quietly she can voluntarily "bring up" (eructate), a mouthful of the now semi rough contents (a cud) from her rumen. This she chews over and over until it becomes a fine mush. Heavier now, and slippery with saliva, when swallowed it drops down her throat into the "*reticulum*", the second chamber of her stomach. Here, masses of sand paper rough, leaf like tissue rub together transforming the cud into an even thinner paste. Next, it passes into the "*omasum*", the third chamber, where excess moisture is removed and replaced into the blood stream. In the fourth chamber, the "*abomasum*", the now fermenting material, having consistency of soup, is devoured by billions more bacteria and protozoa, that use it for their own livelihood. This is a perfect example of "symbiosis", dissimilar life forms living together, totally supporting each other.

It was found from Dr. Kuhen's work with the cow having the

observation window in her stomach that up to this point, in the abomasom, during the digestive process the alfalfa, oats and clover do not contribute one calorie to the physiology or well being of the cow. It is the vast amount of "good bugs" living in harmony within the cow's digestive system that process the cellulose of the plant material now resting in the abomasum that do this. It is only what we consider to be highly undesirable waste, the huge volumes of excreta from the bacteria, protozoa and mold that is absorbed from the small intestine into the bloodstream of the cow that becomes the thick cream, rich milk and the steaks we enjoy so much.

The cow with the window in her stomach provided a major new insight into the largely unknown physiology of how meat and milk is made by cattle from the cellulose they eat. Professors from almost every school of veterinary medicine in the United States and Canada came to Pullman to see the famous cow with the window in her stomach. Dr. Kuhen's work greatly advanced the knowledge of the digestive process so important to the economy in the raising of all types of cattle.

In the Advanced Bacteriology class, we worked with extremely hazardous and potentially deadly, living organisms. One of them, Brucella abortis, is the cause in cattle of "Bangs disease", also called contagious abortion. This bacterium is transmissible to humans causing a disease called "undulant fever". It can be fatal.

In the laboratory where we worked with this germ stood a five-gallon crock of disinfecting agent, a derivative of Phenol. Working with the organism we were instructed not to touch our gloved hands to our eyes, nose or mouth because this "bad bug" can be transmitted by all of these routes. If eyes, nose or mouth itch, we were told to remove our rubber gloves and never to scratch without first soaking our hands in the Phenolic solution for three minutes. However, one of the two girls in our class forgot the instructions and without removing her rubber glove, rubbed her eye with contaminated material. Halfway through the senior year, she contracted a severe case of undulant fever. She had to drop out of the class of 1955, was hospitalized in Spokane and nearly died. But she survived, returned to school a year later, again as a senior and married a member of her new class. After graduation they established a very successful companion animal practice in south Seattle on Military Road.

Another incident associated with Brucellis abortis happened during the last month of the senior year. A dairy farmer brought a milk cow to the Large Animal Clinic. Five months pregnant she recently aborted her calf. Thin, almost to emaciation and with great gobs of greenish yellow, pus filled mucus, hanging in rope like masses from her nose, in the laboratory her blood sample tested positive for Bangs disease.

As usual, my "Great Benefactor", Dr. Kuhen assigned Julio Gabbato, Loren Brown and me to give the old cow her daily treatment. By passing a stomach tube down her esophagus every day and pouring the medication into it through a funnel, we were able to give her help. Of course Gene the city kid had the dubious honor to pass the long stomach tube, generously coated with mineral oil, through one of her nostrils. As I stepped in front of the thin cow, restrained in a pipe stanchion and began to insert the tube into her nose she gave a loud snort and shook her head violently. This startled me. I opened my mouth ready to blurt out, "Aw, shit", because this had pulled the tube out of her nose. The words never came. Instead, just as I got ready to cuss, one of the big slimy ropes of greenish yellow, pus filled mucus flung itself straight into my mouth filling it almost completely. The speed and pressure of the warm mucus, as it hit the back of my throat, caused the normal involuntary swallowing reflex and I gulped down most of the smelly, slimy mass. With my mouth now empty I got the words, **AW SHIT**!!, out several times loudly and in no uncertain terms while gagging and trying, without success, to vomit up my germ laden stomach contents.

Shocked I asked rhetorically "Will I get undulant fever?" Brown and Gabbato told me to get right over to Dr. Kuhen's office and I didn't hesitate. He seemed only a little concerned, "There's nothing we can give you to kill the bacterium, but the digestive juice in your stomach is so highly acid it will tend to do this. You can only wait and see. Not everyone who is exposed gets undulant fever." He concluded, "Though it may be possible, in my 40 years as a veterinarian I've never known anyone who caught it from swallowing the mucus from a Banger cow."

Though somewhat encouraged by his council I lived during the weeks of the incubation period with a lot of apprehension. I didn't contract the disease but did get one benefit. Dr. Kuhen, my benefactor who I certainly could have done without for the entire junior and senior years, never again called on me, the city kid, to do any more work as part of a team in large animal clinics.

❖ A LITTLE HORSING AROUND ❖

About two miles from the main campus, the college of veterinary medicine at the newly designated and named Washington State University, had a horse breeding and evaluation facility. One of the services performed could determine whether an old stallion still had the potential to reproduce. Many horses, usually Thoroughbreds no longer able to race, possibly from injury or age but big money winners in their prime, were brought here to have their sperm tested. This also had to be done for those being sold that were not "proven sires", that is during their life, never had the opportunity to successfully produce offspring.

Getting a sperm sample from a high strung, fractious stallion is not easy. In the barn a mare in season, ready to accept the male for breeding, or one with a cystic ovary, causing her to be in season every day of the year, is led to and secured in a sturdy steel pipe stanchion. The stallion to be tested is brought in and positioned behind her. The scent of her pheromones arouse him and it quickly becomes evident he is eager and ready to perform.

The entire amount of his sperm specimen must be caught and analyzed under a microscope. Checked are shape (morphology), speed of motion (motility), number of dead, (viability) and the total volume. Every 30 minutes a motility test is repeated until no living sperm remain (longevity).

The Trojan Co., a well-recognized maker of condoms for the human market, also makes a much larger version for horses. Three feet long and about two and a half inches in diameter they are the same general shape as those produced for man with the exception of a much larger reservoir tip.

With the stallion in full erection he will rise to the mare, but before he can penetrate, the huge condom must quickly be rolled on to his massively engorged organ. At a teaching session one day, to determine who would be the lucky one to perform this task our instructor, Dr. Kuhen, had us draw straws—I "won"??

With the mare standing quietly in the stanchion the Thoroughbred stallion to be tested, in position behind her, reared up on his hind legs, jerked his head back and forth snorting and whinnying, while eyeing everything with suspicion. Because of my long continuing fear of horses, which began in grade school, to me he looked like a raging monster.

Dr. Kuhen explained, "Gene, take the condom out of the box and roll it up until it looks like a large rubber donut and leave only the reservoir tip hanging down. When the stallion rises to the mare just step under him then quickly roll it on all the way back to his testicles."

I thought to myself, "Step under this massive beast and position a tightly rolled up condom over the full length of his two and a half foot long penis while it flails around beneath his belly? Did Dr. Kuhen manipulate the drawing of the straws? How do I keep from being stepped on by the two huge steel shod rear hoofs as this sex crazed beast jumps up and down eagerly attempting to enter his penis into the mare?"

With two helpers, one holding a twitch on the soft, tender nose of the stallion and one with a twitch on an ear acting as restraints, it caused him to be a little less wild. As the Thoroughbred attempted to be successful in the task before him Dr. Kuhen raised his voice and rapidly instructed, "Now Gene, now!! Quick, get under there and roll it on all the way making sure you leave the reservoir tip hang off the end so it can catch the entire sample."

As I crouched beneath, I grasped clumsily at the bright red, blood engorged, slippery sex organ trying to hold the thing in place with one hand and roll the condom on with the other.

For a moment I thought, "At times it's not even easy for a human, wild with passion and raging hormones, having good hand-eye coordination, who can use both his hands and has the very focused cooperation of an eager and willing partner, to quickly and successfully complete this task. To put a condom on this wild and sex crazed animal, using only one hand, is next to impossible."

Making matters worse several pretty young co-eds, attending other agricultural classes in this facility, put their hands to their mouths and snickered as they watched, obviously with keen interest, as I continued to fumble with the fully erect organ in an attempt to roll the condom on.

Finally I had it in place. The twitches were released and I sprang backward from beneath the snorting monster as he lunged forward, instantly entering the mare. Surging forward and back within her, his teeth grasped the mane and skin on her neck. Holding on, whinnying excitedly he performed before a fascinated mixed audience. It was over in less than a minute and he dropped to a normal standing position. However, for me, the worst was yet to come. I now had to crawl back under him, this time in a much lower and more restricted area, to perform the even more difficult task of removing the heavily loaded condom without spilling any of its contents.

Squatting under the animal I called to my helpers, "Hold him still. There's not much room to work under here and I feel like a Russian doing a Cossack dance." Making reference to his rapidly shrinking organ I continued, "This darn thing is getting small real fast."

The big condom, now only loosely clinging, sagged as the reservoir tip swung back and forth from the weight of the stallion's large sperm deposit.

With both hands I grasped the open end of the condom close to his testicles and without loosing a drop, quickly slid it off the now drooping organ then backed out fast from beneath a much more contented stallion.

"O.K., now tie a tight knot in the condom so we won't loose any of the sample on the way back to the lab," Dr. Kuhen instructed.

After making the knot, like a referee holding up the hand of a winning fighter, I held up the prize. The dangling reservoir tip bulged with the large sample of thick, slippery white fluid. As they turned to leave more snickers came from the pretty co-eds and for a moment the trace of a smile flitted across Dr. Kuhen's face.

The lab gave the stallion an excellent report. He'd be a fine sire. Our teaching session had been a success.

But Dr. Kuhen, I'm still afraid of horses!!

❖ THE SPIRITUALIST MEETING ❖

PART I

A 1913 graduate of Carleton College in Northfield, Minnesota, Uncle Alfred had many interests. To the family some were controversial. For example, he sought out people who could supposedly bring messages to the living from persons long passed away.

After reading the book *There is a River*, by Edgar Cayce, Alfred became determined to contact relatives on "the other side". He believed if one could communicate with the dead, the Christian concept of everlasting life would, for him, be much more meaningful. Throughout his life, searching for truth, for the most part he remained Agnostic.

After his twentieth birthday in 1915, he frequently visited people dealing in spiritualism who called themselves Mediums. He did not seek "fortune tellers" who he believed were charlatans.

When I left Olinda at age 17 to live in Seattle with my biological dad, Harry, I entered College and soon volunteered to join the Navy. For many years, no matter where I was, in the military or later as a civilian, I always carried on a flourishing correspondence with Alfred who remained on his small farm in California.

During the three-month summer vacations from the veterinary medical school in Pullman, Washington I always went back to work at Western Gear Works in Seattle.

Employed with me at the machine shop, Bill Wamhoff was a member of The Church of Spiritualism. He and I were good friends and I told him how Alfred often sought out people with spiritualistic values. On several occasions Bill told me that his church had members who were Mediums and they could communicate with the dead. He said he and fellow church members had meetings at one of their homes each month and usually conducted a séance. I'd chide Bill asking him if he really believed such nonsense. "Eugene, it's not nonsense. You can come to my house anytime we have a meeting and see for yourself." I regret I never went.

At work one day Bill said, "How would you like to be my guest at the annual National Convention of Spiritualists this year?"

"When will it be held?" I asked.

"Saturday and Sunday, August 17th and 18th in Tacoma. Mr. Williams, recognized as the best Medium in the United States, will be our special guest. When you hear him talk with those on the other side, you'll realize everything I've told you is true." He added, "This is a restricted group so I'll have to give the church your name and address and get their approval for you to attend. You'll be able to speak with your guardian angel if you wish. Everyone has one, you know."

I told him I didn't believe it.

I remembered the many years while growing up on Alfred's little farm that he did seek knowledge in this field and asked Bill if I could bring my Uncle along who was visiting from California. I said, "He's been interested in this for nearly 30 years."

"Sure, give me his name and address and I'll see if I can get approval for you both."

"Do you need our full names along with the address?"

"No, we only want your first name."

On August 17th Alfred and I arrived at the Spiritualist retreat in Tacoma. At the gate we were stopped by a guard who asked for our names and whether we were members or guests. I said, "We're guests of Bill Wamhoff." Finding our names, Eugene and Alfred on his list the man waved us on indicating, "O.K., go right in."

Bill saw us enter. "You're just in time" he greeted. Pointing to a building he said, "Mr. Williams is going to take questions in about 10 minutes. I'll see you inside."

In the large hall we sat on benches placed against the walls on either side. Alone at the center, Mr. Williams sat. He announced, "You may ask any question you wish about any subject. It will be answered from the other side. Through me you can speak with any departed loved one. On a table at the far end of the room behind me you will find three by five inch cards and pencils. I will tell you when to use them. Please write just one question. Sign only your first name then place the card face down on the table. Is there anyone here who has never been to a Spiritualist gathering?" Several of us raised our hands.

Pointing to me Mr. Williams said, "Would you please come forward and tape my eyes shut then tie this light proof blindfold over the tape?"

As both a fourth year senior veterinary medical student and ex-Navy Medical Corpsman, I knew very well how to cause the two inch wide tape on the roll I picked up from the stand beside Mr. Williams, to stay securely in place. The secret to make tape stick exceptionally well is to first warm it under an armpit before applying. While Mr. Williams gave more instructions I did this for several minutes. After securing the warm and sticky tape tightly over his eyes I made sure it covered his bushy eyebrows.

"Check the blindfold before you put it on to be sure it's not possible to see through," he instructed.

Examining it carefully, before I put it over the tape already covering his eyes, I made absolutely sure no possibility existed that Mr. Williams could see through the blindfold. Holding his chair by the arms he stood for a moment facing away from us and from the table far at the back of the room. Then he sat down.

"All right, now is the time. Please go to the table at the back of the room and write your questions."

When everyone finished writing an assistant, who had been standing far enough away so he could not possibly see what we wrote, stepped over to the table and shuffled the cards. At all times the writing remained face down. Selecting one card he carried it forward with the writing face down so the helper could not see it. Mr. Williams heard him walking and extended his hands behind himself to accept the card. At no time did Mr. Williams bring the card in front of himself. Behind his back he ran his fingers over the writing.

"Is Alfred Becker here?" Mr. Williams asked.

Because he had written only his first name on the card Alfred became startled when he heard his last name, Becker and silently raised his hand.

Hearing no answer and unable to see, Mr. Williams repeated the question.

Alfred then answered, "Here."

With the card remaining behind him face down Mr. Williams said, "Alfred, I'm not going to answer your question about your Dad because there is someone on the other side who is extremely eager to communicate with you. Does the name Umm— Huuu— Herr"

At that moment Alfred blurted out, "Herman!!"

"No Alfred, it's not Herman, your Father—it's, Ummm, Herr, ah, yes, it's Herbie."

Herbert Hansen, my Cousin and Alfred's nephew, during WWII became a navigator on a B 24 bomber. He died when his plane crashed, shot down by the Germans during a botched up raid on the oil fields at Ploiesti, Rumania. His body was never listed by the War Department as recovered.

Shocked by hearing the nickname, "Herbie", Alfred jumped to his feet.

"Herbie? Herbie?" he questioned loudly.

"Yes," Mr. Williams replied. "It's Herbie. He wants you to tell the family that he's fine. He says to let them know it's beautiful and very peaceful here. He says he experienced no suffering as he crossed to the other side. By the way Alfred, you know that swallowing problem you've had all your life? Don't worry, it isn't cancer and will never hurt you."

Alfred looked totally surprised. Leaning toward him from behind I whispered, "What swallowing problem?"

For 23 years, since I was 6 years old, I never knew he had this problem though he and I were very close and Mother and I lived with him in Olinda, California for many years. Later that day he told me the problem worried him constantly but that no one in the family knew about it because during his lifetime he never mentioned it to anyone, not even Dr. Kay, his physician. "That sure is strange. I didn't even ask Mr. Williams about the problem. It wasn't written on my card and no one in this world, not even you, knew about it."

My Cousin Herbert was a big, good-natured boy of German and Danish descent. Before moving to California Alfred lived in St. Paul, Minnesota a few years, with Clara, his sister, her husband Pete and their young son Herbert. Little Herbert and Alfred were great pals. But this must be emphasized. Herbert allowed no one, family or friends, to ever call him "Herbie". Only his special Uncle Alfred had this privilege.

Still standing Alfred asked Mr. Williams, "Is my dad Herman there for me to speak with?"

Mr. Williams said, "Yes, he's here. He says hello but cannot speak with you right now." After a few moments of silence Mr. Williams lowered his head saying with finality, "Thank you Alfred, I'm unable to give you more."

The reading completed, Alfred took his place sitting beside me. Questions came to my mind. How could the totally blindfolded Medium know that the card belonged to Alfred BECKER when he couldn't see it behind his back even had he not been blindfolded? In addition, Alfred hadn't written his last name on the card. No one at the meeting but me knew it was Becker and I had never told Bill Wamhoff. How could he know the name Herbie, the very personal name of endearment only Alfred was allowed to use many years ago when addressing young Herbert? Lastly, how did he know to tell Alfred, "No, it's not your dad,

Herman, it's Herbie," only a moment after Alfred loudly blurted out "Herman?" Neither the name Herbie or Herman were on the card. Alfred's card simply read, "I'd like to get in touch with my dad." It was signed "Alfred".

But the greatest mystery of all was, how did Mr. Williams know Alfred had a swallowing problem? No one in the family or even his physician knew, because never in his life had he mentioned it to anyone.

Later Mr. Williams held my card. With hands behind him, after feeling the writing he called, "Gene?"

I answered, "Here."

Nodding he said, "The answer to your question is, you will be successful in whatever you choose to do in life."

Breaking the rules a little to see if I could trick Mr. Williams into making a mistake I signed my card, E.E. Curnow. To his credit, before giving the answer, he never hesitated before calling me by my nickname, Gene. How did he know this name? I gave my name to Bill for the guest roster as Eugene, the only name he ever called me during the many years we worked together.

When the time came to remove the blindfold and tape everyone had a laugh at Mr. Williams' expense. The blindfold came off easily. Removing the tape became a different matter. It stuck so tightly he had to pull hard and a lot of his bushy eyebrows came out by the roots clinging to the very sticky surface. When that happened Mr. Williams grumbled and used a few choice expletives, including one that implied I most assuredly had to be the male offspring of a female dog.

I do hope the good people on the other side forgave his indiscretion.

❖ THE SPIRITUALIST MEETING ❖
PART II

In late afternoon on Sunday, August 18th, Alfred and I returned to the Spiritualists meeting in Tacoma, Washington. That evening Mr. Williams would be channeling during two scheduled séances. A channeler is someone, spiritualists say, whose voice is used by people who have passed away to speak with the living. We were again told that through him we could ask questions of or speak directly to friends or relatives on the other side. Later in the evening, during the second séance we would be given an opportunity to hold a brief conversation with our guardian angel.

During the first séance, in a small room, eight of us sat in a half circle holding hands. In one corner of the room Mr. Williams sat in a chair. Beside him stood a trumpet of silver-like metal about three feet tall. Four feet in front of the chair and about six feet overhead a wire stretched across the corner about three feet below the ceiling. A heavy lightproof black curtain hung from it that could be pulled across on brass rings to hide Mr. Williams during the session.

"Is there anyone here who has never attended a séance?" I raised my hand.

"Please come forward Gene." He again called me by my nickname probably remembering the sticky tape incident that pulled out a lot of his eyebrows the day before.

In his hand he held a large, slightly damp and pliable sponge. "Please stuff this into my mouth. Press it in so tightly you'll know for sure I cannot speak. It's moistened and soft making it easy to get it in every area. Before you start, check the moisture in it by squeezing. When you're done seal my mouth with this duct tape." Continuing he said, "With this pen, containing highly water soluble ink, make four marks on the tape. Continue them onto my skin, two above it to my upper lip and two below to my chin. They will indicate exact match up points. If the tape is moved the delicate ink will be disturbed and partially washed away. The marks can never be perfectly re-aligned by a human hand." Offering a pair of handcuffs he said, "Use these to secure each wrist to a leg at the back of the chair." Then, he told me to place the trumpet out of reach in front of and to one side of him. I then made four marks at random with the pen on its bell and continued them off of the trumpet onto the floor and also made the four marks on the tape over his mouth.

When I completed the tasks an assistant drew the black curtain across the corner area in front of Mr. Williams. Hanging from the overhead wire it touched the floor totally hiding him from view. About three feet of space above the curtain's suspending wire remained open to the ceiling. The bright lights in the room stayed on. No other entry existed to get into the corner except to go past the curtain. To make sure of this, after the séance Alfred and I carefully checked both in and outside the building using a small but bright flashlight he always carried.

With the curtain drawn shut we again joined hands and remained quiet. Moments later the bell end only of the silver trumpet appeared shakily in the open space just above the curtain where it continued to waver throughout the séance'.

The assistant, who remained in the room with us announced, "Mr. Williams is ready to channel from the other side with anyone to whom you wish to speak."

A woman to my left asked to hear from her daughter Emily, who had passed away thirty years ago at age five.

Immediately, an obviously very child-like female voice came from the trumpet overhead.

"Hello Mommy, this is your Schnickelfritz. I'm glad you came here tonight."

The conversation continued using many other names of endearment that only mother and daughter could possibly have known from thirty years in the past.

Obviously shaken by the experience, with her turn completed, the mother burst into tears.

On my right, Alfred asked to speak with his dad, Herman.

A booming bass voice, obviously male having a thick German accent and using the correct syntax and idiom from the part of Germany in which Herman lived growing up, came from the trumpet. "Canst du mir haern? Ist Herman, sine Fater, Alfred."

Smiling joyfully Alfred replied, "Jah, ich herst du Fatter." Alfred grinned broadly obviously happy having immediately recognized the tone of voice and unusual phrasing of the words coming through the trumpet. The voice made reference to the furniture store in Elgin, Minnesota and of the apartment above it where Alfred, his dad, mother and eight brothers and sisters lived when he was a child. Then it spoke of the embalming room in the undertaking parlor downstairs at the back of the store where Herman prepared bodies for burial.

Alfred became convinced that for the first time in his life he had made contact with his dad who had an unusual booming voice and spoke in a distinctive way. Alfred never mentioned to anyone at the Spiritualist Convention, the town of Elgin, Minnesota, the furniture store, living above it or the fact that his dad, Herman, was an undertaker.

When the séance concluded everyone in the room believed they had made contact. The variety of sounds, unusual accents and nuances, foreign languages perfectly spoken, as well as the special words of endearment, in their opinion, could not have been known or voiced by only one living individual, Mr. Williams. During this séance I made no request.

The trumpet, still wavering as though floating in air, slowly dropped from sight behind the curtain that the assistant quickly drew aside. Mr. Williams sat in exactly the same position as before the séance. He appeared slightly dazed. His eyelids, partly closed, fluttered. The assistant handed me the key motioning that I should remove the handcuffs and then the sponge. With his hands free Mr. Williams rubbed them together as though to increase circulation. I leaned down to look at the four random marks I made earlier on the trumpet bell and the floor. All marks still remained and matched perfectly.

Pointing to his mouth Mr. Williams indicated I should remove the tape and sponge. Looking carefully at the marks that extended from the tape to the skin above his upper and below his lower lip I found them all exactly in place. I carefully took the tape off of his mouth then removed the sponge, heavy now, and dripping wet with slippery saliva. Beneath it, the assistant holding a pan instructed, "Now squeeze and see how much fluid comes out." When I compressed the sponge a huge amount of semi-thick, warm saliva poured into the pan. There could be no question about the sponge having remained in his mouth the entire session. Alfred and I could find no falsification at this session.

Later in the evening in a different building along with many members of the Spiritualist Church, Alfred and I attended our final séance. We were told here we each could speak with our guardian angel and she would tell us her name. Mr. Williams explained all guardian angels are created female so are always spoken of in the feminine gender. The previous day we were asked to bring something tonight that we used in our present trade or profession. Sitting in silence one of our feet had to rest on the item at all times. For example, as a gear-cutting machinist during this time while on summer vacation from veterinary medical school, I brought a small crescent wrench. An electrician brought a little roll of wire and a plumber a short piece of pipe. All lights were turned off, making it impossible for Mr. Williams to see the objects beneath our shoes as he was led into the nearly pitch black room.

One at a time we were asked to stand, keeping a foot on the symbol of our work and give only our first name. Mr. Williams would then tell how we made our living. My turn came and I stood saying, "My name is Gene."

Mr. Williams, sounding perplexed said, "Gene, I can't seem to clearly see how you make your living. I hear the clattering of machinery but it keeps fading. Then I see very bright lights over your head. They look like those a doctor uses in surgery. The two working conditions fade in and out yet many times they blend. I'm very sorry I can't do better." (I should point out here that in fact I was currently working in Seattle during my summer vacation in my eighth year with Western Gear Works, now as a journeyman gear-cutting machinist. However, in a few weeks I would return to the veterinary medical school in Pullman, Washington and re-enter as a graduating senior the following June to receive my degree, Doctor of Veterinary Medicine. Though he was never told this, Mr. Williams had been absolutely correct in his assessment of both my current and future way of making a living).

My turn came to speak with my guardian angel. I carefully made my way to one corner of the darkened room where a white sheet hung from ceiling to floor. Behind it, in the background a very dim, slightly bluish light glowed. In silence I stood as close to the front of the sheet as I could while trying to see through it. Then, from behind it a mature female voice said, "Gene, I'm Maid Marian, your guardian angel. If you're ever in danger call my name, and I'll protect you. I can tell you no more."

On the thirty mile drive back to Seattle I asked Alfred what he thought about the events of the last two days. Usually very talkative with me, he seemed deep in thought and in the form of questions gave his answer.

"How could Mr. Williams know about Herbert being killed when his plane was shot down during WWII in a raid over Ploiesti? How did he know only I was allowed to call him Herbie? How did he know about my swallowing problem? I've never even told you or my doctor about it. No one in this world knew about it. How could that voice be identical to the one my Dad used, deep bass, always booming and in his peculiar 'Berliner houchdeutch' idiom? I was always happy as a child when I heard his voice and loved it when he spoke to me. Then too, how could he perfectly join together for you the noise at your work in the machine shop and the lights like a doctor uses in surgery? It's all very convincing."

I said to Alfred I too had been impressed.

There was only one thing that happened during the last two days that puzzled me. When it passed through the sheet why did the breath of Maid Marian, my guardian angel, definitely smell like Wrigley's spearmint gum?

❖ A LESSON IN FUTILITY ❖

"Outcall service", provided by the College of Veterinary Medicine and overseen by a Professor of Large Animal Medicine and Surgery, a licensed veterinarian on the college staff, was available to all farms within about 50 miles of Washington State University. A full size station wagon, equipped with everything needed to treat each problem we were scheduled to see that day, served as our transportation. The senior class, divided into teams of three, took turns every few weeks to get this "hands on" experience working with large animals, remaining on call 24 hours a day for three days in a row.

One of my turns came during the miserably cold weather of calving season late in January of 1955 when the temperature frequently dropped to 20 degrees below zero or colder.

At 2:30 in the morning a loud knock on our apartment door woke me. As I opened it, bitter cold wind rushed past blowing stinging sleet-like snow onto my face rapidly reviving my sleep-dulled senses. The unwelcome visitor was fellow classmate Ken Creer, who with Loren Brown, made up our team for outcall duty.

"Don't tell me we're going on call at this hour in weather like this?" I complained.

"Yes we are," came the answer. "So hurry up. The sooner we get there and finish what we have to do, the sooner we'll all get back home and in bed."

As Dr. Bracken drove he spoke. "As I understand from the phone call, the farmer's young cow has been trying to give birth to her first calf for three days. So far she's managed to get only one front leg to appear. It sounds like a textbook case of dystocia, a condition that prevents a calf from passing through the birth canal. It is most commonly caused when a leg or the head and neck is caught on the pelvic bone inside of the mother. At other times the uterus gets so tired it can't contract strongly enough to push the calf out. When the farmer realized his young cow was unable to expel her calf, he attached one end of a rope to the exposed front leg, got out his fence stretcher, attached the other end of the rope to a solid object and began to ratchet away on the leg attempting to pull the calf out. A fence stretcher exerts hundreds of pounds of pull and a force this strong often causes massive injury to both the unborn calf and the uterus of the cow."

Dr. Bracken finished his assessment as we arrived at the farmhouse. The farmer rushed out bundled in thermal wear topped by a heavy, sheepskin lined coat.

"Cold night, huh boys?" he greeted.

"Wow, it is cold!!" Ken called over the howling wind while pulling on the sanitized boots we were required to wear at each farm to prevent the spread of any disease. Adding the wind chill factor, the 20 degrees below zero weather felt much colder and no one disagreed.

Clouds of snow, blown from the ground by the wind, swirled around us as the farmer led the way to a creaky old shed where the young cow lay. He had spread a little extra straw beside and behind her knowing she couldn't get on her feet and that we would have to lie down in back of her to do our work. By the feeble light from the dirt encrusted 25-watt bulb hanging from a rafter we saw the young cow, prone on the floor, breathing heavily.

Weather like this provided a reason for some good humored fun as the other two students razzed the one they were to assist because the "operator", by necessity, had to strip bare to the waist to work. Unfortunately, tonight, I was the operator. The first thing I did after stripping off coat, shirt and underwear, was put on the full arms length, very cold rubber glove that extended all the way to my shoulder. Held on securely by an extra band of nearly freezing rubber two inches wide, this surrounded my bare chest. Hanging on a rusty nail, I noticed what appeared to be an unused, ragged and dirty old sheepskin coat and thought of how warm it would be if I could wear it now.

All procedures first were discussed and approved or disapproved by Dr. Bracken, the licensed veterinary instructor.

Now came the time to cope with the problem.

As I stood bare-chested, shivering in the intense cold and ready to work Dr. Bracken questioned, "Gene, what are you going to do and how will you make your determination?"

"First I'll get her TPR, temperature, pulse and respiration. Then I'll check her gums and the mucus membranes surrounding her eyeballs to determine color that can indicate yellow jaundice, anemia or possibly lack of oxygen. Next, with my stethoscope I'll check her stomach for motility and sound because the stomach of a cow, if she's not too sick, moves vigorously making a gurgling noise called "tympani". Finally, I'll check her lungs listening for abnormal bubbling or rattling sounds, called "rales", that could indicate the onset of bronchitis or pneumonia." Dr. Bracken nodded agreement and with Ken as my number one assistant all procedures were done.

"Now I'm going to lie down behind her" I said "then pass my gloved hand and arm into the birth canal to see if I can determine exactly what the calf is caught on that prevents it from coming out." Again Dr. Bracken approved.

I knew that many times a stuck calf can be pushed back a short distance into the birth canal, in veterinary medical terms called, "repelling the calf", and after repositioning the two front feet into correct alignment and the head properly placed between the front legs it can easily be removed.

Loren poured some almost ice-cold mineral oil, made thicker by the cold, over my gloved hand and arm. I could tell he was glad it was not him but me who lay behind the young cow bare to the waist and chilled to the bone. As I slipped my hand between the calf and the wall of the birth canal what I had anticipated to be the problem proved correct. The cow had no uterine contractions and her calf, hugely swollen and bloated with gas, was dead. Making matters worse, one foreleg extended upward above its head, securely caught on the inside aspect of the young cow's pelvic bone, making birth in the normal manner impossible. I also found the uterus of the young cow badly swollen both from infection and traumatic injury caused by the farmer pulling on the leg of the calf with the powerful fence stretcher. Because of this I had little room to work and couldn't push the calf back to reposition it. My right arm, while working inside the cow whose temperature read 104 degrees, was much warmer than my bare chest and other arm both totally numb now with cold.

I removed my arm and told Dr. Bracken what I'd found. "Looks like it's going to be the palm knife and the wire saw." He agreed.

The palm knife, a surgical instrument curved in shape, when not in use, is safely encased in its own metal sheath. Fitting easily in the closed hand it can be inserted safely into the area of work. Pushing a slide-button on one side of the metal sheath allows the razor sharp scalpel blade to be extended.

Prone on my side, behind the young cow I struggled to get the knife past the swollen uterus and calf. Successful at last, I made an incision through its belly wall then removed and withdrew the abdominal organs. The stench of gas, released by cutting into the dead and rotting calf, overwhelmed everyone.

Brown made the comment, "Geeze Gene, that smell is enough to drive a maggot off a gut cart."

"How do you think I feel?" I said. "I'm right here with my nose next to the opening where that gas is coming from."

The release of gas and removal of the organs made the bloated calf shrink to a smaller size but it still wouldn't budge. It became obvious the wire saw must be used. Made from fine, very flexible stainless steel wire, hundreds of tiny teeth protrude from it in every direction. Using it, legs, hipbones and spinal vertebrae all can be cut through and removed, further reducing the size of any dead and bloated calf.

With great difficulty, as well as feeling I was freezing everywhere except for the one arm inside the feverish cow, I worked the saw between the rear legs of the calf and over its hipbone. After attaching a handle at each end of the flexible saw and pulling it back and forth, I began to cut. When finished I removed one rear leg. Two hours of struggle elapsed and very little protective straw remained behind the cow to cover her soft, sticky and recently passed bowel contents in which I lay. Most of it had been mashed with my shoulder and chest into the small amount of underlying straw close to and behind her. More of the rotting mass, frozen almost solid lay in abundance throughout the shed as one cold, tired and very stinky veterinary student continued to work. Having been successful in removing both hind legs of the decaying calf, only the head, chest and front legs remained inside.

Painfully cold and near exhaustion I complained, "Dr. Bracken, I just can't saw anymore. My hand and arm have been so tightly pressed between the swollen uterus and the dead calf they're numb and almost useless. Could someone relieve me?"

"Ken, go ahead and take over," Dr. Bracken instructed. As I stood up the farmer came from behind and wrapped the most welcome, filthy and ragged heavy old sheepskin coat over me. "Hey, thanks," I said. "That sure feels good."

Ken handed me the one liter bottle of glucose and saline he had been holding as it drained into the jugular vein of the young cow. In his new role he worked the wire saw into a new area across the center of the backbone of the dead calf and cut through it. With more than half of the calf's body removed the front leg, trapped by the pelvic bone of the cow, dropped down to the normal position and the rest of the rotting mass passed easily out the birth canal. As the last of the intravenous fluid I held drained from the bottle, Loren administered an injection of antibiotic.

The job was finished and three tired veterinary medical students, shivering with intense cold, were proud of their success accomplished under very adverse conditions. However, as Ken and I wiped away a lot of grime and manure, preparing to wash off the rest and get back into our clothes, the young cow gave a muffled groan, her eyes rolled back in her head and she died.

Stunned, in silent disbelief we looked at each other. A moment ago we were pleased to have saved a life, the task for which we were rigorously and extensively trained for almost four years. With the patient dead our moment of triumph quickly became a moment of defeat. Embarrassed and at a loss for words we could offer the farmer no explanation.

However, I'll never forget his words as he attempted to console us.

A slight grin played across the leather like skin of his deeply lined face. "Oh hell boys it's O.K., don't feel bad I was going to shoot her anyway." You can imagine what the three of us were thinking as "that silly bastard" talked with our instructor.

Using the welcome bucket of hot water and soap the farmer provided, Ken and I washed from our chilled bodies, the remainder of grime and manure and put on our clothes. Three hours of miserable, almost intolerable work under the worst possible conditions, turned out to be pointless.

Long after I graduated and became a practicing doctor of veterinary medicine, in my mind there always remained a question about this case. Would our only reward be the experience we gained from one of life's many lessons in futility?

Ken Creer spent his career practicing large animal medicine and surgery in Provo, Utah and became the Mayor for three terms. He rejected requests for him to serve several more.

Loren Brown spent his career practicing large animal medicine and surgery in Everson, Washington specializing in the treatment and management of large commercial dairy herds, including the famous "Carnation Dairy Farm" Holsteins, successfully treating many cases of dystocia.

As for me, I've always wondered why the farmer called us out at 2:30 in the morning, in dangerous winter conditions of howling wind and temperature of 20 degrees below zero, to work on the young cow if he already knew "he was going to shoot her anyway". It simply made no sense. One thing the experience carved in stone is that I promised myself that night I'D NEVER, UNDER ANY CIRCUMSTANCES, consider going into large animal practice. I vowed to practice only small animal medicine and surgery, treating cats and dogs inside a modern facility, warm in the cold of winter and air conditioned in the heat of summer. The promise was never broken.

❖ GRADUATION & ENTERING PRACTICE ❖

On June 5, 1955, graduation day arrived. In the forenoon Dr. Ernest Stone, Dean of the veterinary medical school, called a conference with the graduates to give us his farewell address. I remember well his admonishment, the message clear and so typical of this outstanding humanitarian and teacher.

"Today, if you meet me on campus before the graduation ceremony and we talk, you will address me as Dr. Stone. But after the ceremony if we meet, I insist that you call me Ernie."

Many years later, now a successful practitioner, I attended the National Convention for veterinarians held in Seattle. At a table a short distance away I saw Dr. Stone and went over to say hello. While reminiscing I mentioned how I clearly remembered the farewell speech given on the morning of graduation when he said that after we received our diploma, now as equals, he'd insist that we call him "Ernie". Obviously pleased, we conversed for about 15 minutes recalling things that happened long ago.

As I rose to leave he said, "Gene, thanks for coming to talk awhile. It's always good to see any of the graduates who went through school while I was Dean."

"It's been great visiting with you Dr. Stone—woops!! Ernie." He smiled and nodded an acknowledgement.

I didn't know this brief conversation would be our last. Four months later "Ernie" died of cancer.

Only by chance on graduation day, because of random seating in Bohler Gymnasium, I became the first in the class of 1955 to step onto the stage and receive from Dean Ernest Stone the degree, Doctor of Veterinary Medicine. The building was not air-conditioned and at 2:30 that afternoon the outdoor temperature was 102 degrees, inside even hotter. Dressed in the only suit I owned, made of pure wool, perspiration poured down my back. There was no place in the Gym to hang the suit jacket so it hung heavily on my shoulders adding even more heat under the black graduation gown. But it didn't matter because the class had sweated out four long years anticipating this event.

Before the ceremony, at noon the class met in the bookstore expecting to pick up our mortarboard cap, special light gray gown and a cape to be worn around the neck having the distinctive bright colors of Washing State College as well as the other colors indicating our veterinary medical degree. But there were so many doctorates (PhD degrees) in other fields to be awarded this day that the bookstore earlier ran out of the light gray gowns with the thick velour black stripes on the sleeves and frontal area.

As a result the class of 1955 is the only one, up to that time to graduate with an advanced degree wearing a plain black undergraduate gown while draped around the neck hung the special cape with the school colors in addition to those of our advanced degree Doctor of Veterinary Medicine, (D.V.M.)

After the ceremony I walked through the halls of the veterinary medical school for the last time. Some of my instructors had already returned to their office. As I passed by Dr. Klaveno's, the instructor in Materia Medica and Pharmacology, he called, "Gene, come on in, I'd like a word with you." As I entered he motioned to a chair beside his desk. "Here, sit down, I want to tell you something you might like to know." Relaxed, he leaned comfortably back in his swivel chair and continued.

"When your application came before the admissions committee four years ago, as a member, I voted not to accept you. My reason?, I thought Dr. Ehmer's letter of recommendation asking Dean Stone, as a personal favor to admit you, bordered on financial blackmail. The rest of the committee, including Dean Stone, though somewhat reluctant, voted to admit you because of Dr. Ehmer's fame, influence and great financial support. What I want to tell you is this. I was against you being admitted in 1951, but now four years later, I'm sorry to see you leave." Leaning forward and extending his hand he said, "Welcome to the profession. I know you'll be an asset. Drop by and see me any time you're back in Pullman."

"Thank you, I sure will. I appreciate your honesty."

As I left his office I remembered how more than four years ago I smugly thought, "It's not what you know, but who, that makes the difference." However, after this brief visit with Dr. Klaveno I realized the letter from Dr. Ehmer requesting "A personal favor from the Dean" could just as easily have been a liability and prevented me from being admitted.

All we cared about immediately after graduation was to take and pass State Board Examinations in the States where we thought we might want to practice. In Washington State it was held on June 6th, 7th and 8th at the veterinary medical school. In Oregon, the 10th, 11th and 12th at the Multnomah Hotel in Portland and in California the 21st, 22nd and 23rd at the veterinary medical school in Davis. My reason for taking the tests in all three States was to have the option, if successful, to be able to practice anywhere on the west coast. In addition, taking the tests right after graduation seemed important because the four years of veterinary medical instruction would still be fresh in my mind. As it turned out, that thought proved correct. I passed all of them on the first try.

Starting in mid-January of 1955, the bulletin board in the hall of the veterinary medical school began to fill with letters from practitioners offering employment. Most were from the west coast. I answered one from Dr. Alfred C. Ruggles in Portland, Oregon and arranged a meeting and interview there in April. He hired me contingent on my success of passing the Oregon State Board Examination in June.

Results of the State Board Examinations would not be available for at least three weeks. During this time Glennie and I rented a small house at 3110 N. E 86th St. in Portland and anxiously waited. I asked that the results from all three States be mailed to our home in Seattle where Glennie's Mother now lived. We had no telephone in the rented house in Portland and instructed her Mother to call from Seattle to Dr. Ruggles because he too anxiously waited for the results since he'd already hired me to be his assistant.

On Friday July 15, 1955, at ten o'clock in the morning Dr. Ruggles knocked at our door. Glennie's Mother had phoned from Seattle to tell him the letter arrived saying I passed the Oregon State Board and now held an active, current license. Qualified to practice veterinary medicine and surgery in Oregon, one more hurdle lay ahead. I had to satisfactorily complete a one year internship before I could practice unsupervised.

Dr Puls, who had worked with Dr. Ruggles for several years, left to establish his own practice in Colorado. As a result Dr. Ruggles worked seven days a week for several months at his hospital at 2965 N.E. Sandy Boulevard with no relief. He hoped nothing would happen to keep me from passing the Oregon State Board.

The head of the Board of Veterinary Medical Examiners, Dr. C. F. Milleson, was not friendly with Dr. Ruggles and knew he was desperately looking for a new associate. I was cautioned that Dr. Milleson, who would give me the oral part of the examination, would make sure anyone taking the Oregon State Board would not pass if he found out the candidate would be going to work for Dr. Ruggles. To prevent this from happening I was told emphatically,

"Gene, be sure you don't tell Dr. Milleson or anyone else that you are going into practice with me. If he finds out he'll invent a reason to make sure you fail. He can't do anything about your written answers because they run through a machine and are corrected automatically. But even if you get every one right he can and will fail you on the oral portion."

I took this advice seriously and it became clear during the oral examination that what I had been warned about certainly was true.

At the oral examination Dr. Milleson began, "Dr. Curnow, you've done well on the written part. Now I'd like to talk about your plans and what you expect to contribute to the community in which you live while practicing veterinary medicine."

To myself I thought, "This sounds like it might lead to an opening for him to ask where I'll practice and with whom, just as I've been warned." After several easily answered questions he hit me with "the zingers."

"Do you have employment yet?" he leaned forward and smiled disarmingly.

"Yes sir, I have employment." I volunteered nothing in this cautiously worded answer. By his body language I sensed, as he continued to lean toward me, that he expected me to tell him the location and name of the veterinarian who hired me. He paused several seconds looking at me expectantly. I remained silent.

His next question came, "If you are successful and pass the Oregon State Board, where would you like notification sent?"

"Clearly," I reasoned to myself, "An attempt to see if the address is in Portland."

"Please send it to my home in Seattle, 2805 West Elmore Street Zone 99."

Jotting this down he asked, "You say you have employment Dr. Curnow. Wouldn't you like notification sent directly to your employer?"

At this question, now so very obviously asked to find out who I'd be working with, I put on an act in an attempt to make it seem to him that I had become flustered and frightened by his great authority.

I stammered on purpose, "Ye--ye, yes, I have employment. Ple--ple, please just send it to my home in Seattle. Uh--uh huh, I'll be in Seattle if I'm successful. Yes, I have employment." I repeated lowering my gaze to the floor.

Apparently satisfied I wouldn't be practicing in Portland he asked, "Is that address 2805 West Elmore Street, Seattle, Washington Zone 99?"

Meeting his gaze as though greatly relieved, I quickly and brightly replied "Yes sir."

During the interview it became more than obvious that what Dr. Ruggles warned about was correct because Dr. Milleson didn't ask one question about any plans or what I hoped to contribute to the community in which I lived.

❖ TESTED IN THE GOLDEN STATE ❖
AND ON THE HOME FRONT

In 1955, with many classmates I took the test given by the California State Board to obtain licensure. In that year, a license to practice in California, "The Golden State", was eagerly sought. Hundreds of candidates from throughout the United States and from foreign countries arrived in Davis to take the examination.

The difficult test that began on June 21st lasted three days, from eight o'clock in the morning until four o'clock in the afternoon. At the end of the daily session most of us returned to the motel to relax awhile in and around the swimming pool. Among the motel guests also at the pool was a beautiful, dark haired young lady. It quickly became obvious that she didn't know how to swim. Her presence in the shallow part while attempting to learn did not go unnoticed by several of my unmarried classmates and the "gaggle" of young, well-proportioned veterinarians certainly did not go unnoticed by her. Wiping the water from her eyes with the left hand, to make it obvious she wore no ring, made her very attractive to these hot-blooded males.

With two of my unmarried classmates seated at poolside close to where she splashed, she chose just the right moment to back slowly into deeper water. Flailing her arms she called, "Oh dear, I can't swim. Can you help me?"

They immediately jumped in the water and successfully "helped" the young lady. I then heard her ask, "Could you walk me back to my room, I'm a little shaky?"

She had obviously made a remarkably rapid recovery because soon I saw all three walking toward her room laughing and joking, while clinging to each arm was a most attentive young veterinarian.

Unknown to me, all had not gone well at our home in Seattle in which Glennie's Mother now lived and where Glennie and our two daughters were staying while I took the California State

Board Examination. Our second daughter, two-year old Yvonne had been playing in the back yard. Because of our limited income we had only a few toys for the children so Glennie improvised by letting them play with various sturdy household utensils. For example, a two-quart stainless steel, copper bottom saucepan and a small wooden spoon made a wonderful drum to "bang on." The combination also could be used to dig a little sand and transport it someplace else in the yard. Empty cereal boxes that once held Cheerios or Shredded Wheat along with tall round ones, originally containing Quick Quaker Oats, were used to build a make-believe village. Glennie always provided fun for our children, no matter how poor we were.

Among the things Yvonne sometimes played with after it had been washed, was a plastic bowl our Cocker Spaniel, "Sandy", ate from. One day, Glennie fed him, as always, on the opposite side of the house as far away as possible from where Yvonne usually played. For some reason she wandered all the way around the house to where the little dog was eating. Bending down she attempted to pick up the bowl. With her head next to his he objected to having his food taken, jumped at her, knocked her down and bit her in the face.

One sharp top fang penetrated her right cheek only an inch below her eye going almost all the way through into her mouth. She cried out loudly and Glennie ran to her aid. Sandy quickly backed away but did not threaten. Checking the freely bleeding wound Glennie found it was very deep and knew the potential for massive infection. Because I had the car in California and all of the neighbors were at work she had no transportation. There was no bus service close in our area and Glennie couldn't afford a taxi. She reasoned since the wound bled profusely this would wash out most of the bacteria introduced by Sandy's germ laden tooth. After thoroughly flushing the wound with soap and water and applying Mercurochrome, she hoped for the best. But next morning the right side of Yvonne's face had swollen to twice the normal size. It looked like she had two heads instead of one and the odor from the wound was overwhelming. Fortunately a neighbor, now at home, took Glennie and Yvonne to our Pediatrician, Dr. Banks.

Everyone has experienced "Murphy's Law", "If anything can go wrong, it certainly will." Dr. Banks did an antibiotic inhibition test using a culture to identify the organisms in the wound. Would it be a routine case needing only commonly used antibiotics against a few simple bacteria?

The inhibition test revealed only Chloramphenicol could wipe out the unusual Gram-negative bacterium causing the now raging fever, massive swelling and infection close to Yvonne's eye and brain. But Chloramphenicol has the potentially nasty side effect to kill the patient by causing the red blood cell producing bone marrow to die leading to irreversible and fatal aplastic anemia. Only a single large dose of this antibiotic could be given safely to our two-year old child. Then, for nearly a month after the incident, Glennie had to clean out the deep wound four times a day using a Q tip dipped in Phisohex and re-open it all the way to the bottom making it heal from the deepest part outward to prevent a pocket from developing which could become re-infected. After every treatment, she had to boil out the wound with Hydrogen Peroxide.

The result of the long healing process resulted in a special bond between Mother and daughter. Yvonne always cooperated lying quietly every time the wound had to be treated. Glennie would say to her, "It's O.K., everything will be all right" and Yvonne would look into Glennie's eyes as though knowing no harm would come to her.

The outcome? We had some good news and some bad. The good news, the fang that caused the wound followed the smile line in Yvonne's right cheek perfectly so the scar would not show. In addition, while the wound healed a letter came from the California State Board saying I passed the examination and had been awarded an active veterinary medical license.

The bad news: we knew Sandy suffered from heart trouble and had recently been forced to move with us to new surroundings. After living four years in his familiar home in Pullman he had a right to be cranky. But as a result we could never again trust our cherished pet and had to make the decision to have him put to sleep, a most difficult and sad task.

During our junior year in veterinary medical school we were given the opportunity to spoof or mimic our professors at an annual play we called, "The Veterinary Medical School Follies of 1954." That year on stage in front of hundreds of people our little dog performed flawlessly, many unique and unusual tricks that Glennie taught him at home while I attended classes.

For example, she'd have him sit up then would place a small dog biscuit on his nose. Walking away, she'd turn her back to him and talk at length with someone. He'd never move even after many minutes of being totally ignored. When she'd turn to look at him only his eyes moved to meet her gaze. When she'd again turn away he'd continue to sit like a stone statue. Finally, with her back still toward him and making no motion with her hands or body she'd say, "O. K Sandy." He'd hear her then toss the treat high. Then in mid air he'd catch and eat it. Everyone loved this trick.

Told to play dead, on command he'd collapse in a heap onto one side. Standing over him Glennie slammed her foot down again and again only about an inch away from his head. Having total and complete trust he'd never flinch, knowing she wouldn't harm him and he'd never move until told.

Next, she'd position him behind and a little to one side, point to her feet and say, "Serpentine walk." Then she'd walk away at a regular, slow or fast pace while he'd move in and out between her ankles always correctly adjusting his speed to match hers, never touching Glennie's legs or missing a step. This trick brought cheering and clapping.

He knew 15 routines and had a rare talent to learn and Glennie had a real talent to teach this extraordinarily intelligent little dog.

After I put him through his lengthy "repertoire" on the stage at "The Follies" I stepped to the microphone and announced that my wife Glennie had taught Sandy all the tricks. She received a standing ovation from everyone attending, including all the Professors in the veterinary medical school. When the play ended,

Dr. Ott, Head of Department of Small Animal Medicine and Surgery and several other Professors sought Glennie out wanting to know the method she used to teach Sandy such unique and unusual tricks that he would not only perform for her but also for me or anyone that "asked him." She told them, "he was so easy to teach and I used only the "reward" system, never raising my voice or giving discipline with my hand or any object."

At Seattle Veterinary Hospital I held Sandy in my arms gently petting and softly talking to him. Dr. Kraft gave the final I.V. injection that ended the life of our little dog. Though having my own degree now as a veterinarian, I was saddened remembering that six years ago Glennie and I lived in this hospital while I worked as night attendant for Drs. Kraft and Ehmer. Sandy lived here with us and because he was AKC registered we were able to sell his stud service for $25.00 each time.

He produced many offspring and I like to think there are other blonde Cocker Spaniels playing somewhere and enjoying life who still carry in their bloodline his genetic makeup and unique intelligence.

❖ A TRIBUTE TO SPOTTY ❖

She was the smallest among the litter of five kittens, this three day old, beautifully marked black and white ball of soft fur.

The moment I reached for her she pressed her small black nose against my hand and instantly began to crawl up my arm. Hooking her tiny "pins" into my shirt to keep her balance I became fascinated as she shakily but persistently made her way to the top of my shoulder. She had made great effort and it was more than obvious that she really wanted to do it. On my shoulder she began to rub her silky face against my neck and tried to purr.

Experienced cat owners know that many times a kitten will choose one person to be its master and this was a classic example. When weaned, along with one brother, she came to live in our home. It became clear from the time I first saw her that she chose me. She was my cat.

As months passed and she grew, she would lie on the carpet, usually about eight feet away constantly watching me with her unusually colored big green eyes. She didn't watch anyone else.

Two things set her apart from all other cats I have known during fifty-one years of veterinary practice. First, although I made no sound or motion, whenever I looked across the room directly into her eyes she would purr instantly. Her purr was so loud it could be heard from anyplace in the room. I marveled at how such a small cat could have such a loud purr that I very much enjoyed hearing

Her second unusual attribute was that she would run to me, like a dog when I'd call to her. She wouldn't respond to a call from anyone else. I could be sitting quietly on the couch reading, stop, look across the room at her and softly say, "Here Spotty." Instantly she'd bound toward me like a fully-grown Panther then leap magnificently, the last three feet, onto my lap. From here she'd walk her front feet up my chest "making bread", kneading it all the way. As soon as her head was under my chin she'd place it on my bare neck and close her eyes all the while continuing to purr. I've always loved cats that purr loudly and this made her special.

In her bed one morning she was listless. She didn't come running to greet me as she had before, every day of her life. But when our eyes met she purred. I examined her and saw that her gums were slightly yellow. A laboratory test confirmed she had contracted a disease that rapidly kills red blood cells. Even though given blood transfusions and supportive therapy she died that night in her sleep. I buried her in our back yard beneath her favorite rose bush where she so often played.

It has been several years but I continue to miss this small creature. Perhaps some other time, in another place on a different plane, our eyes will meet again—and she'll purr.

Photos & Illustrations: Veterinary School & Practice

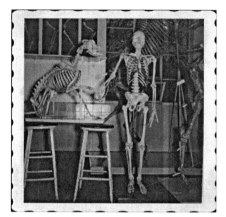

Dog and Man

First Year
Comparative Anatomy

Horses and Man

Senior Year
Surgical Table

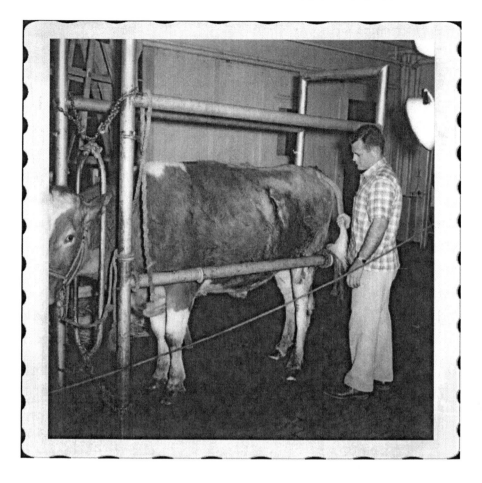

1955 Physiology of Digestive Process

Dr. Kuhen suggested we place a "window to the stomach" in one side of a cow. Narrative: *The City Kid in Senior Year*, p. 394

Gene Curnow, Senior Year, 1955
Age 30

This photo was taken two days before graduation as a Doctor of Veterinary
Medicine (D.V.M.) Gene Curnow practiced for 51 years in Portland, OR.

House Party

On the left is Glenora Curnow. On the right, in black, is Doris Carlon, the only woman graduating with a D.V.M. in the same class as Gene Curnow,

The photo above was taken at a party the Curnow's hosted at their home in Seattle when the National Convention for Veterinarians was held in Seattle. Narrative: *Graduation and Entering Practice*, p. 422.

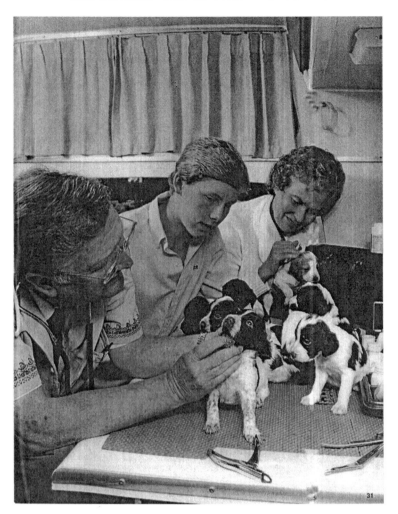

National Geographic's World Magazine
1985 Feature Article
"Freewheeling Vet"

Gene Curnow pioneered the mobile veterinary clinic. Pictured above are
Gene Curnow, a client and his puppies, and Glenora Curnow.

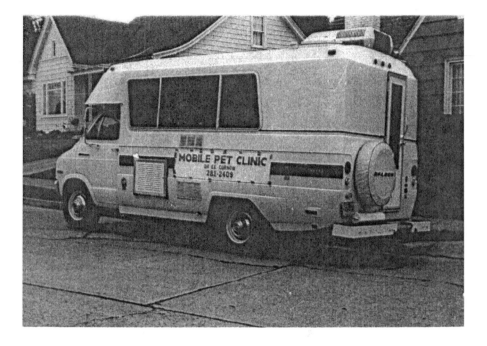

Original Mobile Veterinary Clinic

Gene Curnow was the first to have 100% mobile veterinary practice. The veterinary profession became highly interested in the concept, and there are now more than 800 similar veterinary clinics around the world.

PART VI
EPILOGUE

❖ A BIG SHAGGY DOG STORY ❖

I had been in practice only a short time and was young, eager and hungry. At 2:30 in the morning I reached for the telephone ringing on the nightstand beside the bed.

A voice greeted, "Hello, is this the doctor?"

"Yes."

"Can you meet me at your office? I've got kind of an emergency with my big dog."

"Sure. About how long will it take you to get there?"

"About 20 minutes."

"What kind of an emergency do you have?" I asked.

"I think my dog swallowed something that might make him sick."

"How long ago?"

"Only a few minutes."

Not wanting to waste more time with questions I said, "O.K., I'm on my way."

Driving to the clinic I envisioned a simple case of little consequence. An older Volkswagen van waited as I pulled to the curb. Two young people, a long haired and unshaven young man, dressed in shabby, thread bare military fatigues and a lady dressed in a colorful tie-dyed tee shirt, unkempt and wrinkled slacks and with hair under a brightly colored bandana tightly pressed against her head, clothes and grooming indicative of the then popular counter-culture, stepped from the van. Followed by a large longhaired male German shepherd and St. Bernard mix they stepped close behind me as I unlocked the clinic door.

In the examination room the question came, "Can you pump his stomach Doc?"

"I won't have to" I answered. "I'll just drop a tiny pill of Apomorphine under one of his lower eyelids and I assure you he'll do the rest."

The unusually cooperative dog was then placed in an outside run and soon began to vomit large and small chunks of a tightly packed, greenish-brown and yellow substance.

It was over quickly and when the vomiting stopped I asked, "Is that about as much as you think he ate?"

"Yeah Doc, that looks like it could be all of it."

"Well then," I said, "He looks fairly bright though he does react a bit slowly. To be safe, leave him here until eight o'clock in the morning so my night attendant can keep an eye on him. I'll check him over in the morning as soon as I get here. There'll be no extra charge." Pointing to the larger chunks of stomach contents I asked the young man, "By the way, what kind of stuff is that?"

"Oh it's just some kind of plant material, and we don't know if it could be poisonous for dogs. Better to get it out of his stomach and be safe than take a chance," he laughed feebly.

The couple didn't offer to identify the "plant material" and seemed reluctant to talk about it so I didn't press the issue.

"Can we take some of the bigger chunks home?" the young lady asked.

"Yea, can we?" the young man echoed.

"You don't want any of that slimy old stuff," I said. "I'll have my kennel boy throw it in the garbage for you when he comes in to clean out and wash the run first in the morning." After a little hesitation they paid their fee from a large roll of cash and left. With the dog resting comfortably in a large kennel inside the clinic I left a note for the daytime kennel boy, John, to clean and wash outside run number three, as soon as he arrived.

A little before seven in the morning when I entered the clinic John, obviously excited, approached. "Dr. Curnow, what's that stuff I just cleaned out of number three run?"

"Oh, I had an emergency night call and I guess it's some kind of plant material. The couple, sort of hippie types, wanted the dogs stomach emptied in case the stuff could be something that would make him sick."

Now obviously agitated John asked, "Don't you know what that stuff really is?"

"No, I don't know exactly. Why?"

"I'll tell you why. It's almost a kilogram of pure hashish and it's worth a whole lot of money." (I was told later perhaps $2,000 to $3,000).

I suddenly realized why the couple so eagerly wanted to take some of the bigger chunks home and I was embarrassed by my lack of knowledge. I had heard of hashish but having never seen any, remained totally unaware of how it looked. Though he was above suspicion, an asset to the practice and an excellent worker, I thought it best not to ask John how he knew so much about it.

"By the way, how is the dog?" I said

"Well, they came to get him about six-thirty, just after I cleaned his kennel. He seemed fine but they kept whispering something about, "Geeze, all that money, all that money. But having seen that stuff out in the run I knew why right away."

In an effort to check on the big dog, later that morning I dialed the number the couple gave but the telephone company's recording said, "the number you have reached is disconnected and there is no new number." On my lunch hour I drove to the address written on their record. It was an empty lot.

A day later my garbage pick up man had no idea how valuable and illegal the cargo was he hauled to the city dump.

In almost forty-five more years of veterinary practice I never saw any more hashish. But I'm confident that if I do, thanks to John, two hippies and a big shaggy dog, next time I'll be able to identify it.

❖ EPILOGUE ❖

The hands of time creep relentlessly along destroying that which yesterday was young. We resist the disintegration and each memory grows more meaningful and cherished with the passing of our years. I enjoy recalling the many adventures my family and I had. Some days I am able to remember even the smallest detail. A sentence, a scene, the sound of familiar music heard while growing up or an aroma, such as that of freshly baked bread, can propel to mind a vast flood from yesteryear. Thoughts tumble as a swirling river of crystal clear water and from the depths memories from long ago passing in review well up and gradually disappears beneath the foam as yet another surfaces. With closed eyes before going to sleep, visions of days long gone sometimes rush in to entertain me and I view them as a movie on the private silver screen of memory.

Many people gain money, power and beautiful possessions. It doesn't matter. At your demise none will go with you. I'm not afraid of death. I'm ready to go any time God calls me home. I have no enemies and am at peace within, satisfied with the work I have done.

May you experience life fully in the time you are given and relive your treasured memories that echo from a distant past.

1107289

Made in the USA